MOUNTAIN BIKE!
Washington

MOUNTAIN BIKE!
Washington

A GUIDE TO THE CLASSIC TRAILS

ALAN BENNETT

CHRIS AND LAURIE LEMAN

Menasha
Ridge
Press

Library of Congress Cataloging-in-Publication Data:
Bennett, Alan, 1962–.
Mountain bike! Washington: a guide to the classic trails/
Alan Bennett, Chris and Laurie Leman.
p. cm.—(America by mountain bike series)
Rev. ed. of: The mountain biker's guide to the Pacific Northwest/Laurie Leman.
Includes index.
ISBN 0-89732-280-0(pbk.)
1. All terrain cycling—Washington—Guidebooks.
2. Bicycle trails—Washington—Guidebooks. 3. Washington—Guidebooks.
I. Leman, Chris. II. Leman, Laurie.
III. Leman, Laurie. Mountain biker's guide to the Pacific Northwest.
IV. Title. V. Series:
GV1045.5.W2B45 1998
796.6'3'09797—dc21 98-45034
CIP

Photos by the authors unless otherwise credited
Maps by Brian Taylor
Cover and text design by Suzanne Holt
Cover photo by Tom Jacobs

Menasha Ridge Press
700 South 28th Street
Suite 206
Birmingham, Alabama 35233

All the trails described in this book are legal for mountain bikes. But rules can change—especially for off-road bicycles, the new kid on the outdoor recreation block. Land access issues and conflicts between bicyclists, hikers, equestrians, and other users can cause the rewriting of recreation regulations on public lands, sometimes resulting in a ban of mountain bike use on specific trails. That's why it's the responsibility of each rider to check and make sure that he or she rides only on trails where mountain biking is permitted.

CAUTION

Outdoor recreational activities are by their very nature potentially hazardous. All participants in such activities must assume the responsibility for their own actions and safety. The information contained in this guidebook cannot replace sound judgment and good decision-making skills, which help reduce risk exposure, nor does the scope of this book allow for disclosure of all the potential hazards and risks involved in such activities.

Learn as much as possible about the outdoor recreational activities in which you participate, prepare for the unexpected, and be cautious. The reward will be a safer and more enjoyable experience.

CONTENTS

AMERICA BY MOUNTAIN BIKE · Map Legend

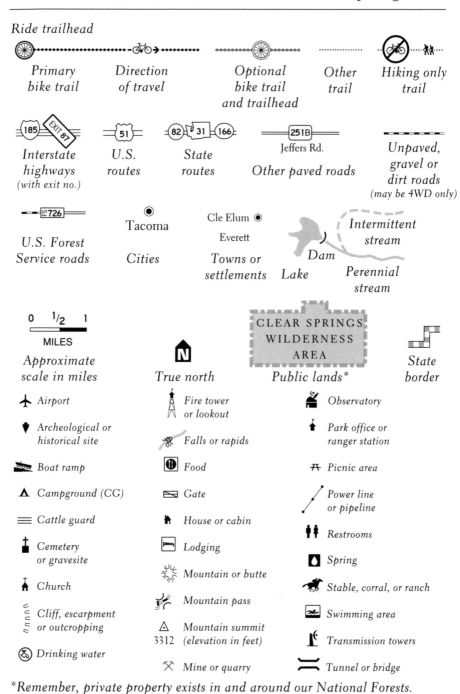

Ride trailhead

| Primary bike trail | Direction of travel | Optional bike trail and trailhead | Other trail | Hiking only trail |

| Interstate highways (with exit no.) | U.S. routes | State routes | Other paved roads — Jeffers Rd. | Unpaved, gravel or dirt roads (may be 4WD only) |

| U.S. Forest Service roads | Cities — Tacoma | Towns or settlements — Cle Elum, Everett | Dam / Lake | Intermittent stream / Perennial stream |

| Approximate scale in miles — 0 ½ 1 MILES | True north — N | Public lands* — CLEAR SPRINGS WILDERNESS AREA | State border |

- ✈ Airport
- ♥ Archeological or historical site
- Boat ramp
- ▲ Campground (CG)
- ≡ Cattle guard
- Cemetery or gravesite
- Church
- Cliff, escarpment or outcropping
- Drinking water

- Fire tower or lookout
- Falls or rapids
- Food
- Gate
- House or cabin
- Lodging
- Mountain or butte
- Mountain pass
- △ Mountain summit 3312 (elevation in feet)
- ✕ Mine or quarry

- Observatory
- Park office or ranger station
- ⊼ Picnic area
- Power line or pipeline
- Restrooms
- Spring
- Stable, corral, or ranch
- Swimming area
- Transmission towers
- Tunnel or bridge

Remember, private property exists in and around our National Forests.

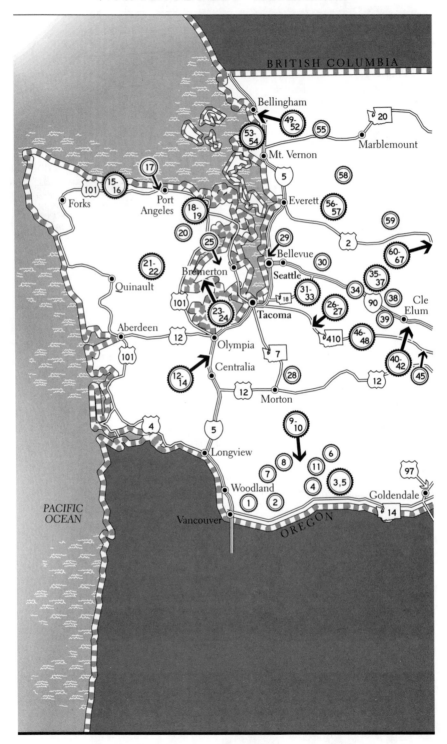

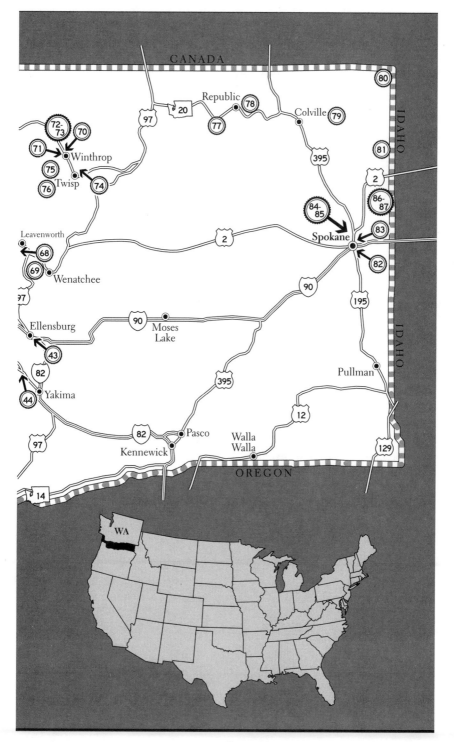

LIST OF MAPS

ACKNOWLEDGMENTS

I dedicate my efforts to my wife and best friend, Tamara Blum, for her support, understanding, encouragement, and enthusiasm. Baby, you are the best wife, friend, and "mountain bike widow" any man could ever hope for.

Thanks also to Dennis Coello, for everything; Jim Sullivan and the WHIMPS gang; Jim Slagle, Gifford Pinchot National Forest; Mark Flint; Joe Nollette and John Gasioroski, REI Spokane; Tom McFadden, Two Wheel Transit, Spokane; Steve Merriam, Mike Curley, Brian Snyder, Single Track Mind Cycling Club, Tacoma; Phil Wolff; "Field Guide" Brad Sauber; Brent McCord; Jem Rockholt, Sagebrush Cycles, Yakima; Jim Dole and the Greatful Tread Mountain Bike Club in Yakima; the gang from The Recyclery, Ellensburg; Craig Nunes; administrative assistant Anne Bennett; Jordan Bennett, for her support from afar; and "mother-in-love" Carol Blum (look at all the words I made, Carol!).

Alan Bennett

FOREWORD

Welcome to *America by Mountain Bike*, a series designed to provide all-terrain bikers with the information they need to find and ride the very best trails around. Whether you're new to the sport and don't know where to pedal or an experienced mountain biker who wants to learn the classic trails in another region, this series is for you. Drop a few bucks for the book, spend an hour with the detailed maps and route descriptions, and you're prepared for the finest in off-road cycling.

My role as editor of this series is simple: First, find a mountain biker who knows the area and loves to ride. Second, ask that person to spend a year researching the most popular and very best rides around. And third, have that rider describe each trail in terms of difficulty, scenery, condition, elevation change, and all other categories of information that are important to trail riders. "Pretend you've just completed a ride and met up with fellow mountain bikers at the trailhead," I told each author. "Imagine their questions, be clear in your answers."

As I said, the *editorial* process—that of sending out riders and reading the submitted chapters—is a snap. But the work involved in finding, riding, and writing about each trail is enormous. In some instances our authors' tasks are made easier by the information contributed by local bike shops or cycling clubs, or even by the writers of local "where-to" guides. Credit for these contributions is provided, when appropriate, in each chapter, and our sincere thanks goes to all who have helped.

But the overwhelming majority of trails are discovered and pedaled by our authors themselves, then compared with dozens of other routes to determine if they qualify as "classic"—that area's best in scenery and cycling fun. If you've ever had the experience of pioneering a route from outdated topographic maps, or entering a bike shop to request information from local riders who would much prefer to keep their favorite trails secret, or if you know how it is to double- and triple-check data to be positive your trail info is correct, then you have an idea of how each of our authors has labored to bring about these books. You and I, and all the mountain bikers of America, are the richer for their efforts.

You'll get more out of this book if you take a moment to read the Introduction explaining how to read the trail listings. The "Topographic Maps" section will help you understand how useful topos will be on a ride, and will also tell you where to get them. And though this is a "where-to," not a "how-to" guide, those of you who have not traveled the backcountry might find "Hitting the Trail" of particular value.

In addition to the material above, newcomers to mountain biking might want to spend a minute with the glossary, page 395, so that terms like *hardpack*, *single-track*, and *waterbars* won't throw you when you come across them in the text.

Finally, the tips in the Afterword on mountain biking etiquette and the land-use controversy might help us all enjoy the trails a little more.

All the best.

Dennis Coello
St. Louis

PREFACE TO THE SECOND EDITION

This guide is an updated and expanded version of half of *Mountain Bike! The Pacific Northwest*, which included rides in both Oregon and Washington. Chris and Laurie Leman, who did the original research for the book, filled out the Oregon entry in the *America by Mountain Bike* series, while I got the opportunity to ride some of the best single-track and dirt roads in the Evergreen State.

The era of trail user fees has arisen since Chris and Laurie's original edition. National Forest budgets have plummeted in recent years. Districts are consolidating to absorb the shortfall. Congress authorized a three-year demonstration program allowing National Forests to collect fees for trailhead parking, which began in 1997. It's controversial, and some are working to repeal it, but once the government gets its paws on a funding source, it's not likely to give it up. My guess is it will continue, but possibly in a modified form.

The three-year demo project requires fees of $3 per day or $25 per year for parking near most National Forest trailheads, with an additional $8 monument pass required for certain sites at the Mount Saint Helens National Volcanic Monument (none of the listed Mt. St. Helens area rides require the monument pass). Check with ranger districts, Forest Service headquarters, or outdoor retailers for information on obtaining trail park passes. Having said that, don't blame me if you don't get one and come back to your car with a ticket on your windshield!

If you've ever followed a mountain bike guidebook before, you'll know that your mileage readings don't always correspond with the book's counts (if in fact you use a cyclometer). In our case, you'll see that the odometers on our vehicles differed as Chris and Laurie, and then I, tracked mileages on rides at similar locations. Whichever reading you follow, know that the cyclometer reading on your bike may not exactly correspond to what is listed here. It is a guideline to follow in that you should be anticipating junctions and landmarks before the mileages listed, even though they may not appear until afterwards!

We also relate slightly different ways of going the same way. Some of my

Approaching Cooney
Lake Trail on Martin
Creek Trail.

directions rely on clock positions (e.g., "the trail takes off to the right at the 4 o'clock position"). Imagine yourself at the center of a clock, where 12 o'clock is directly in front of you, 6 o'clock is behind you, 9 o'clock is directly left, and 3 o'clock is directly right. This makes it easy to visualize directions; in the example above, you would know to look to the right and back to see the trail at the 4 o'clock position.

Clock directions tie into the concept of "hard" turns versus "soft" turns. For example, you may come to a junction where your options are turning "hard" left, "soft" left, or going straight. Again, straight ahead would be the 12 o'clock position; the "hard" left would be at about the 8 o'clock or 9 o'clock position, while the "soft" left would be the 10 o'clock or 11 o'clock position. A *real* hard left would be at about the 7 o'clock position. Those 7 o'clockers to the left and 5 o'clockers to the right require extra attention to find, and I generally note these turns using clock directions.

Another way my directions differ is by my citing "deltas" at certain intersections. Deltas, named for the Greek letter, can be triangular in nature, but can be any shape. The deltas are usually patches of grass, trees, or any other objects in

Single-track excitement.

the trail. These patches tend to come in the middle of **T** junctions, where the delta will veer the rider gradually either left or right. They make for distinctive landmarks; if you're not familiar with the concept, you will be as soon as you see one on the trail.

Along with differences in mileages and directions, we also showed different preferences for maps. While we both freely used national forest maps, ranger district maps, Department of Natural Resources maps, and other, more area-specific maps, I tended to use Green Trails maps in their coverage areas, while Chris and Laurie favored U.S. Geological Survey (USGS) maps.

In national forest districts within range of Green Trails maps, frequently both the district map and the Green Trails will guide you through. The color aspect of the Green Trails maps versus ranger district maps makes them a lot easier to read, and their smaller size make them easier to tote along. Their disadvantage is that they cover a smaller area, per map, than ranger district maps. Of course, you can always photocopy sections of either map and take them along to keep your originals intact.

When deciding which map to purchase, find out the latest revision dates of your choices. They're usually noted on the bottoms of the maps; if you have to buy maps sight unseen, call and ask your map retailer or land manager for revision dates before making your selection.

It's possible to go out without a map, but I've heard about too many cases, even on rides with seemingly easy directions, where a simple outing became an odyssey the rider would rather have forgotten. I note on some rides that only a fool would go out without a map; on a few others, I am confident enough to say you can make it without one. As long as there is a map available for a particular ride or area, I list it for your convenience, the self-confidence of giving you your bearings, and as a potential tool for nothing less than your very survival. Look for the suggested maps at your favorite map store or map library, bike or outdoors shop, Forest Service district office or headquarters, or contact the producers directly:

Custom Correct Maps
3492 Little River Road
Port Angeles, WA 98363
(360) 457-5667
(Olympic Peninsula maps only, but very good 7.5 minute quadrangles)

Green Trails, Inc.
P.O. Box 77734
Seattle, WA 98177
(15 minute quadrangle, trail-specific maps of the Cascades and Olympic Peninsula areas)

U.S. Geological Survey
Branch of Information Services
P.O. Box 25286
Denver, CO 80225
(800) 435-7627 (for the numerologically challenged it translates to HELP-MAP)

As a time- and effort-saving suggestion, almost any single-track ride that intersects a road at both ends can be done as a car shuttle. I shuttled only one route, the Little Bald Mountain loop, so I could share the experience of the entire ride as often as possible, and, well, because I love to ride!

I had to bypass some choice Washington single-track, though. Mt. Constitution, at Moran State Park in the San Juan Islands, was open with restrictions during my research period, but was slated to be off-limits to mountain bikers soon. In addition, the Middle Fork Snoqualmie Trail, despite trail work and political efforts by the Backcountry Bicycle Trails Club of Seattle, was closed to mountain bikers due to the efforts of the Sierra Club. Fellow riders, the trails are political animals, and those individuals and groups working the hardest and in biggest numbers get the results. One hopes that these situations will change in the near future, but to maximize riding on open trails, these areas were excluded from research. I hope the political climate improves and that these and other trails will be included in the next update.

Before you ride, it's always a good idea to call the land managers to inquire about conditions. As a service to mountain bikers, sign in at the trailhead when trailhead registers are provided. It lets land managers know what kind of use the trails are getting, which will help give us our due in the decision-making process. Post-ride, call trail or recreation personnel, or other land managers, and tell them what you saw; as great as their jobs are, they can't get out on every trail. If you had a great ride, tell them (and tell them thank you—it's great fat-tire PR);

if there are sections that need maintenance, or you found any other conditions of note—including trailhead thievery or vandalism—tell them.

Unfortunately, vandalism and "car-clouting"—smashing a vehicle's window and grabbing anything of value inside—have become common at trailhead parking areas and campgrounds. Take your wallet with you and don't leave valuables in plain view in your vehicle while you ride. I've even read a recommendation that trail users record license numbers of other cars at the trailhead. It seems a bit extreme, and I've never done it, but I throw it out as a security precaution. Remember, just because you're paranoid, doesn't mean they're *not* out to get you!

I hope you're like me in that when I use a route in a guidebook, I follow it, but I sometimes explore the side trails and roads along the way. If I find something that leads to another route and yet another route, I'll mark my way with rocks or twigs and disconnect my cyclometer so I can keep track of the described route when I return to it. The beauty of our trail descriptions, though, is that you (generally) don't need an accurate cyclometer to keep track of the mileage; distance between landmarks, instead of cumulative mileage, is noted, so once you get back on the described route you don't have to be a math whiz as well as a mountain biker.

In my research I didn't have time to explore all side-trip options, but I encourage you to do as many as time and fitness allow. If you find a gem of a side trip, please contact Menasha Ridge Press and let me know.

In my travels, I got two great tips from my newfound friends at the Single-Track Mind Cycling Club in Tacoma. The first is buying a small key ring compass and attaching it to the plastic strap tensioner of your CamelBak (or other backpack-style hydration system) for easy access and use. The other is buying a handheld pump sprayer at a hardware store or garden supply store. Fill it with water and bring it along for those muddy rides. After your ride, you can rinse the mud off your bike before it becomes encrusted and harder to remove when you get home. You can also rinse the sweat off and give yourself a mini-shower so you look presentable at the restaurant at your post-ride feast.

I also got tips on extra equipment. Of course, you should always carry the "ten essentials" (extra clothing, extra food and water, map, compass, matches, fire starter, flashlight, first aid kit, sunglasses, and pocket knife) and standard bike repair paraphernalia (spare tube and flat repair kit, tire levers, spare chain links, spare cables, and chain tool; spoke wrench, appropriate allan wrenches, and screwdrivers or all-encompassing multi-tool; plus good ol' duct tape). Another helpful item is a folding pruning saw. You can strap it to your bike, put it in your fanny pack or attach it to your Camelbak; it allows you to cut away some of the smaller blowdown and overhanging brush along the trail. If you're using the trails, it's your responsibility to help maintain them.

In addition, another helpful bit of equipment is some cold, hard cash. It's always good to carry a couple of bucks with you on a ride in case of emergency, and one of those emergencies could be a blown sidewall of your tire. A folded dollar bill (a foil energy bar wrapper will work as well) between the tube and the tire at the point of the split will keep the tube from protruding. It could mean the difference between making it back on the saddle and trudging back on foot.

Any longtime mountain biker will have had the experience of walking back from what was to have been a wonderful ride. But that's part of the adventure. Here's hoping your adventures keep you on your bike, with the wind at your back. Happy trails!

Alan Bennett

PREFACE TO THE FIRST EDITION

The Pacific Northwest is rich with public lands and opportunities for active recreation. The mountain biking in this region is exceptional. Gravel roads crisscross forests, climb mountains to stunning views, and reach across deserts. An inviting array of trails is found here. Single-tracks follow rivers, traverse rocky canyons, and wind through rainforests. Easy or demanding, long or short, road or single-track—the cycling opportunities in Washington are limitless. Some places in the Pacific Northwest are home to networks of bike routes, making them attractive vacation destinations. Other areas offer trips through remote backcountry, longer trails over ridge tops, or easy pedals down forest roads. This part of the country offers routes suited to all skill levels and tastes.

We spent a year looking for outstanding mountain bike rides in Washington. We visited ranger stations and bike shops, scoured guidebooks and brochures, and consulted maps. People we met recommended favorite outings. We rode the routes that seemed most promising—about 100 excursions in all. Thirty-five of those rides have been selected for this guidebook.

We have made every attempt to portray accurately the difficulty of each ride. Keep in mind that "difficulty" is a subjective matter. Some cyclists will find our descriptions understated, while others will find them overly cautious. We suggest that you start with an easier ride, especially if your fitness level is low or if your bike handling skills could use some work. This will give you a feeling for our rating scale and provide you with a setting in which to strengthen your riding abilities.

Mountain biking can be arduous. After logging many miles researching guidebooks, we half expected to tire of the sport. On the contrary, increased strength and bike handling ability make mountain biking more fun. Now we find ourselves looking for longer rides and technical terrain. Our explorations have become more fulfilling. Here's hoping that your adventures are gratifying.

The Book, above the Kittitas Valley.

SAFETY, COURTESY, AND RESPONSIBILITY

Be completely self-sufficient. Be prepared to find your own way if you get lost. Use all available maps. Information is often inaccurate on maps; check their data and make comparisons. Take note of landmarks and keep track of where you are and where you have come from. Stop often and look behind you; it may be necessary to turn around and retrace your path. Tell someone where you plan to go, your route of travel, and your anticipated time of return. Tell them what to do if you do not return by the specified time. Ride with others who may be able to provide help in an emergency, especially in remote areas. Always call ahead to check on trail and road conditions, closures, or special circumstances that could affect your ride. Learn first aid and how to deal with hypothermia, dehydration, heat stroke, snake and tick bites, and other ailments and injuries that could befall backcountry users. Carry a good first-aid and repair kit. Keep your bicycle in good working order and know how to make roadside repairs (like how to fix a flat). Develop a checklist of what to take with you when you go riding. Wear a helmet, cycling gloves, and protective eyewear.

Ride within your limitations. Turn around if the weather becomes threatening or if you find the ride more difficult than you had expected. Keep your speed under control at all times. Play it safe on narrow roads and when approaching blind corners; someone may be coming from the other direction. Stay to the right and ride defensively and predictably. If the route involves highway or city riding, avoid rush-hour traffic. Wait until the off-season to visit areas popular with tourists. Steer clear of ongoing logging operations and backcountry rides during hunting season.

As relative newcomers, mountain bikers should make an extra effort to be courteous and ride safely. Announce your presence when approaching other trail users. Yield the trail when you meet others head-on. Be mindful of the special needs of equestrians. Horses have poor eyesight, are easily spooked, and can cause serious injury when startled. If you meet horses on the trail, dismount and move well off the trail to the downhill side. Take up a position where the horse will have a clear view of you. Ask the rider if the horse is spooked easily. If you come upon equestrians from behind, stop well in back of them. Do not attempt to pass until you have announced your presence and asked for permission. Pass on the downhill side if possible. Give these animals a wide berth, for they may kick out at you.

Be prepared for extreme riding conditions. Weather conditions can change rapidly—especially at higher elevations; carry raingear, warm gloves, and other protective clothing to change into. Dress in layers so you can adjust your clothing to meet any number of riding conditions. Ultraviolet radiation from the sun becomes more intense as you climb higher; wear protective sunglasses and apply sunscreen with an SPF of 15 or higher. Reapply sunscreen frequently. Lower air humidity and loss of water through increased respiration can cause rapid dehydration at higher elevations. Carry water from a safe source and bring more than you expect to need. Force yourself to drink even if you are not thirsty, especially on hot days. Once you become dehydrated, you will not be able to rehydrate and continue cycling. Carry high-energy foods and eat often; drink water with your snacks and meals.

Respect the environment you are riding through. Bicycles are not permitted in Wilderness Areas or on the Pacific Crest Trail. Some public lands restrict bicycle use to designated trails and roads only. Obey all signs indicating road or trail closings. Never trespass on private property or block access with your parked vehicle. Always stay on trails and roads; trailblazing is inappropriate and often illegal. Never travel on worn trails where cycling will cause further damage. Carry your bike over degraded sections of the trail or turn around and return the way you came. Do not shortcut switchbacks or ride around waterbars placed in the trail; help control erosion instead of creating further degradation. It is never appropriate to skid your tires. If you cannot control your speed without skidding, dismount and walk your bike down the hill to gentler terrain. Skidding through switchbacks is extremely hard on trails. If switchbacks are too tight to roll through, walk your bike down them. Resource damage can result from riding on wet trails; call ahead to check on trail and road conditions. Wait until the spring thaw is over and trails are dry before riding. Pack out your own trash and, when possible, remove other people's litter as well. Leave gates as you find them—close them behind you if they were closed.

Call or visit the ranger station (or other land management office) that is responsible for the lands you will be traveling on. Ask to speak with a trail coordinator or a recreation specialist. Find out when the trail was last maintained and what condition it is in. It is also a good idea to inquire about ranger station office hours, for they vary widely from district to district. Forest Service maps are great sources of information. Obtain both the general map of the forest and the district map (district maps are sometimes referred to as "fire maps"). The general map will provide you with an overview of the region and helpful infor mation about the area. The district map (topographic) is more detailed and is helpful as a directional aid. Feedback about trail conditions and your impressions of the ride are helpful to the rangers.

Become an informed participant and get involved in managing the lands you use for recreation. Many groups are active in trail building and maintenance efforts. Non-ATB off-road-vehicle users and equestrians have a record of involvement that speaks well of their concern for public lands. As newcomers, mountain bikers need to make an extra effort to get involved in volunteer activities and in the managing of our common lands. Get in touch with a local cycling club or bike shop that works to keep trails open to mountain bikes and promotes responsible riding. Attend meetings where management and recreation plans are discussed. Ask to be placed on a mailing list for volunteer work building or repairing trails.

Conflicts and closures are still with us, but mountain biking has grown out of its infancy to become an accepted form of recreation. We seem to be getting along better with other trail users. Land managers across Washington welcome mountain bikers; they only ask that cyclists ride responsibly.

Laurie and Chris Leman

P.S. In our trail descriptions you will come across the term pummy (rhymes with tummy). Volcanic activity in the Pacific Northwest produces soils with a high content of pumice. In some areas, trails become thick with pumice dust. These dusty (pummy) conditions usually occur during prolonged dry spells and on routes receiving heavy use. Negotiating a bike on a pummy trail is like riding through sand, but pumice is light, and it can often be pedaled.

Loops

2 Three Corner Rock (17-mile loop if omitting 6.5 miles of gravel road and 2.1-mile single-track, each way, to the top)
3 Gotchen Creek Trail
6 Valley Trail #270
8 Toutle Trail Loop
11 Lewis River Trail (using road return)
12 Mima Loop
13 Mt. Molly Loop
14 Middle Waddell Loop
15 Mt. Muller Loop
17 The Foothills
18 Gold Creek Trail
19 Lower Dungeness Loop
21 Lower South Fork Skokomish Trail (using gravel and paved road return)
22 Wynoochee Lakeshore Trail
23 Howell Lake Lollipop (either from Howell Lake Camp and Picnic Area, or as the middle 7.3 miles of the combination route starting from Tahuya Horse Camp)
24 Mission Creek Single-Track (lower loop of a figure eight)
25 Green Mountain (loop with two out-and-back spurs)
26 Skookum Flats
27 Dalles Ridge
28 High Rock Lookout
29 St. Edward State Park/Big Finn Hill County Park (numerous small loops possible)
31 Tiger Mountain State Forest: Preston Railroad Trail/Northwest Timber Trail Loop
36 Kachess Ridge Loop

37 Cooper River Trail (using road return)
40 North Fork Taneum Creek Loop
41 Taneum Ridge Loop
42 Lookout Mountain Loop
43 "The Book"
48 Little Bald Mountain (loop plus out-and-back spur)
50 Lake Padden Loop
51 Lake Padden Single-Track
52 Galbraith (many loops possible)
53 Cranberry Lake
60 Pole Ridge
61 Lower Chiwawa Trail (if using road return)
62 Chikamin Creek Loop
63 Minnow Ridge Loop
65 Rock Creek Area Trails (can be routed as 10.6-mile loop)
69 Devil's Gulch/Mission Ridge Trail (either as full single-track loop or as gravel road and single-track loop)
70 Pearrygin Lake Loop
72 Buck Lake Loop
73 Goat Wall Loop
74 Lightning Creek Trail
75 Twisp River Trail
77 Swan Lake Trail/Lakes Area Mountain Bike Routes
78 Kettle Crest/Sherman Trail
79 Frater Lake
80 Hall Mountain Loop
81 Bead Lake Loop
83 Minnehaha Park/Beacon Hill
84 Riverside State Park
85 Riverside State Park: "Rattlesnake"
86 Mt. Spokane State Park
87 Mt. Spokane State Park: Mt. Kit Carson/Day Mountain Loop

Figure Eights

2 Three Corner Rock Trail
17 The Foothills (can be rerouted as a figure eight using connector trails)

24 Mission Creek Single-Track
32 Tiger Mountain State Forest: Iverson Railroad Trail

Out-and-Backs

1 Tarbell Trail
2 Three Corner Rock Trail (9.2 miles each way if done as all single-track)
10 Ape Canyon/Plains of Abraham
11 Lewis River Trail
16 Spruce Railroad Trail
20 Lower Big Quilcene Trail
21 Lower South Fork Skokomish Trail
30 Snoqualmie Valley Trail
33 Tiger Mountain State Forest: Poo Poo Point
34 Iron Horse State Park: Snoqualmie Tunnel
37 Cooper River Trail
38 Coal Mines Trail
39 Iron Horse State Park: John Wayne Pioneer Trail
44 Tieton Nature Trail
45 Bethel Ridge
47 Old River Road
49 Interurban Trail and Fragrance Lake
55 Mt. Josephine
57 Monte Cristo
58 North Mountain
59 Johnson Ridge Trail
61 Lower Chiwawa Trail
64 Mad Lake from the North
65 Rock Creek Area Trails
66 Mad Lake from the South
67 Wenatchee River Road
71 Methow Trail/Sun Mountain Trails
76 Cooney Lake
83 Minnehaha Park/Beacon Hill
85 Riverside State Park: "Rattlesnake"

Family Rides

16 Spruce Railroad Trail
30 Snoqualmie Valley Trail
34 Iron Horse State Park: Snoqualmie Tunnel
38 Coal Mines Trail
39 Iron Horse State Park: John Wayne Pioneer Trail
47 Old River Road
49 Interurban Trail and Fragrance Lake
50 Lake Padden Loop
57 Monte Cristo
70 Pearrygin Lake Loop

Novice and Beginner

5 Forlorn Lakes
8 Toutle Trail Loop (not for first-timers)
11 Lewis River Trail
12 Mima Loop (short loop)
16 Spruce Railroad Trail
20 Lower Big Quilcene Trail (experienced beginners)
23 Howell Lake Lollipop (Loop portion only; not for first-timers)
29 St. Edward State Park/Big Finn Hill County Park
30 Snoqualmie Valley Trail
34 Iron Horse State Park: Snoqualmie Tunnel
38 Coal Mines Trail
39 Iron Horse State Park: John Wayne Pioneer Trail
44 Tieton Nature Trail
45 Bethel Ridge
47 Old River Road
49 Interurban Trail and Fragrance Lake
50 Lake Padden Loop
53 Cranberry Lake (experienced beginners)
57 Monte Cristo
58 North Mountain
61 Lower Chiwawa Trail (experienced beginners)
63 Minnow Ridge Loop
67 Wenatchee River Road
77 Swan Lake Trail/Lakes Area Mountain Bike Routes
78 Kettle Crest/Sherman Trail
84 Riverside State Park
87 Mt. Spokane State Park: Mt. Kit Carson/Day Mountain Loop

Intermediate and Advanced (Short Rides)

- 3 Gotchen Creek Trail
- 13 Mt. Molly Loop
- 17 The Foothills
- 25 Green Mountain
- 29 St. Edward State Park/Big Finn Hill County Park
- 32 Tiger Mountain State Forest: Iverson Railroad Trail
- 37 Cooper River Trail
- 41 Taneum Ridge Loop
- 43 "The Book"
- 51 Lake Padden Single-Track
- 52 Galbraith (can be routed short or long)
- 53 Cranberry Lake
- 59 Johnson Ridge Trail
- 67 Wenatchee River Road
- 77 Swan Lake Trail/Lakes Area Mountain Bike Routes
- 79 Frater Lake
- 83 Minnehaha Park/Beacon Hill
- 84 Riverside State Park
- 85 Riverside State Park: "Rattlesnake"
- 86 Mt. Spokane State Park
- 87 Mt. Spokane State Park: Mt. Kit Carson/Day Mountain Loop

Intermediate and Advanced (Long Rides)

- 1 Tarbell Trail
- 2 Three Corner Rock Trail
- 4 Buttes Loop
- 6 Valley Trail #270
- 10 Ape Canyon/Plains of Abraham
- 11 Lewis River Trail
- 14 Middle Waddell Loop
- 18 Gold Creek Trail
- 19 Lower Dungeness Loop (if done as single-track route using Gold Creek Trail)
- 21 Lower South Fork Skokomish Trail (if done as single-track out-and-back)
- 22 Wynoochee Lakeshore Trail
- 24 Mission Creek Single-Track (described route can be expanded)
- 26 Skookum Flats
- 27 Dalles Ridge Loop
- 28 High Rock Lookout
- 35 Amabilis Mountain
- 36 Kachess Ridge Loop
- 40 North Fork Taneum Creek Loop (by itself or combined with Lookout Mountain Loop)
- 46 Raven Roost
- 48 Little Bald Mountain
- 52 Galbraith (using all trails in network)
- 55 Mt. Josephine
- 56 Schweitzer Creek Loop
- 60 Pole Ridge
- 62 Chikamin Creek Loop (described route can be expanded)
- 64 Mad Lake from the North (described route can be extended)
- 66 Mad Lake from the South (described route can be extended)
- 68 Boundary Butte
- 69 Devil's Gulch/Mission Ridge Trail
- 71 Methow Trail/Sun Mountain Trails
- 72 Buck Lake Loop
- 73 Goat Wall Loop
- 74 Lightning Creek Trail
- 75 Twisp River Trail
- 76 Cooney Lake (described route can be expanded)
- 78 Kettle Crest/Sherman Trail
- 80 Hall Mountain Loop
- 81 Bead Lake Loop

Technical Heaven

- 2 Three Corner Rock Trail
- 7 Siouxan Trail #130
- 10 Ape Canyon/Plains of Abraham
- 13 Mt. Molly Loop
- 14 Middle Waddell Loop
- 15 Mt. Muller Loop
- 18 Gold Creek Trail
- 21 Lower South Fork Skokomish Trail

Technical Heaven (continued)

22 Wynoochee Lakeshore Trail
24 Mission Creek Single-Track
26 Skookum Flats
27 Dalles Ridge Loop
31 Tiger Mountain State Forest: Preston Railroad Trail/Northwest Timber Trail Loop (on ungraveled portion of Preston Railroad Trail)
32 Tiger Mountain State Forest: Iverson Railroad Trail
36 Kachess Ridge Loop
37 Cooper River Trail
40 North Fork Taneum Creek Loop
42 Lookout Mountain Loop
48 Little Bald Mountain
51 Lake Padden Single-Track
52 Galbraith
53 Cranberry Lake
54 Heart Lake/Whistle Lake
59 Johnson Ridge Trail
64 Mad Lake from the North
66 Mad Lake from the South
75 Twisp River Trail
80 Hall Mountain Loop

High-Speed Cruising

4 Buttes Loop
9 Marble Mountain (on gravel descent)
28 High Rock Lookout
30 Snoqualmie Valley Trail
33 Tiger Mountain State Forest: Poo Poo Point
38 Coal Mines Trail
39 Iron Horse State Park: John Wayne Pioneer Trail
46 Raven Roost
35 Amabilis Mountain
55 Mt. Josephine
56 Schweitzer Creek Loop
58 North Mountain
60 Pole Ridge
73 Goat Wall Loop
74 Lightning Creek Trail

Wildlife Viewing

39 Iron Horse State Park: John Wayne Pioneer Trail
44 Tieton Nature Trail
53 Cranberry Lake
54 Heart Lake/Whistle Lake
70 Pearrygin Lake Loop
76 Cooney Lake

Great Scenery

1 Tarbell Trail
2 Three Corner Rock Trail
4 Buttes Loop
7 Siouxan Trail #130
8 Toutle Trail Loop
9 Marble Mountain
10 Ape Canyon/Plains of Abraham
11 Lewis River Trail
15 Mt. Muller Loop
18 Gold Creek Trail
19 Lower Dungeness Loop
20 Lower Big Quilcene Trail
21 Lower South Fork Skokomish Trail
22 Wynoochee Lakeshore Trail
25 Green Mountain
27 Dalles Ridge Loop
28 High Rock Lookout
30 Snoqualmie Valley Trail
33 Tiger Mountain State Forest: Poo Poo Point
35 Amabilis Mountain
36 Kachess Ridge Loop
37 Cooper River Trail
40 North Fork Taneum Creek Loop
41 Taneum Ridge Loop
42 Lookout Mountain Loop
43 "The Book"
44 Tieton Nature Trail
45 Bethel Ridge
46 Raven Roost
48 Little Bald Mountain
53 Cranberry Lake
54 Heart Lake/Whistle Lake

Great Scenery (continued)

55 Mt. Josephine
57 Monte Cristo
58 North Mountain
59 Johnson Ridge Trail
64 Mad Lake from the North
65 Rock Creek Area Trails
66 Mad Lake from the South
68 Boundary Butte

69 Devil's Gulch/Mission Ridge Trail
71 Methow Trail/Sun Mountain Trails
73 Goat Wall Loop
75 Twisp River Trail
76 Cooney Lake
80 Hall Mountain Loop
87 Mt. Spokane State Park: Mt. Kit Carson/Day Mountain Loop

Single-Track

1 Tarbell Trail
2 Three Corner Rock Trail (9.2 miles each way)
3 Gotchen Creek Trail
4 Buttes Loop
6 Valley Trail #270
7 Siouxan Trail #130 (all but the first 3 miles)
8 Toutle Trail Loop (9 miles of loop)
10 Ape Canyon/Plains of Abraham (all but 3.4 miles)
11 Lewis River Trail
12 Mima Loop
13 Mt. Molly Loop
14 Middle Waddell Loop
15 Mt. Muller Loop
16 Spruce Railroad Trail
17 The Foothills
18 Gold Creek Trail
19 Lower Dungeness Loop (6.7 miles of loop)
20 Lower Big Quilcene Trail
21 Lower South Fork Skokomish Trail
22 Wynoochee Lakeshore Trail
23 Howell Lake Lollipop
24 Mission Creek Single-Track
25 Green Mountain
26 Skookum Flats
27 Dalles Ridge Loop
29 St. Edward State Park/Big Finn Hill County Park
31 Tiger Mountain State Forest: Preston Railroad Trail/Northwest Timber Trail Loop (5.9 miles of loop)
32 Tiger Mountain State Forest: Iverson Railroad Trail (2.2 miles of figure eight)

36 Kachess Ridge Loop (6.7 miles of loop)
37 Cooper River Trail
40 North Fork Taneum Creek Loop (11.7 miles of loop)
41 Taneum Ridge Loop (3.8 miles of loop)
42 Lookout Mountain Loop (6.2 miles of loop)
43 "The Book" (2.1 miles of loop)
44 Tieton Nature Trail
48 Little Bald Mountain (10.8 miles)
51 Lake Padden Single-Track
52 Galbraith
53 Cranberry Lake
54 Heart Lake/Whistle Lake
59 Johnson Ridge Trail (6.8 miles)
61 Lower Chiwawa Trail
62 Chikamin Creek Loop (8.7 miles; can route as all single-track)
63 Minnow Ridge Loop (3.9 miles of loop)
64 Mad Lake from the North
65 Rock Creek Area Trails
66 Mad Lake from the South
69 Devil's Gulch/Mission Ridge Trail (all single-track or about 12 miles of single-track on road/trail loop)
71 Methow Trail/Sun Mountain Trails
74 Lightning Creek Trail
75 Twisp River Trail
76 Cooney Lake
77 Swan Lake Trail/Lakes Area Mountain Bike Routes
78 Kettle Crest/Sherman Trail
79 Frater Lake

Single-Track (continued)

80 Hall Mountain Loop
81 Bead Lake Loop
82 South Hill
83 Minnehaha Park/Beacon Hill
    (about 2.8 miles each way)

84 Riverside State Park
85 Riverside State Park: "Rattlesnake"
87 Mt. Spokane State Park: Mt. Kit
    Carson/Day Mountain Loop (1.9
    miles of loop)

Rail-Trails

16 Spruce Railroad Trail
30 Snoqualmie Valley Trail
34 Iron Horse State Park: Snoqualmie
    Tunnel
38 Coal Mines Trail

39 Iron Horse State Park: John Wayne
    Pioneer Trail
49 Interurban Trail and Fragrance
    Lake

Spaghetti Systems (Many Configurations Possible)

12 Mima Loop
13 Mt. Molly Loop
14 Middle Waddell Loop
23 Howell Lake Lollipop
24 Mission Creek Single-Track
29 St. Edward State Park/Big Finn Hill
52 Galbraith
53 Cranberry Lake
54 Heart Lake/Whistle Lake

64 Mad Lake from the North
65 Rock Creek Area Trails
66 Mad Lake from the South
71 Methow Trail/Sun Mountain Trails
82 South Hill
84 Riverside State Park
85 Rattlesnake
86 Mt. Spokane State Park

INTRODUCTION

TRAIL DESCRIPTION OUTLINE

Each trail in this book begins with key information that includes length, configuration, aerobic and technical difficulty, trail conditions, scenery, and special comments. Additional description is contained in 11 individual categories. The following will help you to understand all of the information provided.

Trail name: Trail names are as designated on United States Geological Survey (USGS) or Forest Service or other maps, and/or by local custom.

At a Glance Information

Length/configuration: The overall length of a trail is described in miles, unless stated otherwise. The configuration is a description of the shape of each trail — whether the trail is a loop, out-and-back (that is, along the same route), figure eight, trapezoid, isosceles triangle, decahedron . . . (just kidding), or if it connects with another trail described in the book. See the Glossary for definitions of *point-to-point*, *combination*, and *out-and-back*, or see "Ride Configurations" on page 4.

Aerobic difficulty: This provides a description of the degree of physical exertion required to complete the ride.

Technical difficulty: This provides a description of the technical skill required to pedal a ride. Trails are often described here in terms of being paved, unpaved, sandy, hard-packed, washboarded, two- or four-wheel-drive, single-track or double-track. All terms that might be unfamiliar to the first-time mountain biker are defined in the Glossary.

    Note: For both the aerobic and technical difficulty categories, authors were asked to keep in mind the fact that all riders are not equal, and thus to gauge the trail in terms of how the middle-of-the-road rider — someone between the newcomer and Ned Overend—could handle the route. Comments about the trail's length, condition, and elevation change will also assist you in determining the difficulty of any trail relative to your own abilities.

Scenery: Here you will find a general description of the natural surroundings during the seasons most riders pedal the trail, and a suggestion of what is to be found at special times (like great fall foliage or cactus in bloom).

Special comments: Unique elements of the ride are mentioned.

Category Information

General location: This category describes where the trail is located in reference to a nearby town or other landmark.

Elevation change: Unless stated otherwise, the figure provided is the total gain and loss of elevation along the trail. In regions where the elevation variation is not extreme, the route is simply described as flat, rolling, or possessing short steep climbs or descents.

Season: This is the best time of year to pedal the route, taking into account trail conditions (for example, when it will not be muddy), riding comfort (when the weather is too hot, cold, or wet), and local hunting seasons.

Note: Because the exact opening and closing dates of deer, elk, moose, and antelope seasons often change from year to year, riders should check with the local fish and game department or call a sporting goods store (or any place that sells hunting licenses) in a nearby town before heading out. Wear bright clothes in fall, and don't wear suede jackets while in the saddle. Hunter's-orange tape on your helmet is also a good idea.

Services: This category is of primary importance in guides for paved-road tourers, but is far less crucial to most mountain bike trail descriptions because there are usually no services whatsoever to be found. Authors have noted when water is available on desert or long mountain routes and have listed the availability of food, lodging, campgrounds, and bike shops. If all these services are present, you will find only the words "All services available in . . ."

Hazards: Special hazards like steep cliffs, great amounts of deadfall, or barbed-wire fences very close to the trail are noted here.

Rescue index: Determining how far one is from help on any particular trail can be difficult due to the backcountry nature of most mountain bike rides. Authors therefore state the proximity of homes or Forest Service outposts, nearby roads where one might hitch a ride, or the likelihood of other bikers being encountered on the trail. Phone numbers of local sheriff departments or hospitals are hardly ever provided because phones are usually not available. If you are able to reach a phone, the local operator will connect you with emergency services.

Land status: This category provides information regarding whether the trail crosses land operated by the Forest Service, Bureau of Land Management, or a city, state, or national park; whether it crosses private land whose owner (at the time the author did the research) has allowed mountain bikers right of passage; and so on.

Note: Authors have been extremely careful to offer only those routes that are open to bikers and are legal to ride. However, because land ownership changes over time, and because the land-use controversy created by mountain bikes still has not completely subsided, it is the duty of each cyclist to look for and to heed signs warning against trail use. Don't expect this book to get you off the hook when you're facing some small-town judge for pedaling past a Biking Prohibited sign erected the day before you arrived. Look for these signs, read them, and heed the advice. And remember there's always another trail.

Maps: The maps in this book have been produced with great care and, in conjunction with the trail-following suggestions, will help you stay on course. But as every experienced mountain biker knows, things can get tricky in the backcountry. It is therefore strongly suggested that you avail yourself of the detailed information found in the 7.5 minute series USGS topographic maps. In some cases, authors have found that specific Forest Service or other maps may be more useful than the USGS quads and tell how to obtain them.

Finding the trail: Detailed information on how to reach the trailhead and where to park your car is provided here.

Sources of additional information: Here you will find the address and/or phone number of a bike shop, governmental agency, or other source from which trail information can be obtained.

Notes on the trail: This is where you are guided carefully through any portions of the trail that are particularly difficult to follow. The author also may add information about the route that does not fit easily in the other categories. This category will not be present for those rides where the route is easy to follow.

ABBREVIATIONS

The following road-designation abbreviations are used in *Mountain Bike! Washington:*

CR	County Road	I-	Interstate
FS	Forest Service Road	US	United States highway

State highways are designated with the appropriate two-letter state abbreviation, 0followed by the road number. Example: WA 35 = Washington State Highway 35.

SPECIAL TERMS

The following terms are used throughout this book and deserve special attention:

BLM	Bureau of Land Management, an agency of the federal government
carsonite sign	a small, thin, and flexible fiberglass signpost used extensively by the Forest Service and BLM to mark roads and trails (often dark brown in color)
decomposed granite	an excellent, fine- to medium-grain, trail and road surface material; typically used in native surface road and trail applications (not trucked in); results from the weathering of granite
pummy	soil with high pumice content produced by volcanic activity in the Pacific Northwest and elsewhere; light in consistency and easily pedaled; trails with such soil often become thick with dust
recreation opportunity guides (R.O.G.)	handouts which identify and describe resources available to the public on national forest lands (camping facilities, trails, wildlife viewing opportunities, etc.); often available for the asking at Forest Service ranger stations throughout the Pacific Northwest
skid road	the path created when loggers drag trees through the forest with heavy equipment

RIDE CONFIGURATIONS

Combination: This type of route may combine two or more configurations. For example, a point-to-point route may integrate a scenic loop or an out-and-back spur midway through the ride. Likewise, an out-and-back may have a loop at its farthest point (this configuration looks like a cherry with a stem attached; the stem is the out-and-back, the fruit is the terminus loop). Or a loop route may have multiple out-and-back spurs and/or loops to the side. Mileage for a combination route is for the total distance to complete the ride.

Loop: This route configuration is characterized by riding from the designated trailhead to a distant point, then returning to the trailhead via a different route (or simply continuing on the same in a circle route) without doubling back. You always move forward across new terrain, but return to the starting point when finished. Mileage is for the entire loop from the trailhead back to trailhead.

Out-and-back: A ride where you will return on the same trail you pedaled out. While this might sound far more boring than a loop route, many trails look very different when pedaled in the opposite direction.

Point-to-point: A vehicle shuttle (or similar assistance) is required for this type of route, which is ridden from the designated trailhead to a distant location, or endpoint, where the route ends. Total mileage is for the one-way trip from the trailhead to endpoint.

Spur: A road or trail that intersects the main trail you're following.

Ride configurations written by Gregg Bromka.

TOPOGRAPHIC MAPS

The maps in this book, when used in conjunction with the route directions present in each chapter, will in most instances be sufficient to get you to the trail and keep you on it. However, you will find superior detail and valuable information in the 7.5 minute series USGS topographic maps. Recognizing how indispensable these are to bikers and hikers alike, many bike shops and sporting goods stores now carry topos of the local area.

But if you're brand new to mountain biking you might be wondering "What's a topographic map?" In short, these differ from standard "flat" maps in that they indicate not only linear distance, but elevation as well. One glance at a topo will show you the difference, for "contour lines" are spread across the map like dozens of intricate spider webs. Each contour line represents a particular elevation, and at the base of each topo a particular "contour interval" designation is given. Yes, it sounds confusing if you're new to the lingo, but it truly is a simple and wonderfully helpful system. Keep reading.

Let's assume that the 7.5 minute series topo before us says "Contour Interval 40 feet," that the short trail we'll be pedaling is two inches in length on the map, and that it crosses five contour lines from its beginning to end. What do we know? Well, because the linear scale of this series is 2,000 feet to the inch (roughly 2 3/4 inches representing 1 mile), we know our trail is approximately 4/5 of a mile long (2 inches × 2,000 feet). But we also know we'll be climbing or descending 200 vertical feet (5 contour lines × 40 feet each) over that distance. And the elevation designations written on occasional contour lines will tell us if we're heading up or down.

The authors of this series warn their readers of upcoming terrain, but only a detailed topo gives you the information you need to pinpoint your position exactly on a map, steer yourself toward optional trails and roads nearby, plus let you know at a glance if you'll be pedaling hard to take them. It's a lot of information for a very low cost. In fact, the only drawback with topos is their size — several feet square. I've tried rolling them into tubes, folding them carefully, even cutting them into blocks and photocopying the pieces. Any of these systems is a pain, but no matter how you pack the maps you'll be happy they're along. And you'll be even happier if you pack a compass as well.

In addition to local bike shops and sporting goods stores, you'll find topos at major universities and some public libraries where you might try photocopying the ones you need to avoid the cost of buying them. But if you want your own and can't find them locally, contact:

USGS Map Sales
Box 25286
Denver, CO 80225
(800) HELP MAP (435-7627)

VISA and MasterCard are accepted. Ask for an index while you're at it, plus a price list and a copy of the booklet *Topographic Maps*. In minutes you'll be reading them like a pro.

A second excellent series of maps available to mountain bikers is that produced by the United States Forest Service. If your trail runs through an area designated as a national forest, look in the phone book (white pages) under the United States Government listings, find the Department of Agriculture heading, and then run your finger down that section until you find the Forest Service. Give them a call and they'll provide the address of the regional Forest Service office, from which you can obtain the appropriate map.

TRAIL ETIQUETTE

Pick up almost any mountain bike magazine these days and you'll find articles and letters to the editor about trail conflict. For example, you'll find hikers' tales of being blindsided by speeding mountain bikers, complaints from mountain bikers about being blamed for trail damage that was really caused by horse or cattle traffic, and cries from bikers about those "kamikaze" riders who through their antics threaten to close even more trails to all of us.

The authors of this series have been very careful to guide you to only those trails that are open to mountain biking (or at least were open at the time of their research), and without exception have warned of the damage done to our sport through injudicious riding. My personal views on this matter appear in the Afterword, but all of us can benefit from glancing over the following International Mountain Bicycling Association (IMBA) Rules of the Trail before saddling up.

1. *Ride on open trails only.* Respect trail and road closures (ask if not sure), avoid possible trespass on private land, obtain permits and authorization as may be required. Federal and state wilderness areas are closed to cycling.

2. *Leave no trace.* Be sensitive to the dirt beneath you. Even on open trails, you should not ride under conditions where you will leave evidence of your passing, such as on certain soils shortly after rain. Observe the different types of soils and trail construction; practice low-impact cycling. This also means staying on the

trail and not creating any new ones. Be sure to pack out at least as much as you pack in.

3. *Control your bicycle!* Inattention for even a second can cause disaster. Excessive speed can maim and threaten people; there is no excuse for it!

4. *Always yield the trail.* Make known your approach well in advance. A friendly greeting (or a bell) is considerate and works well; startling someone may cause loss of trail access. Show your respect when passing others by slowing to a walk or even stopping. Anticipate that other trail users may be around corners or in blind spots.

5. *Never spook animals.* All animals are startled by an unannounced approach, a sudden movement, or a loud noise. This can be dangerous for you, for others, and for the animals. Give animals extra room and time to adjust to you. In passing, use special care and follow the directions of horseback riders (ask if uncertain). Running cattle and disturbing wild animals is a serious offense. Leave gates as you found them, or as marked.

6. *Plan ahead.* Know your equipment, your ability, and the area in which you are riding—and prepare accordingly. Be self-sufficient at all times. Wear a helmet, keep your machine in good condition, and carry necessary supplies for changes in weather or other conditions. A well-executed trip is a satisfaction to you and not a burden or offense to others.

For more information, contact IMBA, P.O. Box 7578, Boulder, CO 80306; (303) 545-9011.

HITTING THE TRAIL

Once again, because this is a "where-to," not a "how-to" guide, the following will be brief. If you're a veteran trail rider these suggestions might serve to remind you of something you've forgotten to pack. If you're a newcomer, they might convince you to think twice before hitting the backcountry unprepared.

Water: I've heard the questions dozens of times. "How much is enough? One bottle? Two? Three?! But think of all that extra weight!" Well, one simple physiological fact should convince you to err on the side of excess when it comes to deciding how much water to pack: a human working hard in 90-degree temperature needs approximately ten quarts of fluids every day. Ten quarts. That's two and a half gallons—12 large water bottles, or 16 small ones. And, with water weighing in at approximately 8 pounds per gallon, a one-day supply comes to a whopping 20 pounds.

In other words, pack along two or three bottles even for short rides. And make sure you can purify the water found along the trail on longer routes. When writing of those routes where this could be of critical importance, each author has provided information on where water can be found near the trail—if it can be found at all. But drink it untreated and you run the risk of disease. (See *Giardia* in the Glossary.)

One sure way to kill the protozoans, bacteria, and viruses in water is to boil it. Right. That's just how you want to spend your time on a bike ride. Besides, who wants to carry a stove, or denude the countryside stoking bonfires to boil water?

Luckily, there is a better way. Many riders pack along the inexpensive and only slightly distasteful tetraglycine hydroperiodide tablets (sold under the names Potable Aqua, Globaline, and Coughlan's, among others). Some invest in portable, lightweight purifiers that filter out the crud. Unfortunately, both iodine *and* filtering are now required to be absolutely sure you've killed all the nasties you can't see. Tablets or iodine drops by themselves will knock off the well-known *Giardia*, once called "beaver fever" for its transmission to the water through the feces of infected beavers. One to four weeks after ingestion, *Giardia* will have you bloated, vomiting, shivering with chills, and living in the bathroom. (Though you won't care while you're suffering, beavers are getting a bum rap, for other animals are carriers also.)

But now there's another parasite we must worry about—*Cryptosporidium*. "Crypto" brings on symptoms very similar to *Giardia*, but unlike that fellow protozoan it's equipped with a shell sufficiently strong to protect it against the chemical killers that stop *Giardia* cold. This means we're either back to boiling or on to using a water filter to screen out both *Giardia* and crypto, plus the iodine to knock off viruses. All of which sounds like a time-consuming pain, but really isn't. Some water filters come equipped with an iodine chamber, to guarantee full protection. Or you can simply add a pill or drops to the water you've just filtered (if you aren't allergic to iodine, of course). The pleasures of back-country biking—and the displeasure of getting sick—make this relatively minor effort worth the few minutes involved.

Tools: Ever since my first cross-country tour in 1965 I've been kidded about the number of tools I pack on the trail. And so I will exit entirely from this discussion by providing a list compiled by two mechanic (and mountain biker) friends of mine. After all, since they make their livings fixing bikes and get their kicks by riding them, who could be a better source?

These two suggest the following as an absolute minimum:

tire levers
spare tube and patch kit
air pump
Allen wrenches (3, 4, 5, and 6 mm)
six-inch crescent (adjustable-end) wrench
small flat-blade screwdriver
chain rivet tool
spoke wrench

But, while they're on the trail, their personal tool pouches contain these additional items:

channel locks (small)
air gauge
tire valve cap (the metal kind, with a valve-stem remover)
baling wire (ten or so inches, for temporary repairs)
duct tape (small roll for temporary repairs or tire boot)
boot material (small piece of old tire or a large tube patch)
spare chain link
rear derailleur pulley
spare nuts and bolts
paper towel and tube of waterless hand cleaner

First-aid kit: My personal kit contains the following, sealed inside double Ziploc bags:

sunscreen
aspirin
butterfly-closure bandages
Band-Aids
gauze compress pads (a half-dozen 4" × 4")
gauze (one roll)
ace bandages or Spenco joint wraps
Benadryl (an antihistamine, in case of allergic reactions)
water purification tablets / water filter (on long rides)
moleskin / Spenco "Second Skin"
hydrogen peroxide, iodine, or Mercurochrome (some kind of antiseptic)
snakebite kit

Final considerations: The authors of this series have done a good job in suggesting that specific items be packed for certain trails—rain gear in particular seasons, a hat and gloves for mountain passes, or shades for desert jaunts. Heed their warnings, and think ahead. Good luck.

Dennis Coello

AND NOW, A WORD ABOUT CELLULAR PHONES . . .

Thinking of bringing the Flip-Fone along on your next off-road ride? Before you do, ask yourself the following questions:

- Do I know where I'm going? Do I have an adequate map? Can I use a compass effectively? Do I know the shortest way to civilization if I need to bail out early and find some help?

- If I'm on the trail for longer than planned, am I ready for it? Do I have adequate water? Have I packed something to eat? Will I be warm enough if I'm still out there after dark?

- Am I prepared for possible injuries? Do I have a first-aid kit? Do I know what to do in case of a cut, fracture, snakebite, or heat exhaustion?

- Is my tool kit adequate for likely mechanical problems? Can I fix a flat? Can I untangle a chain? Am I prepared to walk out if the bike is unridable?

If you answered "yes" to *every* question above, you may pack the phone, but consider a good whistle instead. It's lighter, cheaper, and nearly as effective.

If you answered "no" to *any* of these questions, be aware that your cellular phone does little to reduce your risks in the wilderness. Sure, being able to dial 911 in the farthest corner of the Cascade Mountains sounds like a great idea, but this ain't downtown, friend. If disaster strikes, and your call is routed to some emergency operator in Portland or Hillsboro, and it takes awhile to figure out which ranger, sheriff, or search-and-rescue crew to connect you with, and you can't tell the authorities where you are because you're really not sure, and the closest they can come to pinpointing your location is a cellular tower that serves 62 square miles of dense woods, and they start searching for you but dusk is only two hours away, and you have no signaling device and your throat is too dry to shout, and meanwhile you can't get the bleeding stopped, you are out of luck. I mean *really* out of luck.

And when the battery goes dead, you're on your own again. Enough said.

Jeff Faust
Author of Mountain Bike! New Hampshire

YACOLT BURN STATE FOREST

The southern border of the Yacolt Burn State Forest lies roughly five to ten miles north of the Columbia River and Oregon. It is easily accessible from Vancouver, the oldest city in the "Evergreen State," and from over the bridge into Portland. The western border is north of Camas; the forest extends eastward almost to Carson, about 50 miles east of Vancouver on WA 14.

The Department of Natural Resources (DNR) roads within the forest are numbered with the prefixes of **L** for the Larch Mountain area in the western region of the forest, **W** for the Washougal area in the central region, and **CG** for the Columbia Gorge area in the eastern region.

The Yacolt lies in a unique area that makes it susceptible to fire. The area has recovered from nine major burns in the first half of the twentieth century to become a vital commercial forest.

The Columbia River Gorge can reverse the moist, cool winds that normally blow from the west, and funnel in dry winds from east of the Cascades. When the arid winds hit the forest, they take the last of the moisture from the dead-wood and brush, already dry from the summer heat, and turn the forest into a wildfire waiting to happen.

One of the worst fires in Washington's history, the 1902 Yacolt fire, was thought to have started when sparks from smoldering burn piles were blown into nearby timber. Other theories hold that it started in the sheep country in the eastern Cascades; that flames from Oregon wildfires jumped the river; and that a boat crew taking on wood on the Columbia River set fire to a wasp's nest and the fire got out of control. However it started, the fire was blown by the "Devil Wind," as pioneers called it, across a total of 393,000 acres. Smoke shrouded all of western Washington; street lamps in Seattle were lit in the middle of the day. Interestingly, winds shifted and the fire spared the tiny town of Yacolt, after which the fire was named

The area recovered strongly. Timber rules here, but recreation abounds. While not especially rich in single-track, the area holds some excellent riding. In addition to the Tarbell Trail and Three Corner Rock Trail, the Jones Creek off-road vehicle system includes about 12 miles of trails, and the Tarbell Trail connects with others leading into the adjoining Gifford Pinchot National Forest. The top of the Three Corner Rock Trail ties into the Pacific Crest Trail, which is off-limits to bikes.

Wildlife has also recovered from the area's devastation; populations include black bear, mule deer, coyote, chipmunk, badger, and marmot. Bald eagles are sighted, as are hawks and owls. Besides mountain biking, activities in the forest include hunting, fishing, picnicking, hiking, horseback riding, and motorcycle riding (motorcycles are not allowed on the Tarbell and Three Corner Rock Trails, but are legal on the more than 350 miles of forest roads and in the Jones Creek off-road vehicle system).

Beacon Rock State Park, just east of Skamania, is a scenic destination near the southeast side of the forest. Here you'll find camping, boating, hiking, biking, and dramatic views of the Columbia River Gorge from the top of Beacon Rock.

RIDE 1 · Tarbell Trail

AT A GLANCE

WA

Length/configuration: Best option is an all single-track 21.6-mile (total mileage) out-and-back; other options include a 26.7-mile loop using the Larch Mountain Trail

Aerobic difficulty: Moderately difficult initial climb; tough 2.1-mile climb out of Hidden Falls

Technical difficulty: Some rocky areas near the start; tight switchbacks

Scenery: Second-growth forest; brief high Cascades views; Pyramid Rock; Silver Star Mountain

Special comments: Some of the best state forest riding in Washington; adjoining trails lead into the Gifford Pinchot National Forest

---

The Tarbell Trail was named for George Lee Tarbell, who, in the early 1900s, lived alone in a shack accessible only by a path that roughly follows the present day trail. Tarbell surely enjoyed some beautiful views along his trail, of Sturgeon Rock (3,100 feet elevation), Pyramid Rock (3,503 feet), Larch Mountain (3,496 feet), and Silver Star Mountain (4,390 feet). Views stretch from the surrounding valleys to the high Cascades.

The Tarbell Trail, like the Three Corner Rock Trail to the east, is among the best Department of Natural Resources (DNR) riding in the state. The trail is mostly hardpack with some rocky and uneven sections. It climbs and descends through second-growth forest with some scattered old growth Douglas fir. It also sports the above-mentioned views, as well as scenic Hidden Falls, to entertain the eyes while exercising the legs and lungs.

I enjoyed this trail from the start, and I was determined to share it with you— routing it was the problem. I first included it in a loop, utilizing the adjacent Larch Mountain Trail, for a 26.7-mile outing. Due to the horse traffic on the Larch Mountain Trail, many sections are merely rough under dry conditions; when the trail is even moderately wet, as during my research ride in late July, the trail sucks wheels down, forcing extreme efforts or dismounts along the trail. In fact, the lower Larch Mountain Trail and the lower portion of the Tarbell Trail, near Rock Creek Campground, are the most horse-scarred trails I have ever ridden. Frankly, I would not recommend it; thrill-seeking hard cores, do that loop at your own peril.

RIDE 1 · Tarbell Trail

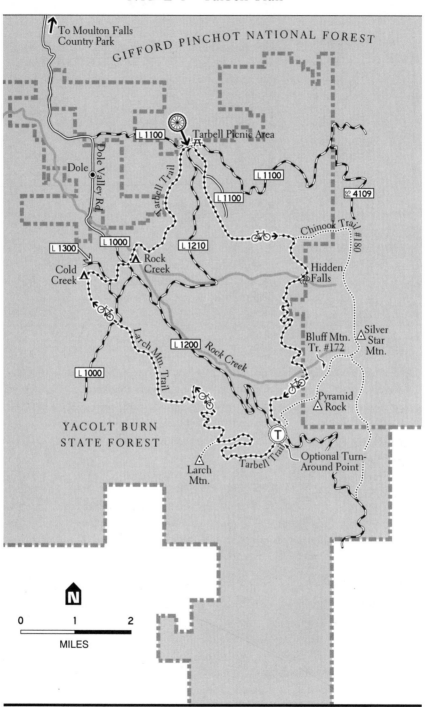

To Moulton Falls
Country Park

GIFFORD PINCHOT NATIONAL FOREST

L 1100 Tarbell Picnic Area

Dole

Dole Valley Rd.

Tarbell Trail

L 1100

L 1100

FS 4109

Chinook Trail #180

L 1300

L 1000

L 1210

Rock Creek

Hidden Falls

Cold Creek

Larch Mtn. Trail

L 1200

Rock Creek

Bluff Mtn. Tr. #172

Silver Star Mtn.

L 1000

Pyramid Rock

YACOLT BURN
STATE FOREST

T

Larch Mtn.

Tarbell Trail

Optional Turn-Around Point

N

0   1   2
MILES

Not giving up, I rode the trail again as a gravel road/single-track loop from the Rock Creek Campground, using DNR roads L-1000 and L-1210. The gravel road section was rough in spots, but it made for a moderate, pleasant, mostly middle-ring climb. However, the final 3.4-mile, 860-foot, horse-scarred descent (which the out-and-back avoids), and the cold, deep ford across Rock Creek were not worthy trade-offs for the road climb.

In the end, I would advise riding the Tarbell Trail as a strong intermediate-level, 21.6-mile round-trip from the Tarbell Picnic Area to Grouse Creek Vista and back; it's a great ride in both directions. If you want to explore further, try a side trip to the east by way of the recently cut Chinook Trail. It leads into the adjacent Gifford Pinchot National Forest and to Silver Star Trail #180, Ed's Trail, Bluff Mountain Trail #172, and Silver Star Mountain.

General location: The Tarbell Picnic Area is approximately 35 miles northeast of Vancouver.

Elevation change: The described route starts at the Tarbell Picnic Area (elevation 1,765'), climbs 790' in 2.4 miles to Squaw Butte (2,552'), and then drops to Hidden Falls (2,460'). The trail rises about 900' out of Hidden Falls to the final descent before the turnaround. Climbing on the return brings total elevation gain to about 3,400' for the out-and-back. For the Tarbell–Larch Mountain Loop, total elevation gain is at least 3,500'—and feels like more!

Season: The trail is open year-round, but you'll find the best riding conditions as the season progresses and the trail dries out. On my second journey here, in late September, I was treated to a beautiful display of fall colors, courtesy of the willow, wild dogwood, red alder, and big leaf maple along the route.

Services: Water is available from a hand pump next to the parking area at the Tarbell Picnic Area, and adjacent to campsite 13 at Rock Creek Campground. Limited services are available in Yacolt, approximately 10 miles northwest of the Tarbell Picnic Area on County Road (CR) 16 (north off Lucia Falls Road where N.E. Sunset Falls Road turns south). Services are also available in Battle Ground, and everything you need, including bike stuff, is in Vancouver.

Hazards: Horses along the trail have been a hazard to the trail itself; mountain bikers can be hazardous to the horses, so ride with care. If you brave the Larch Mountain Trail, some dismounts are necessary not only on the climb to the top but on the descent, where a dangerous scree slope is best walked. Rocky, rooty switchback drop-offs afterward give more reasons to dismount.

Rescue index: A solitary house sits along L-1100 Road. Residents along Dole Valley Road may summon help. The camp host at Rock Creek Campground can also call for help if needed. Help can be obtained in Yacolt, Battle Ground, and Vancouver.

Land status: Yacolt Burn State Forest.

Maps: DNR Yacolt Burn State Forest Map.

Finding the trail: From Interstate 5 in Vancouver, take Exit 9/WA 502. Follow

Hidden Falls.

WA 502 north and east approximately 6.5 miles to Battle Ground, then turn left (north) on WA 503. From I-205 in Vancouver, exit at WA 500. Drive east 1.2 miles to WA 503, then take WA 503 north; you will come to WA 502 in approximately 8 miles. From the intersection of WA 502 and WA 503 in Battle Ground, travel 5.8 miles north on WA 503 (about 2.5 miles north of Lewisville County Park) to Rock Creek Road. Turn right, following the signs to Moulton Falls County Park (Rock Creek Road turns into Lucia Falls Road). In 8.7 miles, at the junction past the park, turn right at CR 12, N.E. Sunset Falls Road (where a left turn brings you to Yacolt). Travel 2.1 miles to Dole Valley Road; turn right, and take it 2.5 miles until you see a gravel road veer left at the 11 o'clock position where Dole Valley Road starts curving to the right. Follow the gravel road, L-1100, signed toward the Tarbell Picnic Area. Stay on the main gravel road, past the spurs and past a solitary house, for 2.2 miles until the **T** intersection with L-1210 at the Tarbell Picnic Area. Turn right on L-1210 and make use of the parking area immediately on the left.

Source of additional information:

Washington State Department of Natural Resources
Southwest Region
601 Bond Road, P.O. Box 280
Castle Rock, WA 98611-0280
(800) 527-3305 or (360) 577-2025 (direct)

Notes on the trail: From the parking area, ride 0.1 mile down L-1210, past the hand pump, to a trail crossing. Begin to the left. The trail starts climbing in a wooded area with a hard-packed surface, and breaks into an exposed, logged area as you climb. The 2.4-mile climb to Squaw Butte is broken up with some downhills and views of the high Cascades and Dole Valley. As you descend to Hidden Falls, you pass the junction with the Chinook Trail and its side-trip possibilities at 3.9 miles. A switchbacking descent of another 1.7 miles brings you to scenic Hidden Falls, and a bench beside the trail beckons you to stop and savor it. Climbing on the other side of the falls, stop and bite into a leaf of tangy, three leaf clover–shaped wood sorrel that lines the trail. At 2.0 miles past the falls, a road crossing signals another descent, with views of Pyramid Rock to the east. Descend to a bridge over Rock Creek and shortly come to the end of the trail. The trail dumps out onto Gifford Pinchot National Forest Trail #172, Bluff Mountain Trail (actually a steep, rocky roadbed). Turn right, and in about 100' come to L-1200 at Grouse Vista, the turnaround point on the described route. Frankly, I didn't see the vista, but it's a great ride, so I didn't grouse!

The Larch Mountain Trail continues on the other side of L-1200 and climbs to its peak in 3.0 miles, where the trees and transmission towers snatch the panoramic view from you (another reason to stick with the Tarbell Trail.) It descends to Cold Creek Campground, continues to Rock Creek Campground, and climbs back to the Tarbell Picnic Area 3.4 miles after fording Rock Creek. I tell you this because the two trails are adjacent, but you'll be a much, much happier camper having done an out-and-back to Grouse Vista on the Tarbell Trail.

RIDE 2 · Three Corner Rock Trail

AT A GLANCE

Length/configuration: 9.2 miles of single-track; can be done as a 25.9-mile road and single-track figure eight, a 21.2-mile road and single-track loop with out-and-back spur to top on single-track, or an 18.4-mile (total mileage) out-and-back

Aerobic difficulty: Difficult initial climb to the trail crossing; climb gets tougher as you ride the road to the top

Technical difficulty: Switchbacks—lots of switchbacks; some loose, rocky sections

Scenery: Meadow and Cascades views at the top; deep woods, canyons

Special comments: Great workout for the legs and eyes; not too far from Vancouver

Do you like riding switchbacks? I mean, do you really, really like riding switchbacks? The Three Corner Rock Trail will test your switchbacking ability as it offers an unofficial 65 of 'em in 9.2 miles of scenic, challenging single-track. Three Corner Rock, perched atop the mountain at the upper end of the trail, can be accessed all on trail, by a part gravel road/part single-track climb, or all on gravel road, which routes the ride as a 25.9-mile figure eight.

Generally, the trail surface is a nice, forest-floor hardpack; toward the bottom some areas are rocky. Even if you're not a switchback master, the woods along the trail and the view from the top make it a beautiful place to polish that skill.

If you choose to ride the trail as an out-and-back, you get some respites from the climb on two one-mile sections on the lower portion of the trail. Other than that, you'll have quite a few uphill switchbacks to navigate. Those with less-than-expert technical proficiency are best off doing the road climb/trail descent.

The length of the climb, the switchbacks, and total distance of up to 25.9 miles make this an advanced level ride.

General location: The ride begins approximately 36 miles northeast of Vancouver along the Washougal River.

Elevation change: The lower trailhead sits at 940' and climbs to 3,505' at Three Corner Rock. Undulations on both the road and trail add another 600', for a total elevation gain of 3,165'.

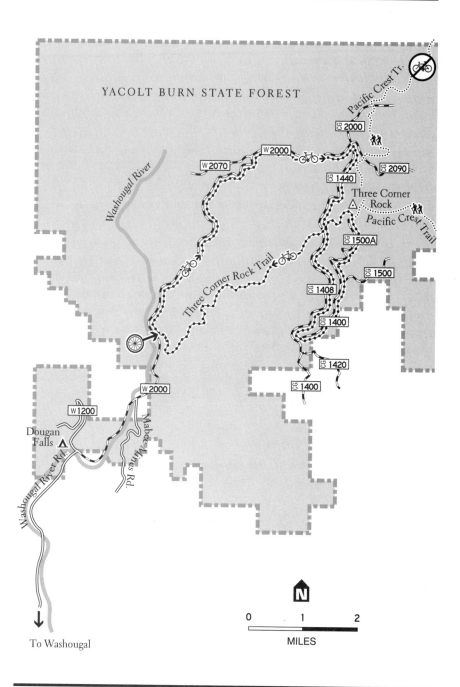

Season: I've been told that the lower portion of the trail stays free of snow and is rideable year-round, though winter precipitation and trail-consciousness may dictate against it. For the entire loop, both you and the trail will be happiest from late spring to fall.

Services: Water, gas, and groceries are available at the Washougal River Mercantile, 10 miles from the trailhead on Washougal River Road. Services are available in Washougal; all services are in Vancouver.

Hazards: On the road, most of the last mile to the top is steep and rocky. Some of the switchbacks, especially on the upper portion of the trail, are rutted, while a few on the lower section are rocky and treacherous.

Rescue index: The in-season campground host at Dougan Falls Campground, 3.3 miles from the trailhead, has a phone. Residences are close by the campground. A pay phone is located at the Washougal River Mercantile.

Land status: Washington Department of Natural Resources, Yacolt Burn State Forest.

Maps: DNR Yacolt Burn State Forest Map.

Finding the trail: From I-5 or I-205 in Vancouver, go east on WA 14 to Washougal. Turn north on 15th Street, which winds around and turns into 17th Street, which turns into Washougal River Road. Travel 17 winding miles (a couple of miles past the Department of Fisheries Salmon Hatchery) until the pavement ends, just past Dougan Falls Road on the left and a bridge over the river. Turn right on gravel road W-2000 after the bridge (where road W-1200 goes left), following the directional sign to Three Corner Rock. The trailhead is at 3.3 miles on road W-2000 alongside the Washougal River. Park on the left, 0.2 miles beyond the lower trailhead on the right, where a parking pullout and outhouses are offered for your convenience.

Source of additional information:

Washington Department of Natural Resources
Southwest Region
601 Bond Road
P.O. Box 280
Castle Rock, WA 98611-0280
(800) 527-3305 or (360) 577-2025 (direct)

Notes on the trail: Begin by continuing north on W-2000. Follow the main road, where a low- to middle-ring climb is broken up with short, fun descents. At 7.5 miles come to a three-way junction: a left on CG-2000, a soft right on CG-2090, and a hard right on CG-1440. Take the hard right. At about 8.7 miles, look up at the one o'clock position for a brief glimpse of the rock, which teases you from above. At 9.9 miles, come to Three Corner Rock Trail. Decision time: you can descend for 7.1 miles back to the start, turn up the trail for 2.1 tough miles of switchbacking to the rock, or continue for 6.6 more miles on the road. For the figure eight, go straight, continuing the road climb on CG-1440, which

Three Corner Rock Trail.

turns into CG-1408. Three miles after the trail crossing (12.9 miles total), a road branches off to the right; veer left, continuing the climb on the main road. In another 1.7 miles, CG-1500 curves right; go straight, around the gate, onto CG-1500A. The trail starts in 1.8 more low-ring miles, just before the rock, to the left. (The famous Pacific Crest Trail, a big-time no-no for bikes, takes off to the right.) Before the descent, though, dismount and climb up the rock to reap your reward of incredible high Cascades views. Now hop on the trail and snake your way down. In 2.1 miles cross CG-1440, the trail picks up just a little to the left. In about 0.5 mile, look for the sign to the viewpoint to the right. Dismount or try to ride the steep 200 yards to get a good last look at Three Corner Rock. In 2.7 more miles, shortly after a footbridge, 1 mile of uphill switchbacking awaits. Then, after a short descent, a rolling 1-mile climb brings you to your final descent. At the lower trailhead you can ride the short 0.2 mile to the right to your vehicle, or cross the road for a bonus 0.2 mile of single-track, which also leads to the parking area.

MT. ADAMS AREA RIDES

The jump-off point for exploring the area around Mt. Adams is Trout Lake, Washington. This town is about 23 miles north of Hood River, Oregon. From Portland, Trout Lake is a few hours' drive away.

At 12,307 feet, Mt. Adams is a massive bulk of a mountain, the third largest peak in the Cascade Range. To the east of Mt. Adams is the Yakima Indian Reservation. To the west is the Gifford Pinchot National Forest, named for the first chief of the U.S. Forest Service. Pinchot was an active conservationist. He played a key role in establishing environmental awareness as a cornerstone of forest management.

The forests blanketing the lower slopes of Mt. Adams contain several varieties of trees of high commercial value. While the economy of the region has long centered around timber, logging of the great forests has slowed. You still encounter logging trucks and hear chain saws, but the woods seem quieter than they were a few years ago. Ranger districts throughout the Pacific Northwest are welcoming people to come and take part in their favorite recreational pursuits.

One very popular activity in this part of the forest is berry picking. The hillsides leading up to Mt. Adams contain vast open areas thick with huckleberry bushes. Large numbers of people come to gather the berries when they ripen (usually around Labor Day). Many of the pickers are Native Americans. In the old days, berries of all kinds were an important part of the Indian diet. The Indians would arrive on horseback and foot, then set up camps on the slopes of the mountain. Huge quantities of huckleberries were gathered and then dried. These berries were formed into cakes that sustained the Indians through the long months of winter.

Today a couple of bed-and-breakfasts, a café, and a general store meet the needs of travelers to this part of the world. Camping facilities are plentiful, and the fishing in the area's many mountain lakes and streams is good. Thanks to the timber industry, miles of gravel roads await two-wheeled adventurers. Trails wander for miles through the woods and make for some good mountain biking.

RIDE 3 · Gotchen Creek Trail

AT A GLANCE
———————

Length/configuration: 9.6-mile loop; gravel roads and single-track

Aerobic difficulty: Moderate; a steady 4-mile climb

Technical difficulty: Forest roads are easy; single-track is moderate to difficult

Scenery: Wooded forest; limited views of Mt. Adams through the trees

Special comments: Classic forest road climb with single-track descent

WA

Combining Gotchen Creek Trail with fire roads makes for a moderately difficult 9.6-mile loop. Well-maintained gravel and dirt roads account for 6.6 miles of the trip. Gotchen Creek Trail descends overall and is in fair shape. The path is bumpy and hoof-worn in places.

The trip begins with a four-mile climb to the upper trailhead. This grade begins easily with a nice warm-up; the remaining three miles are moderately difficult. There are some views of Mt. Adams through the trees as you near the top of the climb. For a trail that drops over 1,000 feet in three miles, Gotchen Creek Trail contains a surprising number of short ascents, some steep. The ride from the lower trailhead back to your vehicle is an enjoyable descent along winding dirt roads.

General location: The ride begins approximately 7 miles north of Trout Lake, Washington. Trout Lake is located about 23 miles north of Hood River, Oregon.

Elevation change: The ride starts at 3,160' and reaches a high point of 4,660' just past the start of Gotchen Creek Trail. Ups and downs add approximately 300' of climbing to the loop. Total elevation gain: 1,800'.

Season: This trail is open to recreational use by equestrians, hikers, and cyclists from June 1 to November 1.

Services: Food, lodging, limited groceries, gas, showers, and pay phones can be found in Trout Lake.

Hazards: Sections of the trail descend sharply and are rough; control your speed. Expect technical riding on the trail, which contains embedded, loose, and moss-covered rocks; soft conditions; creek crossings; and forest litter, including windfall. You may encounter vehicles on the roads.

RIDE 3 · Gotchen Creek Trail

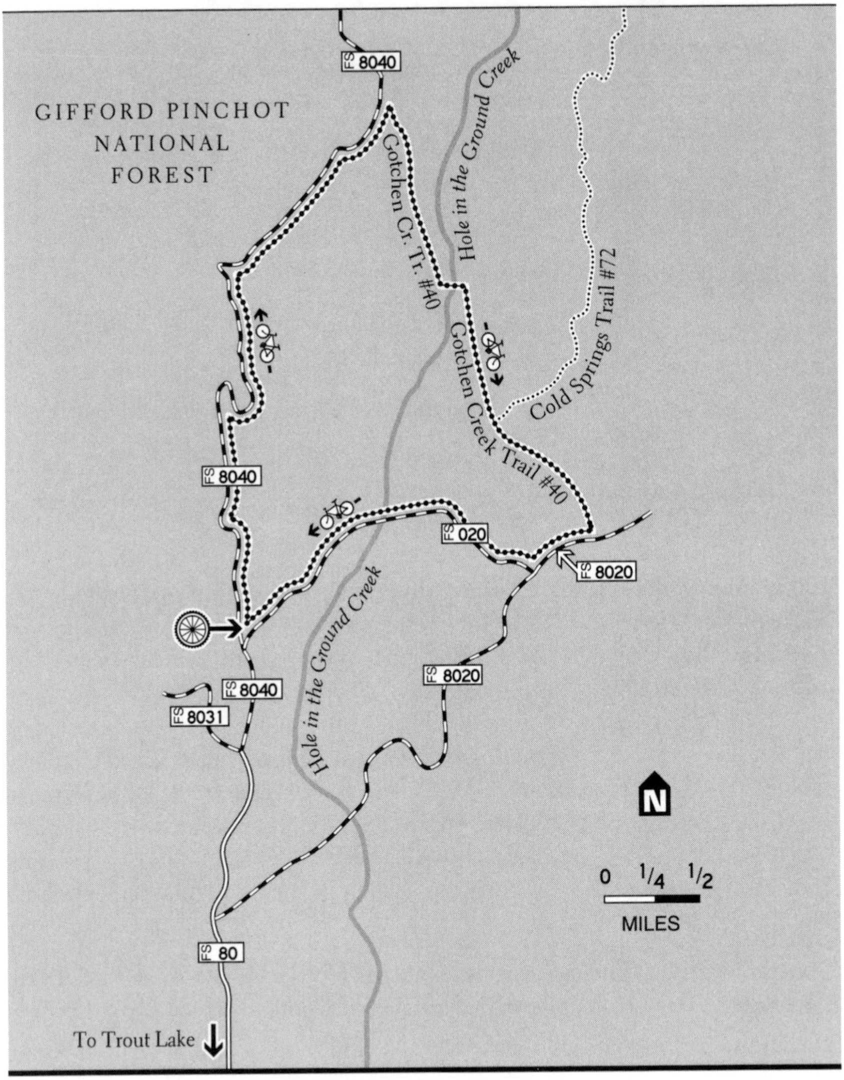

GIFFORD PINCHOT
NATIONAL
FOREST

FS 8040

Hole in the Ground Creek

Gotchen Cr. Tr. #40

Gotchen Creek Trail #40

Cold Springs Trail #72

FS 8040

FS 020

FS 8020

FS 8040

FS 8031

Hole in the Ground Creek

FS 8020

N

0   1/4   1/2
MILES

FS 80

To Trout Lake ↓

Rescue index: Help is available in Trout Lake.

Land status: Gifford Pinchot National Forest.

Maps: The district map for the Mt. Adams Ranger District is a good guide to this route. USGS 7.5 minute quads: King Mountain and Trout Lake.

Finding the trail: From the ranger station in Trout Lake, turn right onto WA 141. In 0.9 mile, turn left at the gas station and head north on Forest Service (FS) Road 17. You will arrive at the intersection of FS 17 and FS 23 in another

Southern trailhead of
Gotchen Creek Trail.

1.3 miles. Bear right, taking FS 17 toward the Mt. Adams Recreation Area. Turn
left in 0.6 mile onto FS 80. Follow FS 80 for 3.7 miles to the end of pavement;
here you will see FS 8040. Turn right onto FS 8040 and drive 0.6 mile to FS 020
(on the right). Park on the left at this intersection.

Source of additional information:

Mt. Adams Ranger District
2455 Highway 141
Trout Lake, WA 98650
(509) 395-2501

Notes on the trail: Follow FS 8040 uphill for 4.1 miles to the upper trailhead for
Gotchen Creek Trail #40 (on the right). There is a weathered wooden signpost
next to the road. Push your bike up the dirt slope to find a larger trailhead sign.
After 2 miles on the path, continue straight on Gotchen Creek Trail #40 as Cold
Springs Trail #72 goes left. In another mile you will reach the lower trailhead. Ride
past the corrals and up to the road. Turn right onto FS 8020 and descend. In 0.5
mile turn right onto FS 020 and follow it back to its intersection with FS 8040.

Creek crossing on Gotchen Creek Trail.

RIDE 4 · Buttes Loop

AT A GLANCE

WA

Length/configuration: 15-mile combination on single-track, double-track, and gravel roads; a 13.2-mile loop with a 1.8-mile out-and-back (0.9 mile each way)

Aerobic difficulty: Mostly moderate with some demanding, sustained climbs

Technical difficulty: Moderately difficult to difficult; single-track has some exciting and technical aspects

Scenery: Panoramic views of big mountains from West Twin Butte

Special comments: A great mix of roads and trails

This 15-mile loop begins with 5 miles on Squaw Butte Trail, which is a single-track in some places and an old double-track in others. It starts with a mod-

RIDE 4 · Buttes Loop

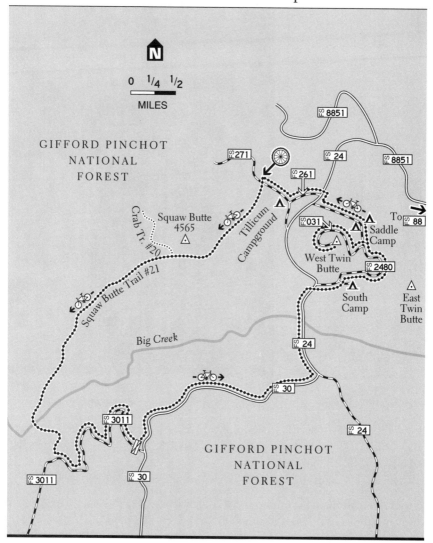

N

0 1/4 1/2

MILES

GIFFORD PINCHOT
NATIONAL
FOREST

FS 8851

FS 271

FS 24   FS 8851

FS 261

Crab Tr. #20

Squaw Butte
4565

Tillicum Campground

FS 031   To FS 88

Saddle
Camp

West Twin
Butte   FS 2480

Squaw Butte Trail #21

South
Camp

East
Twin
Butte

Big Creek

FS 24

FS 30

FS 3011

FS 24

FS 3011   FS 30

GIFFORD PINCHOT
NATIONAL
FOREST

erately difficult mile-long climb around the southern flank of Squaw Butte. This rise contains 0.2 mile of steep climbing. The trail levels out and begins a long descent that is both thrilling and technical. Erosion has created ditchlike conditions — there are steep drop-offs, rocks, and menacing roots. The last part of the trail involves easy to moderately difficult climbs as well as level riding. There are some pummy sections of trail in the last quarter mile.

The remainder of the circuit is on gravel and paved roads that are evenly split between ups and downs. There are a couple of demanding, sustained climbs. The

Mt. Adams from West
Twin Butte.

second is steeper and leads to the summit of West Twin Butte. A short hike through thick brush takes you to the remains of an old lookout. The view is panoramic; Mt. Adams, Mt. St. Helens, Mt. Rainier, Goat Rocks, and Sawtooth Mountain are prominent. The loop ends with a 2.3-mile descent back to your vehicle.

General location: The trailhead for Squaw Butte Trail is approximately 20 miles north of Trout Lake, Washington.

Elevation change: The ride begins at 3,760' and climbs to 4,360' in 1 mile. The trail drops for about 3 miles to a low point of 3,260' at Big Creek. The route follows roads to 4,120', then descends to 4,040' before the ascent to the top of West Twin Butte (4,716'). Ups and downs add about 100' of climbing to the loop. Total elevation gain: 2,236'.

Season: The roads and trails are usually free of snow from July through October. The area is popular with mushroom hunters in the spring and huckleberry pickers in the late summer.

Services: Water is available seasonally at Tillicum Campground. Food, lodging, gas, showers, and limited groceries can be obtained in Trout Lake. All services are available in Hood River.

Hazards: The descent on Squaw Butte Trail is treacherous—ideal conditions for being thrown over your handlebars. There is no bridge where Squaw Butte Trail crosses Big Creek; you must either wade through deep water or cross one of the logs that span the creek. Some of the roads contain large amounts of loose gravel. Watch for traffic on the roads.

Rescue index: Help can be found in Trout Lake.

Land status: Gifford Pinchot National Forest.

Maps: The district map of the Mt. Adams Ranger District is a good guide to this ride. USGS 7.5 minute quad: Lone Butte.

Finding the trail: Turn left out of the Mt. Adams Ranger Station in Trout Lake and head west on WA 141. In 0.8 mile, turn right onto Trout Lake Creek Road/FS 88. Follow FS 88 for 12.4 miles to Big Tire Junction—you will see FS 8851 on the left. Turn left onto FS 8851. You will pass Mosquito Lake after 3 miles on FS 8851. Then you will arrive at a **Y** intersection where FS 8851 goes right and FS 24 goes left. Turn left and proceed on FS 24 for 1 mile to a sign on the right that directs you toward Tillicum Campground and Squaw Butte Trail #21. Turn right onto this road, which is FS 261. Follow FS 261 for a short distance to an intersection where FS 261 meets FS 271. Turn right onto FS 271 and drive through Tillicum Campground for 0.2 mile to the trailhead for Squaw Butte Trail #21 (on the left). Park in the campsite on the right. Additional parking can be found off of FS 271.

Source of additional information:

Mt. Adams Ranger District
2455 Highway 141
Trout Lake, WA 98650
(509) 395-2501

Notes on the trail: Follow the trail and stay to the left at the first two intersections. After 1.6 miles you will come to Crab Trail #20 on the right; continue straight on Squaw Butte Trail #21. You will cross Big Creek in another 2.6 miles. In 0.3 mile from Big Creek, cross a small wooden bridge over a lesser creek. The trail becomes faint after the bridge, but well-placed trail markers make it is easy to follow. Follow the markers out to a trailhead sign at unsigned FS 3011. Turn left onto the road and climb. The road contains a lot of loose gravel for the first 1.5 miles, then becomes a degraded double-track, then changes to a cinder road. You will reach paved, unsigned FS 30 after 2.4 miles of pedaling on FS 3011. Turn left onto the pavement and ride 1.7 miles to a **T** intersection and FS 24. Turn left onto FS 24 (paved). In 1.1 miles, turn right and climb on FS 2480 toward South Camp and Saddle Camp. After 1.1 miles, FS 2480 levels out and comes to an unsigned spur road on the left. Turn left here onto FS 031. (This turn is easy to miss; you will enter Saddle Camp if you go too far.) Take FS 031 to its terminus and look to the right for an overgrown trail. Walk up the steep path to the summit of West Twin Butte. Return the way you came down FS 031, and turn left onto FS 2480. Enter Saddle Camp and stay on the main road through it. Cross through a trench at the lower end of the camp and continue to descend, now on a closed road. Turn right when you reach pavement, then make a quick left onto FS 261 to enter Tillicum Campground and complete the loop.

RIDE 5 · Forlorn Lakes

AT A GLANCE

Length/configuration: 9.2-mile gravel road combination; an 8-mile loop and a 1.2-mile out-and-back (0.6 mile each way)

Aerobic difficulty: Easy to moderately difficult

Technical difficulty: Easy; all on gravel roads

Scenery: A forested pedal past many small lakes; views of Lemei Rock and Mt. Adams

Special comments: A good ride for beginners with moderate stamina

WA

This is a 9.2-mile loop on gravel roads. The 1.5-mile climb to Forlorn Lakes basin involves easy and moderately difficult climbing. The remainder of the ride is easy. The roads are in good condition, with some ruts, rocks, and loose gravel. Level pedaling through the basin takes you past several small lakes with good fishing and campsites. The descent from Forlorn Lakes affords some nice views of Lemei Rock and Mt. Adams.

General location: This ride begins at Goose Lake, approximately 13 miles southwest of Trout Lake, Washington.

Elevation change: This loop begins at 3,130'. You reach Forlorn Lakes basin at 3,700', then descend to 3,040' at the intersection of Forest Service roads 6615 and 6621. Ups and downs add about 60' of climbing to the ride. Total elevation gain: 720'.

Season: The summer is a good time for visiting the area—bring your fishing tackle.

Services: There is no water available on this ride. Water, food, lodging, limited groceries, gas, and pay phones are available in Trout Lake.

Hazards: Watch for motorists. Control your speed while descending—FS 6035 contains some areas of loose rock.

RIDE 5 · Forlorn Lakes

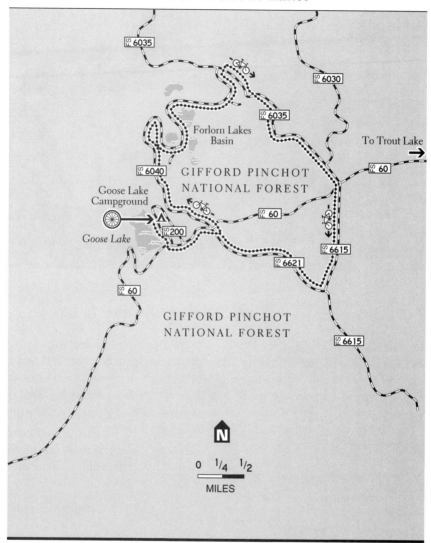

Rescue index: Help is available in Trout Lake.

Land status: Gifford Pinchot National Forest.

Maps: The district map of the Mt. Adams Ranger District is a good guide to this ride. USGS 7.5 minute quads: Little Huckleberry Mountain and Gifford Peak.

Finding the trail: From the Mt. Adams Ranger Station in Trout Lake, turn left (west) onto WA 141. Continue straight on WA 141 where FS 88/Trout Lake Creek Road goes right (follow the signs for Carson/Huckleberry Fields). The

Lovers Stump, Forlorn Lakes.

road's designation changes from WA 141 to FS 24 where it enters the Gifford Pinchot National Forest. You will arrive at an intersection after passing Peterson Prairie Campground. At this junction, continue straight onto FS 60 toward Goose Lake (FS 24 goes right). The remaining intersections are well marked— simply follow the signs to take FS 60 toward Goose Lake. Turn right into Goose Lake Campground and park on the left across from the vault toilets. Do not block the boat ramp.

Source of additional information:

> Mount Adams Ranger District
> 2455 Highway 141
> Trout Lake, WA 98650
> (509) 395-2501

Notes on the trail: Pedal out of the campground and turn left onto FS 60. In 0.6 mile, turn left onto FS 6040 toward Forlorn Lakes. Pedal past the lakes to a T intersection (4 miles into the ride). Turn right and descend on FS 6035. Continue straight where FS 6035 meets FS 6030. When you arrive at FS 60, go straight across FS 60 onto FS 6615. Follow FS 6615 for 1.2 miles to FS 6621. Turn right onto FS 6621 and follow the signs back to Goose Lake.

RIDE 6 · Valley Trail #270

AT A GLANCE

Length/configuration: 16.5-mile loop; half off-road vehicle trail, half paved road

Aerobic difficulty: Moderate to advanced; lots of ups and downs

Technical difficulty: Moderate to advanced; some sandy sections and water crossings

Scenery: Trail rolls through forest; some distant views at clear-cuts

Special comments: Fun and challenging trail

Valley Trail is an off-road vehicle route in the Randle District of the Gifford Pinchot National Forest. A moderately difficult 16.5-mile loop is formed by following the trail for 8.5 miles and then returning on pavement. The path contained some sandy sections but was still in good shape at the time of our research. Expect more degraded conditions as the trail becomes more popular with off-road vehicle enthusiasts.

This is a fun and challenging route for intermediate and advanced mountain bikers. The single-track goes up and down like a yo-yo. The path loses elevation overall as it heads north, but its rolling character creates about 1,000 feet of climbing. Through clear-cuts you can see Burley Mountain, Surprise Peak, and Juniper Peak.

General location: The trailhead is located approximately 25 miles southeast of Randle, Washington.

Elevation change: The trip begins at 2,700' at Cat Creek Campground. The high point along the trail is 2,900'. The single-track portion of the loop ends at 1,920'. The pedaling on Valley Trail contributes an estimated 1,000' of climbing to the loop. Ups and downs on the roads add about 100' of climbing to the ascent back to Cat Creek Campground. Total elevation gain: 1,880'.

Season: The heaviest off-road vehicle use is on summer weekends. This is a good early season ride.

Services: There is no potable water on the ride. Water is available seasonally at Adams Fork and Blue Lake Creek Campgrounds (en route to the trailhead). Food, lodging, groceries, gas, and pay phones can be found in Randle.

Hazards: Watch for other trail users. Control your speed while descending— there are rocky stretches and pummy areas. Expect some traffic on the paved roads.

RIDE 6 • Valley Trail #270

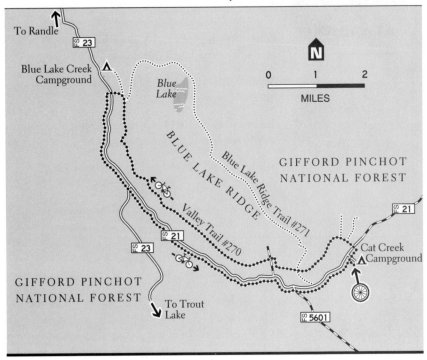

Rescue index: Help is available in Randle.

Land status: Gifford Pinchot National Forest.

Maps: The forest map of the Gifford Pinchot National Forest is a good guide to this ride. Valley Trail #270 is not delineated on the Randle District map or USGS quads.

Finding the trail: From US 12 in Randle, head south on WA 131, following the signs for Cispus Road/Mount St. Helens/FS 23/FS 25. Cross the bridge over the river; here the road's designation changes to FS 23. In 0.8 mile, turn left, taking FS 23 toward Cispus Center/Trout Lake. Stay on FS 23 for another 17.3 miles to FS 21. Turn left onto FS 21. Follow FS 21 for 6 miles to Cat Creek Campground. Turn right into the campground and park your vehicle.

Source of additional information:

Cowlitz Valley Ranger District
10024 Highway 12
Randle, WA 98377
(360) 497-1100

Valley Trail.

Notes on the trail: Turn right onto FS 21, then immediately turn left onto Valley Trail #270. A couple of trails branch off to the right near the start of the ride; stay left on the main trail. You will cross Blue Lake Ridge Trail #271 in less than a mile of riding; continue straight on Valley Trail #270. The route meets a gravel road in another 0.7 mile. Pick up the trail on the opposite side of the road, a little to the right and uphill. Follow the trail for nearly 7 miles to an intersection with several signs. Turn left and descend. You will immediately arrive at another intersection. Stay left and downhill. Soon you will reach a trailhead and a parking area for Valley Trail. Ride out to the pavement and turn left onto FS 23. After 1.8 miles on FS 23, turn left onto FS 21 at a **Y** intersection. Follow FS 21 back to Cat Creek Campground.

MT. ST. HELENS AREA RIDES

The eruption of Mt. St. Helens shook not only Washington, but the entire northwest. The explosion, on May 18, 1980, sent an ash column 17 miles into the air. The wind scattered it throughout the region, turning day into night as the ash cloud blocked out the sun. The blast leveled 230 miles of forest within minutes; woods, meadows, and streams were obliterated; hundreds of miles of roads and trails, 221 homes, 27 recreation sites, and 12 bridges were lost. Fifty-seven people died due to the explosion, mostly of suffocation from ash inhalation.

As the first volcano in the continental United States to erupt since California's Mt. Lassen in 1921, the blast sparked an explosion of interest and use in the area. Congress designated the Mt. St. Helens National Volcanic Monument out of the Gifford Pinchot National Forest in 1982. The 459,721-acre monument provides the opportunity to observe the violent forces of nature that destroyed the land, and the gentle forces that are regenerating it.

There are numerous scenic accesses to the Mt. St. Helens National Volcanic Monument from Interstate 5 at Woodland, Castle Rock, and Toledo, and from US 12 at Randle (from Yakima, US 12 over White Pass to Randle is the most direct route).

For mountain bikers, the most inviting areas of the monument are on the south and east sides of the volcano, about an hour's drive northeast of Vancouver. The fastest access is by way of I-5 to WA 503 at Woodland, from both up and down the I-5 corridor. It's about four hours from Seattle, but it's not unknown for hardy Seattle-area mountain bikers to make a day trip to ride the Lewis River Trail or Ape Canyon/Plains of Abraham. It's well worth the travel time, especially when done on a weekday, when the area is much less crowded. To really enjoy the area, though, come and spend a few days. As a mountain biker, you can have no better camping trip than an outing in and around the Mt. St. Helens National Volcanic Monument. The area holds numerous activities for off-bike time, including cave exploration (Ape Cave, off Forest Service Road 83, about 11 miles northeast of Cougar, is the longest intact lava tube in the continental United States), boating, swimming, fishing, interpretive walks, and just being lazy amid the beauty.

The size of the designated monument area has recently been increased. The challenging, tree-shaded Siouxan Trail, formerly located in the Wind River

Ranger District, is now within monument boundaries. This is advantageous for mountain bikers, as you pass right by the monument headquarters on the way to the trail.

North of the Siouxan Trail, FS 8100 climbs to the Kalama Horse Camp just before the town of Cougar. The Toutle Trail loop, which starts at the horse camp at the western border of the monument, can be ridden by advanced beginners, and provides excellent single-track through old growth woods, lava fields, and along the Kalama River.

East of the Toutle Trail, Marble Mountain provides an intermediate-level gravel road ride to incredible views of the Cascades Peaks above, and rivers and lakes below. Some of the best riding you may ever do is located just east of Marble Mountain, as the Ape Canyon/Plains of Abraham ride puts you beside and in the middle of the blast zone, while the gorgeous Lewis River Trail provides smooth trail through old growth and rock formations, and beside cascading waterfalls.

Summer weekend traffic on WA 503 can get heavy; vehicles with boats in tow on the way to Lake Merwin, Yale Lake, and Swift Reservoir compete with the motor homes and numerous cars and trucks bringing people from all over the world to view Mt. St. Helens.

The eight-dollars-per-person Monument Pass applies to specific developed sites within the monument but does not apply to the described rides. The Lewis River Trail requires a trail park pass at the Curly Creek Falls Trailhead. Changes will probably be made in the future to require passes in other areas, so check with the Monument Headquarters or the Gifford Pinchot National Forest Headquarters for the latest information.

RIDE 7 · Siouxan Trail #130

AT A GLANCE

WA

Length/configuration: 6.2-mile paved road and single-track loop, then 4-mile (each way) out-and-back; total of 14.2 miles, with 11.2 miles of single-track

Aerobic difficulty: Gentle to moderate paved road climb, strenuous climbs of up to 0.3 mile, other rolling climb

Technical difficulty: Some tricky water crossings, steep side-cut trail sections

Scenery: Old-growth and second-growth forest, waterfalls

Special comments: A luscious ride in a lush forest; the deep tree canopy makes for great hot-weather riding. The mostly roller-coaster creek trail ties into a network of ridge trails

The Siouxan (pronounced Soo-sawn) Trail is, in its entirety, an 11.7-mile trail that descends from its 1,700-foot elevation start to 1,200 feet, and eventually climbs to 3,400 feet, with 1,900 feet of rise in the last three miles. The trail has a nice hard-packed surface, with some roots, rocks, and water crossings to keep your attention. The trail becomes overgrown, though, after a slippery, treacherous creek crossing at 6.2 miles, so that is the recommended turn-around point. The natural routing of this ride, then, is an intermediate-level, gentle-to-moderate 3-mile paved road warm-up leading to the western trailhead. The single-track loops back to the parking area and continues with a rolling out-and-back to Wildcat Creek, for a total outing of 14.2 miles.

The described route is a challenging ride through old-growth and second-growth forest, ferns, mosses, waterfalls, and beautiful pools; some of the water crossings demand dismounts.

If this sweet single-track doesn't do it for you, you can make a day of it with a 2,800-foot climb on Huffman Peak Trail #129 or a 2,000-foot climb on Horseshoe Ridge Trail #140. Chinook Trail #130A also takes off just after the turn-around point.

This route is a good choice for a hot summer day because the deep tree canopy keeps the heat at bay. Because the trees block the sun, though, don't start too late in the day without a light; that tree canopy will rob you of some late-afternoon sunlight as the sun sets over the ridge to the west.

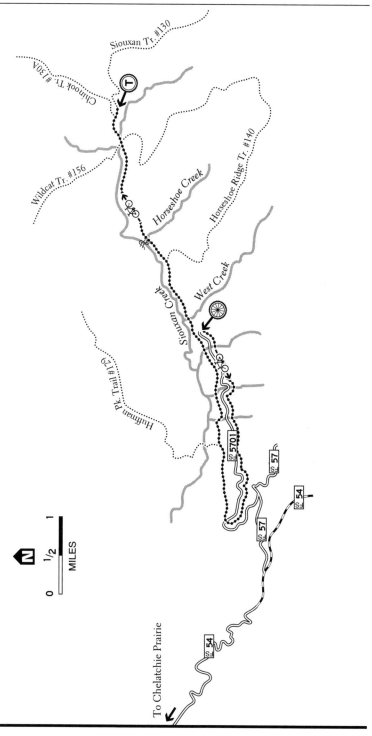

Pool below Horsehoe
Falls.

General location: The ride starts close to 60 miles northeast of Vancouver by way of Interstate 5, or 45 miles northeast of Vancouver via slower, winding WA 503.

Elevation change: The initial road climb rises about 500 feet in 3.0 miles. You descend it in the first 1.3 miles of trail, and then roll the rest of the way with both sharp and gentle rises and descents. Total elevation gain is estimated at 1,400'.

Season: The earlier in the season you ride, the higher the water will be, so later is better. Locals recommend a June through November riding season.

Services: No potable water is available along the ride. Bring a filter or, better yet, stock up in Vancouver or Chelatchie Prairie, where you can also find gas and food. All services are available in Vancouver.

Hazards: Some sharp turns come at you quickly on the initial trail descent. Clear 'em with foresight not by locking up the brakes. Numerous water crossings along the way can be tricky; some demand dismounts.

Rescue index: Help is available in Chelatchie Prairie.

Land status: Mt. St. Helens National Volcanic Monument, recently transferred from the Wind River Ranger District of the Gifford Pinchot National Forest.

Maps: Green Trails #396 Lookout Mountain and the Wind River Ranger District map are equally good choices for the entire trail network. The ranger district map has the advantage of showing a greater amount of area roads as well as the trails. With the recent change in jurisdiction of the area, check with the monument headquarters to see if the latest revision of their map encompasses this area.

Finding the trail: From I-5, take Exit 21, the Woodland/Cougar exit and WA 503. Twist along WA 503 east for 23.1 miles to the junction of WA 503 south (at Jack's Restaurant and Store), and turn right. Travel 6.4 miles on WA 503 south to N.E. Healy Road in Chelatchie Prairie, a block north of the Mt. St. Helens National Volcanic Monument Headquarters. Turn left on N.E. Healy Road as it winds around to the left at a paper mill in 0.4 mile and continues on, eventually turning into FS 54. In 8.9 miles after the paper mill, FS 54 turns to gravel and heads straight as paved road FS 57 climbs to the left. Veer left on FS 57 and stay on it for 1.2 miles. After cresting a climb, just after a gravel quarry on the left, come to the left-hand junction of FS 5701. Take the left on FS 5701. Just after the road switchbacks to the right in about 0.8 mile, keep your eye out for the Siouxan Trail, which takes off to the left at the 7 o'clock position. To get to the ride start, however, take FS 5701 another 3 miles to its end, where parking is available.

Chelatchie Prairie is also accessible via WA 503 from the south, approximately 31 miles northeast of Vancouver.

Sources of additional information:

Mt. St. Helens National Volcanic Monument Headquarters
42218 N.E. Yale Bridge Road
Amboy, WA 98601
(360) 247-3900
(It's actually in Chelatchie Prairie, but has an Amboy mailing address.)

Gifford Pinchot National Forest Headquarters
10600 N.E. 51st Circle
Vancouver, WA 98682
(360) 891-5000

Notes on the trail: From the parking area at the end of FS 5701, ride back up the road. At 2.3 miles you heading right toward a sheer rock face, but then the road veers north (whew!). In another 0.7 mile, just before the road switchbacks left, the single-track takes off to the right at the one o'clock position. Start with a fast 500' descent in the first 1.3 miles, but watch your speed and the trail ahead—some sharp turns come quickly. At 1.3 miles, pass Huffman Peak Trail #129 on your left. From this point the trail is a roller-coaster with many seasonal water crossings. In 1.9 miles after the Huffman Peak Trail junction, hit a **T** intersection. A right (and the next two quick spurs to the right) brings you back to the car in a short 50', but you won't want to do it because you're in the middle of a yahoo-inducing descent. Stay left and keep descending. In 0.3 mile cross the bridge over West Creek and pass the primitive campsite to the left. Now you're alongside Siouxan Creek, riding upstream. In another 0.7 mile pass Horseshoe Ridge Trail #140 to the right. (The Horseshoe Ridge Trail is a 6.9-mile trail that rejoins the Siouxan Trail 2.2 miles farther. From this side, the trail rises 2,200' in 1.5 miles. The gain from its eastern junction with the Siouxan Trail is less severe.) In another 0.5 mile, cross a bridge over Horseshoe Falls. Enjoy the view from here, or continue on for 0.1 mile and down the spur trail to the left for 0.1 mile to enjoy the falls from below.

Back on the main trail, continue on for another 0.4 mile to a little log bench on the left as the trail veers right. The log bench provides a view of a waterfall that cascades down into a rock-banked pool; it's tailor-made for a snack stop or a dip. In 0.3 mile, look for another pool as you ride along. Keep rolling along the trail, and in another 0.9 mile pass the junction of Siouxan Ford Trail #156A, a connector to Wildcat Trail #156. In another 0.1 mile the Horseshoe Ridge Trail rejoins on the right. Continue on, and in 0.7 mile, come to a slick creek crossing. This is the turnaround point on the described ride, but just afterward a bridge to the left marks the start of Chinook Trail #130A. Proceed if you dare, or turn around and retrace the trail just past the low-ring climb after the bridge over West Creek. Take any of the three spurs to the left to return to your vehicle, or continue up the trail for more.

RIDE 8 · Toutle Trail Loop

AT A GLANCE

Length/configuration: 13.6-mile loop, including paved road, gravel road, and 9 miles of single-track; additional single-track and ski trails are accessible from the described route

Aerobic difficulty: Easy paved road and gravel road climb; a few short, steep climbs on the trail

Technical difficulty: Very uneven lava section at Red Rock Pass; pummy, rocky sections; a few switchbacks

Scenery: Great views of Mt. St. Helens, mudflows, the lava field, old-growth woods, McBride Lake, and Kalama River views

Special comments: Gorgeous scenery; a can-do loop for the hardy beginner

RIDE 8 · Toutle Trail Loop

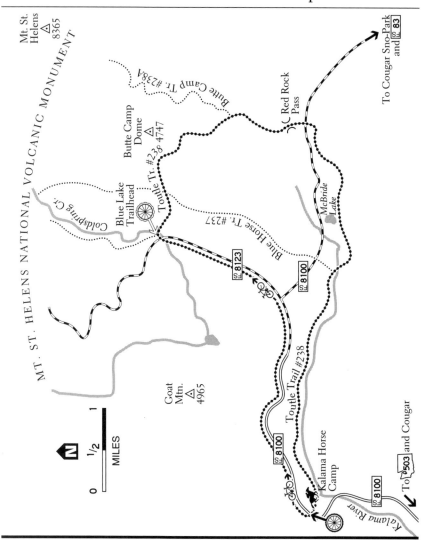

The Toutle Trail loop combines a gentle 4.6-mile paved road and gravel road climb, and an undulating nine sweet miles of trail. The 13.6 miles, with a few steep single-track descents and technical areas, will be a challenging outing for the hardy beginner. It's a beautiful jaunt through a variety of landscapes—and trail surfaces—for riders of all levels. If beginners—and it is not recommended for *true* beginners—tire midway through the loop, Blue Horse Trail #237 and FS 81 provide bailouts.

The loop encircles Kalama Spring—the headwaters of the Kalama River—

Toutle Trail #238, from
the Blue Lake Trailhead
parking area.

and parallels the Kalama on the southern section of the trail. The single-track
and cross-country ski trails you pass throughout the loop provide numerous
exploration opportunities, while the mudflows, lava field, noble fir forest, and
the Mt. St. Helens–dominated scenery give constant cause for viewing pause.
The trail is mostly a rooty hardpack, with rocky, pummy sections and a taste of
lava-rock riding at Red Rock Pass.

General location: The ride starts at the Kalama Horse Camp Trailhead, 9 miles
north of Cougar and about 50 miles northeast of Vancouver.

Elevation change: Start at approximately 2,100' elevation from Kalama Horse
Camp and climb to 3,210' at the trailhead. Hit Red Rock Pass at 3,198', and
make some sharp climbs as well as descents back to the trailhead. Total elevation gain is estimated at 1,350'.

Season: You'll find great riding here from June through October. Check with
the national monument headquarters for conditions.

Services: Water, gas, and groceries are available in Cougar. Camping is available at Kalama Horse Camp, but, as it has corrals and horse troughs, it gives pri-

ority to equestrians. Dispersed camping is available nearby; a dispersed site off of FS 81 just east of the horse camp is close enough that you can make use of the toilet facilities at the campground. All services are available in Vancouver.

Hazards: Lava rock at Red Rock Pass can do a number on flesh and bone if you fall hard; a few spots here are best walked. The loop starts and ends at a horse camp, and it gets a lot of use from equestrians. Blind corners abound, so be on the lookout and show the appropriate courtesies.

Rescue index: The camp host at Kalama Horse Camp can summon help. If the host is not on site, as was the case at the time of research, help can be found in Cougar.

Land status: Mt. St. Helens National Volcanic Monument.

Maps: The Mt. St. Helens National Volcanic Monument map is a sufficient guide for this loop, as is the Gifford Pinchot National Forest map. Neither show the ski trails in the area, but they show the other Forest Service trails, and are good general guides.

Finding the trail: From I-5, take the Exit 21 (Woodland) and travel east on WA 503 approximately 27.5 miles to FS 81 (signed here as FS 8100), 0.8 mile after milepost 35, just before the town of Cougar. Turn left on FS 81 and travel 8.75 miles to Kalama Horse Camp. If you're coming from the Ape Canyon–Marble Mountain Area, turn off FS 83 at Cougar Sno-park (FS 81) and travel 11.5 miles northwest to Kalama Horse Camp. Parking is available in the campground.

FS 83 is also accessible from the north and east via FS 90, 12.1-miles west of the junction of FS 25 (to Randle and US 12).

Sources of additional information:

Gifford Pinchot National Forest Headquarters
10600 N.E. 51st Circle
Vancouver, WA 98682
(360) 891-5000

Mt. St. Helens National Volcanic Monument Headquarters
42218 N.E. Yale Bridge Road
Amboy, WA 98601
(360) 247-3900.

Notes on the trail: Exiting the horse camp, ride right on FS 81, with its smooth pavement and easy grade, enjoying the views of Goat Mountain and Butte Camp Dome. At 2.2 miles the pavement ends and a road goes off to the right. Stay straight on FS 81—the 30 mph speed limit sign and milepost 11 are your landmarks. At 3.0 miles, a right turn continues FS 81, but ride straight on FS 8123, following the Blue Lake Trailhead sign. In 1.6 miles, pass a spur road to the right. Go straight, and immediately after the road, reach the Blue Lake Trailhead parking area. Turn right onto Toutle Trail #238. To the north is Coldspring Creek and the continuation of the Toutle Trail. On this loop, however, travel east, away from the creek, at the trailhead. In 0.1 mile cross the spur road you passed just before the trailhead; the orange snowmobile trail sign points the way. The trail surface is soft here, but traction is good, and you can easily navigate the rocks strewn about the trail. In 0.2 mile pass the intersection of the Blue Horse Trail, which reconnects with the Toutle Trail for a shorter loop. In 0.6 mile come to a mudflow crossing courtesy of Mt. St. Helens. Dismount and cross; the trail continues slightly to the left.

While you're off your bike, enjoy the view of Mt. St. Helens to the north, and, on a clear day, views to the east; unfortunately, I was not blessed with the eastern view on my research ride. In another 0.2 mile cross an area untouched by the wrath of the mighty volcano, containing dense old-growth noble fir and a hard-packed trail. In 1.0 mile, pass the Butte Camp Trail #238A. A descent after the dense woods leads to mudflows, lava rock, and forested hardpack. In 0.7 mile, a beargrass meadow leads to Red Rock Pass. Descend to FS 81 after Red Rock Pass. Ride right on FS 81 as a bailout, or better yet, cross and continue.

The trail returns to a mainly hard-packed trail surface, but with some horse-scarred and softened sections. At 1.5 miles after the road crossing, look down through the trees to the still waters of McBride Lake. Shortly beyond, the trail parallels the Kalama River. Cross the southern intersection of the wide Blue Horse Trail as you cross over the river and continue on the Toutle Trail. The blue diamond ski trail markers in the trees lead the way here. At 2.3 miles beyond the Blue Horse Trail junction, with a clear-cut peak in front of you, the trail is bordered on your left by a waist-high ridge. Dismount and look over it for a stark view of an eroded hillside down to the river. In 0.4 more miles the trail splits. You can follow the diamond markers, which bring you back to the Toutle Trail in 0.9 mile, but go left and switchback down to the river. An equestrian I encountered said the continuation of the ski trail was even more scenic than this section of the Toutle Trail; it must be something really special to beat what I rode, so you can explore it out and back for an extra 1.8 miles (total) when the trails rejoin. Just past a couple of wooden bridges, a short sandy rise brings you back to the trailhead at Kalama Horse Camp.

RIDE 9 · Marble Mountain

AT A GLANCE
_____

WA

Length/configuration: 13.2-mile combination route: 8.2-mile paved road, dirt-road, and gravel-road loop, with a 2.5-mile out-and-back (each way) gravel-road spur

Aerobic difficulty: Moderate gravel road climbing; gets steeper at the top

Technical difficulty: Some fast and loose turns

Scenery: Outstanding Mt. St. Helens and other high Cascades views, looks into Swift Reservoir

Special comments: Some of the best non-single-track riding in the area, with some of the best views

The trip up Marble Mountain is an intermediate-level ride with advanced-level views. The 13.2-mile route is a reverse lollipop configuration, with the sweeter part on the stick! The out-and-back section leads to the top of Marble Mountain, which, on a clear day, provides views of nearby Mt. St. Helens, and also Mt. Rainier, Mt. Adams, Mt. Hood, and other high Cascades peaks and ridgelines. You've got to believe what I'm telling you here; on the day of research it was cloudy enough that I was only able to see the lower part of Mt. St. Helens to the north. On a clear day, it dominates the views along the way. Even on my cloudy adventure, I had a good workout and nice views down into Swift Reservoir to the west.

An added bonus on this ride is that you both begin and end with a descent!

General location: Approximately 60 miles northeast of Vancouver.

Elevation change: The June Lake Trailhead parking area sits at 2,720'. Marble Mountain peaks out at 4,116', for a total climb of 1,396'. The climb out of the initial descent adds an extra 120' of climbing, for a total of 1,516'.

Season: June through October, and maybe a little longer both ways, depending on the weather. Do it on a clear day if possible!

Services: No water is available along the route. Primitive campsites abound in the area. Gas, food, and overnight accommodations are available in Cougar. Everything your heart desires is available in Vancouver.

Hazards: Gravel FS 8312 is very rocky; although it's not single-track, you still need to pay attention and watch your line on the fast, curving descent; also,

Climbing Marble Mountain.

watch for motor vehicles along the route. I found evidence of shooting activity along the way so keep your ears, as well as your eyes, open and alert.

Rescue index: Marble Mountain Sno-park provides an emergency phone. Personnel are on duty during daylight hours during the season at the Ape Cave Interpretive Center, off of FS 83, about 2 miles north of FS 90.

Land status: Mt. St. Helens National Volcanic Monument.

Maps: Green Trails #364 Mt. St. Helens is the best map for this route. It's a good map to have for wintertime recreation, too, as it shows a network of cross-country ski, snowshoe, and snowmobile trails you can access from the same area.

Finding the trail: From I-5, take Exit 21 at Woodland, and travel east for 37.4 miles on WA 503 East/WA 503 Spur/FS 90 (all contiguous; WA 503 Spur turns into FS 90 past Cougar). Turn left on FS 83, 8.2 miles past the town of Cougar. Stay on FS 83 for 7 miles, about 4 miles past FS 81 and Cougar Sno-park, to the June Lake Trailhead turnoff to the left. Make the left, and reach the parking area in 0.1 mile.

FS 83 is also accessible from the north and east via FS 90, 12.1 miles west of the junction of FS 25 (to Randle and US 12).

Sources of additional information:

Mt. St. Helens National Volcanic Monument Headquarters
42218 N.E. Yale Bridge Road
Amboy, WA 98601
(360) 247-3900

RIDE 9 · Marble Mountain

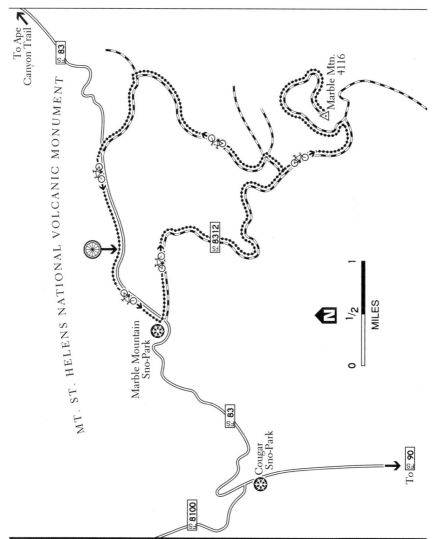

Gifford Pinchot National Forest Headquarters
10600 N.E. 51st Circle
Vancouver, WA 98682
(360) 891-5000

Notes on the trail: Out of the June Lake Trailhead parking lot, turn right and descend 1.0 mile. Immediately past Marble Mountain Sno-park on your right, turn left on FS 8312 and continue your descent for another 0.5 mile until you cross a creek routed under the road. Now starts the climbing! Stay on the main road, past all spurs. Pay attention to the only four-way intersection on the route, at 4.2 miles. At this point, keep going straight (on the descent you'll turn on what is now the road to your left). In another 0.9 mile pass a dirt road to your right; orange snowmobile arrows point you left and to a clear-cut view of the clear-cut peak of Marble Mountain. In another 0.7 mile a steep dirt road to your left invites you on a short, tough climb and a fast descent. Explore if you desire, but, for the described route, keep on the main road. The steepest part of the climb is at the peak; there's no shame in walking this final 0.1 mile. Set your bike down by the tower; take a break and wander around the overgrown trail to the north for some lofty views. Descend with care to that four-way intersection and turn right on the unsigned road. Just past a spur road on your right in 0.2 mile, take the first left, spur road 380; the dirt road is marked with an orange snowmobile sign and a black-on-yellow **T**-intersection sign. Descend to the gravel road **T** intersection and go left. Continue west on this road until you come to paved road FS 83 at milepost 8. Descend leisurely back to milepost 7 and the June Lake Trailhead parking lot.

RIDE 10 · Ape Canyon/Plains of Abraham

AT A GLANCE

Length/configuration: 21.2-mile (total mileage) out-and-back, including 17.8 miles of single-track and 3.4 miles of dirt road

Aerobic difficulty: A strenuous, 1,350' climb up the ridge to Ape Canyon viewpoint; rolling, pummy climbs along the blast zone; 1.7-mile climb to Windy Ridge Viewpoint

Technical difficulty: Uphill switchbacks on initial climb; pumice rocks on the blast zone can hurt if you fall; "hogback" sections of trail, with steep drops on either side; vertical sand stairs are rideable by only the most technically superior riders

Scenery: Old-growth and regenerated forest on the climb up to Ape Canyon viewpoint; in-your-face views of Mt. St. Helens as you travel through regenerating blast zone; views of volcanic neighbors Mt. Rainier and Mt. Adams; more dramatic vistas from the Windy Ridge Viewpoint

Special comments: If you do only one ride in this book, do this ride—especially in clear conditions, this will be an unforgettable experience

You could say that May 18, 1980, was an eventful day in this neck of the woods. This route gives you the unique opportunity to experience what the Mt. St. Helens area looked like before the eruption on that date, and to see the intense effect of its fury.

Of course you won't be able to see what Mt. St. Helens itself looked like before the eruption—it lost 1,300 feet of its elevation that day. The eruption, triggered by a 5.1 magnitude earthquake, had the force to send an ash column 17 miles into the sky. The landscape of trees, meadows, and streams, devoured by mudflows, was rendered a lifeless, post-armageddon-like moonscape.

The ride through this area starts with a climb on regenerated forest and old growth untouched by the eruption. It travels on the east side of the Lahar mudflow, which you can spy through the woods. Breaking out of the trees, past a delicate meadow, the full effect of the eruption emerges. The overlook atop Ape Canyon dramatically shows the path of a mudflow to its depths; the regenerating but stark blast zone shows the cycles of nature at its most dramatic. Mt. Rainier and Mt. Adams lie beyond the moonscape before you, as Mt. St. Helens rules the view.

The Ape Canyon Trail is difficult right off the bat and throws in steep sections along with more gradual climbs. The soft, pummy climbs through the blast zone demand extra energy; loose rocks and treacherous crossings demand extra bike-handling savvy. You will be forced from the saddle at times, which, here, is not a bad thing.

This ride is not for beginners. You don't have to make the whole trip to appreciate the grandeur of the location, though. If you're a strong intermediate-level rider with a sense of adventure, go for it—there's no shame in turning back before Windy Ridge Viewpoint.

The journey ends with a fast final 5.5 miles on the Ape Canyon Trail. It's a popular trail, so watch your speed, especially around the switchbacks and blind corners. Sacrifice some speed to avoid skidding and user conflict.

I've had the thrill of riding this trail twice—so far. On my first trip it was clear and the views were overwhelming. On my second trip the clouds rolled in and stayed, so it was merely awesome. This area creates its own weather conditions and they can change rapidly over the course of the ride, so come prepared for cold and rain as well as hot conditions on the exposed blast zone. Clear conditions can never be guaranteed, but they are bliss. Either way, a camera is essential equipment. And don't forget lunch, so you can relax midride and listen to the interpretive talk at the Windy Ridge Viewpoint.

General location: The ride starts on the southeast side of Mt. St. Helens, about 65 miles northeast of Vancouver.

Elevation change: The route starts at 2,850' at the Ape Canyon Trailhead and meets the Loowit Trail at 4,200'. Climbing along the blast zone up to Windy Ridge Viewpoint and on the return brings the total elevation gain to about 2,000'.

Season: The trails are generally open from June through October. You're more likely to find clearer conditions from July through September.

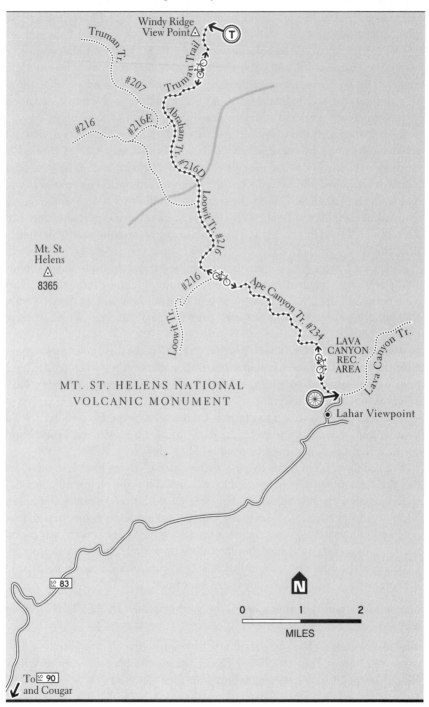

Windy Ridge
View Point △

Truman Tr.

Truman Trail

#207

#216E

#216

Abraham Tr.

#216D

Loowit Tr. #216

Mt. St.
Helens
△
8365

#216

Loowit Tr.

Ape Canyon Tr. #234

LAVA
CANYON
REC.
AREA

Lava Canyon Tr.

MT. ST. HELENS NATIONAL
VOLCANIC MONUMENT

Lahar Viewpoint

83

N

0   1   2

MILES

To 90
and Cougar

Old-growth along the Ape Canyon Trail.

Services: Bring lots of water; it's not available at either end of the route. Dispersed camping and campsites can be found throughout the area. Water, gas, food, and overnight accommodations are available in Cougar. All services are available in Vancouver.

Hazards: Allow plenty of time; you'll want to stop often, and you won't often go too fast on the soft stuff. As you approach the view over Ape Canyon, 1,000' below, either ride smoothly or, better yet, walk your bike so you can take in the view. Sharp rocks will make falls hurt; "hogback" sections on the far end of the Abraham Trail challenge you with steep drops on either side. Once on the blast zone you are at the mercy of the elements; bring plenty of water and sunscreen as well as a jacket in preparation for any type of weather.

Rescue index: Forest interpreters at the Lahar Viewpoint, adjacent to the Ape Canyon Trailhead, are on-site at posted times. The Marble Mountain Sno-park, about 3 miles from the trailhead off FS 83, has an emergency phone; personnel are on-site at the Apes' Headquarters, by Ape Cave on FS 83, about 7 miles from the trailhead, daily from 10 A.M. to 5:30 P.M. from May 17 through September 30.

Land status: Mt. St. Helens National Volcanic Monument.

Maps: The Mt. St. Helens National Volcanic Monument map is a sufficient guide for this route. Green Trails #364, Mt. St. Helens, is more detailed, and shows the route more completely than both the monument map and Green Trails special series map #364S.

Finding the trail: Exit I-5 at Exit 21, the Woodland/Cougar exit and WA 503. Travel east on WA 503, WA 503 Spur, and FS 90 for 37.4 winding miles (all contiguous; WA 503 Spur turns into FS 90 past Cougar) to the junction of FS 83, 8.2 miles east of Cougar. Turn left on FS 83 and follow it for 11.6 miles, nearly to its end. Trailhead parking is to the left, past the Lahar Viewpoint and just before the parking lot for the Lava Canyon Recreation Area (which has toilets).

FS 83 is also accessible from the north and east via FS 90, 12.1 miles west of the junction of FS 25 (to Randle and US 12).

Sources of additional information:

Mt. St. Helens National Volcanic Monument Headquarters
42218 N.E. Yale Bridge Road
Amboy, WA 98601
(360) 247-3900

Gifford Pinchot National Forest Headquarters
10600 N.E. 51st Circle
Vancouver, WA 98682
(360) 891-5000

Notes on the trail: There's no warm-up on this ride; start with a short, sharp, pummy climb with the Lahar mudflow on your left. It gives way to wildflowers, young forest, and old growth along a hard-pack trail, concealing the devastation nearby. After the initial push, the trail levels out before the major grunt up the ridge, starting at 1.7 miles. Look to the east and southeast for glimpses of Mt. Adams and Mt. Hood on some switchbacks on the way up. At about 4.0 miles the views of Mt. St. Helens start to open up. At 4.8 miles the trail ends into the Loowit Trail #216. To the left, the trail descends to June Lake by way of some unrideable lava areas, so go right, toward Abraham Trail #216D. At this point, the pummy surface competes with the incredible views for your attention. This is mostly an on-the-bike experience but with some tests of strength and technique that may force you off momentarily. The short water crossing 0.8 mile beyond the junction marks the view down into Ape Canyon. Traverse along the Plains of Abraham, staying straight on Abraham Trail #216D as the Loowit Trail cuts left, about a mile beyond the Ape Canyon overlook. The trail dumps out at the Truman-Abraham Saddle onto Truman Trail #207, actually the auto-free, dirt road continuation of FS 99 (the single-track portion of the Truman Trail is off-limits to bikes). Climb to the right on the road, and reach the Windy Ridge Viewpoint in 1.7 miles. Eat lunch, snap some photos, and listen to the interpretive talk at the Windy Ridge outdoor amphitheater (weekends from May 17 through June 23, and daily from June 24 through September 1) before the return trip. On the way back you'll expend some more energy both technically and physically. Your climbing effectively ends with the descent on the Ape Canyon Trail—an exhilarating way to end a most memorable experience.

RIDE 11 · Lewis River Trail

AT A GLANCE
WA

Length/configuration: 27.2-mile (total mileage) single-track out-and-back; gravel-road and paved-road loop return option

Aerobic difficulty: The lower end of the trail is generally flat, with short, steep climbs and descents on the upper portion; the middle section contains the toughest climbing, including some hike-a-bike sections

Technical difficulty: This is, for the most part, a baby-bottom-smooth trail with only a few technical challenges; some steep edges along the side of the trail on the middle and upper sections require extra attention; true beginners are best off on the lower portion of the trail

Scenery: Old-growth forest, rock formations, waterfalls at both the lower and upper ends of the trail

Special comments: A scenic feast on which even beginners can dine

It's a good thing that "eye candy" has no calories, because the Lewis River Trail #31 is chock-full of fattening views of old-growth forest, rock formations, and waterfalls. The trail itself is also a sweet treat, with a beginner-friendly smooth surface almost all the way through. In fact, the only arguments against beginners riding the entire 27.2-mile round-trip are some steep sections in the middle portion of the trail and the length of the entire round-trip. One way to avoid both of these potential beginner pitfalls is doing the trail as an out-and-back as far as you feel comfortable riding, knowing that you have to ride back as far as you came! (Another option of course is a shuttle ride starting from the upper trailhead.)

On my research outing in the autumn of 1997, much of the trail was closed for repairs of major damage caused by the previous winter's storms. I had heard about the trail damage, but I had also heard many fellow riders tell me of the wonder of the trail. So I ventured out and was able to ride the open sections: the lower three miles from the trailhead to the Bolt Camp Shelter, and the upper section from the FS 90 road crossing to the end of the trail, also at FS 90. Without a doubt, the trail lived up to its billing; some call this the best stretch of single-track in the state, and it certainly ranks right up there.

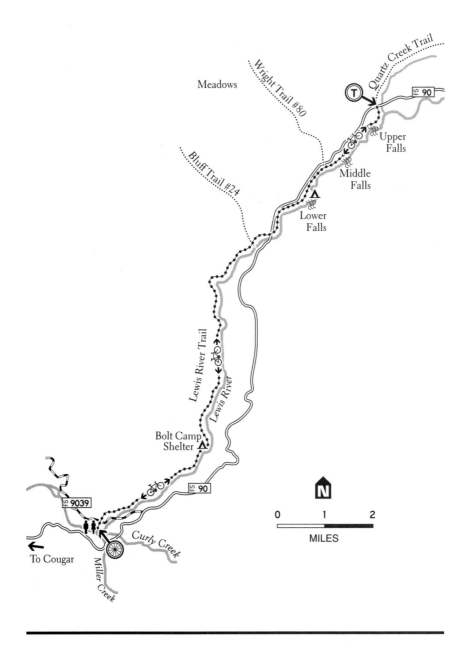

The only drawback, if there is one, is that the trail is no secret, so expect to encounter other trail users. When you come to FS 90 either at the bridge over the Lewis River 9.2 miles up the trail or at the upper trailhead, you can use the road as a loop or bail-out option. Experienced beginners can start at the bridge and ride the top section as an 8.8-mile out-and-back that includes some of the most incredible scenery on an incredibly scenic outing.

General location: The lower trailhead is approximately 70 miles northeast of Vancouver, 35 miles north of Carson, and 50 miles south of Randle.

Elevation change: Elevation at the trailhead parking at Curly Creek Falls is 1,200'. The trail ends at FS 90 opposite the Quartz Creek Trail at 1,800'. Additional climbs along the way make for a total elevation gain of about 860'.

Season: I read one write-up that said you can ride the Lewis River Trail all year long. It would be irresponsible, politically incorrect, and environmentally unfriendly to ride it in the rainy season, so save it for dry conditions from late May or June through October. Check with the Mt. St. Helens National Volcanic Monument Headquarters for trail conditions.

Services: Camping is available throughout the area, including the Lower Falls Recreation Area (which has water), right along the trail and off of FS 90, about 1.2 miles up from the bridge over the Lewis River, adjacent to the trail crossing. Limited services are available at the Eagle Cliff General Store on FS 90, 0.7-mile east of junction of FS 25. Gas is available in Cougar, 18.7-miles west of the FS 90/FS 25 junction. Your nearest big-city amenities are in Vancouver.

Hazards: Some steep side-cuts on the upper middle and upper portions can be intimidating for beginners, as can the short, steep gains and drops.

Rescue index: Help can be summoned from the Eagle Cliff General Store. In addition, a Skamania County Sheriff District Headquarters Emergency Station is located off of FS 90, just south of the junction of FS 25.

Land status: Gifford Pinchot National Forest.

Maps: Green Trails #365, Lone Butte, is a good general guide, but the undated, most recent update only showed the trail as far as its junction with FS 90 near the bridge. You can just draw a line on the north side of the river to the trail's terminus at FS 90 at the Quartz Creek Trail and be accurate.

Finding the trail: From I-5 take Exit 21, the Woodland/Cougar exit and WA 503. Travel east on WA 503, WA 503 Spur, and FS 90 for 46.9 miles (all contiguous; WA 503 turns into WA 503 Spur in 23 miles, which turns into FS 90 past Cougar) to the junction of FS 25. Turn right, staying on FS 90, and travel 5.2 miles to the junction of FS 9039 (to the left only). Turn left on FS 9039; in 0.7 mile, FS 9039 passes over the Lewis River and crosses the trail. Continue for another 0.3 mile and turn left into the Curly Creek Falls parking area. You can also continue on FS 90 for about 9.2 miles northeast of FS 9039 and park just past the bridge to access the upper section of the trail.

From Chehalis and points north, you can exit I-5 at Exit 68E. Take US 12 for

Bridge over Lewis River
in Upper Falls area.

48.3 miles to WA 131 (Cispus Road) in Randle and turn right. In 1.1 miles the road divides. Go right on FS 25 and stay on it for 43.7 miles to the junction of FS 90. Turn left on FS 90 and proceed as above. This route is more scenic, but even from the north the more direct route is via I-5 to WA 503.

From Yakima take US 12 over White Pass to Randle, turn south on Cispus Road, and proceed as above.

From Carson, travel north on CR 30, Wind River Road, about 14 miles to the Carson National Fish Hatchery. Turn right (north) on Meadow Creek Road (CR 30) and travel about 15 miles, approximately 4 miles north of Oldman Pass, to Curly Creek Road (FS 51). Turn left and drive about 6 miles to FS 90. Turn left, and in 0.3 mile, turn right onto FS 9039.

Sources of additional information:

Gifford Pinchot National Forest Headquarters
10600 N.E. 51st Circle
Vancouver, WA 98682
(360) 891-5000

Mt. St. Helens National Volcanic Monument Headquarters
42218 N.E. Yale Bridge Road
Amboy, WA 98601
(360) 247-3900

Notes on the trail: Before you get the bike out, starting near the toilets, take a short walk to the right (bikes aren't allowed) to view Curly Creek Falls and Miller Creek Falls. Then come back and mount your steed. About 100' to the left of the toilets is the signed start of the Lewis River Trail. Take it and ride the straightforward route upriver. Pass the junction of Bluff Trail #24 shortly before crossing FS 90 9.2 miles into the route. From FS 90 it's about 1.2 miles to the Lower Falls Recreation Area where a spur trail provides a view of the falls. Continuing up the trail, you'll find other short accesses to the falls—dismount and explore. About 1.1-miles upriver from the Lower Falls Recreation Area, a trail to the left and uphill crosses FS 90 and accesses Wright Meadows Trail #80, but stay on the main trail. From here it's about 0.5 mile to Middle Falls and another 1.2 miles to Upper Falls. The trail comes out to FS 90 alongside Quartz Creek, about 0.9 mile after Upper Falls, across the road from the Quartz Creek Trailhead. Return on the trail, or on the road if you must.

CAPITOL STATE FOREST

The 80,000-acre Capitol State Forest lies just south of Olympia, Washington, in an area known as the Black Hills. This forest is a favored destination for Puget Sound's more skilled and powerful mountain bikers. The northern half of the forest is an off-road vehicle area, while the southern half is designated for hikers and equestrians (with some trails open to mountain bikes).

This recreation area contains miles and miles of demanding single-track. The woods are filled with unsigned and unmapped trails. Only seasoned locals really know their way around, but even the old hands spend part of their time getting un-lost.

Like many off-road vehicle areas, the trails take a beating, but they are well maintained. Off-road vehicle permit fees and one percent of Washington gas tax revenues pay for off-road maintenance. A high clay content in the soils of Capitol State Forest makes for slippery conditions when the trails are wet. In places, cinder blocks have been set into the trail. Buried flush, the blocks provide excellent traction and help hold unstable ground in place.

RIDE 12 · Mima Loop

AT A GLANCE

WA

Length/configuration: 13.9 miles of single-track, including a 0.6-mile out-and-back (each way) leading to a 12.7-mile loop; 6-mile beginner route skips the hardest of the climbing

Aerobic difficulty: Some short, steep climbs; longest continuous climb is about 1.2 miles (after the beginner loop turnoff); one of the toughest climbs is the 0.1 mile from the parking area to the campground!

Technical difficulty: Rooty challenges, some pebbly sections

Scenery: Soft fern and salal-covered woods; Cascades view snack stop; Mima Falls

Special comments: Some of the best trails in the forest; full loop is for intermediate-level riders; beginners can tackle the shorter loop

This 13.9-mile single-track route will be a satisfying outing for the intermediate cyclist, while the shorter version, which eliminates much of the climbing (but also much of the fun descents), will make a challenging ramble for the beginner.

Trail #10, which allows for the shorter loop, was not surveyed on the research outing. It is well marked, however, and appears to level out after the initial climb (it only crosses one contour line on the topographical map after the first hill!). Without having researched it myself, I'd be confident splitting from my sweetheart at the beginner loop turnoff and meeting her at Mima Falls as I pedal the longer loop. (She'd be OK with that, too—that's why she's my sweetheart!)

Mima Falls is not imposing, as are so many waterfalls in the region, and the water may not even be falling under extended dry conditions, but it's certainly a pretty rest stop and a nice sidelight to a very pleasant outing.

The trail passes through numerous clear-cuts but also through soft, fern- and salal-covered, Douglas fir woods. There are a few wheel-sucking, muddy sections and some loose, pebbly sections, but it is mostly firm, good-quality single-track.

This area of the forest is motorcycle-free, and the trails are in noticeably better condition than in the motorcycle-legal sections.

RIDE 12 · Mima Loop

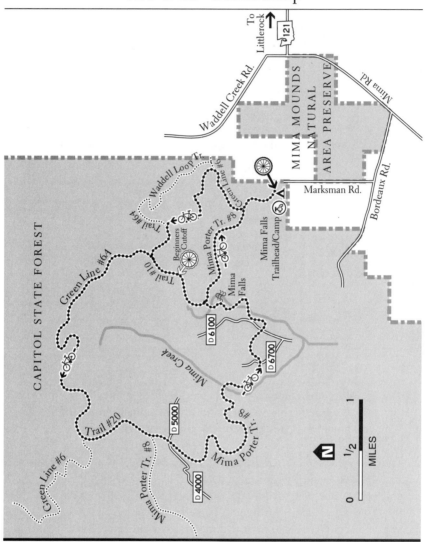

General location: The ride starts about 15 miles southwest of Olympia.

Elevation change: The parking area is at about 300' elevation. The route reaches a high point of 1,150'. Total climbing is estimated at 1,170'. On the short loop prepare for about 600' of climbing.

Season: Year-round. Horses are *verboten* on the trails from November 30 through March 31, so you'll only encounter hikers and other mountain bikers during this time.

Services: Water is available seasonally from a hand-pump at the Mima Falls Trailhead Camp. Camping is available here, but it is geared for equestrians, so use another location if the camp is getting full. (An RV camp is just up the road from the trailhead, and the Margaret McKenney Campground, on Waddell Creek Road, 2.5 miles north of the junction of 128th Avenue S.W. and Mima Road, is not far away.) Gas and grub are available in Littlerock. All services are available in Olympia.

Hazards: At the start and finish, watch for human and horse traffic near the horse camp and along the trail. Root challenges along the way include angled roots, which can be slippery when wet, and a few drop-offs.

Rescue index: The trailhead is located near residences, and also near a gun club—there's a comforting thought! Littlerock has pay phones.

Land status: Washington Department of Natural Resources, Capitol State Forest.

Maps: DNR Capitol State Forest.

Finding the trail: From the north or south, take Interstate 5 to Exit 95 and proceed west toward Littlerock on WA 121. In about 2.8 miles, in Littlerock, go straight at the stop sign onto 128th Avenue S.W. (where Littlerock Road curves to the left). In 0.9 miles come to a **T** intersection. Waddell Creek Road goes right and Mima Road goes left. Take the left onto Mima Road, and travel 1.2 miles to the junction of Bordeaux Road to the right. Make the right on Bordeaux Road and drive 0.7 mile, then turn right onto Marksman Road (so named for the gun club just beyond the trailhead). In 0.9 mile, as Marksman Road curves to the right, bear left, pass the gate, and park at the trailhead parking area to the left.

Source of additional information:

Washington Department of Natural Resources
Central Region Office
1405 Rush Road
Chehalis, WA 98532
(800) 527-3305 or (360) 748-2383 (direct)

Notes on the trail: For some challenging single-track from the first pedal strokes, take the trail to the right of the signboard at the parking area, which climbs to the campground road in less than 0.1 mile. For an easy warm-up, take the paved road from the parking lot. The trail meets and crosses the road, but turn left, then ride to the right of the hand pump. Almost immediately, opposite the end of campsite 5, turn right onto the smooth, gravelled, formal start of the trail. In 0.5 mile, in a clear-cut, come to a junction to the right. You'll return on the trail that is now straight ahead of you, but to start the loop, turn right onto Green Line #6. Cross a road in 0.1 mile, then cross another road in 0.2 mile and pick up the trail about 100' to your right. Descend on a pebbly path out of the clear-cut and come to a **Y** junction in 0.2 mile. Stay left, cross the creek, and make a short climb on the now hard-packed trail. In 0.2 mile pass the junction

Green Line #6.

of the Waddell Loop Trail on your right. Beyond the junction 0.3 mile, skirt a gravel road to your right; bear left when a short trail connects with the road, and then cross the road within 0.1 mile. Make a short descent to a wide puddle—at least it was wide on the February research ride—in a thinned stand of Douglas fir, and cross another road in 0.2 mile. After crossing a bridge over a creek, Trail #6A takes off to the right and meets the Waddell Loop Trail. Stay straight, though, on the gentle climb. In 0.5 mile, ride near a creek to your right that has carved out a small gorge. Very shortly, come to the junction of Trail #10.

Beginners, turn left onto Trail #10, cross the old roadbed, and climb; your more-advanced riding buddies will meet you on the other end of the trail. Hammerheads, turn right, staying on Green Line #6 for the longer loop. In 1.2 miles, after some climbing in a pretty wooded area, come out to a clearing, where you view clear-cut hillsides to the northwest (Little Larch Mountain), west, and south. Start on the most sustained climb on the ride, 1.2 miles up the hill to the left (south). After you switchback, you can spy some views to the north, to Olympia and beyond. At 0.9 mile into the climb, the trail winds to the right as it skirts a road; stay on the main trail as a short access trail joins the road here. Cross the road in another 0.1 mile; or, even better, don't cross it yet. Ride up the road to the right for less than 0.1 mile and stop at the pullout to the right as the road curves left. Clouds limited my view on the research ride, but I still got nice views north to the Puget Sound Basin, east, and northeast at this ready-made rest stop. From this vantage point you can also see the trail on which you just climbed, down and to the right. Pat yourself on the back, ride back down and turn right onto the trail. In another 0.1 mile you'll cross the same road from above the rest stop. If you haven't had an eyeful yet, ride back down. If so, continue straight across the road. The trail traverses a clear-cut hillside, with one very short, very steep rise and some steep, steady climbing bringing you to the same road. Don't cross it, though; the trail continues to the right after it kisses the road. At the next road crossing, the trail continues about 30' to your left. Climb out of that road crossing, and as you make your next descent, bear left at the **Y** intersection, onto Trail #20, where Green Line #6 climbs to the right. Trail #20 makes a rolling, rooty descent, with a small root drop-off just before a creek crossing. In 0.4 mile come to the junction of Mima Porter Trail #8, both straight and up to the left. Veer left and climb. At the next road crossing, the trail continues to the right, between the junction of roads D-4000 and D-5000. Shortly after the crossing, break into a clear-cut; cross a rocky spur road off D-4000, with a view of the main road ahead of you. Not far beyond the road crossing, commence a yahoo-fun descent that leads back into the woods. Start on a hillside over a creek, cross a couple of bridges, and continue a rolling descent on the opposite side. The descent rolls to a road crossing in 1.8 miles. Cross the road, and descend to a bridge over Mima Creek in 0.1 mile. Cross another bridge in 0.1 mile at the edge of a clear-cut. Exercise those legs on the other side of the bridge and quickly get back into the trees on a rolling climb. Cross road D-6700, 0.8 mile beyond the bridge; in 0.3 more miles, come out to a regenerating clear-cut and start a short, fast, fun descent down the hill and past road D-6100. Come to a bridge over East Fork Mima Creek, and, in 0.2 mile, beyond another bridge, come to Mima Falls. (Beginners, make a hard right at the 5 o'clock position as Trail #10 ends into Trail #8, and ride about 0.4 mile to reach the falls).

At Mima Falls, you can dismount and descend a short spur trail to its base for another perspective. Back on the bike, a short, sloppy section of trail brings you to a new bridge over the creek in 0.3 mile. Shortly thereafter, meet the south end of Trail #10, which comes in at the 7 o'clock position on your left. Continue straight, climbing gradually on a wide section of trail. The trail levels out in about 0.3 mile and, in another 0.3 mile, descends to a bridge over a creek, climbs out of it, and levels out again. At the next road crossing, the trail continues at the 1 o'clock position to your right. It's gravelled and well-maintained here, and leads to the junction of Green Line #6 and the end of the loop. Continue straight for the short "back" leg of the out-and-back, coming out opposite campsite 5 on the graveled trail. Descend by road or trail to the lower parking lot and ride's end.

RIDE 13 · Mt. Molly Loop

AT A GLANCE

WA

Length/configuration: 8.3-mile loop on single-track trails, gravel roads, and paved roads

Aerobic difficulty: Moderate; some short steep bursts

Technical difficulty: Intermediate to advanced; trails contain an abundance of ruts, rocks, and roots

Scenery: Second-growth forest and clear-cuts criss-crossed by off-road vehicle trails and roads

Special comments: Plan on getting lost; take a compass and the best map you can get your hands on

The 8.3-mile Mt. Molly Loop is in the northern half of the Capitol State Forest. Locals consider this ride one of the area's easier outings, but in our opinion, it is difficult. The route follows single-track trails for over 6 miles and ends with paved and gravel roads.

Challenges and thrills are commonplace on this route. There is a lot of climbing, but most of it is moderately difficult to easy. The really steep stuff comes in short bursts, adding up to about one mile of strenuous climbing. There are some nice downhills, rolling terrain, and level stretches too. The circuit includes ditchlike conditions, deep ruts, mud holes, big rocks, roots, and howling motorcycles.

General location: Capitol State Forest is about 15 miles southwest of Olympia, Washington.

Elevation change: The ride starts at 180' and tops out at 880' near the halfway point of the loop. The trip is full of lesser undulations that add about 500' of climbing to the ride. Total elevation gain: 1,200'.

Season: The early fall is a good time for a visit, especially on weekdays. The wettest seasons are typically the winter and spring. Off-road vehicle use is heaviest on summer weekends.

Services: There is piped water at the trailhead in Bordeaux Camp. Gas and limited groceries are available in Littlerock. All services are available in Olympia.

Hazards: The trails are chock-full of obstacles and dangerous conditions (like deep ruts on severe descents). The tread is very slick when wet. Give motorized

RIDE 13 · Mt. Molly Loop

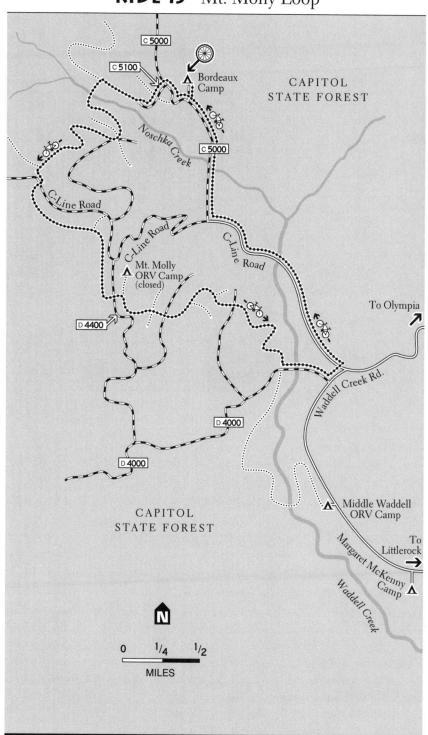

C 5000

C 5100

Bordeaux Camp

CAPITOL STATE FOREST

Noschka Creek

C 5000

C-Line Road

C-Line Road

C-Line Road

Mt. Molly ORV Camp (closed)

D 4400

To Olympia

Waddell Creek Rd.

D 4000

D 4000

Middle Waddell ORV Camp

CAPITOL STATE FOREST

To Littlerock

Margaret McKenny Camp

Waddell Creek

N

0   1/4   1/2

MILES

Miles of ORV trails run
through Capitol State
Forest.

vehicles a wide berth. Be especially careful when crossing roads. The area is a maze of unmarked trails, and new trails are being blazed all the time. Getting lost is a real possibility. Travel with others and be prepared for emergencies.

Rescue index: Help is available in Olympia. The nearest pay phone is in Littlerock.

Land status: Lands administered by the Washington State Department of Natural Resources.

Maps: Check bike shops in Olympia for the latest editions of locally produced maps and directions. USGS 7.5 minute quad: Littlerock.

Finding the trail: Follow I-5 south from Olympia. Take Exit 95 and proceed west on WA 121 toward Littlerock. In Littlerock, go straight at the stop sign and keep going straight, following the sign for Capitol State Forest. The road passes a gas station and a tavern, then crosses some railroad tracks. Drive 0.6 mile beyond the railroad tracks and bear right onto 128th Avenue at a **Y** intersection. You will immediately arrive at a stop sign; turn right onto unsigned Waddell Creek Road. Proceed for 4 miles to a **T** intersection at C-Line Road. Turn left and go another 1.3 miles to the end of the pavement at unsigned C-5000. (The

Trail maintenance in Capitol State Forest.

intersection is marked with an incomplete directional sign on the northwest corner and a "Dead End" sign on C-5000.) Turn right onto C-5000. Follow C-5000 for 0.8 mile; continue straight into Bordeaux Camp to park your vehicle.

Source of additional information:

Washington Department of Natural Resources
Central Region Office
1405 Rush Road S-3
Chehalis, WA 98532
(360) 748-2383 or (800) 527-3305

Notes on the trail: Ride out of Bordeaux Camp to C-5000 and turn right. Climb to C-5100 and turn left. Stay on the road as side trails branch off. Shortly, C-5100 enters the woods and becomes a wide single-track. Pedal into the woods for about 0.5 mile to an intersection of trails. Turn left and descend to a creek crossing. Cross the creek, then climb for 0.6 mile to an intersection where the trail meets a spur road. Several trails take off from here. Look to the right for a pile of roots blocking the road. Go around the roots on the right-hand side. This puts you on a switchbacking single-track that climbs away from the road. Ascend for 0.6 mile to a **Y** in the trail; bear left. When you arrive at a road, turn left then immediately bear right to get back onto the trail. (You will pass a rail fence soon after regaining the trail.) After a stretch of downhill riding and some easier climbing, you will reach another **Y**. Stay right and downhill—the trail skirts D-4400 and the now closed Mt. Molly Camp. Stay on the main trail as side trails branch off to access Mt. Molly Camp. Soon the trail crosses D-4400. Cross the road and turn right at the **T** intersection of trails. Climb moderately, then drop a short way and continue straight across another trail to begin a more demanding and technical climb. The trail crosses a spur road, continues to climb, then arrives at a **Y** intersection of trails. Stay left and ascend steeply to the top of the climb. Crest and follow the trail downhill. (Some trails branch off, but they climb.) From the top, it is 0.25 mile to a **Y** intersection where both trails descend. Bear right, following the trail that is wider and less steep. Stay right at the next **Y** intersection, descend through a clear-cut, and cross a spur road. It is 0.4 mile from this spur road crossing to another road, unsigned D-4000. Turn left onto D-4000 and ride out to paved Waddell Creek Road. Turn left onto unsigned Waddell Creek Road, then left again onto C-Line Road. Ride back to your vehicle at Bordeaux Camp (see "Finding the trail").

To expand your riding options in the Capitol State Forest, find single-tracks that take off from main roads. Use maps and a compass and allow plenty of time for route finding. A good way to quickly get to know some of the trails in the area is to tag along with local mountain bikers. Visit bike shops in Olympia; some of them conduct group rides in the forest.

RIDE 14 · Middle Waddell Loop

AT A GLANCE

Length/configuration: 26.2-mile loop, virtually all single-track and off-road vehicle trail

Aerobic difficulty: Advanced-level climbing; some technical, some muddy, some slick

Technical difficulty: Roots, rocks, rutted trail, slippery clay

Scenery: Second-growth forest interspersed with clear-cuts (hey, it's a working forest), some views east to the high Cascades

Special comments: A physically, technically, and mechanically demanding outing for the advanced rider

Not many rides in Capitol State Forest can be considered easy. The 26.2-mile Middle Waddell Loop can be considered difficult physically (more than 2,000 feet of tough climbing), technically (some of the climbing, and some of the descending, is on slick clay), and mechanically (the mud and clay can cake onto your drivetrain, wearing out equipment and requiring extra effort). The challenges of this ride make it a rewarding outing for the advanced rider.

Along with the clay and mud, you also ride on hard-packed trail surface. You ride through some clear-cuts, but you also ride through dense, wooded areas, across creeks, and by a couple of spots that open up distant views. The ride includes challenging climbs and fun descents, serpentine trails and fast straightaways. It's an inspiring ride and a helluva workout.

The trails are less rutted at the top, because inexperienced motorcyclists tend to stay toward the bottom of the mountains and tear up the trails, while the better, more experienced riders venture to the higher elevations and impact the trails to a much lesser degree.

Like any loop, you can do this ride either way, but the described clockwise route will save you some slippery descents at the end, when you might be toasted.

General location: The Middle Waddell off-road vehicle camp is located approximately 9 miles south of Olympia.

Elevation change: The loop starts at 150' elevation and hits a top elevation of about 1,700', but the numerous climbs and descents along the way bring total elevation gain to well over 2,000'. Be prepared to climb!

Season: Year-round; some sections are slick and sloppy even during the dry months. If you don't mind riding in wet conditions (and if you live in the Pacific Northwest, you shouldn't!), you'll have the trails to yourself from November 1 through March 31, as they are closed to horses and motorcycles during this time. February and March are good times to ride because the trails will have been free of motorcycles and horses for a few months by then, and your fellow mountain bikers will have been packing down the trails.

Services: Water is available at the Middle Waddell off-road vehicle camp. Camping areas abound. Food and gas are available in Littlerock (try the Farm Boy Restaurant, right off of I-5, Exit 95, for a preride breakfast). All services are available in Olympia.

Hazards: On the clay, slick slopes send cyclists slipping and sliding. I walked a couple of descending sections due to the sketchiness of the trail surface. Bring a map and a compass; the trail is a working forest, so new trails and roads are opened and old ones are closed on a regular basis.

Rescue index: You'll find houses on the way to the trailhead to both the north and south. You'll find pay phones in Littlerock and at the Black Lake Grocery, on Black Lake Boulevard, about 7.1 miles from the ride start.

Land status: Washington Department of Natural Resources, Capitol State Forest.

Maps: DNR Capitol State Forest.

Finding the trail: From I-5 in Olympia, take Exit 104/US 101. Travel about 1.5 miles and exit at Black Lake Boulevard. Turn left (south) off of the exit and drive about 3.7 miles to where Black Lake Boulevard turns into 62nd Avenue S.W. as

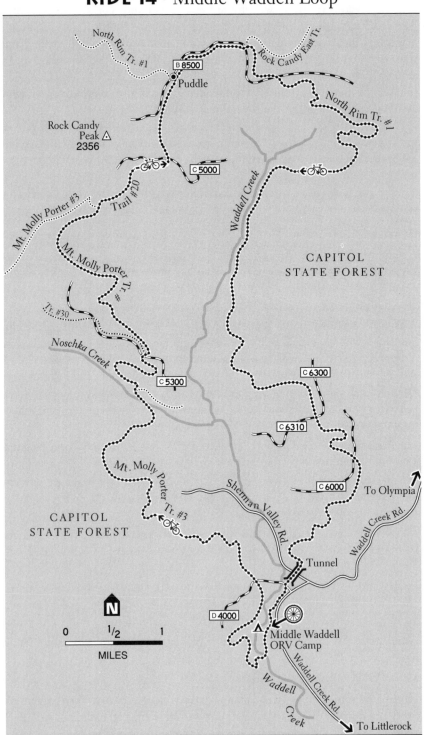

North Rim Tr. #1

B 8500

Puddle

Rock Candy East Tr.

North Rim Tr. #1

Rock Candy
Peak △
2356

C 5000

Trail #20

Waddell Creek

Mt. Molly Porter #3

Mt. Molly Porter Tr. #

Tr. #30

Noschka Creek

C 5300

CAPITOL
STATE FOREST

C 6300

C 6310

C 6000

Mt. Molly Porter Tr. #3

Sherman Valley Rd.

To Olympia

CAPITOL
STATE FOREST

Waddell Creek Rd.

Tunnel

N

0   1/2   1

MILES

D 4000

Middle Waddell
ORV Camp

Waddell Creek Rd.

Waddell
Creek

To Littlerock

it curves to the right and then ends at a **T** intersection at Delphi Road. Turn left onto Delphi Road and travel 2.1 miles, then turn right on Waddell Creek Road. In 2.6 miles, past a pullout with a signboard on the right, turn left, staying on Waddell Creek Road. (Sherman Valley Road continues straight.) In 0.7 mile turn right into the Middle Waddell off-road vehicle camp. Pass the trail on which you'll start and end the loop, pass a gate, and park in the parking area straight ahead. Parking is also available on the left side of the road.

From Shelton and Aberdeen, the Black Lake Boulevard exit is about 4 miles west of the US 101/WA 8 junction.

From the south, take I-5 to Exit 95 and head west on WA 121 toward Littlerock. In about 2.8 miles, in Littlerock, go straight at the stop sign onto 128th Avenue S.W. (where Littlerock Road curves to the left), following the sign toward Capitol State Forest. In 0.9 mile come to a **T** intersection and turn right onto Waddell Creek Road (where Mima Road goes left). Enter Capitol State Forest in 2.3 miles, pass Margaret McKinney Campground in another 0.2 mile, Middle Waddell Day Use Area parking 0.6 mile farther, and turn left into the Middle Waddell off-road vehicle camp in another 0.4 mile.

Source of additional information:

Washington Department of Natural Resources
Central Region Office
1405 Rush Road
Chehalis, WA 98532
(800) 527-3305 or (360) 748-2383 (direct)

Notes on the trail: Backtrack past the gate and turn right (south) onto the trail in a sparsely wooded area, with the road and a clear-cut hill to your left. At a junction at 0.4 mile, turn right and wind around the back of the campground (if you go straight you'll come to the day-use parking area). Come to a bridge after a 100' climb at the 1.1-mile mark, and in another 0.5 mile come to a delta junction. To the right is the old trail and to the left is a reroute, so take the left. At a road crossing 0.3 mile farther, gear down for a steep climb as the trail picks up about 20' to the right. At a junction 0.5 mile into the climb, the hard right, at the 4 o'clock position, descends; instead, take the soft right to continue on the main trail. In another 0.1 mile, a trail of hike-a-bike steepness shoots up to the right; continue straight on the steep-but-rideable trail, and you'll eventually switchback and meet the top of the hike-a-bike in 0.4 mile. The climb levels out a bit after you make the left at the **Y** junction 0.1 mile beyond the top of the hike-a-bike trail. Crest the climb 0.3 mile after the **Y** junction, go straight past the skid road, and earn the first of your descending rewards. Hold your line through the slick stuff!

When you pick up the trail after crossing a road in 0.5 mile, you're on Mt. Molly Porter Trail #3, which suffers from heavily scarred spots as it parallels the road. Ride along what used to be Mt. Molly Campground (closed in 1996, partially due to rowdiness among the regulars). The trail continues to the left at a road crossing about 1.2 miles along the Mt. Molly Porter Trail. On the ensuing

Mike Curley traversing a
clear-cut at Capitol State
Forest.

climb you can catch some views of Mt. Rainier to the east as you level out. After
a crest 0.1 mile beyond the road crossing, take the trail to the right at the 1
o'clock position. In 0.7 mile it descends to a road that is part of the trail; it swings
to the left in 100 yards or so, and again narrows into trail. You'll be descending
into the valley you see below you as you wind to the left. Descend, and after
climbing from Noschka Creek at the bottom of the descent, come to a **T** junction. To the right, you'd come to Bordeaux Camp in 0.8 mile—but for this ride,
you're not going that way; turn left and climb.

In 0.8 mile cross a road, then climb up the cinder-blocked trail and come to
a landing at a road crossing in 0.5 mile. Stop for some great views to the east on
a clear day, then cross the road and keep climbing. You cross the same road a
total of three times as you make this climb. As you meet the road for the third
time in another 0.4 mile, climb to the left about 100' to continue on the trail. As
you come back onto the trail, stay straight and climb on Mt. Molly Porter Trail
#3, where Trail #30 climbs to the left. Mt. Molly Porter makes a traversing climb
on nice, narrow trail across a clear-cut and then back into the woods, where it
continues traversing after another road crossing. Riding 1.7 miles beyond that
road, the trail swings around to the right in a wooded section, and then splits;

here, Mt. Molly Porter #3 continues up, but instead, descend on Trail #20. Cross C-5000 in 1.1 miles and continue on Trail #20 for another 0.8 mile, where you come to a four-way intersection: to the right and left are Road B-8500 (mapped on the 1995 Capitol State Forest map as C-4700 — Rock Candy Peak is up to the left. Straight across is North Rim Trail #1, which descends to the Rock Candy Trailhead, and a long ride back to the car; so head right on B-8500 (formerly C-4700), which is actually a part of Trail #1. A puddle to the right as you start always seems full and deep, so ride around it, and enjoy a sweet, fast, rocky descent on the road. The descent gets a bit smoother in 0.8 mile, and has a tree-canopied, trail-like feel to it. Start looking to the left as the descent smoothes out, because in another 0.2 mile (1.0 mile total descending on the road), a trail, also part of Trail #1, picks up to the left. Shortly after climbing onto the trail, it splits; the Rock Candy East Trail breaks left and stays even, but stay with the trail to the right and climb, continuing on North Rim Trail #1.

Climb and descend for 0.6 mile and cross the same road, now wide and graveled, on which you descended. The trail continues straight across and goes into a nice 780', 3-mile descent in fir-, alder-, and dogwood-covered, fern-laden woods with some slick spots to negotiate. After some whoop-de-doos, cross a bridge over Waddell Creek to bottom out the descent, ignoring the trail that goes back to the right at the 5 o'clock position before the bridge; go straight, into a low-ring climb out of the creek. You get some breaks along the climb, but it'll be 3.3 miles until a rolling descent, on which some short bursts are required. On the descent, cross C-6310, where it reaches a junction with C-6300. The trail continues directly across, while the road provides a nice view to the northeast. The trail continues into a short, sharp 30' rise and a 200' descent; then catch another view of Mt. Rainier on a climb through a clear-cut, riding south/southeast. The trail descends again, crossing C-6000, and continues a bumpy, fun descent punctuated by some short climbs.

Another 2 miles from the road crossing, come off the descent and go toward a tunnel under Sherman Valley Road, just west of its junction with Waddell Creek Road. Go through the tunnel and ride straight, following the main trail, as another trail branches off to the right. Stay on the main trail as it bends to the left, roughly paralleling Waddell Creek Road, when a trail goes off to the right. In 0.9 mile past the tunnel, come to a road crossing. Go straight if you're a super-human rider ready for another lap, but here you're back at the Middle Waddell off-road vehicle camp. Turn right, ride a few feet to your vehicle, and bask in the glow of a tough, excellent ride, well done.

OLYMPIC PENINSULA RIDES

The 6,500-square-mile Olympic Peninsula is separated from the rest of Washington by salt water. The main access for the peninsula is US 101. The highway parallels the Pacific coastline on the west, the Strait of Juan de Fuca on the north and the inland waters of Puget Sound on the east. You can also access the peninsula by ferry from Seattle or Victoria.

The area is unique and strikingly beautiful. It encompasses ocean beaches, windy ridges, precipitous mountains, snowfields, glaciers, deep gorges, and verdant forests.

Much of the peninsula lies within the Olympic National Forest. The forest contains a stunning variety of environments within short distances. In the 50 miles that stretch from the summit of Mt. Olympus to the Pacific, the vegetation changes from an arctic environment of lichen and rock to a temperate rainforest.

Precipitation on the Olympic coast averages over 12 feet a year! Rainfall amounts drop dramatically as you move east. Precipitation is heaviest in the winter, decreasing by spring. Summer is the driest time of the year.

While much of the riding on the Olympic Peninsula is on gravel forest roads, we direct your attention to eight excellent trail rides, roughly around the perimeter of Olympic National Park.

From the advanced-level Mt. Muller Trail and the easy Spruce Railroad Trail (which actually lies within the park) on the north end of the peninsula, the rides swing east to the Port Angeles and Sequim area (the intermediate-level Foothills Loop, and beautiful, advanced-level Gold Creek Trail and Lower Dungeness Loop), south to Quilcene (the scenic Lower Big Quilcene Trail), and to the southeast peninsula area (gorgeous single-tracks along the Lower South Fork Skokomish River and Wynoochee Lake).

The Olympic National Forest is participating in the trail park pass fee system, requiring a pass to park at trailheads within the forest. Pick up your day or season pass at a ranger station or outdoors shop before you head out on trails within forest boundaries.

RIDE 15 · Mt. Muller Loop

AT A GLANCE

Length/configuration: 13.6-miles, including 13.2-mile loop (almost all single-track), plus two 0.1-mile (each way) side trails

Aerobic difficulty: Strenuous; initial 3-mile climb switchbacks up 2,200' in first 3 miles—climbing totals 3,150'; if you can make the climb without walking, you are an animal!

Technical difficulty: Difficult; tight switchbacks, both uphill and downhill; some rough, rooty sections along the ridge

Scenery: Views of Mt. Olympus, Lake Crescent, Strait of Juan de Fuca and Vancouver Island, and, on a clear day, Mt. Baker and Glacier Peak in the distance; incredible wildflower displays through the meadows

Special comments: The rewards are directly proportional to the effort. For advanced riders only!

From the get-go, the 13.6-mile Mt. Muller loop is difficult and demanding, but the pleasure is worth the pain.

The pleasure: Climbs and descents through beautiful woods and incredible wildflower-strewn meadows; views of Mt. Olympus, Lake Crescent, the Strait of Juan de Fuca and Vancouver Island, and, on a clear day, Mt. Baker and Glacier Peak.

The pain: With only a couple of pedal strokes worth of warm-up, the initial three-mile climb alternates between difficult and punishing, with just a few short respites. Once on the ridge, there's more climbing and steep roller-coaster sections until a descent with around 30 switchbacks brings you back to the bottom. This is a must-ride for the strong-legged and technically advanced rider.

The trail is hard-packed, with some steep, rooty, and rocky sections. The last three miles roughly parallel US 101 as you make your way, on both dirt road and trail, back to the trailhead.

General location: The trailhead lies about 5 miles west of Lake Crescent, about 30 miles west of Port Angeles, and 24 miles east of Forks.

Elevation change: The trail starts at 1,000' elevation and climbs to 3,200' in the first 3 miles. Sharp climbs along the ridgeline add about 400'. High elevation is 3,748' at the top of Mt. Muller. Total elevation gain is 3,150'.

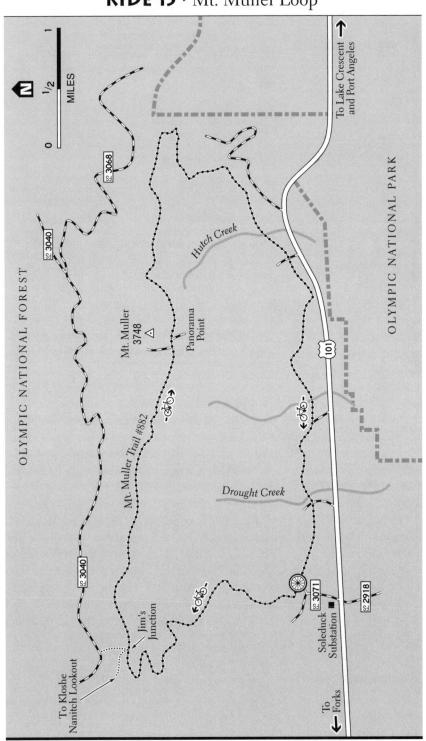

N

0   1/2   1
MILES

FR 3068

OLYMPIC NATIONAL FOREST

FR 3040

FR 3040

Mt. Muller Trail #882

Mt. Muller
3748

Panorama
Point

Hutch Creek

101

OLYMPIC NATIONAL PARK

To Lake Crescent
and Port Angeles

Drought Creek

Jim's
Junction

Soleduck
Substation

FR 3071

FR 2918

To Kloshe
Nanitch Lookout

To
Forks

Brent McCord at Jasmine Meadow.

Season: The best riding conditions are generally found in late spring through early fall. The trail is popular among hikers, equestrians, and mountain bikers on summer weekends, so watch for other users and take appropriate cautions.

Services: There is no water at the trailhead, and no potable water along the trail. Water is available at the Fairholm Campground, at the west end of Lake Crescent, and gas and groceries can be obtained at the Fairholm Store.

Hazards: The trail sports numerous tight switchbacks, both uphill and downhill. The trail on the north side of the ridge, especially, is uneven in spots, which combines with steep grades for some challenging riding. Watch your speed on the downhills—some of the switchbacks come upon you suddenly.

Rescue index: Help can be flagged down on US 101, or from the phone at the Fairholm Store 4.7 miles from the trailhead.

Land status: Olympic National Forest, Soleduck Ranger District.

Maps: The information board at the trailhead shows the loop, and maps are available at the trailhead. Although the loop is pretty straightforward, be prepared with your own map if there are none at the trailhead; get the Mt. Muller handout from the Soleduck Ranger District. The 1987 revision of the Olympic National Forest map did not denote the trail. The Custom Correct Lake Crescent–Happy Lake Ridge map shows all but the westernmost portion of the loop.

Finding the trail: From Port Angeles, travel west on US 101 for 25.8 miles to the Fairholm Store at the west end of Lake Crescent. Continuing on US 101,

4.7 miles beyond the store, turn right onto Forest Service Road 3071 (where FS 2918 goes left). Drive 0.3 mile, past the Soleduck substation, to the Mt. Muller/Littleton Loop Trailhead parking area. The trailhead is approximately 24 miles northeast of Forks on US 101.

Source of additional information:

USFS Soleduck Ranger District
196281 US 101
Forks, WA 98331
(360) 374-6522

Notes on the trail: From the parking area, enter the trail on the wide gravel path and go left, routing the loop clockwise. Climbing starts almost immediately. At Jim's Junction, a four-way intersection at 3.1 miles, veer right to continue the loop. After some steep climbing and descending on Snider Ridge, past Jasmine, Allison, and Markham Meadows (2.5 miles after Jim's Junction) climb on the spur trail to the left for 0.1 mile to the top of Mt. Muller. Walk around to the north for views through the trees of Juan de Fuca and Vancouver Island to the north, and Glacier Peak and Mt. Baker to the east. Return to the main trail and continue the loop. Pretty quickly, as the trail winds to the left, look to the right for the 0.1-mile spur trail down to Panorama Point, where views of Lake Crescent add to the visual wonder. On the descent, 1.6 miles past the signed Mosley Gap, on a right-hand switchback, a 200' walk straight ahead takes you to Fout's Rock House, an imposing rock formation on your left that juts straight up. Continuing the descent, cross Hutch Creek in another mile. About 0.3 mile past Hutch Creek, the trail opens into a clearing; ride straight through and you'll pick up the trail in less than 0.1 mile. Pass a dirt road in another 0.5 mile and continue on the trail through a clear-cut. At the next intersection, follow the road for 0.2 mile, looking for the sign pointing you to the left, just past Drought Creek. Follow this road a short distance to the trail, which veers off to the right. Follow the trail to loop's end in 0.7 mile.

RIDE 16 · Spruce Railroad Trail

AT A GLANCE

Length/configuration: 8-mile out-and-back (4 miles each way); old rail bed (gravel) and some brief sections of single-track

Aerobic difficulty: Easy

Technical difficulty: Mostly easy; a couple of technical spots

Scenery: Peaceful lake with forested mountain backdrop

Special comments: Good outing for energetic families

WA

During World War I, the United States needed Sitka spruce for airplane production. The roadless forests of the western Olympic Peninsula held great promise as a source of this valuable wood. A railway accessing the timber was built with dizzying speed but was completed 19 days after the war ended. A portion of this old railroad bed has been converted into the Spruce Railroad Trail.

This is an easy eight-mile out-and-back ride beside bucolic Lake Crescent. At one point the trail crosses an arched bridge over a lovely rock-walled inlet. Waterfowl may be observed along the shore of the lake, and deer are often seen in the woods. Views across the clear water are of forested hills backed by the majestic Olympic Mountains. Since the ride is in a national park, the scene contains no clear-cuts. The trip is spiced up by a couple of short stretches of technical single-track.

General location: The trail begins on the north side of Lake Crescent, approximately 30 miles west of Port Angeles, Washington.

Elevation change: The trailhead lies at 800'. The route reaches a high point of 860', and small hills add about 100' of climbing to the ride. Total elevation gain: 160'.

Season: The low elevation of the ride makes it suitable for year-round use.

Services: There is no potable water on the trip. Water can be obtained seasonally at Fairholm Campground. Fairholm Store (open during the summer) has limited groceries and gas. All services are available in Port Angeles.

Hazards: Cougars have been encountered at close range in this area. Watch for poison oak growing beside the trail, and check your skin and clothing for ticks. The trail surface does contain some obstacles like loose rocks, roots, and small creek crossings.

RIDE 16 · Spruce Railroad Trail

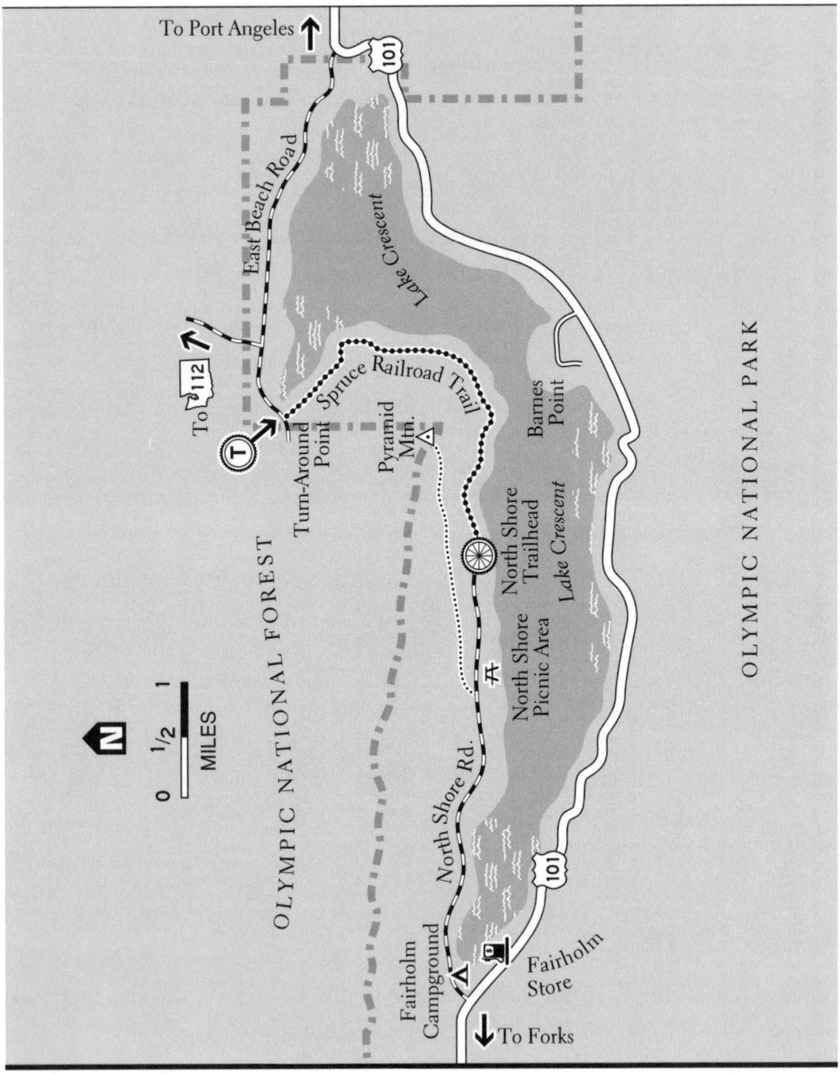

To Port Angeles ↑

101

East Beach Road

Lake Crescent

To 112

Spruce Railroad Trail

Turn-Around Point

Pyramid Mtn.

Barnes Point

T

OLYMPIC NATIONAL FOREST

OLYMPIC NATIONAL PARK

North Shore Trailhead
Lake Crescent

North Shore Picnic Area

N

0   1/2   1
MILES

North Shore Rd.

101

Fairholm Campground

Fairholm Store

↓ To Forks

Rescue index: The Storm King Ranger Station is on the south shore of Lake Crescent; it is open during the summer (from 10 A.M. to 4 P.M.). There are pay phones outside of the Fairholm Store and the ranger station.

Land status: Olympic National Park.

Maps: The Olympic National Forest and Olympic National Park map is an adequate guide. USGS 7.5 minute quad: Lake Crescent.

Finding the trail: From Port Angeles, follow US 101 west for about 25 miles to the west end of Lake Crescent. Pass the Fairholm Store (on your right) and take

Lake Crescent.

the next right onto North Shore Road. Follow the road to its terminus at the North Shore Trailhead of the Spruce Railroad Trail.

Sources of additional information:

Park Superintendent
Olympic National Park
600 East Park Avenue
Port Angeles, WA 98363
(360) 452-4501

Storm King Ranger Station
106 Lake Crescent Road
Port Angeles, WA 98363
(360) 928-3380

Notes on the trail: The 8-mile round-trip starts at the North Shore Trailhead. Starting at the North Shore Picnic Area adds 3 miles to the tour. Beginning at Fairholm Campground makes for a 17-mile out-and-back excursion.

RIDE 17 · The Foothills

AT A GLANCE

WA

Length/configuration: 6.8-mile loop, including 1.2 miles on gravel roads and the remainder on single-track

Aerobic difficulty: Tough 1-mile gravel road climb to upper trailhead; single-track climbs are moderate roller coasters

Technical difficulty: Intermediate; rocky, rooty sections

Scenery: Second-growth woods; fun riding and lack of daytime scenery makes for good night-ride potential

Special comments: Roller-coaster trails include fun, swooping turns and fast, final descent; connector trails intersecting main loop allow you to reroute differently each time

Here's some of what the Foothills Trails do not provide: sweeping vistas, rushing rivers, peaceful lakes, cascading waterfalls, and majestic stands of 400-year-old cedars and pines.

Here's what the Foothills Trails do provide: fun, roller-coaster, intermediate-level mountain biking with swooping turns and a mile-long fast final descent, all close to town.

In other words, don't do this for the views; do it for the riding—this is mountain biking for mountain biking's sake. (The best view, in fact, comes before you ever touch trail, off the gravel road to the left shortly before the trailhead. Wander up that trenched-and-mounded road for looks down into Port Angeles and the Strait of Juan de Fuca.)

The trails are in second-growth woods with some fern- and salal-covered forest floor. They're hard-packed with some roots and ruts to negotiate. Motorcycle usage is apparent in spots, but the trails are in good shape overall.

The 6.8-mile loop won't take a lot of time—maybe an hour to an hour and a half—but if you want to extend the ride, do it again in another configuration. An even longer option is to ride from town on the road, play around on the trails, and descend back to town via the eastern extension of the trail system (not researched for this ride) that leads back to Heart O' the Hills Parkway.

Would I plan an entire weekend around this ride? No. Would I ride here if I was in the area? You bet!

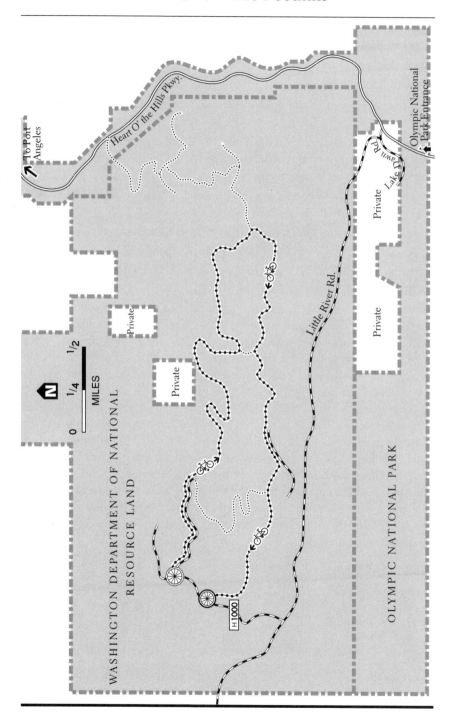

General location: From Port Angeles, a 10-mile drive south will get you to the Foothills.

Elevation change: The loop starts at 1,700'; the initial road climb brings you to 2,300', and after undulations on the trail, the far end of the loop sits at 2,520'. Other climbing brings total elevation gain to near 1,000'.

Season: Year-round.

Services: There is no water available on this ride. All services are available in Port Angeles.

Hazards: With the trails so close to town, you'll likely encounter other users, on motorized and unmotorized wheels, on hooves, and on foot—another reason to do this ride at night. Watch out for all of these along the trail.

Rescue index: Residents on Lake Dawn Road may call for help. Help is available in Port Angeles.

Land status: Washington Department of Natural Resources, Olympic Region.

Maps: Custom Correct, Hurricane Ridge shows the trails on the loop as well as the trails that will eventually get you down to Heart O' the Hills Parkway.

Finding the trail: Driving westbound in Port Angeles, turn south (left) on Race Street from US 101. Veer right onto Heart O' the Hills Parkway, toward the Olympic National Park entrance, where Mt. Angeles Road goes left, just after the Hurricane Ridge Visitor Center. In 5.1 miles turn right onto Lake Dawn Road (if you come to the Olympic National Park entrance you went 0.2 mile too far). Continue straight as Lake Dawn Road veers left in 0.3 mile, putting you on gravel Little River Road. Stay on Little River Road, past junctions, for 3.3 miles. Just after a descent on Little River Road, turn up to the right on H-1000 where a small sign nailed to a tree points you toward the trailhead (if you go too far on Little River Road you'll come to Black Diamond Road in about a mile). Drive up H-1000 for 0.4 mile and park at a small pullout to the left, across from where the trail comes down on your right at the 4 o'clock position. More parking is available about 0.2 mile past the trail after you go left at the **Y** junction.

Coming from the west, go straight onto East Lauridsen Boulevard off of US 101 as US 101 turns north toward town. In about 10 blocks, turn right on Race Street and proceed as above.

Source of additional information:

Washington Department of Natural Resources
Olympic Region
411 Tillicum Lane
Forks, WA 98331
(800) 527-3305 or (360) 374-6131

Notes on the trail: From the parking pullout across from the trail, continue up the steep 1-mile road. Stay right at the **Y** intersection (if you turned left here to park, come back and climb). Pass a road to the left before the trailhead parking, or stop and climb up it for a view. Quickly reach the trailhead parking area at

1.0 mile, and take the trail to the left. After a stair-step initial climb, you twist and swoop and climb and descend to a **T** intersection after 1.9 miles on the trail. Two big firs mark the right side; go left to continue the loop. After a roller-coaster climb, come to a junction in another 1.9 miles. If you go straight, you will eventually drop onto Heart O' the Hills Parkway using your map-reading skills (it's not a direct route); but ride to the right to continue the loop as it snakes its way around. In 0.9 mile from the last junction, continue straight when a connector trail takes off to the right. In 0.7 mile more, the trail dumps into a gravel road. Descend it for 0.2 mile until the trail picks up again to the right. Use your momentum on the road section for the short, steep, rocky 0.1-mile climb that begins this section of trail. In another 0.2 mile, the trail to the right connects to the trailhead on which you started; veer left and reap the fast reward for your hard climbing at the start. The trail dumps out onto the road, and your vehicle, at 6.8 miles. Got time for another lap?

RIDE 18 · Gold Creek Trail

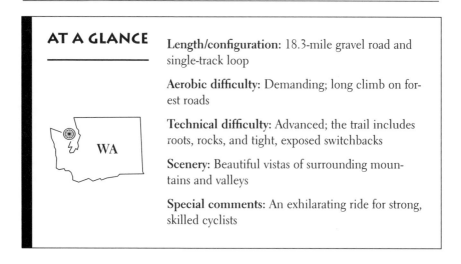

AT A GLANCE

Length/configuration: 18.3-mile gravel road and single-track loop

Aerobic difficulty: Demanding; long climb on forest roads

Technical difficulty: Advanced; the trail includes roots, rocks, and tight, exposed switchbacks

Scenery: Beautiful vistas of surrounding mountains and valleys

Special comments: An exhilarating ride for strong, skilled cyclists

WA

Advanced cyclists will appreciate this demanding 18.3-mile loop. The trip begins with climbing on good gravel roads. Vistas into the snowcapped Buckhorn Wilderness get better as you gain altitude. Twelve miles of difficult climbing and screaming downhills bring you to Gold Creek Trail. The path begins in an area thick with rhododendrons. This single-track includes some short, strenuous climbs, but it is mostly downhill. The trail is exciting, with twists, whoop-de-doos, major root drop-offs, and clifflike experiences.

General location: The ride begins near the first crossing of the Dungeness River on FS 2860. This trailhead is approximately 15 miles south of Sequim, Washington, on the Olympic Peninsula.

RIDE 18 · Gold Creek Trail

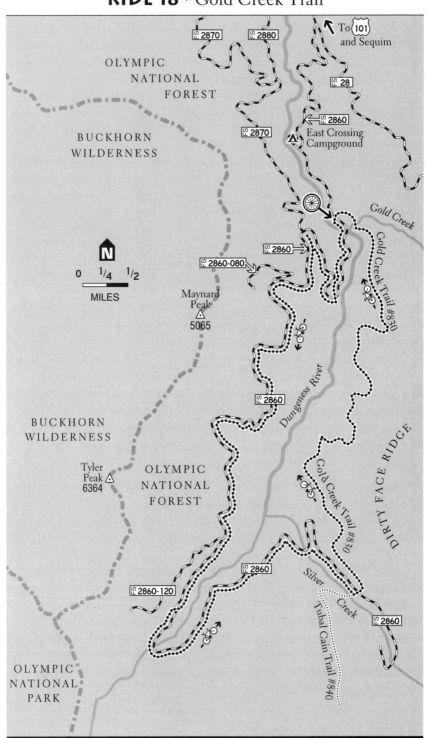

A view into Buckhorn Wilderness from Forest Service Road 2860.

Elevation change: The loop begins at 1,250' and climbs 2,000' in the first 4 miles. A series of descents nets a loss of 700' in the next 4 miles and brings you to a bridge over the Dungeness River. The following 4 miles go up and down, adding up to 1,100' of ascending and 400' of descending. This puts you at the Gold Creek Trailhead at an elevation of 3,200'. Undulations in the trail contribute about 350' of climbing to the trip. Total elevation gain: 3,450'.

Season: The Olympic Peninsula receives large amounts of precipitation, so predicting dry conditions is nearly impossible. The odds for fine weather improve in the late summer and early fall. The rhododendrons should be blooming in June.

Services: There is no water available on the ride. Water can be obtained seasonally at nearby East Crossing Campground. Food, lodging, gas, and groceries are available in Sequim.

Hazards: This circuit is long and hard. You will be gassed by the time you reach the single-track. Gold Creek Trail presents obstacles like roots, rocks, extreme descents, and severe drop-offs. There are situations where a mistake could lead to serious injury. Anticipate others approaching from around the next bend—the trail is open to equestrians, hikers, and motorcyclists, as well as mountain bikers. The lower end of the trail has some switchbacks that are tight and steep. Walk your bike down these fragile sections of the trail.

Rescue index: Help can be found in Sequim.

Land status: Olympic National Forest.

Maps: The district map of the Quilcene Ranger District is a good guide to this route. USGS 7.5 minute quads: Mount Zion and Tyler Peak.

Finding the trail: From US 101, head inland on Louella Road, which is 0.2 mile south of the entrance to Sequim Bay State Park (about 5.5 miles south of the town of Sequim). Climb steeply for 1 mile and turn left onto Palo Alto Road at a **T** intersection. The road turns to gravel after 3.4 miles. Continue on gravel Palo Alto Road for 2 miles to a **Y** intersection. Bear left onto unsigned FS 28 where FS 2880 goes right toward Dungeness Forks Campground. Follow FS 28 for about a mile to another **Y** intersection and turn right onto unsigned FS 2860. Follow FS 2860 for 2 miles to the entrance of East Crossing Campground (on the right). Proceed past the campground on FS 2860 for 1 mile to the lower trailhead for the Gold Creek Trail #830 (on the left). Park on the right.

Source of additional information:

Quilcene Ranger District
P.O. Box 280
Quilcene, WA 98376
(360) 765-2200

Notes on the trail: Gold Creek Trail has the potential to be greatly damaged by inappropriate use. Stay off the trail when it is wet, and tread lightly.

Ride uphill on FS 2860. Follow this road for 12 miles to the upper trailhead for Gold Creek Trail #830 on the left. Turn left onto the single-track. You will arrive at a **Y** intersection after 3.5 miles on the trail; stay left and head downhill. The trail ends at your vehicle.

RIDE 19 · Lower Dungeness Loop

AT A GLANCE

WA

Length/configuration: 14.6-mile loop; 7.9 miles on gravel road, 6.7 miles on single-track

Aerobic difficulty: Difficult climb on first 3.2-mile gravel road section; a low-ring grunt, with respites, on middle portion of single-track

Technical difficulty: Some steep, tricky switchbacks; rough trail in spots

Scenery: Views of Dungeness River Valley from above and below; Buckhorn Wilderness views; old growth; lush, riverside scenery; dry, rugged forest

Special comments: Two single-tracks in one: lush riverside trail and rugged forest ridge trail

This 14.6-mile loop, amid two distinct environments, is as interesting as it is exciting. The initial, strenuous 3.2 miles on gravel road and the steep climbing and descending on the rooty single-track make it suitable for advanced riders. After the initial climbing, the final 4.7 miles on the road is a fun, fast descent and the final single-track descent is a steep, technical thriller.

The Lower Dungeness Trail is in a unique area within the rain shadow of the Olympics. As you start on the single-track alongside the river, you cruise along a rooty, hard-pack trail through a soft, lush area, with stately old-growth cedar and hemlock towering over ferns, mosses, and riverside shrubbery. This area is moist enough to escape much of the effects of the wildfires that have shaped the landscape of the upper reaches of the trail. On the sunny summer day of my research ride, I could feel a difference of at least 10 degrees when I turned off the gravel road onto the tree-canopied single-track alongside the river. The rushing water provided an idyllic soundtrack to an incredible ride.

Climbing steeply away from the river up Three O'Clock Ridge, the Douglas fir–dominated hillsides are arid enough to support Rocky Mountain juniper, which thrives only in drier climates. Past the climb, the loop ends with a fast, steep, technical descent.

Oddly enough, both the Lower Dungeness Trail and the Lower Big Quilcene Trail, both within the Quilcene Ranger District of the Olympic National Forest, are designated as trail #833.

Note: You can make a 17.1-mile, 75-percent-plus single-track ride by starting at the Gold Creek Trailhead, climbing to and onto the Lower Dungeness Trail, descending and climbing FS 2860 for 3.7 miles, and descending the Gold Creek Trail.

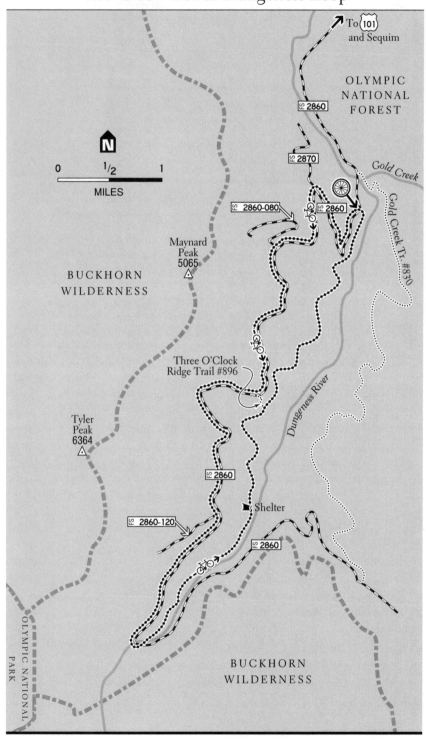

To 101 and Sequim

OLYMPIC
NATIONAL
FOREST

FS 2860

FS 2870

Gold Creek

Gold Creek Tr. #830

N

0   1/2   1
MILES

FS 2860-080

FS 2860

Maynard
Peak
5065

BUCKHORN
WILDERNESS

Three O'Clock
Ridge Trail #896

Dungeness River

Tyler
Peak
6364

FS 2860

Shelter

FS 2860-120

FS 2860

OLYMPIC NATIONAL PARK

BUCKHORN
WILDERNESS

River Camp Shelter along Lower Dungeness Trail #833.

General location: The ride starts approximately 15 miles south of Sequim.

Elevation change: The lower trailhead sits at 1,400' elevation. The road climbs to 3,020' in the first 3.2 miles, then descends to the trail. Single-track climbing accounts for 350' of 1,970' total elevation gain.

Season: The trail is best ridden in dry conditions from spring through fall.

Services: Water is available from a hand pump at East Crossing Campground, on FS 2860, 1.4 miles before you reach the trailhead. All services are available in Sequim.

Hazards: The trail is popular, and hiker-, horse-, and motorcycle-legal. Especially on summer weekends, you're likely to encounter some traffic. Ride in control on the switchbacks toward the steeply descending final section of the trail; don't skid around them.

Rescue index: This area is a popular jump-off point to the Buckhorn Wilderness, so you're likely to find someone who may be of help. Help may be available at East Crossing Campground, and is available in Sequim.

Land status: Olympic National Forest, Quilcene Ranger District.

Maps: Take your pick: Green Trails #136 Tyler Peak, Custom Correct Buckhorn Wilderness, or the Quilcene Ranger District map. They'll all do the job well.

Finding the trail: Traveling northwest on US 101, turn left onto Louella Road, just before Sequim Bay State Park (4.8 miles southeast of Sequim). Climb 0.9 mile to Palo Alto Road and turn left. In 5.6 miles the road divides; Palo Alto Road continues straight and turns into FS 2880, but veer left onto gravel road FS 28. In 0.9 mile, veer right and down onto FS 2860. Pass the Gold Creek Trailhead in 3 miles, then cross the bridge and climb to the Lower Dungeness Trailhead parking area to the left, in 0.4 mile.

From Sequim, turn right off of US 101 onto Palo Alto Road, 2.8 miles southeast of Sequim. Pass Louella Road in 2.3 miles and continue as above.

Source of additional information:

Quilcene Ranger District
295142 US 101 South
P.O. Box 280
Quilcene, WA 98376
(360) 765-2200

Notes on the trail: From the lower trailhead parking area, continue climbing on FS 2860. In 1.4 miles, FS 2870 takes off to the right, but continue to the left on FS 2860, enjoying the views of the peaks in the Buckhorn Wilderness as you climb. At 2.0 miles, a view of the Dungeness River Valley opens up to the south. The climb tops out at 3.2 miles. At 6.3 miles, as road FS 2860-120 rises to the right at 1 o'clock, continue your descent to the left. The upper trailhead is on your left at 7.9 miles, just before FS 2860 crosses over the Dungeness River. The trail continues to the right, but it quickly enters the Buckhorn Wilderness, so go left—you will not be disappointed! The first 2.4 miles of the trail is a gradual descent along the river. About a mile after the River Camp Shelter, the scenery changes to rugged forest as the trail starts a low-ring climb on the lower portion of Three O'Clock Ridge. A little more than a mile after the climbing starts, Three O'Clock Ridge Trail #896 switches back to the left and climbs to road FS 2860 in 0.5 mile; but go straight, where a short descent leads to some more climbing. About 0.2 mile after the Three O'Clock Ridge Trail junction, the trail turns left into a short, steep drop; dismount before the descent and look to the right at the 4 o'clock position, where just a few steps onto the rocks leads to a picturesque view. Some steep sections and tight switchbacks lead back to the lower trailheads and ride's end.

RIDE 20 · Lower Big Quilcene Trail

AT A GLANCE

WA

Length/configuration: 12.4 mile single-track out-and-back (6.2 miles each way)

Aerobic difficulty: Moderate; a few short bursts on the 1,420' gain to the upper trailhead

Technical difficulty: A few rooty and rocky sections, but mostly smoooooooth

Scenery: Classic Northwest forest and riverside scenery

Special comments: Adventurous beginners can blossom on this trail

---

Scenery and sweet single-track make the Lower Big Quilcene Trail #833 a great ride for anyone, but this 6.2-mile (each way) trail presents a special challenge for adventurous, single-track-tested beginners looking for more. It's not for true beginners, but if you have some experience in the saddle and on the trails, this is the place to jump up to the next level of mountain biking.

It's a great trail for such a leap: the scenery is gorgeous riverside and picture-postcard 400-year-old stands of Douglas fir, as well as hemlock and scattered cedar. Much of the hard-pack single-track is baby-bottom smooth but with a few challenges, like water crossings and loose rocks, to negotiate. The 1,420 feet of elevation gain comes gradually, punctuated with anaerobic bursts.

While this may be the trail to expand your riding horizons, you can still hold onto that directional sense of security that a beginner might need: with no junctions between the lower and upper trailhead, chances of getting lost are virtually nil.

Soon-to-be-intermediates will build initial confidence with a smooth, gradual descent at the start, while the Big Quilcene River is only to be heard from below. The trail rolls gently as it joins the river at 2.4 miles. The short, steep climbs come later in the trail, after you're warmed up and ready.

General location: The ride starts 6.6 miles southwest of Quilcene. Quilcene is about 30 miles southeast of Sequim, 50 miles northwest of Bremerton via the Hood Canal Bridge, and 54 miles north of Shelton.

Elevation change: Elevation at the lower trailhead is 1,200'; at the top, 2,500'. Additional climbing makes for a total elevation gain of about 1,420'.

Season: You'll find the best riding conditions from late spring through midfall.

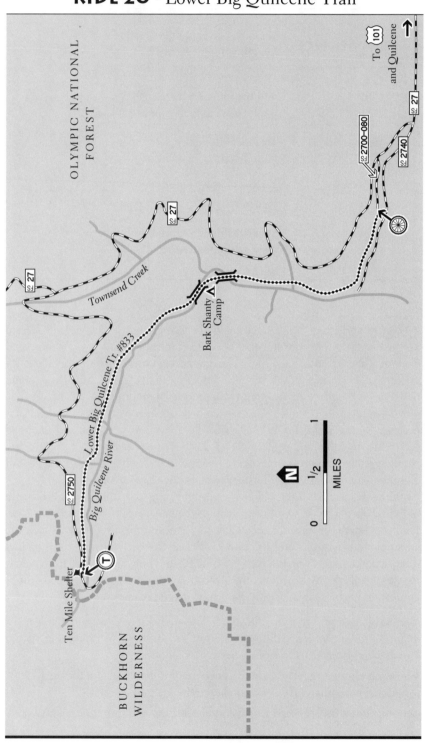

Blowdown, both cut and
uncut, along Lower Big
Quilcene Trail #833.

Services: Services are available in Quilcene. Bike shops are in Sequim, about 35 miles north on US 101, and all the way down in Shelton, about 55 miles south on US 101. Get what you need before you come.

Hazards: A tough creek crossing just before the upper trailhead is best walked. A few shallow water diversion ditches along the trail demand your attention. The trail is open to motorcyclists, and though it is not heavily used by the gas-powered crowd, be aware that you may encounter a throttle-twister or two.

Rescue index: Help is available in Quilcene.

Land status: Olympic National Forest, Quilcene Ranger District.

Maps: Truth be told, if you can get to the trailhead and follow the route, you don't really need a map—you need it more to get to the trailhead than on the trail itself. But in case the unthinkable happens, be prepared with the Custom Correct Buckhorn Wilderness map or the Quilcene Ranger District map, both available at the Quilcene Ranger District Office.

Finding the trail: The Quilcene Ranger District Office is 0.7 mile south of the town of Quilcene on US 101. Heading 1 mile south of the office, take Penny

Creek Road to the right at the 1 o'clock position. When the pavement ends in about a mile, veer left on Big Quilcene River Road (FS 27). In 3.2 miles, go right to stay on narrow FS 27 as FS 2740 continues straight. In another 0.4 mile, turn left on FS 2700-080, just before FS 27 curves up and to the left. Travel 0.3 mile to the trailhead parking at the end of the road.

Source of additional information:

Quilcene Ranger District
295142 US 101 South
P.O. Box 280
Quilcene, WA 98376
(360) 765-2200

Notes on the trail: At 2.4 miles up the trail, cross the bridge over the river. The Big Quilcene River is now on your right as Townsend Creek joins it from the north. In 0.1 mile, just after Bark Shanty Camp, cross back to the other side of the river. Pass a logged area at 4.1 miles. About a mile after that, at a 10-foot-wide creek crossing, an access trail back to the left at 7 o'clock brings you riverside. The trail ends onto FS 2750 just after a short but potentially treacherous creek crossing. I walked it, thank you very much.

On the other side of the road the trail continues into the Buckhorn Wilderness, where bikes are not allowed. But 50 feet to the right of the trailhead, a 1-minute walk to Ten Mile Shelter provides a nice snack stop and turnaround point.

RIDE 21 · Lower South Fork Skokomish Trail

AT A GLANCE

WA

Length/configuration: 20.9-mile single-track, gravel road, and paved road loop, or 10.4-mile out-and-back (each way) all on single-track

Aerobic difficulty: Steep, roller-coaster single-track with lots of low-ring climbing

Technical difficulty: Intermediate; some tight switchbacks, creek crossings

Scenery: Classic, lush Pacific Northwest old-growth setting

Special comments: There is no bad way to ride this route

Y ou can ride the Lower South Fork Skokomish Trail #873.1 as a 20.9-mile loop taking paved and gravel roads up and the single-track down, or as researched, trail up and road down. The trail itself is up and down, up and down, and up and down some more, steeply. The slight road return descent is a nice, smooth contrast—despite a little washboarding—to the sharp roller-coaster trail, and provides some pretty scenery. Hardier riders will tackle 10.4 miles of single-track each way, getting revenge on the steep, barely rideable 0.5 mile from the lower trailhead, on which some walking is required.

This is an excellent, advanced-level trail through lush old-growth stands and across feeder creeks to the river. The ride constantly alternates short, tough climbs with fun, sometimes rooty, rocky, and twisty descents. The trail only comes down to the river when it crosses at a bridge 9.8 miles up; the official trail crosses over the bridge and continues on the other side, while the continuation on the same side of the river is the unofficial, user-built trail that leads to primitive campsites. On our research trip, we first continued past the bridge for 0.5 mile, not wanting to be the ones who put the listing structure into the river (the bridge is slated for reconstruction in 1999), and figured on doing the ride as an out-and-back. Once we got back to the bridge, we tested the waters and decided to ford the thigh-deep river to continue the trail on the other side. We were glad we did; although we all love single-track, we were a little tired by the time we reached FS 2361, and knew we had more than 10 challenging miles to get back to the lower trailhead. The road descent was an ever-so-gradual decline, and only required about a mile's worth of moderate effort toward the bottom.

As you exit the trail to the top of FS 2361, the trail continues to the right, entering the Olympic National Park in 5.5 miles. I was told by a Hood Canal Ranger District representative that, even though there was printed material saying this section of trail was open to mountain bikes to the park's border, it is actually closed. It can be opened, she noted, if mountain bikers make an effort toward it.

General location: You'll be astride the saddle about 25 miles northwest of Shelton, 30 miles southwest of Bremerton, and 25 miles southwest of Hoodsport.

Elevation change: The lower trailhead is at 600' elevation and the upper trailhead (before the 5.5-mile continuation to the park boundary) is at 1,200' elevation. With lots of short, sharp descents along the way, a lot of short, sharp climbs add another 600' of elevation gain for a total of 1,200'. Out-and-backers add another 600', road returners add about 80'.

Season: To let the trail recover from its winter slumber and spring rains, the Hood Canal Ranger District recommends not riding it until June. Enjoy it to the end of the season, which can stretch into November.

Services: Water is available from a hand pump next to the pay station at Brown Creek Campground. A small café sits on US 101 just north of Skokomish Valley Road. Services are available in Shelton to the south, Belfair and Bremerton to the northeast, and Hoodsport to the north (limited service in Hoodsport).

RIDE 21 · Lower South Fork Skokomish Trail

To Olympic National Park

South Fork Skokomish River

Harp's Shelter

Church Creek Shelter

OLYMPIC NATIONAL FOREST

FS 2361

FS 23

Lower South Fork Skokomish Trail #873.1

FS 2353

Brown Creek Campground

FS 23

To 101

N

0   1/2   1
MILES

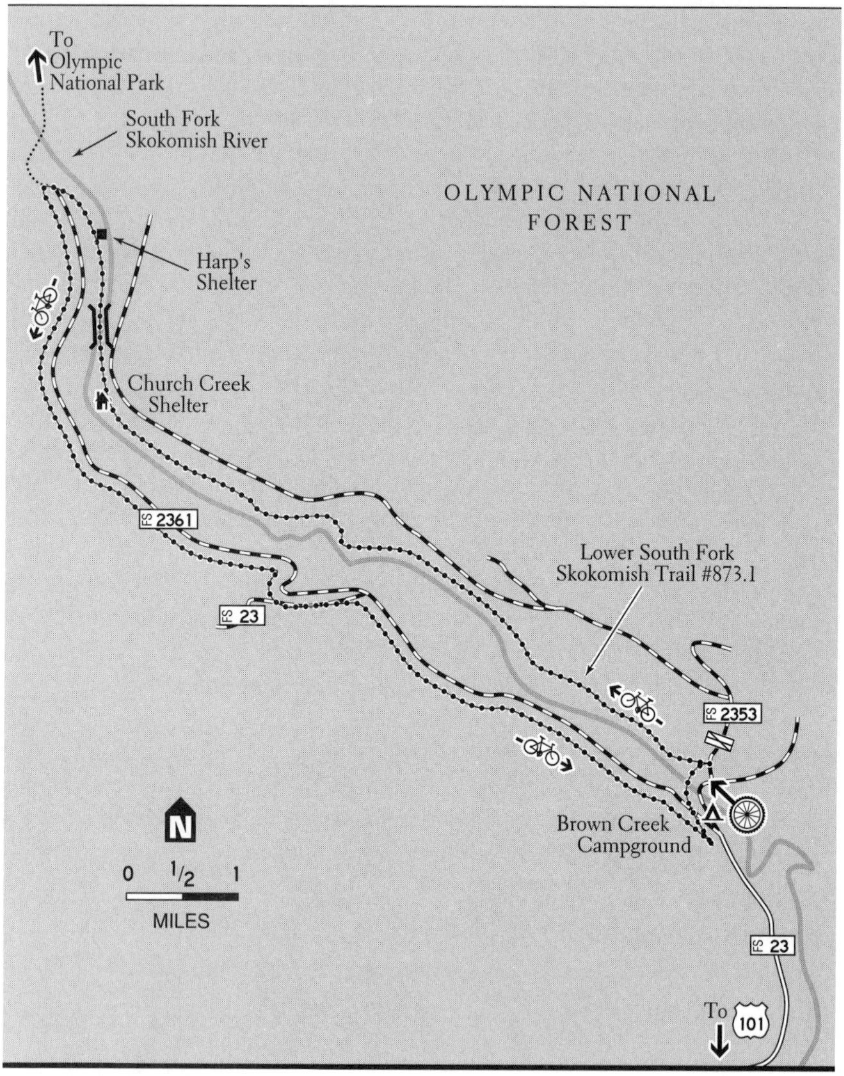

Hazards: The viewpoint at 5.9 miles up the trail is atop a sheer drop. Dismount on the main trail and walk to it for a look. Don't try to cross the bridge in its state of disrepair, and be careful when fording the river—the water was fairly high and the current was swift during the September research outing.

Rescue index: Help might be available at the Brown Creek Campground, 0.2 mile from the lower trailhead. The Fir Creek Guard Station sits 6.9 miles from the trailhead along FS 23. Residents along Skokomish Valley Road may also provide assistance. You'll find a phone at the cafe on US 101. Help is available in Hoodsport, Union, Belfair, and Shelton.

Craig Nunes in fat-tire bliss.

Land status: Olympic National Forest, Hood Canal Ranger District.

Maps: The Olympic National Forest and Olympic National Park map is good enough to get you through this ride and many others in the forest, although it doesn't provide topographical information. For topo info, use Green Trails #199, Mt. Tebo.

Finding the trail: From Shelton, travel north on US 101 for about 8 miles, and go left (west) on Skokomish Valley Road. (The George Adams Fish Hatchery sits on the northwest corner of US 101 and Skokomish Valley Road, directly west of Purdy Cutoff Road.) In 5.5 miles, veer right onto FS 23. Stay on FS 23 (which is paved except for a small portion around FS 2340) past numerous junctions, for 9.2 miles, to the junction of FS 2353. FS 23 continues up and to the left, but go right and down on FS 2353. Cross a one-lane bridge over the river in 0.6 mile, then go left, staying on paved road FS 2353. The pavement ends after another one-lane bridge in 0.2 mile. The trailhead is on the left at the end of the pavement; park at the pulloff by the trailhead. If you drive to the yellow gate you've gone too far.

From Bremerton, drive south on WA 3 for around 12 miles, just south of Belfair, to WA 106. Go right (west) on WA 106, and pass the town of Union in 14.6 miles. Continuing 3.6 miles past Union, turn left on Purdy Cutoff Road. In 2.8 miles reach the junction of US 101. Cross US 101 onto Skokomish Valley Road, and proceed as above.

From Interstate 5 in Tacoma, travel 16 miles northwest on WA 16 to WA 3. Turn left onto WA 3, and come to the junction of WA 106 in about 9 miles. Turn right, and figure out the rest with the directions above.

Driving south on US 101, Skokomish Valley Road is about 0.5 mile south of the bridge over the Skokomish River, about 8 miles south of Hoodsport.

Source of additional information:

Hood Canal Ranger District
150 N. Lake Cushman Road
P.O. Box 68
Hoodsport, WA 98548
(360) 877-5254
(a block off of US 101 on WA 119, about 7miles north of the Skokomish River)

Notes on the trail: You may have to walk on the initial climb anyway, but gear down before you start. Steep rollers abound. At about 5.2 miles, on a climb after a level section, the trail goes up to the right; straight ahead the trail stops abruptly at a steep overlook to the river, so stop and walk to the viewpoint. In 4.6 more miles look to the left to find the bridge over the river near a horse-crossing sign. Turn back, continue forward until the trail ends, go over the bridge, or if it is still not repaired, ford the river to continue the official trail upriver on the other side. Stay on the main trail past a descent on your right to Harp's Shelter. Meet FS 2361 0.6 mile after the bridge. From here ride the trail back or ride down the smoothly descending road. Stay on the obvious main road past the junctions. On the road, stop at the bridge in 1.4 miles and take a look down a deep, beautiful gorge. In another 3.8 miles FS 2361 ends into FS 23, which also continues back to the right. Keep going straight, continuing the descent on FS 23. In 4.4 more miles FS 23 meets FS 2353 just after the gravel road turns to pavement. Turn left on FS 2353 and retrace the last 0.8 mile of the drive to the trailhead, crossing the bridge, then turning left for the final 0.2 mile to the lower trailhead.

RIDE 22 · Wynoochee Lakeshore Trail

The single-track around Wynoochee Lake is 12 miles long and moderately difficult. There are some steep climbs, and pushing your bike will be necessary in several places. Some segments of the trail are technically demanding, while others are smooth and wide. The trail becomes exacting as it nears the north end of the reservoir. Obstacles like roots and rocks are more common, and the path switchbacks through some drainages. In places, the single-track narrows and drops off steeply to the side. The trail crosses the Wynoochee River at the north end of the reservoir. There is no bridge, so you must ford the river to continue the loop.

The scenery is lovely; the best views are at the south end of the lake. The trail offers glimpses of Anderson Ridge to the east and the Olympics to the north. Wynoochee Lakeshore Trail winds through a dense forest and past some magnificent old-growth specimens of Douglas fir and western hemlock.

General location: Wynoochee Lake is 37 miles north of Montesano, Washington, on the Olympic Peninsula.

Elevation change: The trailhead lies at 780'. The route climbs and drops over its entire length and reaches 900' several times. The first half of the loop sees the most elevation gain—about 1,000'. The second half is easier and involves approximately 500' of climbing. Total elevation gain: 1,500'.

Season: Trail conditions are normally best in the summer and fall. The trail is usually cleared of underbrush by midsummer. Prior to this maintenance, windfall can be a problem.

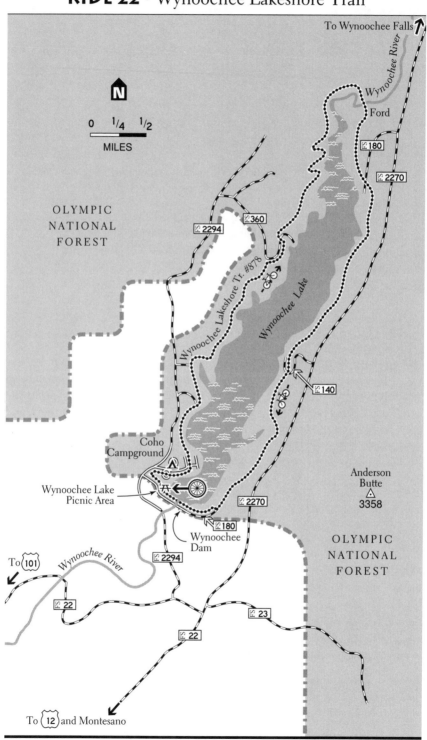

To Wynoochee Falls

Wynoochee River

Ford

☒ 180

☒ 2270

N

0   ¼   ½
MILES

OLYMPIC
NATIONAL
FOREST

☒ 360

☒ 2294

Wynoochee Lakeshore Tr. #878

Wynoochee Lake

☒ 140

Coho
Campground

Anderson
Butte
△
3358

Wynoochee Lake
Picnic Area

☒ 2270

☒ 180

Wynoochee
Dam

OLYMPIC
NATIONAL
FOREST

To 101

Wynoochee River

☒ 2294

☒ 22

☒ 23

☒ 22

To 12 and Montesano

North end of Wynoochee Lake.

Services: Water is available seasonally at Coho Campground and year-round at the visitor center. There are no commercial services at Wynoochee Lake. Food, lodging, groceries, and gas can be obtained in Montesano.

Hazards: There are many small creek crossings. The larger creeks are spanned by simple bridges—one large log with a handrail. Carrying or pushing your bicycle over these bridges can be awkward. The trail takes a turn to the northeast near the north end of the lake and comes close to a high bank of sand and gravel. Stay back from the edge of this unstable slope. The river level at the ford fluctuates; the river is generally too high to cross in the spring. Phone ahead to the Hood Canal Ranger Station for current trail conditions. The district is planning to build a footbridge over the river (eliminating the ford).

Rescue index: Help can be found in Montesano. There is a phone at the Wynoochee Dam Picnic Area that accepts collect or credit card calls. When using the phone, be patient; it may take 15 to 20 seconds for the operator to come on the line. The phone is located near the gate on FS 180. You may be able to obtain assistance in the summer at the Wynoochee Dam Project Office or from the campground host at Coho Campground.

Wynoochee Lakeshore Trail.

Land status: Olympic National Forest.

Maps: The district map of the Hood Canal Ranger District is a good guide to this ride. USGS 7.5 minute quad: Wynoochee Lake.

Finding the trail: From Montesano, drive west for 1 mile on US 12 and turn north on Wynoochee Valley Road/FS 22. Continue on FS 22 for approximately 35 miles to the major intersection with FS 2270. Turn left to stay on FS 22. In 0.4 mile, turn right onto FS 2294. Follow FS 2294 for 1.2 miles and turn right onto FS 180 toward the Wynoochee Lake Picnic Area. Park in the day-use area.

Wynoochee Lake can also be accessed from US 101. The intersection of US 101 and FS 22 is approximately 30 miles north of Aberdeen and 20 miles south of Quinault Lake. Head east on FS 22, driving 21 miles to FS 2294 on the left. Turn left onto FS 2294 and go 1.2 miles to FS 180 on the right. Turn right onto FS 180 toward the Wynoochee Lake Picnic Area. Park in the day-use area.

Sources of additional information:

Hood Canal Ranger District
P.O. Box 68
Hoodsport, WA 98548
(360) 877-5254

Tacoma Public Utilities
(253) 383-2471 ext. 7600
(operates the visitor center and Wynoochee Dam)

Notes on the trail: Exit the day-use area and turn right onto FS 2294. Take the first right into the Coho Campground and follow the sign toward the boat launch. Just before you get to the lake, turn left onto the trail signed "Wynoochee Lakeshore Trail #878." After 2.7 miles, the single-track meets an abandoned road. There is a sign here that reads "Trail." Turn right onto this road and descend for 0.2 mile to an identical sign and the trail. Turn left onto the trail. You will come to the river crossing in about 2 miles. We were turned back by high water at the time of research. We pedaled back to our vehicle, drove around to the other side of the ford, and continued with the trail. The path follows the lakefront for a couple of miles, then parallels FS 140. Soon the route crosses FS 140. The trail continues on the opposite side of the road. (It is hard to see; look for the sign.) The single-track ends at the south end of the lake, on the east side of the dam. Cross the dam to reach the day-use parking area.

KITSAP PENINSULA RIDES

The Kitsap Peninsula is a transitional area in western Washington, lying directly between the urban areas of Seattle and Tacoma, and the pristine environment of the Olympic Mountains. It is bordered by Hood Canal and the Olympic Peninsula to the west, Puget Sound to the north and east, and Mason and Pierce Counties to the south. Washington State Highway 3 accesses the Olympic Peninsula to the south by way of WA 106, and to the north by way of the Hood Canal Floating Bridge. Access to the Kitsap Peninsula from Seattle is via ferry to Winslow (on Bainbridge Island) or, more likely for riding purposes, to Bremerton; from Edmonds by way of the Edmonds-Kingston ferry; from Tacoma by WA 16; and from Olympia and Shelton by way of US 101 to WA 3.

While Seattle-area mountain bikers fight to keep area trails open, the Kitsap Peninsula welcomes mountain bikes. The riding in the area focuses on Department of Natural Resources land, namely Green Mountain and the Tahuya State Forests.

Green Mountain State Forest, located northeast of Bremerton, contains 6,000 acres. It sports about 20 miles of trails, and adds about double that amount in forest roads to vary the riding. The roads are closed to vehicle traffic except on Saturdays and Sundays from June through September. You'll find one of the best views of the Puget Sound Region from the top of 1,690-foot Green Mountain.

The 23,000-acre Tahuya State Forest is just southwest of the town of Belfair. The trails here could be described as "immediate gratification" trails, in that climbs can be steep, but aren't too long, and you immediately enjoy the descending fruits of your uphill labors.

The trails at Tahuya can also be described as abundant; the forest contains around 200 miles of trails, many of which are unmapped.

Rides at Tahuya rarely revolve around particular destinations within the forest; people ride here for the joy of riding in the woods. Come armed with a compass, a map, and a familiarity with the main roads in this area, and your route possibilities will be limitless.

As a working forest, the Tahuya State Forest is constantly changing. The trails that were here when I rode may not be the same as when you ride; some may have been extended, closed, or logged over, and new trails will probably have been added. If you get lost you can find your way back via the roads and a general knowledge of the direction in which the trailhead lies. If you have an idea of which way to ride once you come to a road, you'll find your way back. I know from experience.

The trail accesses you drive by on the way to the Howell Lake ride give an indication of the enormity of Tahuya's trail system. Driving past trail crossings signed with motorcycle icons to start a ride out of a horse camp gives an indication of its usage. But mountain bikes already rival other recreation modes here, and for good reason; you can come back again and again, year-round, and never retrace your route.

RIDE 23 · Howell Lake Lollipop

AT A GLANCE

Length/configuration: The 'stick' is a 2.7-mile out-and-back (each way), leading to the 7.4-mile 'sucker' (loop), for a 12.8-mile single-track total (wide trail in areas); can be done stick-less

Aerobic difficulty: Lots of rollers; some short, steep climbs

Technical difficulty: Whoop-de-doos, loose pebbles, puddles, roots, and mud

Scenery: Howell Lake, Olympic Mountains views, fern-lined woods, clear-cuts

Special comments: Great year-round riding for the intermediate (entire route) or tough beginner (loop only)

WA

Two things a local rider warned me about the Tahuya State Forest: you'll get muddy, and you'll get lost. On my first research trip on the Howell Lake Trail, done in mid-August, neither happened. On my second, in February, both happened. Though you can easily get lost on the seemingly endless web of trails, the Howell Lake Lollipop is fairly well marked and easy to follow; and though my first trip was a dry one, you're more likely to come back wet than dry, so bring a compass and come with a muddy mindset.

This 12.8-mile combination route follows the Howell Lake Trail for almost its entirety and, of course, allows for exploration on some of the many un-mapped trails in the forest. The Howell Lake Trail is designated as a "trunk" trail, that is, a main trail off of which other, minor (and fun) trails branch. The trail is marked intermittently by blue diamonds. They're good general markers, but no match for a map and compass.

The route travels amid Douglas fir, western hemlock, and coastal rhododendron. The wooded, fern-lined areas near the lake and the trailhead are nice, lush contrasts to the clear-cuts you ride through on other sections. Soft pebbly surfaces and whoop-de-doos on wide trails alternate with narrower, steep, roller-coaster conditions on firmer trails. Come in the summer and the soft surfaces get dusty while the firm surfaces dry out. Come in the winter and the dusty areas pack down while the firm surfaces get slick and muddy. Come any time of the year and you'll find great riding that tempts you to return and explore.

In clear conditions look for views of the Olympics to the west along the loop portion of the route, but the trails themselves are entertainment enough regardless of the weather.

RIDE 23 · Howell Lake Lollipop

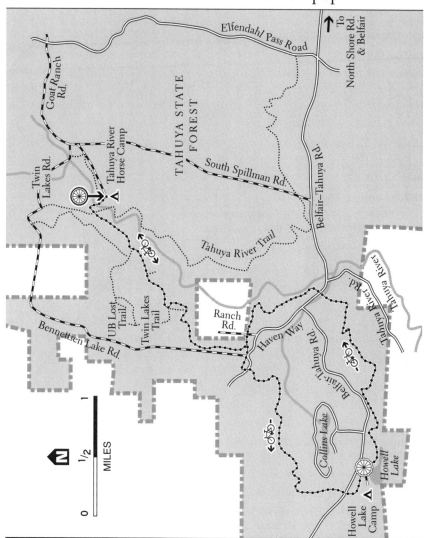

The entire trip will probably be too much for adventurous beginners, but those hardy souls can park at Howell Lake for just the loop portion, and can bail out at a few road crossings along the way.

General location: The Tahuya River Horse Camp is located approximately 21 miles southwest of Bremerton, 33 miles northwest of Tacoma, 35 miles northeast of Shelton and 55 miles north of Olympia.

Elevation change: Elevation at the ride start and at the loop start are both about 220', but it's far from a flat journey. Howell Lake is at 450' elevation.

Total elevation gain on the loop is about 420'; elevation gain for the entire route is approximately 720'.

Season: Year-round.

Services: Water is available at the Tahuya River Horse Camp and at Howell Lake Camp and Picnic Area, adjacent to campsite 5. Limited services are available across from the entrance to Belfair State Park at the Park Place Market. Everything you can use, except a bike shop, is in Belfair; for that, go to Bremerton to the north, off WA 16 in Gig Harbor to the southeast, and in Shelton to the south.

Hazards: Depending on the season, some deep puddles with who-knows-what at the bottom. I've ridden twice here in wet conditions and both times took falls in deep puddles that drenched me!

Rescue index: The Tahuya State Forest is a popular area year-round, so, at least on weekends, you're likely to find someone who can summon help. A phone is located at the Park Place Market.

Land status: DNR Tahuya State Forest.

Maps: The way things change here, there can be no truly accurate map of all the trails. The DNR Tahuya State Forest Map, usually available at the Mission Creek Trailhead and Elfendahl Pass Staging Area, show good coverage of official trails. Tahuya State Forest is a favorite haunt of the Single-Track Mind Cycling Club, and some members told me there are networks of choice single-track that aren't listed on the maps. They also said that if they showed those choice trails to me, they'd have to kill me! Seriously, though, they are a great group, and you're likely to discover many of these trails if you ride with the club. Contact the DNR South Puget Sound Region Office to make sure you get a map before you come out, just in case there are none at the above locations.

Finding the trail: From Bremerton, take WA 310 or WA 304 to WA 3, and drive south. Pass WA 16 in 3.6 miles and continue for another 7.9 miles to N.E. Clifton Lane at the north end of Belfair. Turn right and follow the road for 3.6 miles, as it turns into WA 300 and then into North Shore Road after it passes Belfair State Park. Turn right, 0.5 mile after the state park entrance, on Belfair-Tahuya Road. Pass the Mission Creek Trailhead in 1.1 miles, and continue another 0.7 mile to Elfendahl Pass Road. Turn right on Elfendahl Pass Road and travel 2.7 miles (0.4 mile past the Elfendahl Pass Staging Area) to gravel Goat Ranch Road, and turn left. In 1 mile come to the Tahuya River Horse Camp on the right, 0.1 mile past Twin Lakes Road. Turn right and come to the parking area in 0.5 mile.

From Interstate 5 in Tacoma, exit at WA 16 and drive 16 miles northwest to WA 3. Turn left (south) onto WA 3 and proceed as above.

From Olympia, drive on US 101 north to the junction of WA 3 in Shelton. Drive north on WA 3 for about 26 miles to Belfair. One block north of Belfair Street (signed as a dead-end street), turn left, then make a left at the stop sign onto N.E. Clifton Lane and proceed as above. (If you miss the left after Belfair Street, just continue up to N.E. Clifton Lane and turn left.)

Howell Lake Trail.

To start the loop at Howell Lake, continue on Belfair-Tahuya Road 2.4 miles past Elfendahl Pass Road and turn left, which continues Belfair-Tahuya Road (where straight is Haven Way). Travel 1.7 miles to the Howell Lake Camp and Picnic Area on the left. Look for the trail as the gravel road crosses it on the way to the parking area.

Sources of additional information:

Department of Natural Resources
South Puget Sound Region
950 Farman Street North
P.O. Box 68
Enumclaw, WA 98022-0068
(800) 527-3305 or (360) 825-1631 (direct)

Single-Track Mind Cycling Club
6824 19th Street West #147
Tacoma, WA 98466
(206) 565-5124
http://members.aol.com/STMClub/stmclub.html

Notes on the trail: Start between campsites 3 and 4 on the north side of the campground. After crossing the footbridge, a short climb brings you to a **T** junction with arrows in both directions; turn left. (A right turn will bring you to Twin Lakes Road.) Near a whoop-de-doo section at 0.7 mile, a small map board on your right shows you where you are, and notes that the Single-Track Mind Cycling Club contributed to it—one of its many contributions to these trails. Continue straight, past the Twin Lakes Trail junction to the right after the map board, and come to a **Y** junction, marked by arrows and a tree in the middle, in 0.3 more miles. Take the right fork at this junction. In 0.8 more miles—after passing other trails, including another junction of the Twin Lakes Trail, and climbing out of a creek bed—come to a clear-cut expanse.

As you parallel Bennettsen Lake Road to your right near the loop portion of the route, you'll pass some houses to your left. The loop starts just after a cinder block–reinforced bridge. Turn right for the counterclockwise loop. Cross gravel Bennettsen Lake Road and paved Haven Way within the first 0.1 mile of the loop. Keep following the signs for the Howell Lake Trail. At 0.7 mile into the loop, a trail comes in from the left; veer right—the diamond and arrow keep you on track.

As you crest a hill 1.7 miles into the loop, the Olympic Mountains come into view through the trees. In another 0.9 mile, turn left at the **T** junction; cross Belfair-Tahuya Road in another 0.1 mile. Get back into the trees 0.2 mile beyond the road crossing, and come to the Howell Lake Camp and Picnic Area in another 0.2 mile. Stop and refill your water, take a look across the lake, or just continue the loop as you pass the gravel road entrance to the camp and picnic area. In 0.3 mile, come to an intersection with junctions that are soft left, straight, soft right, and hard right. Hard right backtracks along the lake to the campground/picnic area; up to the left the trail becomes overgrown; straight ahead connects with the continuation of the trail, which is the soft right (this was starting to erode at the time of research; it will most likely be reinforced or re-routed straight). Descend soft right and pedal on. Enjoy a woodsy, ferny section over a creek bed that gives way to a 1997 clear-cut 1.9 miles from the 5-way junction. Come out of the new clear-cut, and an older one, in 0.4 mile. Drop to a bridge over a creek, then climb up to and cross Belfair-Tahuya Road. At gravel Ranch Road, in another 1.1 miles, the trail continues to the right. Complete the loop in 0.2 mile, and go right for the return. If your legs and schedule allow it, explore some of the trails you passed on the way out. As you near the horse camp by end of the return section, turn right at the Tahuya River Trail sign. Descend to the footbridge and ride back to the parking lot, or check out the Tahuya River Trail, which passes through the campground.

RIDE 24 · Mission Creek Single-Track

AT A GLANCE

WA

Length/configuration: 15.2-mile figure eight (7.9-mile lower loop), virtually all single-track, some wide

Aerobic difficulty: Lots of short, steep climbs and descents, gradual rollers

Technical difficulty: Roots, rocks, mud, puddles, steep edges; a lot of off-the-saddle riding; good bike-handling skills required

Scenery: Lush second-growth woods, some clear-cuts

Special comments: Full figure eight and lower loop can be extended or shortened; trail tread test area an interesting feature

This 15.2-mile figure eight joins a trunk trail with some of the newest single-track (that branches off of it), although there is plenty more than what's shown on the maps. Although the Mission Creek Trail is the main artery of the trail system, in most places you'll just call it fun single-track. The ride is an exciting, physical, technical adventure as described, and it can be the starting point for an exploration of any duration.

Tahuya is a working forest, so you'll see your share of clear-cuts. You'll also twist on tight single-track through deep woods and lush drainages; roller-coaster on roots, rocks, and sometimes slow, soft, pebbly sections; and splash through enough puddles and mud to make both biker and bike need postride cleaning.

The trail tread test area along the Mission Creek Trail gives an example of how the foresters here encourage trail use. Foresters Phil Wolff (a mountain biker!) and Jon Byerly and others on the Tahuya trail crew, wanted to find ways to anchor trails threatened by erosion when rerouting is not an option (for example, if salmon habitat would be threatened). This way, they could compare different methods at the same time, and get user feedback as well. Included are shredded tires woven together; cement blocks (not trail-standard cinder blocks); "ground master," a plastic sheet with approximately two-inch diameter holes; and "Geo Web," a honeycomb-shaped, plastic, cellular confinement which gains strength as it is anchored into the dirt. They're also experimenting with recycled asphalt on a nearby trail.

Their conclusion? The shredded tires haven't stood the test of time, but no one other concept is best in all circumstances. Take a minute to study the area when you ride by.

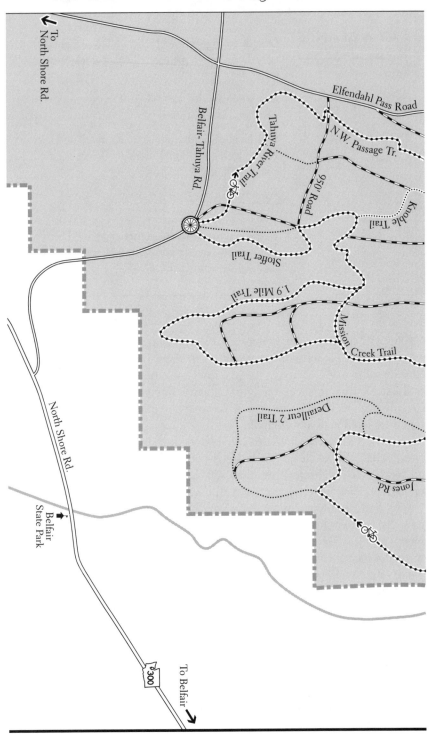

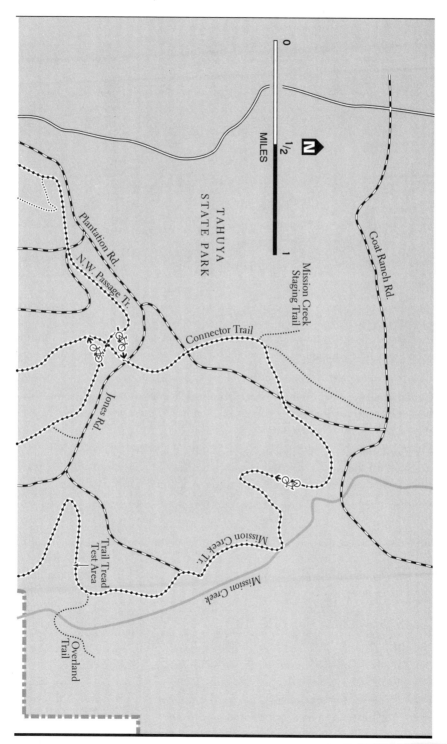

TAHUYA STATE PARK

Mission Creek Staging Trail

Goat Ranch Rd.

Plantation Rd.

N.W. Passage Tr.

Connector Trail

Jones Rd.

Mission Creek Tr.

Mission Creek

Trail Tread Test Area

Overland Trail

0   ½   1

MILES

N

Tahuya State Forest.

If you do just the lower loop of the figure eight, you'll go about 7.9 miles, which can be increased or decreased by either staying on the Mission Creek Trail or riding the single-track that branches off of it.

General location: The Mission Creek Trailhead is approximately 16 miles southwest of Bremerton, 28 miles northwest of Tacoma, 30 miles northeast of Shelton, and 50 miles north of Olympia.

Elevation change: The Mission Creek Trailhead is at 400' elevation. The high elevation on the ride is 495' but the near-constant ups and downs on the trails make total elevation gain on this ride in the neighborhood of 1,600'.

Season: The area is open year-round; each season has its own charm and reason to ride.

Services: There is no water at the trailhead or along the route. If you forgot to fill up on the way, you can get water at the Elfendahl Pass Staging Area, 2.3 miles up Elfendahl Road, 0.7 mile past the Mission Creek Trailhead. Camping is available at numerous areas in the forest. Limited services are available as close as the Park Place Market across from Belfair State Park. Most services, though no bike shops, can be found in Belfair.

Hazards: How deep is that puddle? And what's at the bottom? Probably not motorcyclists, equestrians, or other mountain bikers, but watch out for them, too, especially on weekends.

Rescue index: You're in civilization by the time you're back on North Shore Road. The nearest phone is at the Park Place Market. Help is available in Belfair.

Land status: DNR Tahuya State Forest.

Maps: DNR Tahuya State Forest map.

Finding the trail: From Bremerton, take WA 310 or WA 304 to WA 3, and drive south. Pass WA 16 in 3.6 miles and continue for another 7.9 miles to N.E. Clifton Lane at the north end of Belfair. Turn right and follow the road for 3.6 miles, as it turns into WA 300 and then into North Shore Road after it passes Belfair State Park. Turn right, 0.5 mile after the state park entrance, on Belfair-Tahuya Road. Come to the Mission Creek Trailhead on the right in 1.1 miles. Plenty of parking is available.

From I-5 in Tacoma, exit at WA 16 and drive 16 miles northwest to WA 3. Turn left (south) onto WA 3 and proceed as above.

From Olympia, drive on US 101 north to the junction of WA 3 in Shelton. Drive north on WA 3 for about 26 miles to Belfair. One block north of Belfair Street (signed as a dead end street), turn left, then make a left at the stop sign onto N.E. Clifton Lane and proceed as above. (If you miss the left after Belfair Street, just continue up to N.E. Clifton Lane and turn left.)

Sources of additional information:

Department of Natural Resources
South Puget Sound Region
950 Farman Street North
P.O. Box 68
Enumclaw, WA 98022-0068
(800) 527-3305 or (360) 825-1631 (direct)

Single-Track Mind Cycling Club
6824 19th Street West #147
Tacoma, WA 98466
(206) 565-5124
http://members.aol.com/STMClub/stmclub.html

Notes on the trail: Start on the left, but cut right (north) of the trail that parallels the road. You'll quickly wind to the west on the Tahuya River Trail. Cross a road at 0.2 mile and continue straight. Continue straight at the intersection in another 0.3 mile; a blue diamond marker points the way. Undulate another 0.2 mile, and come to the Northwest Passage Trail on a short descent through a clear-cut, just after a climb. Turn right on the Northwest Passage Trail; if you miss this junction, you'll hit Elfendahl Pass Road shortly. In 0.3 mile (1.0 total) turn left onto 950' Road. The trail continues in 200', after a short rise on the road. In 0.7 mile meet the Knoble Trail at a **Y** junction; bear left to continue on the Northwest Passage Trail, which, in 30', bends to the right where an access trail continues straight and veers left. Stay with the Northwest Passage Trail. In 0.4 mile, after 120' of climbing, come to an unmarked road off of Plantation Road and turn left. Ride about 30' and then make a hard right onto the road that intersects it. In less than 0.1 mile pick up the trail to the left at the 10 o'clock position. Roll for 0.2 mile until a sharp 50' climb leads to a **T** intersection where the natural line takes you left. If you make that left you'll wind up on Plantation Road in 0.1 mile; but go right, continuing on the Northwest Passage Trail. Climb and descend to the junction of the Mission Creek Trail in 0.5 mile.

To do just the lower loop of the figure eight turn right here and pick up the directions below. The only overlapping section of the route starts to the left. For the full figure eight, descend to the left and follow the trail around for about 0.1 mile, until the Mission Creek Trail veers right and the Connector Trail continues straight. You'll get back here on the Mission Creek Trail, but for now, go straight, taking the Connector Trail. In 0.1 mile, cross Jones Road, and pick up the trail about 20' to the right. Cross Plantation Road in another 0.4 mile. In 0.2 mile the Mission Creek Staging Trail takes off to the left; turn right, again picking up the Mission Creek Trail. In 0.2 mile come to a 4-way intersection where the road to the left, at time of research, was blocked by some well-placed logs. Continue straight, and in 0.1 mile, the Mission Creek Trail continues to the right. In 0.2 mile come to a road crossing and pick up the trail about 100' to the left. In another 0.2 mile cross another road and pick up the trail dead ahead. At a junction in 0.2 mile the Mission Creek Trail continues both straight (on a cinder-block reinforced climb), and to the left (on a descent). Gear down and climb up; you'll make a rolling climb and, in about 0.7 mile, descend to a short whoop-de-doo section, followed by a 100' climb. The next descent is along a steep edge to a creek, about 1.4 miles after the Mission Creek Trail split. The trail winds left as it climbs past the creek. About 0.5 mile from the creek the trail widens out and veers right into a 0.1-mile whoop-de-doo section. The trail winds left as a road continues straight and ends quickly.

About 200' after the road junction, the Overland Trail comes in from the left at a delta junction where the Mission Creek Trail winds to the right. Go right, staying on the Mission Creek Trail and climbing after the junction. The climb passes the tread enhancement test area, an interesting place to dismount and see how local foresters are trying to improve trail conditions. Keep climbing and descending; 1.2 miles after the test area the trail widens out into a pebbly road. In 0.4 mile the Mission Creek Trail winds to the right as the Derailleur 2 Trail continues straight and narrows into single-track. If your legs are still fresh, try the Derailleur 2 Trail and the other single-tracks to come; if you're fading, you can take the Mission Creek Trail all the way back to the trailhead. On this outing I compromised: I took the Mission Creek Trail here, but enjoyed the next two trails off the Mission Creek Trail on the return.

To follow this route, bear right on the wide road. In 0.2 mile come to a **T** intersection at Jones Road. Turn left and pick up the trail in about 100', after which it narrows again. In 0.1 mile, the trail splits; to the left, ATVs are allowed; to the right, on the narrower trail, they are not. Go right, choosing the human-powered route. In 0.5 mile, after climbing and descending, come to a **T** intersection. Derailleur 2 reaches a junction with the ATV trail, which joins from the left; turn right, and in 0.1 mile the Mission Creek Trail continues to the left. Make the left, and in about 0.4 mile, pass the Connector Trail, and ride the 0.1 mile overlapping section of the route. (Lower loopers, pick up the directions here.)

Continue on the Mission Creek Trail, heading south, and this time, pass the Northwest Passage Trail, which will take off on your right. Head south for another 0.8 mile, and as the trail curves around to the right, the 1.9 Mile Trail starts to the left. If you're getting spent, continue on the Mission Creek Trail; the 1.9 Mile Trail takes a circuitous route to rejoin with the more direct Mission Creek Trail. The 1.9 Mile Trail, despite its name, meets the Mission Creek Trail again in about 2.6 miles. Climb to the end of the 1.9 Mile Trail and turn left at the junction of the Mission Creek Trail. Roll to the junction of the Knoble Trail in 0.4 mile. The Knoble Trail (which proceeds north to connect with the Northwest Passage Trail) continues straight, as the Mission Creek Trail turns left into a fun descent in a southerly direction. Make the left, descending in the direction of the trailhead. Note 950' Road off to your right 0.3 mile beyond the Knoble Trail junction; just beyond that, the Stoffer Trail takes off to the left as the Mission Creek Trail winds to the right. Ready for one more single-track? Take the left onto the Stoffer Trail. You first ride away from the trailhead, but the trail quickly winds around with more climbs and descents on narrow trail, until meeting up again with the Mission Creek Trail in 0.7 mile. Turn left, and return to the trailhead in 0.1 mile.

RIDE 25 · Green Mountain

AT A GLANCE

Length/configuration: 10.7-mile combination, all on single-track; includes a 2.1-mile out-and-back (each way) leading to a 5.3-mile loop, with a 0.6-mile out-and-back spur (each way) to the top

Aerobic difficulty: Stair-step climbing with some steep sections

Technical difficulty: The rooty Beaver Pond Trail is the more technical of the two, but be prepared for lots of rocks and roots en route

Scenery: Views of the Seattle skyline and Puget Sound, Hood Canal, and the Olympic Mountains

Special comments: Good fitness test and great views, close to town

Green Mountain State Forest is located close to Tahuya State Forest, but it offers quite a different riding experience. While Tahuya's 23,000 acres lay host to a seemingly endless web of trails, none with extensive climbs, the 6,000-

RIDE 25 · Green Mountain

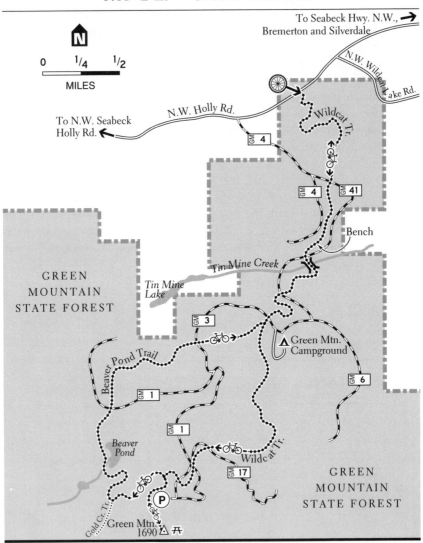

To Seabeck Hwy. N.W., →
Bremerton and Silverdale

N.W. Wildcat Lake Rd.

N.W. Holly Rd.

To N.W. Seabeck
Holly Rd. ←

Wildcat Tr.

GM 4

GM 4   GM 41

Bench

Tin Mine Creek

GREEN
MOUNTAIN
STATE FOREST

Tin Mine
Lake

GM 3

Green Mtn.
Campground

GM 6

Beaver Pond Trail

GM 1

GM 1

Beaver
Pond

Wildcat Tr.

GM 17

GREEN
MOUNTAIN
STATE FOREST

Gold Cr. Tr.

Green Mtn.
1690

P

acre Green Mountain State Forest to the north has just a fraction of the trails—
but some thigh-popping, sustained climbing to the 1,609-foot peak of Green
Mountain, and some fun descending from it.

This ride, a good fitness test for intermediate-level to advanced riders, also
provides less-rutted trails than its Department of Natural Resources cousin to the
south. Like most trails at Tahuya State Forest, Green Mountain's trails are open
to motorcycle use, but most motorcyclists prefer the added mileage that Tahuya
allows. For us human-powered recreationists, though, this 10.7-mile route makes
for an invigorating outing.

A green Green Mountain State Forest.

The loop portion of the journey starts after climbing on the Wildcat Trail past the Green Mountain Campground. Passing the lower junction with the rooty Beaver Pond Trail, it makes its way to the peak on the Vista Trail after passing the top of the Beaver Pond Trail. Returning on the Beaver Pond Trail, the loop portion is complete as you make your final descent on the Wildcat Trail.

The view from the top is a sweeping panorama of Puget Sound, the Seattle area and beyond, plus Hood Canal, and views of the Olympic Mountains as you wander around the picnic area.

One similarity between Green Mountain and Tahuya State Forests is that the Single-Track Mind Cycling Club is instrumental in the upkeep of the trails in both systems. This ride was led by STMCC webmaster and local musician Steve Merriam—he rocks when he works and rolls when he plays!

General location: The trail is located approximately 9 miles northwest of Bremerton, 37 miles northwest of Tacoma, and 45 miles northeast of Shelton.

Elevation change: The trailhead sits at 540' elevation; you'll be perched at 1,690' enjoying the view from the top o' the mountain. Additional climbing both out and back brings the total elevation gain to about 1,500'.

Season: Year-round.

Services: Water is available at the Green Mountain Campground from a hand pump past the toilets by a horse trough. Camping at Green Mountain Campground is by trail access only. Vehicle access to the campground is for group camping, available with reservations from June through September on limited weekends. Gas and snacks are available at the Wildcat Grocery, 0.9 mile from the trailhead. Services are available in Bremerton and Silverdale.

Hazards: The trails, especially the Beaver Pond Trail, provide rooty challenges. The angled roots on the trail can be slippery when wet.

Rescue index: Help can be summoned from a phone at the Wildcat Grocery. Help is available in Bremerton and Silverdale.

Land status: DNR Green Mountain State Forest.

Maps: DNR Green Mountain State Forest map.

Finding the trail: From Tacoma, take WA 16 northwest to WA 3, and travel about 4 miles north on WA 3 to the Kitsap Way exit. Turn left at the exit, and in 1.3 miles, across from the Red Apple Grocery Store, veer left, at the 11 o'clock position, onto North Lake Way. Stay on North Lake Way as it winds to the right in 0.4 miles, and travel another 0.7 miles to a **Y** intersection. Veer left onto Seabeck Highway N.W., and take it for 3 miles to N.W. Holly Road at a flashing yellow light. Turn left onto N.W. Holly Road; pass Wildcat Grocery in 1 mile, N.W. Wildcat Lake Road in another 0.6 mile, and turn left into the Wildcat Trailhead parking area 0.3 mile farther.

From Shelton, take WA 3 north, past Belfair in 26 miles, and past WA 16 in another 8 miles. Continue on WA 3 to the Kitsap Way exit and proceed as above.

From the Hood Canal Bridge, take WA 3 south. In 15 miles, stay on WA 3 past the junction of WA 303 in Silverdale. Proceed about 2 miles beyond WA 303 to the Newberry Hill Road exit. Turn right on Newberry Hill Road and come to Seabeck Highway at a **T** intersection in 3 miles. Turn left on Seabeck Highway and, in 2 miles, come to N.W. Holly Road at the flashing yellow light. Turn right, and come to the Wildcat Lake Trailhead parking area in 1.9 miles.

From Bremerton, hey, you're almost there already! Take WA 310, which turns into Kitsap Way as you head west. Pass WA 3 and proceed as above.

Sources of additional information:

Department of Natural Resources
South Puget Sound Region
950 Farman Street North
P.O. Box 68
Enumclaw, WA 98022-0068
(800) 527-3305 or (360) 825-1631 (direct)

Single-Track Mind Cycling Club
6824 19th Street West #147
Tacoma, WA 98466
(206) 565-5124
http://members.aol.com/STMClub/stmclub.html

Notes on the trail: Start to the left of the map board, in a south/southeast direction. Start on a gentle climb on smooth trails with some nice banked turns. After crossing road GM-41, gear down for some difficult climbing with some loose sections. At 1.2 miles, before you descend to the next road crossing, a bench on the left invites you to sit and look at the Seattle skyline. Have a seat, or descend and again cross road GM-41. The trail picks up about 20' to the left. Cross over a creek and climb steeply on a wood-railed section to a final crossing of GM-41. The trail picks up just to the right. Climb to the next road crossing in 0.9 mile, where you'll find the Green Mountain Campground to the left. About 50' past the road crossing, pass the Beaver Pond Trail, on which you'll return, on your right. The climb continues with some downhill respites; keep your eyes peeled for some good looks into Seattle on the way.

In 1.5 miles beyond the Beaver Pond Trail junction, descend to a road crossing (GM-17); turn right, and ride about 100'. Before the road winds to the left, take the trail to the left that parallels it (if you do any considerable climbing on the road you've gone too far). This section is a short climb that quickly comes to another road. At this junction, a gate is to your left; road GM-17 is right. Ride a few feet to the right and pick up the trail before the paralleling road. After the next road crossing, come to a trail junction in 0.1 mile (at which point the sign indicates 4.3 miles total). You'll take the Beaver Pond Trail, down and to the right, on the return, but right now, climb to the left for the final 0.6 mile to the vista. You'll come up to the vista parking area in 0.3 mile.

The Vista Trail takes off to the left of the signboard and makes a steep 0.3 mile ascent. The trail opens up at the picnic area, and a little higher to the right is the 1,690' peak. Catch a view, have a snack, and proceed back down to the Beaver Pond Trail. Take it as it continues straight and then winds to the left, as the Wildcat Trail curves to the right. Continue descending past the Gold Creek Trail, which climbs to the left at a junction in 0.3 mile. In another 0.6 mile, at the end of the descent, stay to the right on the main trail near the pond as a connector trail to the Gold Creek Trail continues straight. The Beaver Pond Trail stays level near the pond and then climbs up and away from it very shortly. In 0.6 mile cross road GM-1 and continue the moderate climb. In 0.9 mile cross road GM-3 as you climb. Come to a **T** junction in another 0.6 mile, where a primitive trail goes right; turn left and descend, and in 0.3 mile return to the Wildcat Trail at another **T** junction. Descend to the left, and pass the road to the Green Mountain Campground as you continue descending. As you climb past the second road crossing beyond the campground, you'll find the bench to the right, for your viewing pleasure, just before the climb levels out. Another 1.2 miles of rolling descent brings you back to the trailhead.

GREENWATER AND ELBE AREA RIDES

The town of Greenwater is on WA 410 about an hour east of Tacoma. Beyond Greenwater is the north entrance to Mt. Rainier National Park. Just before entering the park, you pass some outstanding mountain bike country. Single-track masters love the challenge of Skookum Flats Trail and White River Trail.

Forest roads and single-tracks are abundant in the area and make for some prime rides for strong cyclists. The mountain roads in this neck of the woods tend to be steep. The trails are no slouches either, but it's their obstacles that leave you gasping. The paths throw everything they have at you, all at once.

Elbe is a small town that lies about 40 miles south of Tacoma on WA 7. The road that heads east out of Elbe leads into Mt. Rainier National Park (by way of the Nisqually River Entrance). This road winds up the south flank of the mountain to Paradise Valley, a rolling parkland mottled with stately fir trees and wildflowers. The valley sits about 9,000 feet below the rounded white summit of the Big Mountain. The area is rich with fascinating day hikes.

Outside of the park, in the adjacent Mt. Baker–Snoqualmie National Forest, is a popular hike that leads to High Rock Lookout. The lookout is one of the forest's few remaining manned fire observation posts. While most people drive to the trail, we recommend mountain bikes. Once you reach the trailhead, you can stash your bike and climb the ridge to the overlook. This view of Rainier is unparalleled.

RIDE 26 · Skookum Flats

AT A GLANCE

WA

Length/configuration: 11-mile loop on single-track trails; the ride includes a short piece of paved highway

Aerobic difficulty: Difficult

Technical difficulty: Skookum Flats Trail is extremely demanding with roots and rocks; White River Trail is much less technical, yet it, too, presents challenges

Scenery: Impressive old-growth and the beautiful White River

Special comments: Exciting ride on varied single-track

Skookum Flats Trail is one of the most entertaining pieces of extreme single-track in the Pacific Northwest. This popular loop utilizes Skookum Flats Trail, Dalles River Trail, a short stretch on WA 410, and White River Trail. This is an excellent and challenging 11-mile circuit.

Difficulty rating for the loop: strenuous. Skookum Flats Trail is a lesson in humility. It is technically demanding, with innumerable roots, rocks, drop-offs, staircase climbs, and switchbacks. Remember, there is no shame in walking; besides, it is better than dying. Beginners and intermediates will enjoy out-and-back excursions from the south end of Skookum Flats Trail.

General location: This ride begins at the intersection of Buck Creek Road/Forest Service Road 7160 and WA 410, about 28 miles east of Enumclaw, Washington.

Elevation change: The trailhead at Buck Creek Road lies at 2,480'. The northern terminus at FS 73 is the low point of the loop, at 2,060'. Hilly terrain produces about 500' of climbing on this trail. The route climbs to 2,280' on FS 7150, then meets up with WA 410 at 2,220'. The ride's high point—2,580'—occurs on White River Trail. Lesser ups and downs contribute about 300' of climbing to the pedaling on White River Trail. Total elevation gain: 1,380'.

Season: Dry spells during the summer and early fall offer good opportunities for low-impact cycling. These trails are popular and can be crowded on weekends.

Services: Water is available seasonally at the Dalles Campground. The nearby community of Greenwater offers food, lodging, gas, limited groceries, and showers. All services are available in Enumclaw.

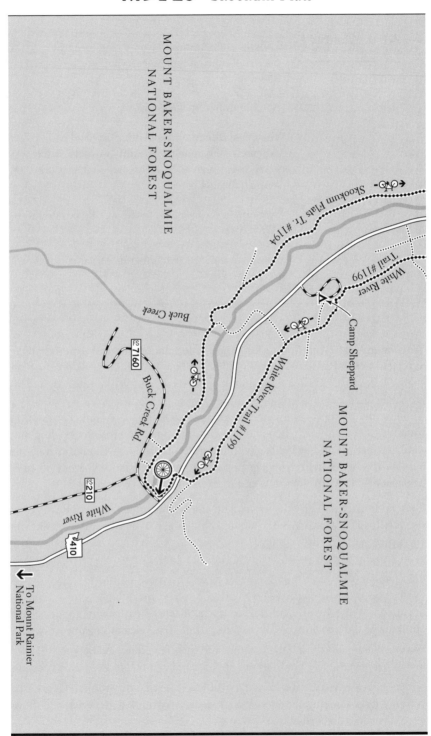

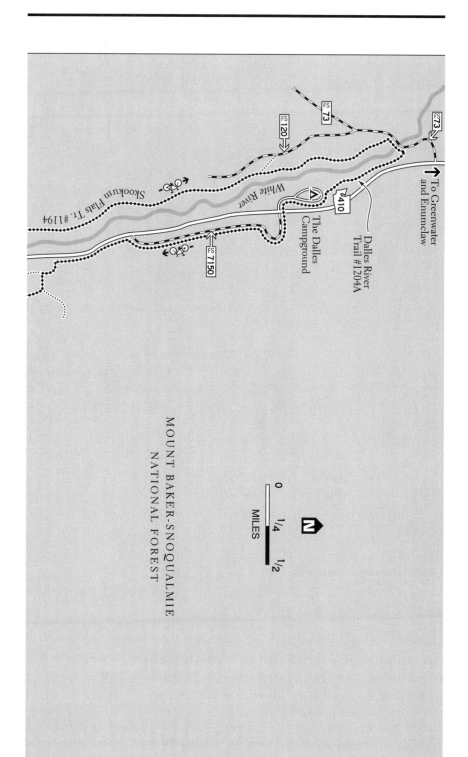

To Greenwater
and Enumclaw

FS 73

FS 73

FS 120

Skookum Flats Tr. #1194

White River

The Dalles
Campground

410

Dalles River
Trail #1204A

FS 7150

MOUNT BAKER-SNOQUALMIE
NATIONAL FOREST

N

0   1/4   1/2

MILES

"Look at me, I can ride
this part!"

Hazards: The single-track portions of the loop are intensely technical. The trails are perilous when wet—bridges and roots become very slick. Anticipate others approaching from around corners. Be extra cautious while riding on the highway.

Rescue index: Help can be found in Greenwater.

Land status: Mt. Baker–Snoqualmie National Forest.

Maps: The district map of the White River Ranger District is a good guide to this ride. USGS 7.5 minute quad: Sun Top.

Finding the trail: From locations to the north, follow WA 410 east from Greenwater. You will pass the Dalles Campground on the right after about 7 miles. Continue for another 3.8 miles to FS 7160/Buck Creek Road (on the right, just beyond milepost 54). From locations to the south, take WA 410 west (toward Seattle) from Cayuse Pass. It is about 11 miles from the pass to Buck Creek Road (on the left, just past milepost 55). Coming from either direction, look for the big wooden sign for Buck Creek Organization Site, opposite Buck Creek Road. Park in the small parking area on the west side of WA 410.

Source of additional information:

White River Ranger District
857 Roosevelt Avenue East
Enumclaw, WA 98022
(360) 825-6585

Notes on the trail: Cross the bridge over the White River, and immediately turn right onto Skookum Flats Trail #1194. Turn right after 0.1 mile to stay on Trail #1194. Turn right again in another 0.2 mile at an unmarked intersection. One more mile brings you to a suspension bridge that leads out to WA 410. Bear to the left before the bridge to remain on Trail #1194. Pedal 0.4 mile to another intersection; here, turn right. The trail enters a camp area after 3 more miles; stay to the right and on the main trail until you reach unsigned FS 73. Turn right onto the gravel road and cross the bridge. Turn right onto Dalles River Trail #1204A immediately after crossing the river. Proceed along this path for 0.5 mile to the Dalles Campground. Turn left and follow the paved road through the campground to WA 410. Continue straight across the highway and ride up FS 7150. This road passes cottages and ends up back at WA 410. Turn left onto the highway and pedal 0.4 mile to a faint trail on the left. The path is hard to find—it looks like a small traffic pullout. Turn left onto the trail and climb very steeply under power lines to the White River Trail #1199. Turn left and follow the trail signs to remain on Trail #1199. After passing through a couple of clearings you'll arrive at a double-track and some power lines. Turn left and ride past a grassy field. Turn left at the next power pole onto a trail, then bear to the right to follow White River Trail as it passes behind Camp Sheppard. Follow the signs and stay on White River Trail #1199 for another 1.6 miles. Leave White River Trail where a sign indicates that White River Trail #1199 continues on to Ranger Creek Trail, Deep Creek Trail, and Corral Pass Road. Turn right at this sign and descend to WA 410. Turn left and ride up the highway 0.2 mile to your vehicle.

RIDE 27 · Dalles Ridge Loop

AT A GLANCE
————————

WA

Length/configuration: 22.3-mile loop on gravel roads, single-track, and paved highway

Aerobic difficulty: Tough; 10-mile climb and other fun challenges

Technical difficulty: Tough; trails offer extreme riding conditions and tons of obstacles

Scenery: Excellent views from clear-cuts on gravel road climb

Special comments: Eat your Wheaties and bring an energy bar or two

This is a demanding 22.3-mile training ride. The loop begins with a real lip-chapper—10 miles of steady climbing on gravel roads (including 3.5 miles of steep climbing). Your stay on Dalles Ridge is brief—one-half mile of moderately difficult to steep uphills. The descent from the mountain involves a great deal of walking and carrying your bike. This is not what most cyclists would call a fun downhill. Ranger Creek Trail descends a steep drainage with severe switchbacks, most of which are too tight to ride. Huge root obstacles are common. We counted over 30 unrideable sections of trail (not including countless dabs). Ranger Creek Trail spits you out onto White River Trail for 3 sweet miles of challenging single-track. The trip ends with 3.2 miles on the highway.

There are excellent views of the White River Valley, Crystal Mountain, and Mt. Rainier on this ride. Clear-cuts dominate the road miles, but the trails pass through lovely stands of old-growth timber. The stretch on White River Trail is a superior piece of technical single-track.

General location: This ride begins approximately 5 miles south of Greenwater, Washington.

Elevation change: The elevation at the trailhead is 2,160'. A high point of 5,500' is attained on Dalles Ridge Trail. Undulations on the roads and trails add about 500' of climbing to the loop. Total elevation gain: 3,840'.

Season: The roads and trails are usually free of snow from late June through September. Avoid the route when it is wet—trail damage and slick roots are concerns. The highway is busy with traffic on summer weekends.

Services: There is no water available on the ride. Water can be obtained seasonally at the Dalles Campground. Food, lodging, limited groceries, and gas can be found in Greenwater.

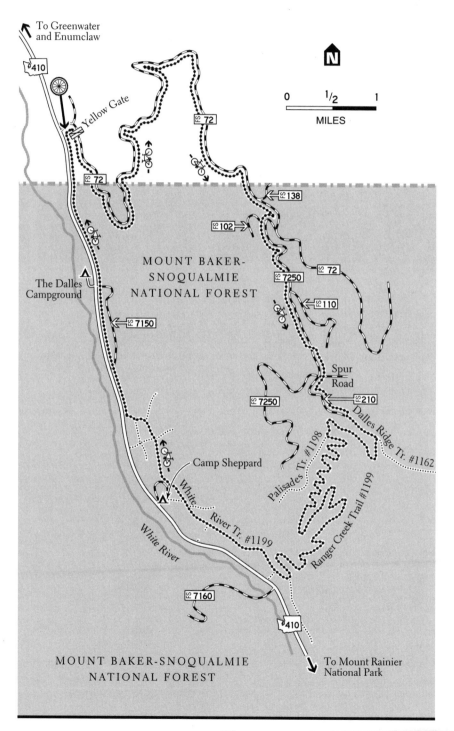

Cloud-cloaked view from Forest Service Road 72.

Hazards: The ride is long and demanding. You will be fatigued by the time you reach the highway. Remain alert for traffic on the roads; be especially careful on WA 410. The single-tracks are treacherous and full of obstacles. Steep drop-offs are commonplace on Ranger Creek Trail.

Rescue index: Help is available in Enumclaw.

Land status: Mt. Baker–Snoqualmie National Forest.

Maps: The district map of the White River Ranger District is a good guide to this ride. USGS 7.5 minute quad: Sun Top.

Finding the trail: From Greenwater, follow WA 410 south for 5.3 miles and turn left onto signed FS 72. Go up the gravel road and park on the right (across from an unsigned spur road on the left).

Source of additional information:

White River Ranger District
857 Roosevelt Avenue East
Enumclaw, WA 98022
(360) 825-6585

Notes on the trail: Carry your bike down the tight switchbacks on Ranger Creek Trail. Skidding around the turns is inappropriate; it causes severe trail damage. Attempting to roll through them does not cut it either—you may clean some of them, but you will miss frequently. When you miss, your foot comes down to catch your fall. Invariably, this damages the hillside above the trail and leads to slope failure (i.e., the trail gets trashed).

Pass through the yellow gate and ride up FS 72. Stay on the main road where spur roads branch off. Turn right onto FS 7250 where FS 72 continues straight (0.4 mile beyond milepost 7). Follow FS 7250 for 2.1 miles to an intersection of three roads. An unsigned spur goes left, FS 210 goes straight ahead, and FS 7250 swings right. Continue straight onto FS 210. You will come to the end of FS 210 in 0.4 mile at a trailhead sign for Dalles Ridge Trail #1162. Proceed up this single-track for 0.6 mile to Ranger Creek Trail #1197, which cuts off just after the crest on Dalles Ridge Trail. Turn right and descend on Ranger Creek Trail for just over 1 mile to a hiker's shelter. Turn left, remaining on Ranger Creek Trail, where Palisades Trail #1198 goes straight. You will reach Little Ranger Creek Viewpoint in 2 miles. Visit the viewpoint, then continue with the descent. You will reach an intersection of trails in 2.5 miles; a sign on the left indicates that you have been following Ranger Creek Trail. Turn sharply to the right onto unsigned White River Trail.

Soon you will find yourself paralleling the highway. Then you will arrive at a junction where a trail goes left and descends to the highway. Continue straight on White River Trail toward Camp Sheppard. In 1.1 miles you will reach an intersection where Buck Creek Trail goes left. Continue straight on White River Trail. You will come to another meeting of trails in 0.3 mile; continue straight on White River Trail and stay to the right at the next intersection, where a path branches left toward Camp Sheppard. Shortly you will pass through the back of the camp—stay on White River Trail. When you arrive at a grassy field, turn right onto a double-track. Immediately turn right into the woods to get back onto the unsigned single-track. (This turn is easy to miss—the double-track continues straight, following some telephone lines). Follow the signs at the next two intersections to remain on White River Trail. Turn right when you arrive at a clearing and power lines. Ride down to the highway. Turn right onto WA 410 and pedal 3.2 miles to FS 72. Turn right and ride to your vehicle.

RIDE 28 · High Rock Lookout

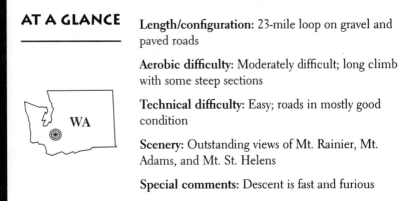

AT A GLANCE

Length/configuration: 23-mile loop on gravel and paved roads

Aerobic difficulty: Moderately difficult; long climb with some steep sections

Technical difficulty: Easy; roads in mostly good condition

Scenery: Outstanding views of Mt. Rainier, Mt. Adams, and Mt. St. Helens

Special comments: Descent is fast and furious

This is a 23-mile road loop. An 11-mile ascent takes you to Towhead Gap and High Rock Lookout Trail #266. The 1.6-mile hiking trail climbs 1,365 feet to the last manned lookout in the Packwood Ranger District. Views of Mt. Rainier, Mt. St. Helens, and Mt. Adams are outstanding. The ride ends with a long, fun descent.

The first nine miles are paved. The remainder of the loop is on gravel roads in mostly good condition. The trip starts with three miles of gently rolling terrain—a nice warm-up for the moderately difficult climb to Towhead Gap. The ascent contains some steep (but short) grades and many easy breath-catching stretches.

General location: This ride begins near Mt. Rainier National Park, approximately 14 miles east of Elbe, Washington.

Elevation change: The ride begins at 1,960' and climbs to Towhead Gap, at 4,300'. Undulations on the route add an estimated 200' of climbing to the loop. Total elevation gain: 2,540' (hike not included).

Season: This ride is best on clear days from July through October.

Services: Limited groceries, gas, a pay phone, and espresso can be found in Ashford.

Hazards: The roads may be busy with logging and tourist traffic. Exercise caution when exploring on High Rock—the north face is a sheer 600' cliff.

Rescue index: Help can be found in Ashford.

Land status: Mt. Baker–Snoqualmie National Forest lands, administered by the Gifford Pinchot National Forest.

Maps: The district map of the Packwood Ranger District of the Gifford Pinchot National Forest is a good guide to this route. USGS 7.5 minute quad: Sawtooth Ridge.

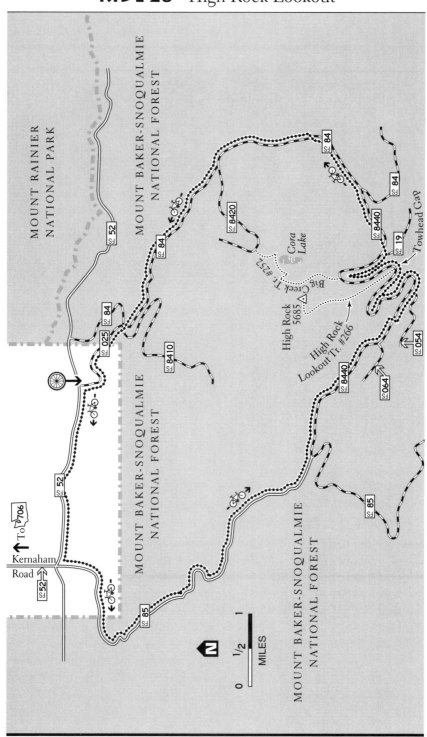

Towhead Gap.

Finding the trail: From Elbe, follow WA 706 east to Ashford. Continue east from Ashford for about 2 miles to Kernahan Road/FS 52 (on the right, just east of milepost 10). Turn right onto FS 52. Proceed on FS 52 for 4 miles to FS 025 (on the right, just east of milepost 4). Turn right onto FS 025 and park on the left.

Source of additional information:

> Packwood Information Center
> 13068 Highway 12
> Packwood, WA 98361
> (360) 494-0600

Notes on the trail: Turn left out of the parking area onto FS 52. Continue on FS 52 to the intersection with FS 85 and turn left to follow the sign for High Rock Lookout. The pavement ends at a **Y** intersection 9 miles into the ride. Bear left onto FS 8440 toward the lookout. Keep left at the next two intersections, staying on FS 8440, until you reach Towhead Gap. Descend from the pass and stay on the main road when side roads branch off. You will pass Big Creek Trail #252, then FS 019 on the right. The next intersection signals the end of FS 8440. Continue onto FS 84, which is straight ahead and hard to the right. Stay on FS 84 for 5.3 miles to FS 025 (just beyond FS 8410 on the left). Turn left and follow FS 025 back to your vehicle.

SEATTLE AREA RIDES

L ying between two major mountain ranges—the Olympics and the Cascades—
Seattle is within fairly easy reach of some of the best riding the state has to offer.
It's just a ferry ride away from the Kitsap Peninsula and its year-round mountain
biking, and the majestic Olympics are shortly beyond it to the west. To the east,
Seattlites can be at Snoqualmie Pass in an hour's time, and over the hill and on
the way to drier, "east of the Cascades" riding just a bit farther. But there's plenty
of riding around town.

Riders can tour around town with slick tires instead of knobbies. Numerous
Seattle landmarks are accessible by bike, including the Pike Place Market,
Pioneer Square, Seattle Center, and too many others to name. (Bring a tour book
and a heavy-duty lock.) A must for mountain bikers is a trip to the Seattle REI
(Recreational Equipment, Inc., 222 Yale Avenue North, right off of Interstate 5;
206-223-1944); the store has an outdoor mountain bike test track, an exhaustive
map selection, and anything you may need for a short bike ride or an extended
tour.

A good place to start on two wheels, though, is the Burke-Gilman Trail. The
paved rail-trail starts just southwest of Green Lake—another popular riding
spot—at 8th Avenue N.W. and Leary Way N.W. It travels by the University of
Washington and skirts the northwest side of Lake Washington, providing some
nice views in its 14.1 miles. In Kenmore, the trail ends into the Sammamish
River Trail, which extends another 10 miles southeast to Marymoor Park on
Lake Sammamish. The trail is used by commuters as well as recreational
cyclists, skaters, and walkers with dogs; it's fun, but it can get crowded at times,
and though it is a good introductory tour, it's not the best road riding that Seattle
has to offer. For extensive road riding information, pick up a copy of one of the
free local bike magazines at area shops, call the Cascade Bicycle Club at (206)
522-BIKE, or contact Terrene Tours, which offers everything from one-day
guided tours around Seattle and Puget Sound to multi-day excursions in the San
Juan Islands and the Cascades. Find them at 117 32nd Avenue East, Seattle, WA
98112; (206) 325-5569.

When you're ready to put some dirt under your tires, the best, hilliest single-
tracking close to town is at Tiger Mountain, southeast of Issaquah off of WA
18. While many trails are closed to mountain bikers, the Preston Railroad

Trail/Northwest Timber Trail loop provides a technically and physically demanding outing. You can add the Iverson Trail to the mix for a 15.3-mile, single-track-intensive ride. Gravel roads in the forest, nearly auto-free, provide enough appeal to entertain riders year-round.

Some great in-town single-tracking with a suburban flavor is offered at St. Edward State Park and Big Finn Hill County Park in Bothell. The trails are of excellent quality and are not as hilly as those at Tiger Mountain. About 20 miles east of Redmond, the nearly flat Snoqualmie Valley Trail is one of numerous rail-trails in the region, and highlights a pastoral, auto-free, family-friendly route to Snoqualmie Falls.

The area holds numerous pockets of low-mileage but fun dirt outings. An especially popular local destination is the privately-owned Victor Falls, east of Tacoma. Trails and trail conditions change constantly here, so check with local bike shops or call the Backcountry Bicycle Trails Council of Seattle or the Single-Track Mind Cycling Club in Tacoma for the most up-to-date information.

RIDE 29 · St. Edward State Park/Big Finn Hill County Park

AT A GLANCE

WA

Length/configuration: Up to 10 miles in the spaghetti-style network of single-track, plus Seminary Trail, a 0.6-mile (each way) road to the shore of Lake Washington

Aerobic difficulty: Easy to moderate, with one short but steep **V** and a couple of short grinders

Technical difficulty: Moderate; lots of rooty challenges and some log crossings; a few dismounts even for intermediate riders

Scenery: Deep forest trails amid suburban backdrop

Special comments: A taste of the forest, and high-quality trails, by the northeast shore of Lake Washington.

With so many nearby Seattle area trails restricted to mountain bikers, these single-tracks provide a great in-town riding experience for mountain bikers of all abilities. Because of its proximity to a huge population base, these trails get a lot of use, and local activists from the Backcountry Bicycle Trails Club of Seattle have had to work, both politically and on the ground, to keep access to the trails. Respectful, trail-sensitive riding is necessary to keep this area open.

St. Edward State Park is just off of Lake Washington but you don't get any real lake views by bike except at the bottom of the Seminary Trail (which is actually a dirt road). The views are of the trails before you, the trees and brush, ferns, and some blackberry brambles. Level and rolling trails are punctuated by a few short bursts and maybe a little walking. It's fun, woodsy riding on hard-packed trails in the midst of the masses. Nearby civilization is not always bad; though the background noise you hear will be auto traffic, the trails are only a few pedal strokes from a midride snack or a postride beverage!

The kiosk by the parking area notes interesting facts about the park and the history of the former seminary. Read about it when you come; it's all well and good, but the really interesting stuff is the fun mountain-biking the area affords. Study the map at the kiosk, and steer clear of the trails off-limits to bikes.

There's more room to roam at Big Finn Hill, where the spaghetti system of trails allow much more improvisation.

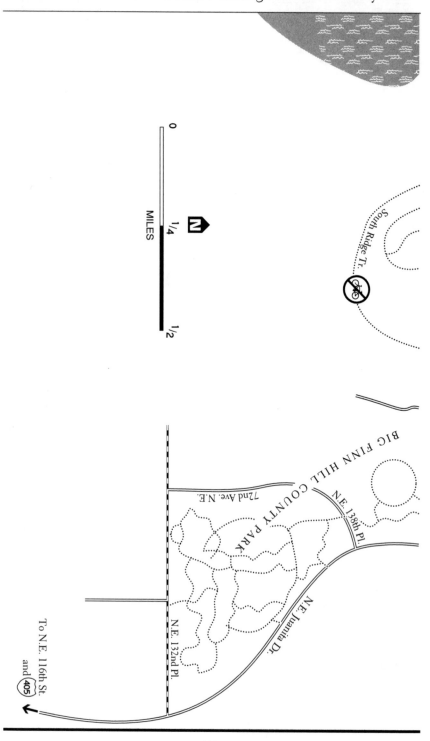

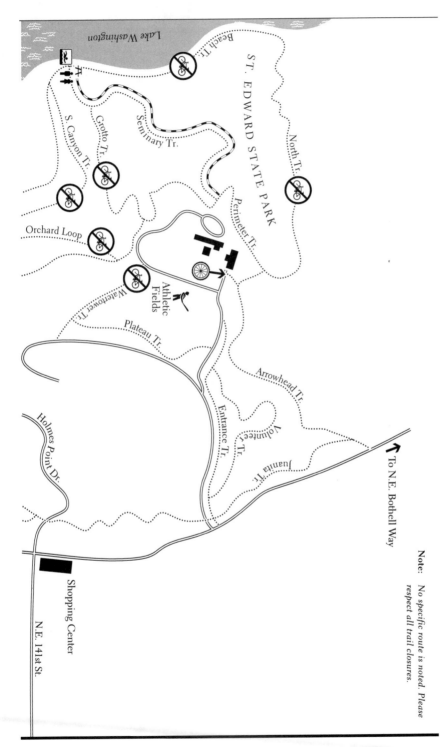

ST. EDWARD STATE PARK

Lake Washington

Beach Tr.

North Tr.

Seminary Tr.

Grotto Tr.

S. Canyon Tr.

Orchard Loop

Perimeter Tr.

Watchtower Tr.

Athletic Fields

Plateau Tr.

Arrowhead Tr.

Entrance Tr.

Volunteer Tr.

Juanita Tr.

Holmes Point Dr.

To N.E. Bothell Way

Shopping Center

N.E. 141st St.

Note: No specific route is noted. Please respect all trail closures.

At the shore of Lake Washington, at the bottom of the Seminary Trail. Trails along the lake are closed to bikes.

General location: St. Edward State Park and Big Finn Hill County Park are located in Bothell, on the northeast side of Lake Washington.

Elevation change: The most extensive climb (and descent) in the system is the 320' on the Seminary Trail, from its junction with the Perimeter Trail to the lakeshore. Other climbs and descents on all the trails add up to a total elevation gain of about 800'.

Season: The trails here are both physically and politically sensitive, so reserve your riding for the dryer conditions.

Services: Water is available at St. Edward State Park. Most services are available adjacent to the trails on Juanita Drive.

Hazards: The short, deep **V** section, a steep 30' drop into and out of a small ravine, can be intimidating for beginning mountain bikers, and even intermediates. Overhanging blackberry bushes can be a nuisance if they're not trimmed back. Not all the trails at St. Edward are open to mountain bikes; again, please be respectful of the closed trails.

Rescue index: Help, if needed, is close at hand at the state park office; a pay phone is located there.

Land status: St. Edward State Park is a part of the extensive Washington State Parks system. Big Finn Hill County Park comes under the jurisdiction of King County Parks.

Maps: There are no accurate maps of the trails at Big Finn Hill. The kiosk by the parking area at St. Edward State Park shows only the trails within the state park boundaries, though the trails in the two jurisdictions are contiguous.

Finding the trail: From Seattle, take either I-90 or WA 520 east to I-405 and travel north to Exit 20A/N.E. 116th Street. Go left (west) on 116th Street. As you cross N.E. 98th Avenue, 116th turns into N.E. Juanita Drive. From here continue on Juanita Drive for 5.4 miles (0.3 mile after a supermarket and shopping center at Holmes Point Drive/N.E. 141st Street). Turn left at the signed entrance to St. Edward State Park (also signed as the entrance to Bastyr University). As you proceed into the park, passing trails and trail accesses as you drive, veer right at the **Y** intersection in 0.4 mile. Drive another 0.3 mile to the parking area to the right.

From the north, from the junction of I-5 and I-405, take I-405 south to Exit 23B, and head west on WA 522 (which turns into N.E. Bothell Way) for 4.2 miles. Turn left (south) at the stoplight at 68th Street N.E. (which turns into N.E. Juanita Drive in 0.4 mile) and proceed 1.8 miles to the entrance to St. Edward State Park on the right, 0.3 mile before Holmes Point Drive/N.E. 141st Street.

On the northwest side of Lake Washington, follow WA 522 (which turns from Lake City Way to Bothell Way at the junction of WA 523) around the north side of the lake; 68th Street N.E. is 3.0 miles from the Lake City Way/Bothell Way split. Turn right (south) on 68th Street N.E. and proceed as above.

Sources of additional information:

St. Edward State Park
14445 Juanita Drive N.E.
Bothell, WA 98011
(425) 823-2992

King County Parks and Recreation Department
Luther Burbank Park
2040 84th Avenue S.E.
Mercer Island, WA 98040
(206) 296-4232

Backcountry Bicycle Trails Club
P.O. Box 21288
Seattle, WA 98111-3288
(206) 283-2995 (activities hotline)
membership:
14241 N.E. Woodinville-Duvall Road #301
Woodinville, WA 98072-8595
http://www.dirtnw.com/bbtc

Notes on the trail: If you know the basic boundaries, you can get lost without *really* getting lost, which is part of the fun of mountain biking—so ride and enjoy.

You can access the Seminary Trail down to the lakeshore by way of the Perimeter Trail, which takes off near the parking lot. The other trails to and on the lakeshore are off-limits to bikes.

To access Big Finn Hill County Park, take Entrance, Arrowhead, Volunteer, or Juanita Trail to the junction of Juanita Trail and Entrance Trail close to the park entrance and Juanita Drive. Cross the entrance road, and continue. At the **T** intersection in 0.4 mile, where a right will bring you back to St. Edward State Park, go left. Cross Holmes Point Drive; from there, numerous loops are possible. You'll find two deep **V** sections on the far side of Holmes Point Drive; they're both steep, and they'll both bring you up to the same spot. As you make your way south, cross the road where N.E. 138th Place becomes 72nd Avenue N.E. Again, numerous loops are possible. The trails end at N.E. 132nd Place, with a residential paved street ahead of you and gravel roads to either side.

If you get lost at any point, well, that's part of the fun. If waning daylight or your schedule force a quick return to your car, use the trail accesses or N.E. 138th Place to the east, and you'll wind up on Juanita Drive, from where you can return to the park.

Ride it, love it, give back to it. Contact the Backcountry Bicycle Trails Council to get involved.

RIDE 30 · Snoqualmie Valley Trail

AT A GLANCE

WA

Length/configuration: 22.6-mile out-and-back (11.3 miles each way), virtually all on gravel rail-trail, with 0.1 mile of single-track leading to the paved 1-mile descent to Snoqualmie Falls; 9.2-mile option (4.6 miles each way) for the true beginner

Aerobic difficulty: Easy; you won't even know you gained 400' on the long route to the falls

Technical difficulty: Easy rail-trail; very short section of technical, walkable single-track

Scenery: Suburbia, pastureland, woods, creek overlooks, Snoqualmie Falls

Special comments: Excellent family or social cruise; good winter workout when area single-tracks are too wet

The Snoqualmie Valley Trail is a lovely jaunt of 11.3 miles each way, but it can be extended or shortened as schedule and fitness allow. For a ride that provides virtually no physical and technical challenges, it can be turned into a vigorous workout with a quick cadence. This is a ride, though, that beckons to be ridden at a slower, recreational tempo.

The nearly all-gravel rail-trail route gently climbs about 400 feet on the 11.3-mile journey to the power-generating, 270-foot rush of Snoqualmie Falls. The trail passes through some residential areas, farmland, and tree-lined logging land, giving it a pastoral feeling. Being in the midst of civilization, though, it gets a lot of use from joggers, equestrians, and dog walkers.

Just before 356th Drive S.E., 6.7 miles into the ride, a picnic table and trash can flank a new concrete bridge over a creek, inviting you to eat, rest, and enjoy. For the true beginner, a leisurely 4.2 miles (each way) from this point to powerful Snoqualmie Falls and back is a lovely way to break in a new pair of wheels or legs. Yet another option is beginning and ending at scenic, touristy, Snoqualmie Falls.

General location: The start of the described ride, in Carnation, is about 20 miles east of Redmond, and about 11 miles north of I-90 at Preston.

Elevation change: Starting at about 100' elevation, a gradual 400' elevation gain on the "out" leg brings you to the slight descent at Tokul Road that leads to the falls.

Season: All year.

Services: Water is available in Carnation and at Snoqualmie Falls. Services are available in Carnation. Food (from snacks to fine dining), picnic areas, rest rooms, and souvenirs are available at Salish Lodge and Snoqualmie Falls Park, adjacent to the falls.

Hazards: Watch for cars on the numerous road crossings, and especially at the oft-crowded Snoqualmie Falls. Watch out, too, for the broken glass in the tunnel under Tokul Road. Most of the land around the trail is private, so stay on the straight and narrow; resist the urge to explore the few side trails along the way.

Rescue index: Residences by the trail can be a source of help. Some of the road crossings lead to WA 202 and WA 203.

Land status: King County Parks.

Maps: Trail-specific maps are not currently available. Use USGS 7.5 minute quads: Carnation, Fall City.

Finding the trail: From I-90 in Seattle, travel east to Exit 22, to Preston and Fall City. Go left (north) at the off-ramp to the **T** intersection and proceed right on Preston–Fall City Road S.E., at first paralleling the freeway east and then turning north. In 4.5 miles, Preston–Fall City Road meets WA 202. Turn right, cross the Snoqualmie River, and immediately turn left onto WA 203. (For the shorter option, continue another 1.1 miles on WA 202 and turn left on 356th Drive S.E. Travel 0.5 mile and park by the trail on either side of the road.)

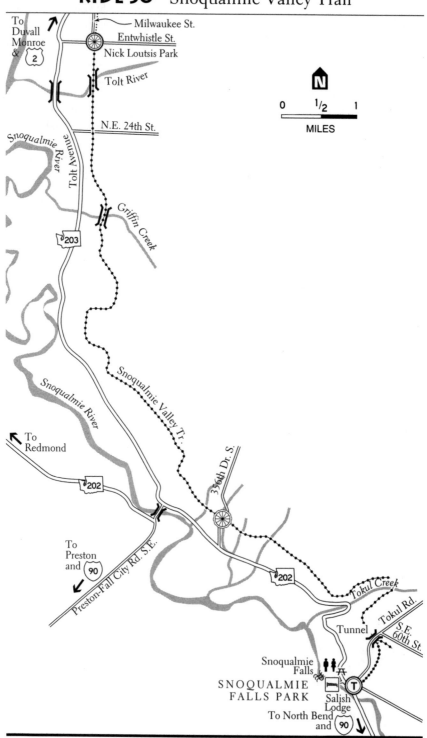

To
Duvall
Monroe
& **2**

Milwaukee St.
Entwhistle St.
Nick Loutsis Park

Tolt River

N.E. 24th St.

Snoqualmie River

Tolt Avenue

Griffin Creek

203

Snoqualmie River

Snoqualmie Valley Tr.

To
Redmond

202

356th Dr. S.

To
Preston
and **90**

Preston-Fall City Rd. S.E.

202

Tokul Creek

Tunnel

Tokul Rd.

S.E. 60th St.

Snoqualmie
Falls

SNOQUALMIE
FALLS PARK

Salish
Lodge

To North Bend
and **90**

T

N

0   ½   1

MILES

Snoqualmie Falls.

Drive for 6.2 miles on WA 203 into Carnation, where it turns into Tolt Avenue. Just after a supermarket and gas station on the left, turn right onto Entwhistle Street. In 0.3 mile, come to Nick Loutsis Park on the right (where Milwaukee Street goes left). You'll see the trail going to both the left and the right immediately after the park. Parking for just a few vehicles is provided at Nick Loutsis Park.

From Redmond, take WA 202 (Redmond-Fall City Road N.E.) about 14.5 miles east to the junction of WA 203, just past the river; then turn left and proceed as above.

From the east, take I-90 to Exit 31/WA 202, in North Bend. Turn right and proceed northwest. WA 202 turns into Railroad Avenue in 2.9 miles, at the corner of Meadowbrook Way. From this junction continue on WA 202, passing Tokul Road on your right in 1.8 miles, and Snoqualmie Falls in another 0.1 mile on your left. Keep going on WA 202, passing 356th Drive S.E. in 2.8 miles (turn right here and travel about 0.5 mile to the trail for the shorter route), and reaching WA 203 in another 1.1 miles. Turn right onto WA 203 and proceed as above.

Source of additional information:

King County Parks and Recreation
Luther Burbank Park
2040 84th Avenue S.E.
Mercer Island, WA 98040
(206) 296-4232

Notes on the trail: Take the trail to the right just east of the park, or ride for 0.1 mile under the trees in the park to join it. Continue past a bridge over the Tolt River in 0.3 mile; to the right a trail connects with Tolt River County Park and WA 203 in 0.3 mile. Pass paved N.E. 24th Street, which connects with WA 203, in 1.2 miles. Cross a bridge high above Griffin Creek at 2.3 miles and continue. Cross a bridge over a scenic creek, with a picnic table and trash can at your disposal, at 6.7 miles, then cross 356th Drive S.E. Gravel parking areas on both sides of the road, 0.5 mile from its junction with WA 202, allow for the shorter option. In 2.7 more miles, another bridge stretches high over Tokul Creek, with views to the west/southwest of Rattlesnake and Tiger Mountains. In another 0.8 mile, approach a tunnel under Tokul Road S.E. You'll take Tokul Road S.E. to what is now on your right, for the gentle, 0.8-mile descent to Snoqualmie Falls. But instead of barreling up alongside the tunnel to the road, go through it. After the tunnel, the trail narrows into a single-track. Keep your eyes peeled to the left, because within 0.1 mile of the tunnel, you'll see an unmarked trail to the left. Take the trail about 100 feet to paved S.E. 60th Street. Go left, doubling back to Tokul Road S.E. Ride left on Tokul Road S.E., over the tunnel, and down the gentle 0.8 mile descent to WA 202, Salish Lodge, and Snoqualmie Falls Park. Watch for traffic! On your return from the falls, Tokul Road S.E. branches off to your left at the 11 o'clock position to begin the journey.

RIDE 31 · Tiger Mountain State Forest: Preston Railroad Trail/Northwest Timber Trail Loop

AT A GLANCE

WA

Length/configuration: 11.3-mile loop, using gravel roads and 5.9 miles of single-track

Aerobic difficulty: Difficult; tough initial 3.1-mile gravel road climb; moderate climbing on the Northwest Timber Trail

Technical difficulty: Preston Railroad Trail is easy on graveled sections; some root drop-offs and narrow, advanced-level, technical sections on the rest; Northwest Timber Trail is much smoother than the ungraveled Preston Railroad Trail section

Scenery: Brief glimpses of Mt. Rainier and valleys below on the initial road climb; trails go under the cover of second-growth woods

Special comments: Challenging, fun loop, pretty close to town; popular among hikers and equestrians as well as mountain bikers

This 11.3-mile loop, suitable for strong intermediates and above, is by far the most entertaining ride available to mountain bikers in Tiger Mountain State Forest. This is partially because it's a great ride, but also because area trails are presently very limited to mountain biking.

The woods and trails are the highlight of the ride, as views are few. The route travels through second-growth clear-cuts, but also Douglas fir, western red cedar, western hemlock, red alder, and big-leaf maple.

At the time of research, the Preston Railroad Trail was gravelled for the first 0.6 mile, but the gravel mounds on the side of the trail along the rest of the way indicated more coverage to come. The gravel trail was fun to ride, but it eliminated the rooty, rocky technical challenges encountered on the rest of the trail. The Northwest Timber Trail was much smoother, and by itself can make for an out-and-back, virtually all single-track route.

General location: Tiger Summit is located about 30 miles east of Seattle, and 30 miles northeast of Tacoma.

Elevation change: From the base elevation of 1,377', the initial road section climbs 1,020' in 3.1 miles. After descending on the Preston Railroad Trail, the

Descending the
Northwest Timber Trail.

road descends to 1,460' elevation and then climbs quickly to the Northwest Timber Trail. The Northwest Timber Trail adds another 120' feet of climbing, for a total of about 1,520'.

Season: The trails are open from April 15 through October 15. Riding on closed trails will prevent expanded access in Tiger Mountain State Forest, and even threaten current access. Don't do it.

Services: Bring enough water; there is none on the ride. All services are available in Issaquah and Auburn.

Hazards: On a hot, sunny day, the climb is made harder by logged, sun-exposed areas. Some tricky roots and rocky dropoffs lie on the ungraveled portions of the Preston Trail. On trails this good, in an area so populated, you will encounter other users.

Rescue index: When the trails are open, people are out. One of the throng may offer assistance. Help is available in Issaquah.

Land status: Washington Department of Natural Resources, Tiger Mountain State Forest.

This, too, is part of the fat-tire experience.

Maps: DNR Tiger Mountain State Forest.

Finding the trail: From downtown Seattle, take I-90 east, past Issaquah, to WA 18 (Exit 25). Go right on WA 18, signed toward Auburn and Tacoma, and proceed 4.2 miles to Tiger Summit. Park in the pullout to the right. A newer parking area, with toilets, is up West Side Road 1000 (past the left gate) about 0.3 mile. WA 18 is approximately 28 miles west of Snoqualmie pass on I-90.

From Tacoma, take I-5 north to Exit 142A, and take WA 18 east (northeast) 23.6 miles to Tiger Summit. Turn left into the parking area.

Sources of additional information:

Washington Department of Natural Resources
South Puget Sound Region Office
950 Farman Street North
P.O. Box 68
Enumclaw, WA 98022-0068
(800) 527-3305 or (360) 825-1631 (direct)

Backcountry Bicycle Trails Club
P.O. Box 21288
Seattle, WA 98111-3288
(206) 283-2995 (activities hotline)
membership:
14241 N.E. Woodinville-Duvall Road #301
Woodinville, WA 98072-8595
http://www.dirtnw.com/bbtc

RIDE 31 • Preston R.R. Trail/ N.W. Timber Trail Loop
RIDE 32 • Iverson Railroad Trail
RIDE 33 • Poo Poo Point

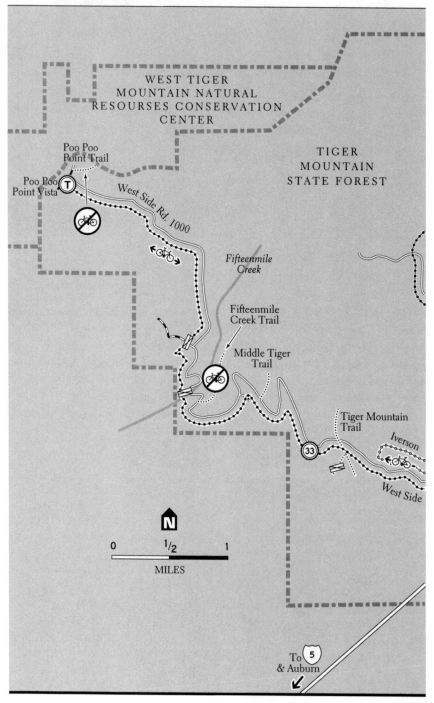

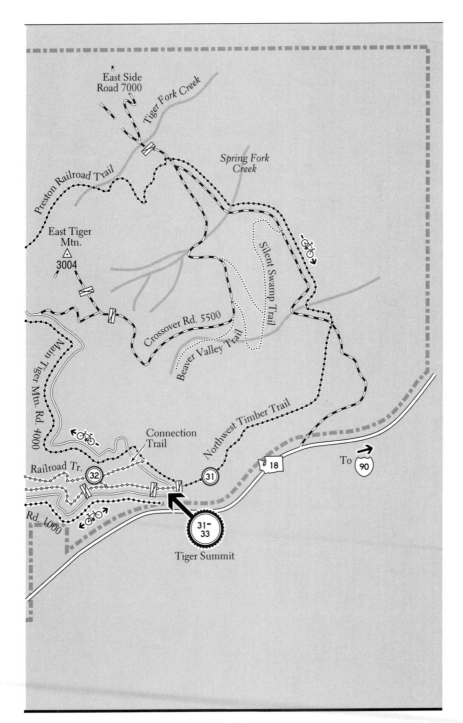

East Side
Road 7000

Tiger Fork Creek

Spring Fork
Creek

Preston Railroad Trail

East Tiger
Mtn.
△
3004

Silent Swamp Trail

Crossover Rd. 5500

Beaver Valley Trail

Main Tiger Mtn. Rd. 4000

Northwest Timber Trail

Connection
Trail

Railroad Tr.

(32)

(31)

18

To 90

Rd. 1000

31–
33

Tiger Summit

Notes on the trail: From the parking area, proceed through the right gate on Main Tiger Mountain Road 4000 and start climbing. At 0.2 mile on the right is the lower trailhead for the Northwest Timber Trail, on which you'll return. Shortly after that to the left is the Connector Trail, which leads to Iverson Railroad Trail (you can add this to the described route for a 15.3-mile total). Catch some views of Mt. Rainier as you wind around at 1.3 miles, and then below you in another 0.1 mile, before a 0.6 mile respite. Continue climbing on Main Tiger Mountain Road past a junction to the left, 0.3 mile after the climbing resumes. In another 0.4 mile come to a **T** intersection. To the right is Crossover Road 5500 and a 1-mile side trip to East Tiger Mountain Vista, the highest point in the forest at 3,004' elevation (check out the view or save it for when the trails are closed). To continue the loop, go left, staying on Main Tiger Mountain Road. In 0.4 mile you'll reach the gated Preston Railroad Trail on your right. The trail rolls for about a mile before it starts its descent. The 3.6-mile-long Preston Railroad Trail ends at Crossover Road. Go left, and very quickly take the right onto East Side Road 7000 where the road ahead is gated. Descend on East Side Road, past spur roads, until it bottoms out in 1.9 miles. Use your momentum for the 0.2-mile climb to the gated Northwest Timber Trail; it takes off to the right as you see Rattlesnake Mountain to the east and hear I-90 off to the north. The 2.3-mile Northwest Timber Trail ends on Main Tiger Mountain Road and completes the loop. Turn left and go 0.2 mile to the parking area and ride's end, or turn right, and go left onto the Connector Trail to add the Iverson Railroad Trail to your day's mileage.

RIDE 32 · Tiger Mountain State Forest: Iverson Railroad Trail

AT A GLANCE

 **WA**

Length/configuration: 4.3-mile gravel road and single-track figure eight, with a 1.1-mile lower loop and a 3.2-mile main loop; single-track totals 2.2 miles

Aerobic difficulty: Moderate to advanced; tough climbing on the technical single-track

Technical difficulty: Difficult rooty, rocky challenges; a steep, final single-track descent

Scenery: Vista along West Side Road at top elevation on the road climb; second-growth Douglas fir forest, clear-cuts

Special comments: Challenging, technical single-track; can be combined with the Preston Railroad Trail–Northwest Timber Trail loop for a 15.3-mile total

The lower loop of this 4.3-mile figure eight is mainly on gravel roads; the main event is the upper loop—the gravel West Side Road climb and descent, and the Iverson Railroad Trail, a single-track known to locals as Fat Hand.

The ride is not for beginners—not because of the short, relatively tough initial climb but much more for the technical, sometimes steep single-track. Even intermediates will be challenged on rocky, rooty sections of trail.

Don't let the low mileage of this ride fool you; the Iverson Railroad Trail ride is short in duration, but it's a fun, advanced-level outing on high quality trail. It can be combined with the Preston Railroad Trail–Northwest Timber Trail loop for a satisfying 15.3-mile day.

General location: Tiger Summit is located about 30 miles east of Seattle, and 30 miles northeast of Tacoma.

Elevation change: The parking area is at 1,377' elevation; climb about 250' before a gravel road descent brings you to the trail. Climb another 250' or so on the trail, for approximately 500' of elevation gain.

Season: Iverson Railroad Trail is open April 15 through October 15. Roads are open year-round.

Services: BYOW (bring your own water); there is no water along the route. All services are available in Issaquah (about 11 miles northwest of the parking area), and in Auburn (on the way from Tacoma).

Hazards: Some tricky roots, rocky drop-offs; a creek crossing 1.2 miles into the trail is best walked by all except the most technically advanced riders.

Rescue index: This is a popular riding area; you'll likely be among people who can assist you. The nearest help is down the hill in Issaquah.

Land status: Department of Natural Resources, Tiger Mountain State Forest.

Maps: DNR Tiger Mountain.

Finding the trail: From downtown Seattle, take I-90 East, past Issaquah, to WA 18 (Exit 25). Go right on WA 18 toward Auburn and Tacoma and proceed 4.2 miles to Tiger Summit (1,377 elevation). Park in the pullout to the right. To do just the upper loop, park in the newer parking area 0.3 mile up West Side Road 1000 (past the gate on the left).

WA 18 is approximately 28 miles west of Snoqualmie Pass on I-90.

From Tacoma, take I-5 north to Exit 142A, and take WA 18 east (northeast) for 23.6 miles to Tiger Summit. Turn left into the parking area.

Sources of additional information:

Washington Department of Natural Resources
South Puget Sound Region Office
950 Farman Street North
P.O. Box 68
Enumclaw, WA 98022-0068
(800) 527-3305 or (360) 825-1631 (direct)

Backcountry Bicycle Trails Club
P.O. Box 21288
Seattle, WA 98111-3288
(206) 283-2995 (activities hotline)
membership:
14241 N.E. Woodinville-Duvall Road #301
Woodinville, WA 98072-8595
http://www.dirtnw.com/bbtc

Notes on the trail: From the parking area, go past the right gate onto Main Tiger Mountain Road. Climb 0.3 mile, just past the Northwest Timber Trail junction to the right, and go left onto the Connector Trail. After a bridge you'll see the final descent on the Iverson Trail to the right. Stay straight, where the trail shortly ends in the parking lot off of West Side Road. Out of the parking lot, go right on West Side Road and climb 0.5 mile, where a view down to Maple Valley and up to Mt. Rainier opens up to the left as the road curves right. Descend from that point to a clear-cut in 0.6 mile and, as the road starts to climb in another 0.3 mile, come to the gated, well-marked Iverson Railroad Trail on the right. The trail starts with a tough, narrow climb back into the woods. At 0.5 mile the trail darts out of the trees to a recent clear-cut, but jumps back under the wooded canopy in 0.3 mile. Stay on the main trail past a couple of short spur trails. On the descent 1.3 miles into the trail, keep your eye out for a very technical, rocky creek crossing. More rooty, rocky challenges await as you descend to a **T** intersection after 1.9 miles on the trail. The short overlap portion of the figure eight starts as you go right, retracing your treads 0.1 mile to the upper parking area. This time, go left at the stop sign and descend on West Side Road to the lower parking area.

RIDE 33 · Tiger Mountain State Forest: Poo Poo Point

AT A GLANCE
———————

WA

Length/configuration: 15.0-mile (total mileage) gravel road out-and-back

Aerobic difficulty: Plenty of climbing in both directions, including some killer-steep sections in the final 2.5 miles to the point

Technical difficulty: None; we're talkin' gravel roads in good condition

Scenery: Second-growth forest with views into Maple Valley and Mt. Rainier; striking views of the Puget Sound Basin and beyond

Special comments: Good winter workout when the trails are closed; good summer outing for views and hang glider watching

---

This 15-mile intermediate-level gravel-road out-and-back travels through clear-cuts and pretty, second-growth woods. It features some moderate climbing and descending, more climbing and better descending, and a punishingly-steep climb to Poo Poo Point for a stunning view.

At Poo Poo Point, Lake Sammamish lies before you to the northwest, and the Puget Sound Basin and Olympic Mountains lie beyond as the view unfurls. Even on my cloudy winter research ride with limited visibility, the view was beautiful; on a clear day, it is majestic. Poo Poo Point is a popular hang-gliding and parasailing area, and in the summer, the airborne folks add to your viewing pleasure.

You'll want to rest and refuel at Poo Poo Point while taking in the view, because that fast 2.5-mile descent before the final 2-mile grunt to the top will soon be an uphill venture.

Some views to the southwest can help you take your mind off your legs as you approach the summit, but they are mere teasers to the Poo Poo view. Conversely, don't let the views to the southeast take your mind off the fast descent at the start of the return.

General location: Tiger Summit is located about 30 miles east of Seattle, and 30 miles northeast of Tacoma.

Elevation change: Elevation at the lower parking area is 1,380'; you'll be at 1,960' after the initial 250' climb to the first vista and final 1000' climb to Poo Poo Point. Total elevation gain is in excess of 2000'.

Season: The roads on Tiger Mountain are open year-round, with enough options to keep you interested and in shape over the winter. Good thing, because the trails are closed from October 15 through April 15.

Services: There is no water along the route. All services are available in Issaquah, about 11 miles northwest of the parking area, and in Auburn on the way from Tacoma.

Hazards: Control your descents, and be aware of vehicles on the road. Even though the roads are closed to the general public, DNR trucks or hang gliders and parasailers, who have a deal with the powers that be, may be on them. There have been cougar encounters in the forest, and bears are no strangers here, either, but autos are much more likely to be a nemesis. If you're screaming down uncontrolled on the right-hand curve at the bottom of the 2.5-mile descent on the way out, you'd better hope that the gate you can't see is open. Exercise caution, as well as your legs!

Rescue index: Hopefully, the mountain bikers you meet will be helpful, as most are, when you're in need. Help is available in Issaquah.

Land status: Washington Department of Natural Resources, Tiger Mountain State Forest.

Maps: DNR Tiger Mountain.

Finding the trail: From downtown Seattle, take I-90 East, past Issaquah, to WA 18 (Exit 25). Go right on WA 18, signed toward Auburn and Tacoma, and proceed 4.2 miles to Tiger Summit. Park in the pullout to the right. There is enough space for many cars here, and that space can be filled on weekends. If that area is full, another parking lot is 0.3 mile up the hill to the left, on West Side Road 1000.

WA 18 is approximately 28 miles west of Snoqualmie Pass on I-90.

From Tacoma, take I-5 north to Exit 142A, and take WA 18 east (northeast) for 23.6 miles to Tiger Summit. Turn left into the parking area.

Sources of additional information:

Washington Department of Natural Resources
South Puget Sound Region Office
950 Farman Street North
P.O. Box 68
Enumclaw, WA 98022-0068
(800) 527-3305 or (360) 825-1631 (direct)

Backcountry Bicycle Trails Club
P.O. Box 21288
Seattle, WA 98111-3288
(206) 283-2995 (activities hotline)
membership:
14241 N.E. Woodinville-Duvall Rd. #301
Woodinville, WA 98072-8595
http://www.dirtnw.com/bbtc

Notes on the trail: From the parking area, ride around the left gate onto West Side Road 1000 and start the initial 0.8-mile stair-step climb. Pass the new parking area, with toilets, in 0.3 mile. The final stair on this climb is the steepest; at the top, as the road curves to the right, ride to the lookout point on the left for some good views into Maple Valley and to the Mt. Rainier–dominated Cascades beyond. Start into a nice descent as the road curves right. Bottom out the descent in 0.8 mile in a research area of regenerating clear-cut. As you start a gradual climb, pass the Iverson Railroad Trail on your right. Pass Tiger Mountain Trail (no bikes allowed), and top out the climb at a quarry. After a few pedal strokes as the road levels out, start into a fast 2.5-mile descent. Glide past Middle Tiger Trail (no bikes allowed here, either) and stay on the main road as a road branches off to the left 0.6 mile beyond Middle Tiger Trail. In another 0.5 mile pass the Fifteenmile Creek Trailhead on your right. (Are bikes allowed? No.) As you keep zooming down, 0.2 mile beyond the trailhead, scrub off some speed on the blind right-hand curve. The gate will most likely be open, but the one time you're not paying attention, you know what'll happen. The descent ends just beyond the gate as you cross Fifteenmile Creek and start a steep climb. In 0.2 mile stay on West Side Road, as a trail and then Road 1500 shoot off to the left. Enjoy a short level area 1 mile into the climb, and grind up to another level spot in another mile. A road veers left and descends as you make your way up the final 0.2 mile on the main road. Straight ahead is the Poo Poo Point Trailhead (you guessed it, no bikes allowed); but up to the left, the picnic area provides a well-earned view.

If you read too many "no-bike" notations, that can change with your help. Contact the Backcountry Bicycle Trails Club to get involved.

SNOQUALMIE PASS TO CLE ELUM

Interstate 90 is the jump-off point for some excellent mountain biking as you head up and over Snoqualmie Pass and east of the Cascade crest, about an hour east of Seattle. The area described in this section starts at Snoqualmie Pass, roughly the western boundary of the Wenatchee National Forest. It represents the start of the transition zone from the wet west side to the dry east side of the Cascades. The eastern border of this section is in the Cle Elum area, which provides easy access to the Cle Elum–Ellensburg area in the following section.

The Ski Acres Mountain Bike and Hiking Center at Snoqualmie Pass has aggressively courted the mountain biking crowd, and has cut enough new trails that national and international mountain biking events have been lured here. The area is located within both the Mt. Baker–Snoqualmie and Wenatchee National Forests.

Within a short pedaling distance of Ski Acres, the easy John Wayne Pioneer Trail starts as a scenic outing—for the first three-quarters of a mile. Then it becomes a mysterious, dark ride, as bikers travel through the 2.3-mile Snoqualmie Tunnel, under Snoqualmie Pass. This rail-trail is the old Milwaukee Railroad corridor that became the 113-mile-long Iron Horse State Park. The park, and the John Wayne Pioneer Trail within it, start about 15 miles to the west of the tunnel near North Bend; the trail itself is targeted to eventually cross all the way over into Idaho via Spokane's Centennial Trail. You can sample another portion of this trail in Easton or South Cle Elum.

As you travel east of Snoqualmie Pass near Easton, Amabilis Mountain treats intermediate cyclists to outstanding views overlooking Kachess Lake. On the other side of the lake, the demanding, exhilarating Kachess Ridge Trail delights the most advanced riders.

About 15 minutes east of Easton is Roslyn. The sleepy little town, the quaint former home of television's "Northern Exposure," has a rich coal mining history. You can explore some of that history at the Roslyn Museum, and ride the same path the trains took as they carried coal from nearby Ronald to Cle Elum. As you drive out of Ronald and north of Cle Elum Lake, the beautiful Cooper River Trail provides a lush, forested alternative to some of the residential scenery on the Coal Mines Trail.

The two described sections of the John Wayne Pioneer Trail are in the linear Iron Horse State Park. For rides in the national forest, trailhead parking areas are subject to the new trail park pass fee system, so come prepared, though neither the Kachess Ridge Trail nor the Cooper River Trail ride descriptions recommend parking at the trailhead.

RIDE 34 · Iron Horse State Park: Snoqualmie Tunnel

AT A GLANCE

Length/configuration: 6.1-mile (total mileage) out-and-back on gravel rail-trail; can be extended in either direction

Aerobic difficulty: Darn near pancake-flat riding; you lose about 100' on the 3-mile trip to the west end of the tunnel

Technical difficulty: None, except the challenge that riding in the dark brings

Scenery: Alpine views on the way to the tunnel, darkness inside, Keechelus Lake nearby

Special comments: Even in the heat of summer, the tunnel is dark and chilly; lights and warm clothing are essential

Ever want to go on a night ride—during the day? The Snoqualmie Tunnel, on the old Milwaukee Railroad grade, affords that unique opportunity with a 2.3-mile tunnel *through*, not over, Snoqualmie Pass. The flat, smooth, gravel rail-trail is suitable for beginners, but provides an experience that even advanced-level riders won't find elsewhere. Advanced riders can also continue west of the tunnel for more than 15 miles each way.

Unfortunately, on my research journey, the tunnel was closed for repairs. On a previous trip, my wife and I made a day of the tunnel ride, a picnic, and a paddle on Keechelus Lake in our inflatable kayaks. On that journey through the tunnel, some wisenheimers thought it would be funny to close the gate to the tunnel and wrap the chains around it as if we were locked in. It *was* kind of funny, after the initial panic wore off and we figured out what they did; then we just unwrapped the chains, swung the tunnel doors back open and breathed a sigh of relief. Don't let the pranksters fool *you!*

For miles of decidedly non-flat riding nearby, tackle the roads and single-track at nearby Ski Acres Mountain Bike and Hiking Center, at the south end of the ski area off of I-90 about a mile and a half west of the trailhead (between exits 53 and 54). The area has hosted national- and international-level competition, both cross-country and downhill. Be like the downhillers and take the ski lifts up, or be like the cross-country riders and climb from the base.

General location: The ride begins just east of Snoqualmie Pass, about 55 miles east of Seattle, adjacent to the northwest side of Keechelus Lake.

RIDE 34 · Iron Horse State Park: Snoqualmie Tunnel

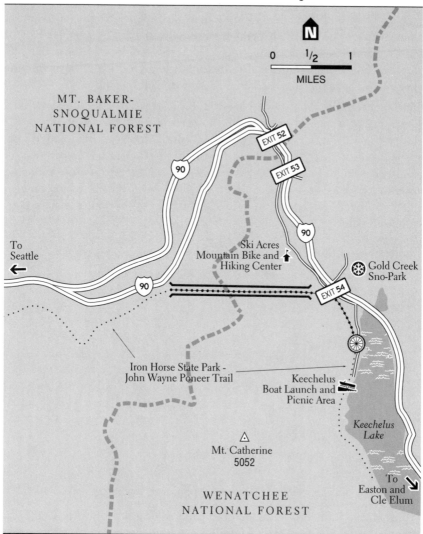

Elevation change: The ride starts at about 2,600' elevation on the east end of the tunnel and descends imperceptibly to 2,500' on the west end.

Season: The tunnel is open from May 1 through October 31, although you can ride in the other direction on the John Wayne Trail so long as conditions allow.

Services: There is no water at the trailhead or the picnic area. Most services are available at Snoqualmie Pass (Exit 52 off of I-90). The Ski Acres Mountain Bike and Hiking Center can help you out in a pinch with bike repairs and supplies.

Hazards: Don't be afraid of the dark!

Rescue index: Help is available at Snoqualmie Pass.

Land status: Iron Horse State Park.

Maps: You can easily do this ride without a map. But if you have any inkling of doing additional riding in this area, use Green Trails #207, Snoqualmie Pass, or the Cle Elum Ranger District map. The Ski Acres mountain bike operation produces a general map of area trails. They've done a good job of expanding the trail system; hopefully future editions of the map will keep up.

Finding the trail: From I-90 in either direction, take Exit 54, the Hyak/Gold Creek exit. Go south at the off-ramp to the stop sign, then turn left on the frontage road. (Turn right to get to Ski Acres Mountain Bike and Hiking Center.) Drive about 0.5 mile and turn right, just before the Department of Transportation Maintenance Division station. Travel for another 0.5 mile to the trailhead parking area on the right, or continue on to the picnic area in another 0.5 mile, to extend the ride and gain easy access to the lake for post-ride frolicking.

Sources of additional information:

Washington State Parks and Recreation Commission
P.O. Box 42650
Olympia, WA 98504-2650
(800) 233-0321

Rails to Trails Conservancy
1400 Sixteenth Street N.W.
Suite 300
Washington, D.C. 20036
(202) 797-5400

Ski Acres Mountain Bike & Hiking Center
P.O. Box 1068
Snoqualmie Pass, WA 98068
(206) 236-7277, ext. 3372
(Friday–Sunday and holidays, Memorial Day through Labor Day, 9 A.M.–6 P.M.)

Notes on the trail: From the trailhead parking area, the tunnel is about 0.75 mile to the right. Add an extra 0.5 mile (each way) if you start from the picnic area.

RIDE 35 · Amabilis Mountain

AT A GLANCE

WA

Length/configuration: 11.2-mile combination on gravel roads; a 5.2-mile loop with two out-and-backs, a 5.6-mile out-and-back (2.8 miles each way), and a 0.4-mile out-and-back (0.2 mile each way)

Aerobic difficulty: Moderately difficult to difficult; most of the climbing is moderately difficult

Technical difficulty: Easy to moderate; some rough and degraded sections of gravel road

Scenery: Clear-cuts and forested hillsides; views from Amabilis Mountain

Special comments: The return descent is exhilarating

This 11.2-mile ride is a combination of two out-and-back spurs and a loop. Of the climbing, 2 miles are easy, 2.5 miles are moderately difficult, and 1 mile is demanding. The route follows good gravel roads, with some exposed rocks and a loose, coarse tread in the steepest areas. There is a short stretch of dirt double-track in good condition. The second half of the ride is a long descent that starts out roughly: the road is washed out and rutted at the top, but it quickly improves.

Freeway noise and views of clear-cut forests are predominant as you climb. Your senses are rewarded with less assaulting stimuli as you near the summit of Amabilis Mountain. At the top, the view of Kachess Lake, with its mountain backdrop, is lovely. To the north you can see the rugged Rampart and Chikamin Ridges, which lie in the Alpine Lakes Wilderness Area. Mt. Rainier looms large on the horizon in the southwest.

General location: This ride begins near Cabin Creek Road, approximately 65 miles southeast of Seattle.

Elevation change: The ride starts at 2,520' and reaches a high point of 4,500' atop Amabilis Mountain. Ups and downs along the way add about 100' of climbing to the ride. Total elevation gain: 2,080'.

Season: Amabilis Mountain is usually free of snow from May through October. A good time to visit is in the late summer or early fall—the weather is drier and the roads are quieter.

Services: There is no water available on this ride. Water, gas, and limited groceries are available in Easton. All services can be found in Cle Elum.

RIDE 35 · Amabilis Mountain

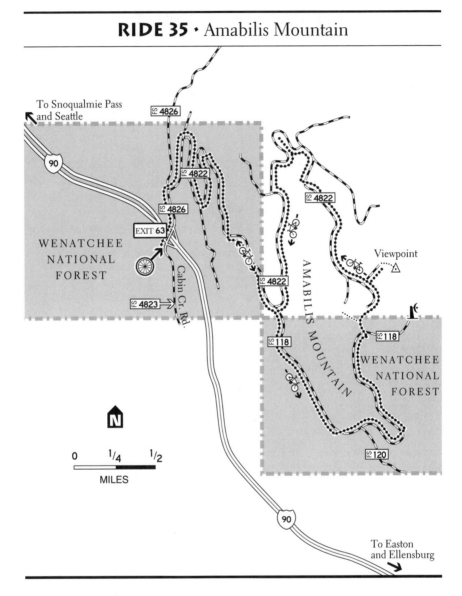

Hazards: Exercise caution while crossing the freeway overpass—keep an eye out for motorists exiting the highway. Expect some traffic on the gravel roads. The descent from the mountain can get very fast. Watch for areas of loose gravel as you descend.

Rescue index: Help is available in Easton (Exit 71), 8 miles southeast of the trailhead on I-90.

Land status: Public and private lands within the boundaries of the Wenatchee National Forest.

Kachess Lake from
Amabilis Mountain.

Maps: The district map of the Cle Elum Ranger District is a good guide to this
ride. USGS 7.5 minute quad: Stampede Pass.

Finding the trail: From Seattle, drive east on I-90 for 63 miles, to Exit 63/Cabin
Creek Road. From Yakima, follow I-82 north for 37 miles to I-90. Proceed northwest on I-90 for 56 miles to Exit 63/Cabin Creek Road. Exit the highway and follow the signs to the Sno-park parking area. This gravel lot lies adjacent to the
freeway on the southwest side.

Source of additional information:

Cle Elum Ranger District
803 W. 2nd Street
Cle Elum, WA 98922
(509) 674-4411

Notes on the trail: Head northeast from the parking area and cross over the
highway. Continue straight onto Forest Service Road 4826. Follow this road for
about 0.25 mile, to FS 4822. Turn right onto FS 4822 and stay on the main road
as side roads branch off. After 2.4 miles, turn right onto FS 118. The sign mark-

Rampart and Chikamin Ridges from Amabilis Mountain.

ing FS 118 is on the right, partially obscured by weeds. The pedaling on FS 118 is more demanding, and the road is rougher. This more demanding section lasts for about 1 mile. At the end of this tougher stretch, you will be pedaling next to a large clear-cut on your left. Proceed to the end of the clear-cut, where FS 118 veers to the right and reenters the woods. Look to your left here and find a double-track that heads west across the clear-cut. Turn left onto the double-track and follow it as it curves around in a more northerly direction. You will come to an intersection after just 0.1 mile. Go right (toward the east, roughly) and climb steeply on a double-track—the woods are on your right, the clear-cut is on your left. From the last intersection it is 0.2 mile to a small knoll and a maintained gravel road. This unsigned road is FS 4822. Follow this road as it swings to the left and goes downhill. Turn right at the first intersection (after 0.1 mile on FS 4822). Pursue this spur road for about 0.2 mile to its terminus at a gravel turnaround. Park your bike and walk up the trail to the right to visit a viewpoint. Return on the spur road to FS 4822. Turn right onto FS 4822 and begin a long descent. Side roads branch off left and right, but you should stay on the main road. After more than 5 miles of downhill coasting, you will arrive at a "Yield" sign at the intersection of FS 4822 and FS 4826. Bear left onto FS 4826 to return to your vehicle.

Bikers can also follow a 16-mile loop around the base of Amabilis Mountain. This loop and other rides in the region are described in a mountain bike pamphlet produced by the Cle Elum Ranger District.

RIDE 36 · Kachess Ridge Loop

AT A GLANCE

WA

Length/configuration: 18.6-mile loop including gravel roads and 6.7 miles of insane single-track

Aerobic difficulty: Near-flat warm-up followed by a strenuous 4.8 miles of road climbing; initial 0.5 mile of trail is a steep climb/hike

Technical difficulty: Roots, drop-offs, sketchy creek crossings, scree

Scenery: Kachess Lake from the near the shore and from high above; meadows; jagged peaks close by and in the distance

Special comments: A rugged trail with rugged scenery makes for an advanced, rugged ride

You'd never guess it from the first 5.9 miles of the loop, but the Kachess Ridge loop is a steep, challenging, advanced-level ride with a strenuous 5.3 miles of climbing (4.8 miles on the road and another 0.5 mile to start the trail) and an exhilarating 6.2-mile descent through meadows, across creeks and loose rocks, down some tight switchbacks and to beautiful views.

As you make the climb, you'll pass numerous spur roads. If you take the wrong road, it'll cost you some climbing but the roads will end, so just turn around and continue up the main road. The trail access is unmarked as well. If you're an advanced rider, don't let it deter you; it's really pretty straightforward, and definitely worth the effort.

By the time the trail is rideable you'll encounter dusty trail in some sections, and some wet trail in other sections as you parallel and cross Silver Creek. On our trip I noticed some unsightly tread marks through wet sections and skid marks through loose, steep sections. Please be a trail-conscious rider and walk your bike where appropriate.

General location: The trail starts approximately 70 miles east of Seattle, 2 miles north of Easton, and 15 miles west of Cle Elum.

Elevation change: The ride starts at 2,200' elevation, and tops out on the trail at close to 5,000 feet. The bulk of the climbing is done in about 5.3 miles.

Season: Check with the ranger district office. Depending on the snowpack, July may be too early, and mid-October may be too late. On our research trip in mid-August we hiked through some snow at the top.

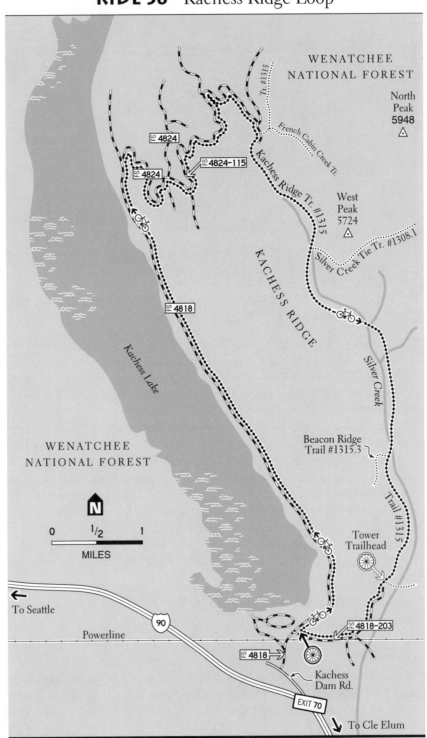

WENATCHEE
NATIONAL FOREST

North
Peak
5948

Tr. #1315

French Cabin Creek Tr.

FS 4824

FS 4824-115

FS 4824

Kachess Ridge Tr. #1315

West
Peak
5724

Silver Creek Tie Tr. #1308.1

KACHESS RIDGE

FS 4818

Silver Creek Tie Tr. #1308.1

Silver Creek

Kachess Lake

WENATCHEE
NATIONAL FOREST

Beacon Ridge
Trail #1315.3

Trail #1315

Tower
Trailhead

N

0   1/2   1
MILES

To Seattle

Powerline

90

FS 4818-203

FS 4818

Kachess
Dam Rd.

EXIT 70

To Cle Elum

An off-the-bike moment on Kachess Ridge Trail.

Services: At 4.3 miles along the route, there is a private (as in the Boeing Corporation) campground. There is water at the campground, but if you need water at this point in the ride you didn't prepare. Camping is available nearby, at Lake Easton State Park on the other side of I-90, and at Kachess Campground off of FS 49 on the other side of the lake. Services are available in Easton. The nearest bike stuff is about 15 miles east in Roslyn, at Central Sundries (see Cooper River Trail for directions) and at Ski Acres Mountain Bike and Hiking Center, about 17 miles west (see Snoqualmie Tunnel for directions).

Hazards: The steep little access onto the trail is pretty sketchy, and is best walked. Skidding down steep sections is destructive to the trail. Watch your line on the scree and steep switchbacks near the bottom.

Rescue index: Help is available in Easton.

Land status: Wenatchee National Forest, Cle Elum Ranger District.

Maps: Green Trails #208 Kachess Lake and the Cle Elum Ranger District map are both suitable guides for the loop, despite the confusing-looking road climb section. Neither map shows the short access that puts you on the trail.

Finding the trail: Traveling I-90 eastbound from Seattle, take Exit 70/Easton. Turn left at the off-ramp, then left at the **T** intersection onto Kachess Dam Road. In 0.5 mile, turn right onto gravel FS 4818, before the "limited winter maintenance" sign. In 0.4 mile, a sign informs you that you'll find the Kachess Ridge and Easton Ridge Trails in 1 mile to the right. Maybe so, but to avoid some rough road, park just ahead on the right by the power lines at the junction of FS 4818 and spur road 203. Easton is approximately 15 miles west of Cle Elum on I-90.

Source of additional information:

Cle Elum Ranger District
803 W. 2nd Street
Cle Elum, WA 98922
(509) 674-4411

Notes on the trail: Saddle up and continue on FS 4818 on the flat forest gravel road warm-up along Kachess Lake that belies the efforts to come. In the 5.9 miles along FS 4818, you'll gain a mere 300'. At that point, just after a road veers down to the left, FS 4824 takes off to the right, and the real climbing begins. From here to Kachess Ridge Trail, you'll climb about 2,400' in 4.8 miles. A mile into the climb the main gravel road switchbacks to the left, while a spur road continues straight. Take the left and keep climbing; you can catch some views of the peaks in back of you as you climb here. In another 0.4 mile, stay on the main road, switchbacking right, while a spur road goes straight. In yet another 0.4 mile, continue on the main road, switchbacking left while a spur road goes straight. Shortly after this turn pass a gate across the road. Stay on the main road, to the left, 0.8 mile after the gate, as a dirt road veers to the right. Then, 1.1 miles farther up, climb to the right at the junction where your other option veers a little to the left. Come to an intersection 0.8 mile farther up, where the road ahead of you climbs and winds around to the left, while the right turn descends just a touch and the road ends quickly. Go right, and immediately start looking left, where a road narrows into a trail within 30'. This is the access to the Kachess Ridge Trail.

Descend the short, steep, rocky trail carefully—walking is recommended—to the Kachess Ridge Trail at a **T** junction, and head right, where you'll climb and hike about to a saddle on the north side of the ridge. You'll enjoy nearby views of North Peak and West Peak, and the Stuart Range in the distance. From here you'll descend through woods and meadows as the trail roughly follows Silver Creek for much of its mileage. Continue on the trail as it passes the junction of Silver Creek Tie Trail #1308.1 at about 12.4 miles into the loop, shortly after the first creek crossing. (Frankly, I never even noticed the junction on our descent, but be aware that it's there.) After a creek crossing 3.9 miles from the top, the unmaintained Beacon Ridge Trail #1315.3 shoots off to the right at the 4 o'clock position and provides a short side trip but, like our group, you might want to just keep grooving on the trail and continue down. The trail loses altitude in a hurry toward the bottom and switchbacks its way down to the lower trailhead. Stay in control, and keep your eye out for a spur trail that goes up and to the right for views of Easton, Manastash Ridge, and Quartz Mountain. From the lower trailhead ride straight down the road, and go right at the 4-way intersection in 0.6 mile, following the power lines back to your vehicle.

RIDE 37 · Cooper River Trail

AT A GLANCE

Length/configuration: 10.8-mile (total mileage) out-and-back, including 7.0 miles of single-track; the described loop is 10.8 miles, including 1.9-mile paved and gravel road warm-up, 3.5 miles of single-track and mostly paved road return; can be extended by up to 8 miles via adjoining trails and/or roads

Aerobic difficulty: No extended climbs, but short, steep rollers

Technical difficulty: Trail surface alternates between smooth and rocky/rooty; both technical and physical conditions may force you off of the bike

Scenery: Old-growth forest, riverside views

Special comments: Do it as an out-and-back, or continue on to Pete Lake Trail #1323 for an approximate total of 19 miles

There is a wealth of riding in the Roslyn area, but much of it is on private land. The land owners, Plum Creek (a subsidiary of Burlington Northern Railroad) and Trendwest Resorts, aren't particularly averse to you riding on their land, but would rather not have specific routes published. Eric Mathes, the owner of Central Sundries in Roslyn (Ruth Anne's General Store in the old "Northern Exposure" television series), is a great source of information on the trails in the area, and has connections with both landowner groups.

The described route is a rolling 10.8-mile (total mileage), mostly single-track out-and-back on a clearly legal trail within the Wenatchee National Forest, near Roslyn. It travels along the Cooper River up to scenic Cooper Lake, utilizing a 1.9-mile paved road and gravel road warm-up and Cooper River Trail #1311. A mostly paved road descent allows for a loop return option. Although there are no extended climbs on the route, the steep rollers and technical trail combine to make this an intermediate-level ride.

Numerous accesses to the river provide scenic rest stops; the primitive camping area 2.5 miles up the trail and the turnaround point at Cooper Lake are real gems.

Even if you do the trail as an out-and-back (which comes out to a solid 7 miles of single-track), the initial 1.9-mile road portion provides a good warm-up

RIDE 37 · Cooper River Trail

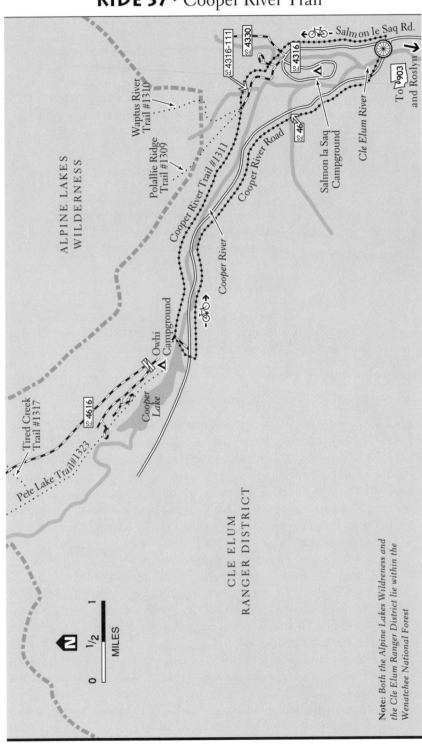

Cooper Lake.

and cool-down. The road return requires a few efforts; it's a smoother, though not as fun, alternative to the single-track return.

Note: At the end of the Cooper River Trail, you can make the short ride up road FS 4616 and turn left onto spur road 113 to access Pete Lake Trail #1323. If you use this route, pass the junction of Tired Creek Trail #1317—which enters the Alpine Lakes Wilderness—then turn right on Road Tie Trail #1323.1, before the Pete Lake Trail crosses the wilderness boundary, and loop back via FS 4616. The Pete Lake Trail was not ridden for research, but it's nearby, it's open to mountain bikes until the Road Tie Trail, and if you still have the legs and the wanderlust, then go for it!

General location: The trail is located about 16 miles northwest of Roslyn.

Elevation change: The route starts at about 2,200' elevation at the parking area. The trail starts at 2,400' and rolls to 2,800' at the upper trailhead, but the near-constant ups and downs on the trail bring total elevation gain to about 860'. There are some efforts required even on the road loop, and many more short, steep, climbs on the single-track return; on the trail, though, you can descend the stuff that took you off of your bike on the way out.

Season: The snow will clear in May, but the best conditions will be found from July through October. Check with the Ranger District Office for trail conditions.

Services: Water is available at Salmon la Saq Campground. The Last Resort, a gas station/restaurant/mini-mart, is located between Ronald and the ride start. The closest true bike shop is in Ellensburg, about 45 miles east of the trail, or on the other side of Snoqualmie Pass, far to the west, but check out Central Sundries in Roslyn. It's a combination general store, liquor store, and minibike shop (what more does a mountain biker need?). If you ask owner Eric Mathes really nicely, maybe he'll use his tools and expertise to make a last-minute repair for you. Camping is available at the Salmon la Saq Campground, Cle Elum River Campground, and Wish Poosh Campgrounds along Salmon la Saq Road. Services are available in Roslyn and in Cle Elum, 4 miles south of Roslyn on WA 903.

Hazards: Be careful when negotiating rock-strewn sections of the trail, both uphill and downhill. They demand good bike-handling skills, and can send you off of your bike if you lose concentration.

Rescue index: When on duty, the Salmon la Saq camp host can provide help. If no one is in the vacation cabins by the campground or by Cooper Lake, help is available in Ronald and Roslyn. You'll find a pay phone at the Last Resort.

Land status: Wenatchee National Forest, Cle Elum Ranger District.

Maps: Cle Elum Ranger District map or Green Trails #208 Kachess Lake.

Finding the trail: From Interstate 90, take Exit 80, the Roslyn/Salmon la Saq exit. Travel north 3 miles to the junction of WA 903. Turn left on WA 903; pass through Roslyn in about 1.5 miles and through Ronald in another 2 miles. From Ronald, WA 903 turns into Salmon la Saq Road in 2.9 miles and travels north along the east side of Cle Elum Lake. In 9.6 more miles, park on the left at the corner of Salmon la Saq Road and FS 46 (Cooper River Road), a total of 12.5 miles northwest of Ronald and 2.6 miles north of the Cle Elum River Campground.

Sources of additional information:

Eric Mathes
Central Sundries
101 Pennsylvania Avenue
Roslyn, WA 98941
(509) 649-2210

Cle Elum Ranger District
803 W. 2nd Street
Cle Elum, WA 98922
(509) 674-4411

Notes on the trail: From the parking area, continue north up Salmon La Saq Road. In 1.0 mile the road ends at the Salmon la Saq Campground. In another 0.2 mile, FS 4330 climbs to the right; stay lower to the left on FS 4316. As you pass over the bridge, take spur road 4316-111, which winds away from the cabins to your right. At 1.8 miles, pass spur road 113, which climbs to the right at the 1 o'clock position, as you continue on spur road 111. Pick up the trail in another 0.1 mile at the south end of the parking area and start riding upriver. Just after a glimpse of a beautiful pool at the start of the trail, come to a trail junction. To the right are Polallie Ridge Trail #1309 and Waptus River Trail #1310, which head into the Alpine Lakes Wilderness. Being the high-minded and respectful mountain biker you are, though, you will stay to the left, along the river, on the Cooper River Trail. After the junction, a short, steep, rocky, rooty section will force you off of your bike, but it is short-lived, and the trail quickly becomes smoother and rideable. The surface alternates between smooth sections and rough, technical sections as you climb and descend. At 2.5 miles on the trail (4.4 miles total), as the trail descends to the river and swings to the right, a primitive campsite to the left makes for a beautiful stopping point amid the old-growth Douglas fir and hemlock that rise above the river and its rocky banks. At 5.4 miles, a smooth tread brings you to FS 4616 and the end of the Cooper River Trail. Before the road descent, though, turn right on FS 4616 for about 100' and turn left on the trail access to the southeast end of Cooper Lake. It's a beautiful view of where the lake drains into the river, and makes for another good stopping point. Then turn around and ride the trail back, continue up to the Pete Lake Trail, or descend on FS 4616 for 0.4 mile to paved FS 46 (Cooper River Road). Turn left, and descend 4.8 miles back to the junction of Salmon la Saq Road and the end of the loop.

RIDE 38 · Coal Mines Trail

AT A GLANCE

Length/configuration: 10.4-mile out-and-back (round-trip) on gravel rail-trail and paved streets

Aerobic difficulty: If you can't tackle the 440' gain from Cle Elum to Ronald, you should be riding an exercycle

Technical difficulty: No technical challenges, but at the time of research, the trail was a little soft on the Cle Elum–Roslyn leg

Scenery: Mostly pastoral setting, some old mine buildings, and the town of Roslyn as the centerpiece

Special comments: Flat, touristy ride; a great way to tour the town of Roslyn

Originally built to carry coal from Ronald and Roslyn, the 4.75-mile Burlington Northern Rail Line was abandoned long ago. In 1987, the rails and ties were removed, and the jurisdictions of Roslyn, Cle Elum, and Kittitas County went about the process of turning the old line into a recreational trail. The trail is still evolving; as of publication date, the determination of whether to

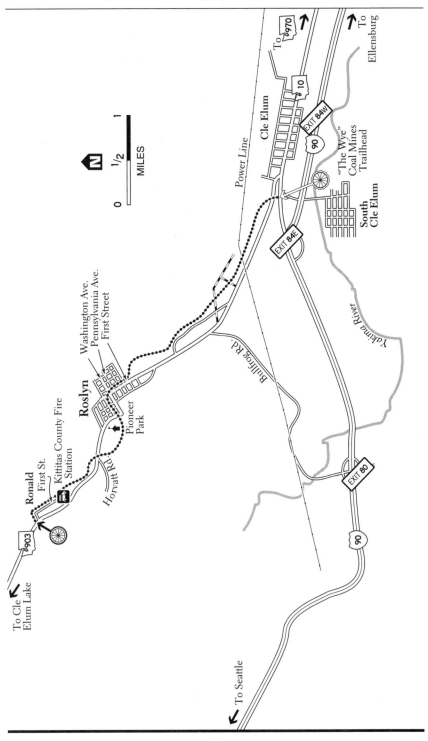

N

0   1/2   1
MILES

To 970

To 10

EXIT 84W

Cle Elum

90

"The Wye" Coal Mines Trailhead

EXIT 84E

South Cle Elum

To Ellensburg

Power Line

Yakima River

Bullfrog Rd.

Washington Ave.
Pennsylvania Ave.
First Street

Roslyn

Pioneer Park

Ronald

First St.

Kittitas County Fire Station

Horvatt Rd.

903

To Cle Elum Lake

EXIT 80

90

To Seattle

pave the trail was still undecided, signage was yet to be posted, and steps to minimize or avoid user conflict were yet to be implemented. But the main goals, of
using the right-of-way to route underground public utilities and using the trail
as a nonmotorized recreational route, were firmly established.

The centerpiece of the trail is the quaint town of Roslyn, which was the site
for filming the old "Northern Exposure" television series. The fictional town of
Cicely, Alaska, is kept alive with the very real Brick Tavern, Roslyn Cafe, and
Northwestern Improvement Company Store, from which the "Chris in the
Morning" radio show on KBHR ("K-BEAR") was broadcast. The James Dean
mural in back of the Roslyn Theater is also a notable attraction, while the Roslyn
Museum, located just west of the Roslyn Cafe, provides a wealth of information
on the area's mining history.

Along with other trail users, you might see deer, elk, skunk, or rabbits along
the trail. Bear and cougar have been spotted, too; look for animal tracks as you
ride.

General location: The trail starts in Ronald, passes through Roslyn, and ends
in Cle Elum, approximately 85 miles east of Seattle and 31 miles east of Snoqualmie Pass.

Elevation change: The trail starts at 2,360' in Ronald, and descends to 1,920'
at the Cle Elum Trailhead.

Season: Only the snow level dictates the riding season. The only exception to
the trail's nonmotorized restriction is the permission for snowmobile use when
snow coverage is adequate.

Services: Along the trail, water is available at Pioneer Park in Roslyn. Plans call
for rest rooms and water along the trail in both Roslyn and Cle Elum. Services
are available in Roslyn and Cle Elum. Limited bike supplies can be obtained at
Central Sundries (Ruth Anne's General Store in "Northern Exposure"), 101
Pennsylvania Avenue, Roslyn.

Hazards: The only real hazards along the route are the cars along WA 903 as
you cross it southeast of Ronald and in downtown Roslyn. Watch for other trail
users as well.

Rescue index: You're never really away from civilization on this ride. Help is
available in Cle Elum, Roslyn, and Ronald.

Land status: City of Cle Elum, City of Roslyn, Kittitas County.

Maps: No trail-specific map has yet been produced. The Cle Elum Ranger
District map is a good general guide for this journey.

Finding the trail: From I-90, take Exit 80, the Roslyn/Salmon la Saq exit.
Travel north 3 miles to the junction of WA 903. Turn left on WA 903; pass
through Roslyn in about 1.5 miles and through Ronald in another 2 miles. Turn
right just before Old #3 Family Dining and Cocktails in Ronald, and park to the
left, on the side of Old #3.

To start from the Cle Elum end, exit I-90 eastbound at Exit 84, Cle Elum.
Continue 0.6 mile from the exit toward town, to what's known locally as "The

Wye," (say "Y") at the junction of Stafford Avenue to the left, at the big flagpole. Parking is available by the flagpole. From the east, exit I-90 westbound at Exit 84, and head toward town. Travel west on First Street for about 12 blocks until you hit "The Wye."

Sources of additional information:

City of Roslyn
13 S. First Street
P.O. Box 451
Roslyn, WA 98941
(509) 649-3105

City of Cle Elum
119 W. First Street
Cle Elum, WA 98922
(509) 674-2262
(You will probably be referred to local resident Don Connor, who is chairman of the Coal Mines Trail Commission, a citizen advisory board)

Notes on the trail: In Ronald, from the parking area in front of Old #3, ride north, and as the street quickly winds to the right, it turns into First Street and parallels WA 903 back toward Roslyn (the trail roughly parallels WA 903 for its duration). In 0.2 mile come to Kittitas County Fire Station, on the corner of First Street and Atlantic Avenue. The trail—unsigned at the time of research— starts to the left of the fire station at the 11 o'clock position. In 1.0 mile, cross WA 903—Horvatt Road is to your right as you cross—and continue on the trail. At 1.8 miles the trail passes behind Pioneer Park in Roslyn. This portion of the trail ends at the park at Washington Avenue. To continue the trail, ride straight on Washington Avenue. When you cross North First Street (WA 903), you pass the back of the Northwestern Improvement Company Store, the big brick building on your right. The first right turn after the store is residential; the second right, at the 1 o'clock position, leads to the continuation of the trail. If you miss it, just turn right on "A" Street and it'll connect in a couple hundred yards. Or, better yet, take a few minutes to ride around Roslyn, and then pick up the trail at Pennsylvania and "B" streets, one block east of The Brick Tavern. As you continue on the trail, you'll cross a road in 1.5 miles, and about 0.3 mile further, you'll pass some old mine buildings, abandoned now, but the hub of a settlement called "Number Five" in their heyday. By the time you reach the Cle Elum Trailhead at "The Wye," you'll have gone 5.2 miles. From here you can turn back, or continue for about a mile to reach the South Cle Elum Trailhead of the John Wayne Trail.

RIDE 39 · Iron Horse State Park: John Wayne Pioneer Trail, South Cle Elum to Easton

AT A GLANCE

Length/configuration: 23-mile (total mileage) out-and-back on gravel rail-trail

Aerobic difficulty: Near-level trail makes constant socializing possible

Technical difficulty: Lack of technical difficulty also makes constant socializing possible

Scenery: Yakima River, pastureland, wetlands, pine transitional forest

Special comments: Excellent for beginners or as an aerobic workout; can also tie in with the Coal Mines Trail in Cle Elum

This ride, like the Snoqualmie Tunnel ride, is a sampling of the John Wayne Pioneer Trail in Iron Horse State Park, the state's first "linear park," on the old Milwaukee Railroad right-of-way. The park begins at Cedar Falls, about 6 miles southeast of North Bend, travels through Snoqualmie Pass via the 2.3-mile Snoqualmie Tunnel, and stretches east to the Columbia River. Organizers envision the John Wayne Pioneer Trail stretching far beyond the bounds of Iron Horse State Park all the way to Idaho.

This 11.5-mile (each way) section of the trail travels by some residences, rural lowlands with mountainous backdrops, pine transitional forest, and makes two passes over the Yakima River and feeder creek crossovers as well. Wildlife viewing can be bountiful, too; on our journey we passed by a small snake on the trail and an eight-point buck just 20 feet away.

The trail is well-suited to the beginner with its nearly flat, nontechnical nature, good scenery, and the opportunity to socialize and learn basic bike handling skills without the burden of auto traffic. If you're a beginner who can do this mileage on a paved road, you can do this ride. The trail is well suited to the advanced rider as well, because it can be extended to a much longer outing (from the South Cle Elum Trailhead another 16 miles east to the Thorp Trailhead) or a fast, aerobic workout. Ambitious riders can also connect with the Coal Mines Trail at "the Wye" in Cle Elum.

At the turnaround point in Easton, picnic tables, water, and toilet facilities beckon you to enjoy a ride half-done, with a slight descent on the return trip. As

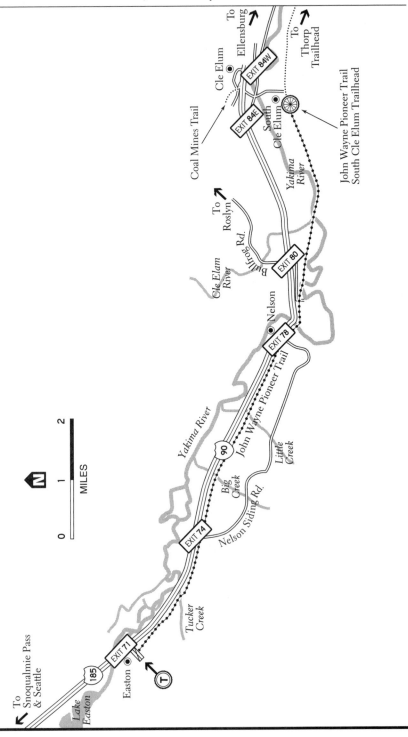

an out-and-back ride, though, you have the option to cut the John Wayne Trail short at any time—but that would make it the John Wayne Bobbit Trail! (Sorry, I couldn't resist. . . .)

General location: This section of the John Wayne Pioneer Trail extends from South Cle Elum (about 24 miles west of Ellensburg) to Easton (approximately 70 miles east of Seattle).

Elevation change: At the South Cle Elum Trailhead, elevation is 1,980'. The trail climbs ever-so-gently to 2,150' at the Easton Trailhead.

Season: The trail is open year-round, but in winter it sees skiing and snowshoeing. Check with the Lake Easton State Park office to make sure the trail is rideable in late fall and early spring.

Services: Water is available at the Easton Trailhead. Services are available in Cle Elum and Easton. You can camp at Lake Easton State Park, which borders both the Easton Reservoir and the Yakima River, 1 mile west of the town of Easton.

Hazards: Besides road crossings and other trail users, the only thing to watch for is the scenery and the wildlife. Be prepared for summer heat, too; the trail is generally sun-exposed.

Rescue index: Help can be secured in Easton, South Cle Elum, and Cle Elum.

Land status: Iron Horse State Park.

Maps: Use the Cle Elum Ranger District map or Green Trails #240 Easton, and #241 Cle Elum. The Washington State Parks and Recreation Commission produces the "Washington State Parks Cross-State Trail System" brochure. It is very basic as a directional aid but contains some good information on Iron Horse State Park, the Centennial Trail (Spokane), and the Pasco-Fish Lake Trail, the envisioned trail system linking western Washington to Idaho.

Finding the trail: Traveling eastbound on I-90, take Exit 84, Cle Elum. Travel 0.6 mile to "The Wye," marked by the big flagpole on your left (which provides parking for the Coal Mines Trail), and turn right toward South Cle Elum. Travel 0.8 mile, under I-90 and over the Yakima River—the road turns into Fourth Street in South Cle Elum—to Madison Avenue, marked on the left by the Christian Missionary Alliance Church. Turn right on Madison Avenue. In 0.2 mile, turn left on Sixth Street, and make a quick right on Milwaukee Avenue. Just after a road veers to the right at the 1 o'clock position, turn left into the Iron Horse State Park trailhead parking area, where toilets are provided.

From the east, drive west on I-90 and make use of Exit 84, 25 miles west of Ellensburg. Travel north off the exit and come to First Street West. Turn left, and travel about 12 blocks to "The Wye." Turn left toward South Cle Elum and follow the directions as above.

Sources of additional information:

Lake Easton State Park (1 mile west of Easton off of I-90)
P.O. Box 26
Easton, WA 98925
(509) 656-2586

Washington State Parks and Recreation Commission
P.O. Box 42650
Olympia, WA 98504-2650
(800) 233-0321

Rails to Trails Conservancy
1400 Sixteenth Street N.W.
Suite 300
Washington, D.C. 20036
(202) 797-5400

Notes on the trail: Straddle your saddle and head west, past an old brick sub-station that you can envision as busy and thriving in the days that the steel wheels of the railroad ruled the day. Pass a few gates and roads along the way, with the continuations of the trail straight ahead. The trail ends at the picnic area on the left at the Easton Trailhead. There is no immediate trail access to the west from the Easton Trailhead.

CLE ELUM TO ELLENSBURG

The Taneum area lies in the Cle Elum District of the Wenatchee National Forest, south of Interstate 90. It's accessible by paved roads traveling about 10 miles east of Cle Elum and then back, south of South Cle Elum Ridge. The described area in this section stretches from the Taneum east to Ellensburg, from the Cascades into the Kittitas Valley.

The Taneum and Manastash Creek drainages start in a series of ridges that reach up to 6,000 feet elevation. They wind their way east to the Yakima River near Ellensburg, through canyons cut out of Columbia River basalts from lava flows 13 million to 16 million years ago. The area is a classic example of the drier east side of the Cascades, with the dominant Douglas fir starting to give way to western larch, lodgepole, white and ponderosa pines, grand fir, aspen, and spruce. As you travel further east to Ellensburg, vegetation becomes sparse on the nearly bald hillsides of Manastash Ridge that bake in the hot summer sun.

The trails in the Taneum are favorites of riders—including equestrians and motorcyclists—from the west to the Puget Sound area and from the east to Ellensburg and Yakima. Summer weekends can get crowded; you'll encounter far fewer trail users if you can make it out during the week.

Ellensburg, in the middle of the Kittitas Valley, is an old west town that retains some of its heritage with the famous Ellensburg Rodeo over Labor Day weekend. The town was situated to become the capital of the new state of Washington in 1889 when a fire gutted its new commerical center. Ellensburg, of course, lost out in its state capitol bid, but the town rebuilt quickly; Central Washington University was established in 1891. Today, Ellensburg is as much a college town as it is a center for central Washington's agriculture and mining industries.

The mountain bike crowd at Central Washington University has easy access to the Taneum, and "The Book," located just south of town, is right in their backyard. "The Book" is a popular local biking and hiking trail that allows riders to sign a register at the top while enjoying views over the Kittitas Valley, the Cascades, and Central Washington, and treats them to a fast single-track descent afterward.

Trails in the Taneum area are in the Cle Elum District of the Wenatchee National Forest, which is participating in the trail park pass fee system. Pick one up at the Cle Elum Ranger Station in Cle Elum on your way out from the west, and from the east, pick one up at the Ellensburg Chamber of Commerce, 436 N. Sprague Street (behind Safeway), Ellensburg. You can reach the chamber office at (509) 925-2002.

RIDE 40 · North Fork Taneum Creek Loop

AT A GLANCE
_____

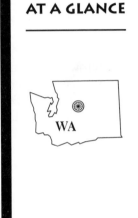

WA

Length/configuration: 21.4-mile loop, including gravel roads, 2.6 miles of double-track, and 11.7 miles of single-track

Aerobic difficulty: A 1,500' grinder (with a few descents) up to Taneum Ridge, some low-ring climbing on the Fishhook Flat Trail, and roller-coaster climbs on the North Fork Taneum Trail

Technical difficulty: A whole lotta water; some crossings can be tricky; some rocky, rooty trail

Scenery: Old-growth and second-growth forest, meadows, and water, water, water

Special comments: You're gonna get wet!

Everyone likes a nice wet one every now and then. The North Fork Taneum Creek Loop provides just that, with roughly 13 crossings of the North Fork Taneum Creek and its feeders along the described section of the trail. Some were hub-high at the time of research in mid-August. I rode some, I sloshed through others on foot. What will *you* do?

Both trails on the loop are dusty and rough in places, but are generally hard-packed and in good condition.

The ride highlights North Fork Taneum Trail #1377; the climbing and descending in the wooded valley, through and around the creek, is sure to keep you soggy and smiling. It's not the only highlight, though. The direct route would be to just take Forest Service Road 3300 for 10.9 miles to the North Fork Taneum Trail, and then take the trail back. But the enjoyment is not in the destination, Grasshopper; it is in the journey. . . .

A variation from the direct route puts you on the Fishhook Flat Trail, which cuts off of the road and then rejoins it after some easy bounding through woods and meadows, some tough climbing, and some steep descending. (To cut the ride short by about 7 miles, you can descend the Fishhook Flat Trail to its terminus at the North Fork Taneum Trail and turn right to complete the loop.) The route also bypasses the main road near the start, on 2.6 miles of wooded double-track—with steep grades—that avoids 3.4 miles of potential vehicle traffic on FS 3300.

Fishhook Flat.

General location: The start of the loop, at the Taneum Junction Camp, is approximately 24 miles northwest of Ellensburg. Taneum Junction is about 23 miles southeast of Cle Elum on the road. As the crow flies it's only about 6 miles from Cle Elum over South Cle Elum Ridge, but then, you're not a crow.

Elevation change: Taneum Junction is at 2,880'. You'll be at 4,230' as you turn onto the Fishhook Flat Trail, and 4,080' at the North Fork Taneum Creek Trail. Total elevation gain is about 1,850'.

Season: You'll find the best riding conditions from July through October. Consider this route a good choice in the heat of the summer.

Services: Water is available at Taneum Campground, 4.1 miles east of Taneum Junction. You can camp at Taneum Junction, and at campgrounds along FS 33. Services can be obtained in Cle Elum to the west and Ellensburg to the east. For bike stuff, check out Central Sundries in Roslyn (see Cooper River Trail for directions), about 30 miles west. In Ellensburg, about 30 miles east, try the Recycle Bike Shop. It has what you need, and you'll swear it's 1971 when you walk inside.

Hazards: This area is popular with a variety of users, so watch for vehicles on the road and hikers, motorcyclists, and equestrians on the trails. Watch your line on the creek crossings, lest you take an unplanned swim.

Rescue index: Campers in campgrounds along FS 33 may be able to help you out. Residents along Thorp Cemetery Road may be of assistance. The nearest pay phones are in Thorp, off of I-90 to the east, and in Cle Elum to the west.

RIDE 40 • North Fork Taneum Creek Loop
RIDE 41 • Taneum Ridge Loop
RIDE 42 • Lookout Mountain Loop

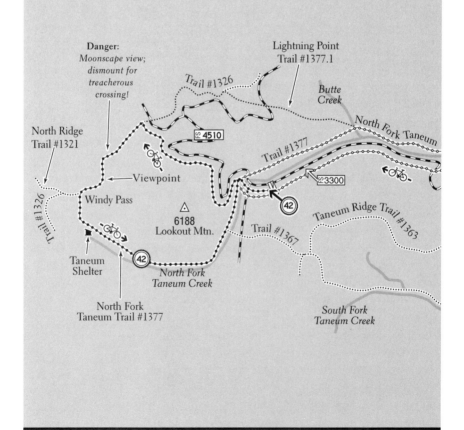

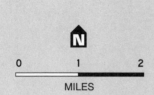

0   1   2

MILES

WENATCHEE
NATIONAL FOREST

Danger:
*Moonscape view;
dismount for
treacherous
crossing!*

Lightning Point
Trail #1377.1

Trail #1326

*Butte
Creek*

North Ridge
Trail #1321

North Fork Taneum

FR 4510

Trail #1377

Viewpoint

FR 3300

Trail #1326

Windy Pass

6188
Lookout Mtn.

42

Taneum Ridge Trail #1363

Trail #1367

Taneum
Shelter

42

*North Fork
Taneum Creek*

North Fork
Taneum Trail #1377

*South Fork
Taneum Creek*

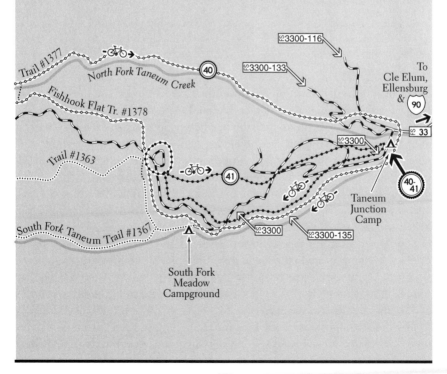

WENATCHEE
NATIONAL FOREST

Trail #1377

North Fork Taneum Creek

40

FS 3300-116

FS 3300-133

To
Cle Elum,
Ellensburg
& 90

Fishhook Flat Tr. #1378

Trail #1363

41

FS 3300

FS 33

Taneum
Junction
Camp

40-
41

Trail #1363

South Fork Taneum Trail #1367

FS 3300

FS 3300-135

South Fork
Meadow
Campground

Land status: Wenatchee National Forest, Cle Elum Ranger District. The land actually has a checkerboard ownership pattern, with about one-third of the area owned by Plum Creek (the logging subsidiary of the Burlington Northern Railroad). It's OK to ride on the trails but don't trailblaze off the beaten path.

Maps: Green Trails #240 Easton and #241 Cle Elum are good choices, as is the Cle Elum Ranger District map. The 1995 revision of Green Trails #241 does not show spur road 116 at the end of the route, as does the district map, but both are worthy guides.

Finding the trail: From Cle Elum, travel 8 miles east on I-90 and take Exit 93/Elk Heights Road. Go left, cross over the interstate, and follow the road to the right. At the stop sign at a **T** intersection turn right toward Thorp, on Taneum Road. In 3.5 miles come to a stop sign at a **T** intersection. Turn right, back over I-90, and again turn right at the stop sign, over the cattle guard, continuing on West Taneum Road. Travel 10.1 miles on paved West Taneum Road (which turns into FS 33 in 2 miles) until the dirt junction of FS 3300 on the left and FS 3300-133 straight ahead. Turn left on FS 3300, cross the bridge over the North Fork Taneum Creek, and park to the left at Taneum Junction Camp.

From Ellensburg, travel 8 miles west on I-90 to Exit 101/Thorp. Turn left (south) on South Thorp Highway and travel 0.9 mile to Thorp Cemetery Road. Turn right (west) on Thorp Cemetery Road, paralleling I-90. Thorp Cemetery Road turns into West Taneum Road in 4.6 miles and into FS 33 in 6.6 miles. From here, proceed as above.

Sources of additional information:

Cle Elum Ranger District
803 W. 2nd Street
Cle Elum, WA 98922
(509) 674-4411

Recycle Bicycle Shop
307 N. Main Street
Ellensburg, WA 98926-3311
(509) 925-3326

Notes on the trail: Warm up on gravel road FS 3300, past the lower Taneum Ridge Trailhead. In 0.4 mile, descend to the left on double-track FS 3300-135. In another 0.4 mile, continue straight, paralleling South Fork Taneum Creek, as a road veers down to the left. Pass an old log cabin as you start a steep climb. Roll along FS 3300-135 until a steep climb brings you back up to FS 3300 at 3.0 miles. Stay on FS 3300 as it climbs over Taneum Ridge and then past the Taneum Ridge Trail #1363 in 1.6 more miles. Pedal on another 0.2 mile, just after a road to the right, to Fishhook Flat Trail #1378. Turn right onto the trail and descend to a meadow (Fishhook Flat), and then make a 0.4-mile, 240' climb. As you descend this hill, after about 2.7 miles on the trail, look for an access trail that goes up to the left as the Fishhook Flat Trail makes a right-hand switchback with a wide arc. Scamper up the 0.1 mile trail back to FS 3300, and turn right to descend on FS 3300. (If you desire, you can cut the ride short by continuing the descent on the Fishhook Flat Trail the short distance farther to its junction with the North Fork Taneum Trail.) Stay on FS 3300, past the spurs, for 3.8 miles to a locked gate. While you're here look down to the right, where the clear-cut provides a view of the creek and the trail you'll be on shortly. Ride around the gate, make the 0.1 mile descent to the junction, and turn right, riding over the creek.

The trail starts to the right, just a couple hundred feet uphill and beyond the creek. (To the left is the continuation of the trail, and the end of the Lookout Mountain Loop. You can combine these two rides for a 31.6-mile outing.) The trail starts in the clear-cut, but gets back into the trees in 0.7 mile. In another 0.5 mile, make your first splash across the creek. Continue past an access trail to the right (to FS 3300) in another 0.1 mile; past the junction of Lightning Point Trail #1377.1 to the left 0.3 mile beyond that; through another dusty clear-cut; and past a pretty meadow that leads to the lower end of the Fishhook Flat Trail. In another 0.9 mile crank those wet pedals across a footbridge, where a rough, rooty, rocky, rideable section shortly gives way to smoother trail. The trail crosses spur road 133, 4.4 miles after the footbridge, and finally dumps out onto spur road 116 in another 0.8 mile. Hammer down to the right on spur road 116 for 0.6 mile, and, as the road curves left, a trail takes off to the right at the 5 o'clock position. This will drop you back to Taneum Junction and ride's end; if you're really getting into the descent and don't want to make the sharp turn, just keep going. You'll end the descent on FS 33, a mere 0.3 mile east of Taneum Junction.

RIDE 41 · Taneum Ridge Loop

AT A GLANCE

WA

Length/configuration: 9-mile loop, with 3.8 miles of single-track, 2.6 miles of double-track, and 2.6 miles of gravel road

Aerobic difficulty: About 1,400' of climbing in 5.2 miles to the trail; another 240' of climbing as you roll your way back down

Technical difficulty: Stutter bumps on the trail provide an upper-body workout as you descend

Scenery: Glacier Peak, the Stuart Range, and other views to the north, courtesy of a clear-cut at the top

Special comments: Fast, fun descending; tough climbing as you follow the ridge down

The Taneum Ridge loop provides a nice contrast to the nearby North Fork Taneum Creek loop. It starts out with the same double-track and road climb, but it's a shorter ride and provides some distant Cascades views that the North Fork loop lacks. It's a more vertical single-track, too; you'll find sharper climbs and faster descents on the trail. The final descent is a screamer!

You'll encounter some dust, stutter bumps and cupped sections of trail as you ride through forest and clear-cuts. Strong legs are necessary to get you up to the trail; good bike handling skills are required to get you back down.

This area can provide days of camping and riding, with many, many trails to explore; bring maps and an adventurous spirit.

General location: Taneum Junction, the start/finish of the loop, is approximately 24 miles northwest of Ellensburg and almost the same distance southeast of Cle Elum via paved roads.

Elevation change: Start at 2,880' elevation from Taneum Junction and climb to about 4,250' at the Taneum Ridge Trail. Additional climbing brings total elevation gain to about 1,620'.

Season: You should encounter good riding conditions from midspring through fall.

Services: Water is available at Taneum Campground, 4.1 miles east of Taneum Junction. You can camp at Taneum Junction, South Fork Meadow Campground, and at campgrounds along FS 33. Services can be obtained in Cle Elum and Ellensburg. Recycle Bike Shop is about 30 miles away in Ellensburg, in the east. Toward the west, Central Sundries is about 30 miles away in Roslyn (see Cooper River Trail for directions).

Hazards: You can get up some serious speed and have some serious fun on some sections of the trail, but let's keep our legal department happy here: ride in control. On weekends, especially, expect to encounter motorcyclists, equestrians, and/or hikers on the trail, and vehicle traffic on the road.

Rescue index: Campers along FS 33 and residents along Thorp Cemetery Road may be of assistance. The nearest pay phones are in Thorp, off of I-90 to the east, and in Cle Elum to the west.

Land status: Wenatchee National Forest, Cle Elum Ranger District.

Maps: Green Trails #241 Cle Elum contains all but the very western portion of the route. If you're here for a few days of riding, spring for that one and #240 Easton. An all-encompassing option is the Cle Elum Ranger District map.

Finding the trail: Follow the directions for the North Fork Taneum Creek loop. To save you some page flipping, here it is again:

From Cle Elum, travel 8 miles east on I-90 and take Exit 93/Elk Heights Road. Go left, cross over the interstate, and follow the road to the right. In 0.3 mile, at the stop sign at a **T** intersection, turn right toward Thorp, paralleling I-90. In 3.5 miles come to a stop sign at a **T** intersection. Turn right, back over I-90, and again turn right at the stop sign, over the cattle guard, continuing on West Taneum Road. Travel 10.1 miles on paved West Taneum Road (which turns into FS 33 in 2 miles) until the dirt junction of FS 3300 on the left and FS 3300-133 straight ahead. Turn left on FS 3300, cross the bridge over the North Fork Taneum Creek, and park to the left at Taneum Junction.

Taneum Ridge Trail.

From Ellensburg, travel 8 miles west on I-90 to Exit 101/Thorp. Turn left (south) on South Thorp Highway and travel 0.9 mile to Thorp Cemetery Road. Turn right (west) on Thorp Cemetery Road, paralleling I-90. Thorp Cemetery Road turns into West Taneum Road in 4.6 miles and into FS 33 in 6.6 miles.

Sources of additional information:

Cle Elum Ranger District
803 W. 2nd Street
Cle Elum, WA 98922
(509) 674-4411

Recycle Bicycle Shop
307 N. Main Street
Ellensburg, WA 98926-3311
(509) 925-3326

Notes on the trail: From the parking area at Taneum Junction, start up FS 3300, past the lower trailhead. In 0.4 mile, descend to the left on double-track FS 3300-135. In another 0.4 mile, continue straight as a road veers down to the left. Pass an old log cabin at 1.6 miles as you start a steep climb. Roll along on FS 3300-135 until a steep climb brings you back up to FS 3300 at 3.0 miles. (If you stayed on FS 3300, you'd have come to this junction in 3.8 miles.) Stay on FS 3300 as you pass the South Fork Meadow Campground and keep climbing. After 1.6 miles on FS 3300, come to Taneum Ridge Trail #1363. The trail continues left, quickly intersecting Fishhook Flat Trail #1378, and intersecting South Fork Taneum Trail #1367 in about 4.5 miles; but for the described route, turn right onto the wide trail. In about 150' it splits; turn left, where it becomes a logging road. In 0.3 mile come to a **Y** intersection. The left fork descends; you, knowing better, will veer right. At this point, you've done the lion's share of the climbing and you've earned your break, so take it here. The clear-cut affords a good look northward, at Mt. Stuart, Glacier Peak, and other inspiring Cascade peaks. Pedaling onward, follow the logging road for another 0.2 mile, and the trail will shoot off to the right. In another 0.1 mile, the trail splits; you can descend steeply straight ahead, or veer right, where the trail will switchback and rejoin quickly. Descend 0.1 mile from the split to a road crossing at a saddle, where you can take a final peek at the peaks to the north. From here, climb for 0.2 mile until the trail narrows out, enters the woods, and descends again—and then again. On a descent 2.1 miles into the trail, cross the junction with FS 3300 to the right, another road to the left, and yet another road to the left of that. Just keep going straight, though, and you'll pick up the trail. You'll again whiz by that lower road on the fast, final descent, and after 9.0 total miles, you'll be back at Taneum Junction, much happier for the experience.

RIDE 42 · Lookout Mountain Loop

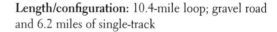

AT A GLANCE

WA

Length/configuration: 10.4-mile loop; gravel road and 6.2 miles of single-track

Aerobic difficulty: A middle- to low-ring 4.1-mile 1,180' gravel road climb; the real hard stuff is on the first 0.5 mile of single-track

Technical difficulty: A rideable 10' section near the top, but the penalty for not clearing it may be death; sheer drops and tight switchbacks on the descent to Windy Pass; rooty, rocky lower trail

Scenery: Moonscape-like scene as you climb the ridge; a near 360-degree view at the top

Special comments: Scenic and downhill thrills; you can combine this ride and North Fork Taneum Creek #1377 for a 31.6-mile outing

A ride that travels a gravel road through a vast clear-cut wouldn't be too enticing in and of itself, and that's how this ride starts. But once on the single-track, a moonscape view, nearly 360 degrees of beautiful scenery, and a fast, thrilling, wooded descent make this 10.4-mile outing a "must-ride" loop.

The ride is rated for strong intermediates, more for the technical climbing and descending on the trail than for the grade of the road climb.

Tacoma resident, Single-Track Mind Cycling Club founder, and Washington trail guru Mike Curley served as the guide for this outing, which starts with a pleasant, low- to middle-ring, 4.1-mile gravel road climb. The clear-cut scenery on the road climb is hardly tonic for the eyes, but it improves dramatically once on the trail.

The steepest of the climbing comes when tires meet trail and you get into the trees. The initial trail section is soft, steep, and cupped, and will probably entail some dismounting. Once you ride (or hike) the initial 0.4 mile on the trail, you'll roll along the ridge, where rock outcroppings beckon you to stop and climb around; you can catch some good views from here, but the best is yet to come. After a short climb along the ridge, a beautiful moonscape holds both close-up and distant visual wonder. A dismount here is strongly recommended, because the ten-foot section that follows can be treacherous; bad things sometimes happen even to good riders, and bad, bad things—like death—will happen if you fall here. Walk it; you'll be happy to be alive to enjoy the incredible views and the descent still to come.

You'll be at the high point of the ride 0.6 mile beyond the crossing. Dismount again before the descent, and drink in the views of Mt. Rainier to the southwest, the Stuart Range to the north, and South Cle Elum Ridge and Manastash Ridge as you wind east. Lookout Mountain towers before you to the left, and Windy Pass lies below you. You might even spy some mountain goats, as Mike did on a previous trip. After the supreme view, some supreme descents await.

The descent to Windy Pass requires control and lower speeds, but once you turn onto the North Fork Taneum Creek Trail you can crank it up a notch on the rooty, rocky trail (remember, riding in control and riding slow are not the same thing!).

At the end of the loop, you can go straight, combining this ride with the North Fork Taneum Creek loop. In that case, start from Taneum Junction.

General location: The ride starts approximately 34 miles southwest of Cle Elum via Taneum Road, and 35 miles northwest of Ellensburg.

Elevation change: Start at about 4,080' at the gate, and descend about 80', passing the trail to start the loop. Top out the elevation at about 5,700' before descending to Windy Pass. Total elevation gain is approximately 1,840'.

Season: The trail should be ready and waiting for your knobbies in mid-June; you'll have a great ride here as late as October. This route is also motorcycle-legal, so, especially on summer weekends, prepare for encounters. Because of the altitude, check with the Cle Elum Ranger District for trail conditions.

Services: The nearest water is at the Taneum Campground, 4.1 miles east of Taneum Junction. You can camp at South Fork Meadow Campground, 7.1 miles from the locked gate that starts the ride; at Taneum Junction; and at campgrounds along FS 33. Services can be obtained in Cle Elum to the west and Ellensburg to the east. If you're in need of bike stuff—and even if you're not—check out the Recycle Bike Shop in Ellensburg. To the west, try Central Sundries in Roslyn (see Cooper River Trail for directions) for your cycling-related needs.

Hazards: The aforementioned perilous 10' crossing on the ridge is not a big deal—unless you fall. The trail down to Windy Pass is steeply side-cut and barren; better to walk the switchbacks than take a long, painful tumble.

Rescue index: Mike Curley is a great guy to ride with because, among other things, he is an emergency medical technician. If you can't ride with Mike, folks in the campgrounds along the way may be of assistance. Residents along Thorp Cemetery Road may be able to help you out. The nearest pay phones are in Thorp, off of I-90 to the east, and in Cle Elum to the west.

Land status: Wenatchee National Forest, Cle Elum Ranger District. The trail is also an easement through some private land, owned by Plum Creek.

Maps: Green Trails #240 Easton and the Cle Elum Ranger District map are equally effective for this outing. Neither, however, show the spur road to the saddle and the start of the single-track.

Finding the trail: Follow the directions for the Taneum Ridge and North Fork Taneum Creek loops. From Taneum Junction, proceed 10.9 miles on FS 3300 to the locked gate. Parking for just a couple of vehicles is available at a pullout near the gate; if necessary, back up and park off of the road.

Source of additional information:

Cle Elum Ranger District
803 W. 2nd Street
Cle Elum, WA 98922
(509) 674-4411

Notes on the trail: Ride around the gate and down 0.1 mile to the junction to the right. Turn right and cross North Fork Taneum Creek. About 200' beyond the creek, cross the North Fork Taneum Creek Trail #1377 both to the left and the right. You'll finish the loop on the trail that is now to your left; the trail to the right is part of North Fork Taneum Creek loop. About 50' past the trail crossing, as the road going straight ends quickly, veer left onto FS 4510. The climb is moderate; the scenery, at this point, clear-cut. Stay on the main road where a road veers off to the left at 1.0 mile. Continue climbing until 3.6 miles, when, as you're climbing in a northwest direction before the road curves right, a road takes off to your left. You can, as we did on our journey, take the left here, or you can extend the road portion and do some extra single-tracking by climbing to the ridge you see up to your right (if you do this, look for the trail and take it left, meeting up with the described route at the saddle). The road to the left comes to a **T** junction in 0.2 mile; to the right, the road climbs; to the left, it descends a little and climbs again. Take the left, and in 0.3 mile, the road meets Cle Elum Ridge Trail #1326 at a saddle. (Signage made it appear as if it were the Granite Creek Trail, but I was assured by a Forest Service representative that it is in fact the Cle Elum Ridge Trail. To avoid confusion let's just call it Trail #1326.) The road continues to the right; the trail veers to the left and commences a steep, soft climb into the tree cover. Top out the climb in 0.4 mile and roll on the ridge. As you start descending you can climb onto the rocks to

"X" marks a steep section
of Trail #1326.

your right for a great view to the north. But wait, there's more! Hop back on the saddle and in another 0.3 mile, after a little climb along the ridge, come to the moonscape in front of you to the left. Walk the next short, precarious 10' section, then saddle up again and continue climbing. In 0.6 mile, you'll find yourself above Windy Pass. After enjoying the view, you'll encounter a couple of rough, loose switchbacks with steep drops to the side.

After a 500', 0.5-mile descent, you're at Windy Pass. At this junction Trail #1326 continues and climbs to North Ridge Trail #1321 in 0.5 mile. Turn left, continuing the descent on North Fork Taneum Trail #1377. Some fun, fast technical descending with some nice, swooping turns brings you to the Taneum Shelter in 0.9 mile. You can stop and take an imposing look up to where you were just moments ago, or you can keep the rhythm going on the descent. As you continue downhill, you'll need the pedals again 1.5 miles after the shelter as you negotiate a crossing of North Fork Taneum Creek. Pass an access for South Fork Taneum Creek Trail #1367 as you roller-coaster back down to the clear-cut and the road that marks the end of this section of trail. Turn right and climb back to your vehicle, or continue straight, using the directions for the North Fork Taneum Creek Loop. If you do the longer ride, start at Taneum Junction.

RIDE 43 · "The Book"

AT A GLANCE

Length/configuration: 8.9-mile loop; 2.1 miles of single-track descent

Aerobic difficulty: Difficult 4.4-mile, 1,800' road climb

Technical difficulty: Loose, rocky climb; a dusty descent with some treacherous side-cuts

Scenery: Barren, sagebrush-lined route; views into and beyond the Kittitas Valley

Special comments: Advanced-level climb; without tree cover, overheating becomes a factor on hot days

WA

At the top of the tough 4.4-mile, 1,800-foot, rocky, gravel-road climb, rest your legs, stop at the rocks, and tell the world you came. It's a tradition to write your name, and anything else that strikes your fancy, in the notebook in the metal box there. When the book is full it goes to the Ellensburg Public Library for posterity, and another book goes up.

The Book rewards you at the top of the climb, but the real reward is the fast 2.1-mile single-track descent that follows—a plunge from the rocks to the road that parallels the South Branch Irrigation Canal and the end of the loop.

The route is through dry, sun-exposed sagebrush country overlooking Ellensburg, the Kittitas Valley, and beyond. The views get better as you climb higher, and are another reward for your efforts.

The directions are from the start and finish of the loop. You may want to start from town, though, as many locals do. (Irene Rinehart Park, on the Yakima River, is a good place to start.) You'll appreciate a warm pair of legs for the steep climb up the lava-cut canyon to the ridge. Being so close to town, the trail gets a lot of use, so watch your speed on the fast, dusty descent—especially when you come to the fence. You can barrel straight down from there, as some members of our research crew did, but almost all of them took spectacular spills. Take the right turn and switchback down at this point, and you're a lot more likely to keep the rubber side of your bike connected to the earth.

General location: The ride starts and ends at the base of Manastash Ridge, at the south end of the Kittitas Valley, just south of Ellensburg. Ellensburg is about 36 miles north of Yakima, 25 miles southeast of Cle Elum, and 75 miles south of Wenatchee.

Elevation change: The ride starts at 1,780' elevation. You'll be at 3,580' elevation when you sign the book. Elevation gain is about 1,800'.

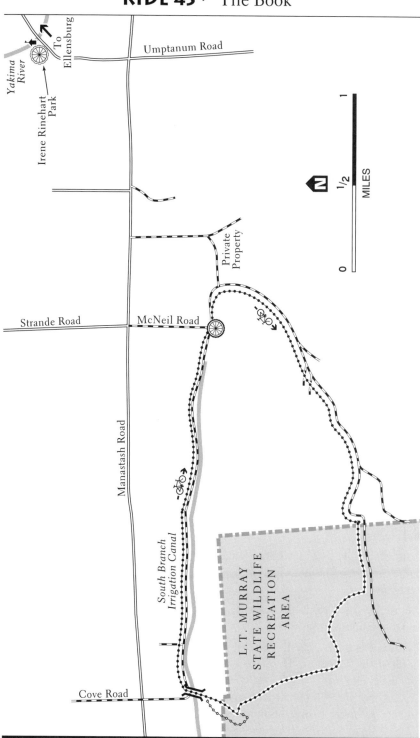

To Ellensburg

Yakima River

Umptanum Road

Irene Rinehart Park

Strande Road

McNeil Road

Private Property

Manastash Road

South Branch Irrigation Canal

L. T. MURRAY STATE WILDLIFE RECREATION AREA

Cove Road

N

MILES

1

½

0

The Recycle Bikeshop gang and The Book, high above the Kittitas Valley.

Season: Early spring to late fall. This is a very sun-exposed ride, and overheating is a danger in the heat of a summer day. If you ride it in summer go early or later in the day.

Services: There is no water available along the ride (not counting the South Branch Irrigation Canal, which you'll ride alongside for the final 2.3 miles). All services are available in Ellensburg.

Hazards: As mentioned, the sun can do more than just give you a cyclist's tan; slap on some sunscreen. Also, be careful when you come to the fence on the descent. To avoid a potential tumble, go right instead of straight down.

Rescue index: Residences are close by the bottom of the trail. Help is available in Ellensburg.

Land status: L. T. Murray State Wildlife Recreation Area. The route also travels some private land, but as long as you're respectful there won't be any negative repercussions.

Maps: USGS 7.5 minute quads: Ellensburg South and Manastash Creek are suitable guides for this ride.

Finding the trail: Take I-90 to Exit 109/Canyon Road, in Ellensburg and travel north about 7 blocks to Umptanum Road. Turn left (west) on Umptanum Road and travel under I-90 in 0.7 mile. From here the road turns south and then winds around past Irene Rinehart Park and the Yakima River, to Manastash Road in another 1.0 mile. Turn right on Manastash Road and travel 1.5 miles to unpaved McNeil Road on the left and paved Strande Road on the right. Turn left, and in

0.4 mile, park to the right near the rock and concrete grain storage area as the road curves left (east) and the road on which you finish the loop goes right.

Sources of additional information:

Recycle Bicycle Shop
307 N. Main Street
Ellensburg, WA 98926-3311
(509) 925-3326

Washington Department of Fish and Wildlife
1701 S. 24th Avenue
Yakima, WA 98902-5720
(509) 575-2740

Ellensburg Public Library
Reference Desk
209 N. Ruby Street
Ellensburg, WA 98926
(509) 962-7250
(For the curious, to check out filled-up books.)

Notes on the trail: Continue east on the road for 0.2 mile, enjoying views past the Kittitas Valley, Mt. Stuart, and the Wenatchee Mountains to the north, and Whiskey Dick Mountain to the northeast. It's flat here, but the climbing starts when it turns to the right. (The turn is at 0.2 mile, across a cattle grate and past a gate, where continuing straight would put you on private property.) At 1.6 miles the road widens out, but narrows again pretty quickly. About 0.1 mile after the road narrows, look for a not-as-well-defined road to the right and take it. Once you're on the road it forks twice in fairly short order; stay low against the fence both times. Keep winding your way up the barren hillside to the ridge. After 1.7 miles from the turn off of the initial road (3.9-miles total), come to a **Y** intersection. The left fork goes south and starts to descend; take the right fork and continue on. After winding up to the left and then to the right, crest the ridge (which you can see from below) at the 4.5-mile mark. The road continues on and starts to descend, but at the top, turn to the right on an ill-defined rocky path that leads to the trail in about 20 yards.(If you start descending on the road you've gone too far.) There are the rocks! There's the box! Take a look; there's The Book! Stop and certify your ride while enjoying the views into the valley and up to the Cascades. The descent starts to the right of The Book. As you descend, in 1.7 miles you'll come to a junction, where the trail ahead of you is fenced on the sides. Turn right, before the fence, and in 0.4 mile come to a footbridge over the South Branch Irrigation Canal. On the other side of the bridge is Cove Road, which leads back to Manastash Road. To finish the loop, parallel the canal, traveling east. Continue to parallel the canal past a road crossing in 0.3 mile, and to the loop's end in 2.3 miles.

YAKIMA–SOUTH WENATCHEE NATIONAL FOREST

The Wenatchee National Forest is an enormous piece of public real estate. It encompasses 2.2 million acres and extends from Lake Chelan in the north to the Yakima Indian Reservation in the south—135 miles!

The chapters in this section focus on rides most easily accessible from the Yakima area. As you drive west of Yakima on US 12, the junction of WA 410 signals two major accesses to the Wenatchee National Forest and over the Cascades.

The gateway to much nearby riding is through the town of Naches, about 13 miles northwest of Yakima. The little farming community, with a population of 710, is little more than a quick stop on the way to the mountains from Yakima. The Naches Ranger District office, though, on the main drag in town—the *only* drag in town—can be a valuable source of information.

The beautiful but controversial Tieton Nature Trail lies just six miles beyond Naches on the Tieton River alongside US 12. It's an excellent, beginner-friendly single-track, and many a love affair with mountain biking has blossomed from a ride on this trail. However, it's under the jurisdiction of the Department of Wildlife, whose mission is to protect wildlife, not mountain bikers. We're still the "new kids on the block," and mountain biking may be restricted if its use affects the habitat or causes trail user conflicts.

About 20 miles farther up US 12, Bethel Ridge provides fun, easy riding and beautiful Cascades views from over 6,000 feet elevation.

The listed rides up WA 410 are within the area where the Little Naches River joins the confluence of the Bumping and American Rivers to form the Naches River. The area holds everything from level gravel-road romps to epic single-track descents.

Yakima, central Washington's most populous city, is hot and dry. It gets only about eight inches of rain per year; summer temperatures get up into the 90s. But the area is far from barren. Irrigation from the Yakima and Tieton Rivers has made the Yakima Valley a prime agricultural region. Cherries, apricots, plums, and peaches, as well as Washington's famous apples, abound. In addition, the Yakima area is the world's fourth-largest producer of hops, so beer drinkers owe the area a debt of gratitude. Presently, five microbreweries offer samples of local suds, while grape producers serve the 26 wineries in the area.

Two-wheeled winery tours are popular in these parts. The Yakima Valley Visitors and Convention Bureau distributes a map with a tour route for Yakima Valley wineries. The visitor's bureau is at 10 North 8th Street in Yakima; call them at (509) 575-3010 or toll free at (800) 221- 0751. For other pavement-pedaling options, the Yakima Chamber of Commerce produces a brochure listing nine road cycling tours from between 10 and 81 miles in length. Stop by the chamber office at 10 North 9th Street in Yakima, a block away from the visitor's bureau, or call (509) 248-2021.

On the dirt, the Cowiche Canyon Conservancy Area, ten minutes west of downtown, offers a fun, challenging network of trails. Grey Rock, in the Ahtanum Multiple Use Area, about 35 miles west of town, and the Manastash Observatory area, north of town, are other local dirt playgrounds. Jem Rockholt, owner of Sagebrush Cycles in Yakima, is a great source of information on local riding, as is Yakima's Greatful Tread—yes, the Greatful Tread—Mountain Bike Club.

RIDE 44 · Tieton Nature Trail

AT A GLANCE

WA

Length/configuration: 1.2 miles of double-track and 5.2 miles of single-track for a 6.4-mile (total mileage) out-and-back, plus a 0.2-mile (each way) side trip, for beginners; advanced riders can continue another 1.4 miles each way from the beginner turnaround point

Aerobic difficulty: Near-level with a few short bursts to the beginner turnaround point; beyond it, a challenging climb to the canal

Technical difficulty: A couple of rocky sections and a log crossing for beginners; the advanced scree section requires finesse

Scenery: Sheer canyon walls, rock formations, Tieton River views

Special comments: A beginner trail doesn't get any better than this; a treat for advanced riders, too—ride with care; it's a highly sensitive trail in a highly sensitive area

This 3.2-mile (each way), beginner-friendly ride is aerobically and physically easy, with a few short leg-burners thrown in. The short stretch of double-track leads to a scenic sampling of honest-to-goodness, high-quality single-track.

I list this ride after much hesitation about its inclusion. On the one hand, it is suitable for first-time single-trackers but through an area beautiful enough that advanced mountain bikers will appreciate it, too. On the other hand, there is a real possibility that this trail could be closed due to overuse by mountain bikers, and by user conflict. As the newest of the trail users, mountain bikers will shoulder the blame for any user conflicts regardless of the origin of the problem.

In the end, I decided that this is a ride so nice I wanted to share it with you, in the hopes that you will ride responsibly and respectfully, so that others may enjoy this trail in the future. Please stay on the trail, ride in control, and dismount and give a friendly greeting when encountering hikers. If at all possible, ride midweek.

The trail is soft and dusty in some spots, and just a touch rocky in others, but generally has a firm, smooth surface. Many spots along the trail invite you to stop and admire the imposing scenery—dry, beautiful hillsides; sheer canyon walls; majestic rock formations; and, of course, the Tieton River. You'll ride by sage-

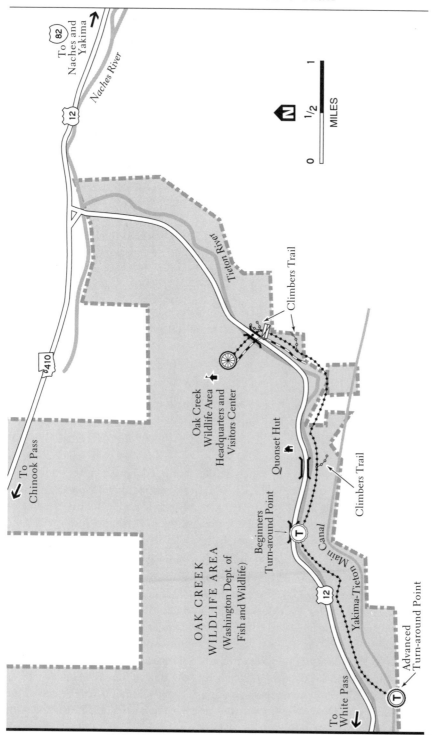

brush, cactus bushes, Oregon white oak, and further up the trail, ponderosa pine. You're also likely to see climbers on the Royal Columns, a popular hiking site.

The route provides easy bailouts, too. It parallels the river and US 12, and has accesses to the road over the bridges at 1.7 miles and the turnaround at 3.2 miles. With a comfortable 160-foot elevation gain on the way out turning into a fun 160-foot descent on the return, there's no reason to use them, though.

The ride starts at the Oak Creek Feeding Center, with an elk viewing area beside the parking lot. If you come in the off-season (*sans* bike) you can watch the elk feedings at 1:30 P.M. from around mid-December through early March.

The trail beyond the beginner turnaround is an access trail to the canal for the Yakima–Tieton Irrigation District. A representative from the district kindly asked me to inform you of the following: DO NOT RIDE ON, OVER, AROUND, OR ALONGSIDE THE CANAL, OR RIDING PRIVILEGES WILL BE REVOKED! Are we straight? Good.

Having said that, it's a tasty bit of trail! It starts with a sketchy ten-foot section along the scree at the base of the canyon wall and then rises away from the river, climbing 380 feet in 1.4 miles to the canal. A landing just below the canal, beautifully situated, invites you to sit and ponder and enjoy the views north and south, up and down, in front and in back.

General location: The trail is located about 20 miles northwest of Yakima, 2 miles south of the US 12/WA 410 junction.

Elevation change: The trail starts at 1,740' elevation and reaches the upper bridge at 1,900'. The trail rises to 2,280' at the canal.

Season: April through October, maybe a little longer with good weather. The trail is closed for all access from February 1 through March 30 and, if eagles nest there, it is closed through April 15. When the hot summer sun is shining, go early or later in the day.

Services: Water is available at the wildlife area headquarters. Limited services are available in Naches. Yakima provides all services, including Sagebrush Cycles for anything "bike" you may need. Owner Jem Rockholt is one of the nicest guys you'll ever meet, and he knows a thing or two about local mountain biking.

Hazards: The sun and heat can be a factor here. Rattlesnakes can, too, but if you stay on the trail and away from brush the risk is minimal. The canal itself could be a hazard, but only if you're doing something you shouldn't be; please heed the above warning (a rider who didn't was almost killed when he was swept away by the fast-moving water). The trail is a popular trail for birders and novice hikers as well as bikers. Help to leave them with a positive image of mountain bikers—ride in control and give a friendly greeting. As you ride out memorize the section beyond the sagging cable across the trail to the bridge at 1.7 miles. It can clothesline you if you're descending at speed and not paying attention on the return trip. Hold your line on the steeply side-cut section just before the

Tieton Nature Trail.

bridge at 3.2 miles. It's always a good idea to heed the IMBA rule of riding in control; on this trail, continued access depends on it.

Rescue index: A pay phone is at the Oak Creek Wildlife Area Headquarters office by the parking area. Personnel are scheduled there from 9 A.M. until 4 P.M. seasonally, but they may be out in the field at times. Help is available in Naches and in Yakima.

Land status: Washington Department of Fish and Wildlife has jurisdiction of the trail to the second bridge. The agency's primary mandate is protection and enhancement of fish and wildlife habitat, and I was warned that if mountain bikers impede these goals, our activity will be restricted on this trail. The Yakima-Tieton Irrigation District controls the trail up to the canal. They, too, warn of restricted access if any problems arise from mountain bike use.

Maps: Green Trails #305 Tieton and the Naches Ranger District map don't show the trail, but they show the roads, the recreation area headquarters, the river and canal, and that'll get you through. The best map I've seen is the one Jem Rockholt drew freehand on a piece of notebook paper! But the route is so straightforward that if you can get inside the elk fencing, you can get by without a map.

Finding the trail: From Interstate 82 on the north end of Yakima, go west on US 12 for 14.7 miles to the junction of WA 410. Turn left, continuing on US 12 for 2.0 miles to the Oak Creek Wildlife Area parking lot on the right. Park in the lot or on the left before the bridge over the Tieton River.

Sources of additional information:

Sagebrush Cycles
1406 Fruitvale Boulevard
Yakima, WA 98902-1927
(509) 248-5393

Washington Department of Fish and Wildlife
1701 S. 24th Avenue
Yakima, WA 98902-5720
(509) 575-2740
(509) 653-2390 (direct to the Oak Creek Headquarters)

Yakima-Tieton Irrigation District
470 Camp Four Road
Yakima, WA 98908
(509) 678-4101

Greatful Tread Mountain Bike Club
118 E. Orchard Street #1
Selah, WA 98942
(509) 697-9695
http://www.ewa.net/users/jdmtnbiker/index.html

Notes on the trail: Cross the bridge over the Tieton River. Pass the climbers' trails on your left, and veer right. Dismount, open the box-wire gate, go through, close the gate, and remount. The route starts with a flat double-track. Pass a climbers' trail on your left at 0.2 mile. The double-track narrows into single-track at 0.6 mile alongside the elk fencing. It starts near the river and then rises above it. After a short burst of a climb at 0.9 mile, come to a **T** junction. A short river access trail is to the right; the main trail continues left. After a little climb at 1.3 miles, descend into the oaks where the trail levels out. Pass another river access trail on your right at 1.5 miles, where you can see a Quonset hut across the river, and pass a climbing access trail to your left at the 7 o'clock position, 0.1 mile farther. In another 0.1 mile come to a footbridge over the river. Make the 0.2 mile side trip (each way) over the river and wind to the right on the double-track to the Quonset hut. Turn back around for a great view to the southwest of the rock faces, the canyon walls, and beyond. Back across the river, continue up the trail, remembering this section, and the overhanging cable, for the return trip. After a short, steep climb, come into a clearing at 2.1 miles that opens up some nice views. In about 0.5 more miles the canal comes into plain view up to the left. Do a little climbing to bring you to an overlook of the river and the bridge at 3.1 miles. Descend to the bridge, cross, soak in another view, and cross back over. Beginners head back; more advanced riders continue up toward the canal. Climb through the pines and the scree for 1.4 miles. A very rough, rocky access trail veers down to the right about 30' before the trail winds to the left and ends at the canal. Pass it, and then dismount and hop onto the rocks to the right to laze and gaze. It's worth saying again: don't mess with the canal—period. On the other side of the canal are some elk trails. Don't even think about it; turn around and ride back, stopping to enjoy more views along the way.

RIDE 45 · Bethel Ridge

AT A GLANCE

Length/configuration: 8-mile out-and-back on gravel roads and double-track (4 miles each way)

Aerobic difficulty: Easy for fit, acclimatized riders

Technical difficulty: Moderate; a mix of good roads and rough roads

Scenery: Excellent views from the ridge

Special comments: In the spring, bring a jacket; in the fall, bring a "hunter orange" jacket

This is an easy eight-mile out-and-back ride. The route follows a compacted dirt and gravel road for two miles to Bethel Ridge. This road is in good condition, with some exposed rocks and loose gravel. Once on the ridge, you follow a dirt double-track that is in poor condition, with large, sharp rocks and lots of ruts.

Bethel Ridge drops off to reveal a sweeping panorama. The view to the south takes in the Tieton Basin and Divide Ridge. Farther to the west lies Goose Egg Mountain, at the eastern end of Rimrock Lake. Vistas extend for many miles; Mt. Adams can be seen in the southwest on clear days.

General location: The ride is about 50 miles northwest of Yakima, Washington.

Elevation change: The trailhead lies at 5,600'. The high point of the trip, 6,160', occurs on Bethel Ridge. Total elevation gain: 560'.

Season: Cooler temperatures at its higher elevation makes the ridge an inviting destination on hot summer days. Cyclists also enjoy exploring the area in the spring and fall.

Services: There is no water on this ride, but it can be obtained seasonally at Hause Campground. There are two convenience stores on US 12. One is located

RIDE 45 · Bethel Ridge

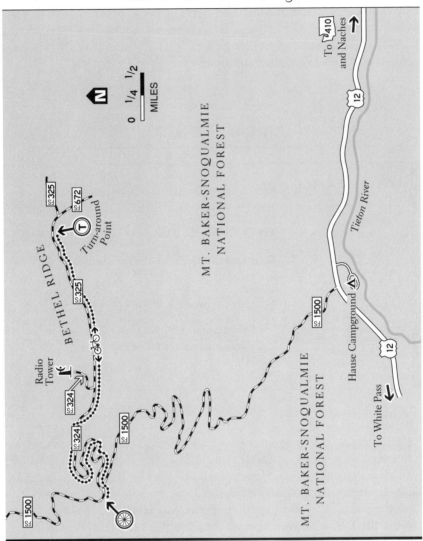

2.5 miles west of Hause Campground, the other 4.5 miles to the east. Food, lodging, gas, and groceries can be found in Naches. All services are available in Yakima.

Hazards: You will cross a cattle guard near the start of the trip. Expect some vehicular traffic on the roads. Control your speed and watch for loose gravel while descending.

Rescue index: The nearest pay phones are at the convenience stores on US 12. Help is available in Naches.

Bethel Ridge.

Land status: Mt. Baker–Snoqualmie National Forest lands administered by the Wenatchee National Forest.

Maps: The district map of the Naches Ranger District is a good guide to this ride. USGS 7.5 minute quad: Tieton Basin.

Finding the trail: From locations to the west, drive approximately 18 miles east of White Pass on US 12 to Forest Service Road 1500 (on the left). FS 1500 is 0.3 mile east of milepost 168. From locations to the east, travel west from Naches on US 12 for about 26 miles to FS 1500 (on the right). Turn north onto FS 1500 and follow it for 6.9 miles to FS 324 (on the right). There is room to park on the left side of FS 1500.

Source of additional information:

Naches Ranger District
10061 Highway 12
Naches, WA 98937
(509) 653-2205

Notes on the trail: Ride up FS 324 to FS 325. Turn right onto FS 325 and ride under the power lines. Stay on the main road that borders the cliff. Ride along Bethel Ridge for about 1.5 miles to where FS 325 enters the woods and begins to descend rapidly. Turn around and return the way you came.

RIDE 46 · Raven Roost

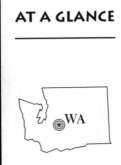

AT A GLANCE

Length/configuration: 27-mile gravel road combination; 10.8-mile loop and a 16.2-mile out-and-back (8.1 miles each way)

Aerobic difficulty: Difficult; long climb

Technical difficulty: Easy; gravel forest roads

Scenery: Spectacular views of rugged Cascade peaks

Special comments: The area is laced with off-road vehicle trails

This demanding 27-mile trip combines a loop and an out-and-back ride. Although this circuit is not technical, the long climb requires strength and stamina. The route is entirely on gravel roads in good condition. The first half of the ride is a long ascent to a viewpoint at Raven Roost. The climbing is mostly easy to moderately difficult, with some short steep stretches. The last 1.5 miles to the summit are steep. The return is an exhilarating downhill cruise.

Vistas extend in every direction from Raven Roost. On the approach, you obtain a spectacular view of Fifes Ridge and Fifes Peaks to the south. From the top, the snowfields of Mt. Rainier are prominent in the southwest. The distant horizon to the north is filled with rugged peaks.

General location: This ride begins at Crow Creek Campground, approximately 45 miles north of Yakima, Washington.

Elevation change: The ride starts at 2,720' and climbs to 6,200' at Raven Roost. Ups and downs encountered along the route add approximately 200' of climbing to the ride. Total elevation gain: 3,680'.

Season: These roads are usually clear of snow from June through October.

Services: There is no water available on this ride. Water may be obtained at Sawmill Flat Campground on WA 410. The Whistlin' Jack Lodge in Cliffdell has food, lodging, limited groceries, pay phones, and gas. All services are available in Yakima.

Hazards: You may encounter some vehicular traffic on these roads. Remain alert for loose gravel, particularly while descending. Be prepared for changes in the weather; it may be windy and cold at the top.

Rescue index: Help can be found in Cliffdell.

Land status: Wenatchee National Forest.

Maps: The district map of the Naches Ranger District is a good guide to this ride. USGS 7.5 minute quads: Mt. Clifty and Raven Roost.

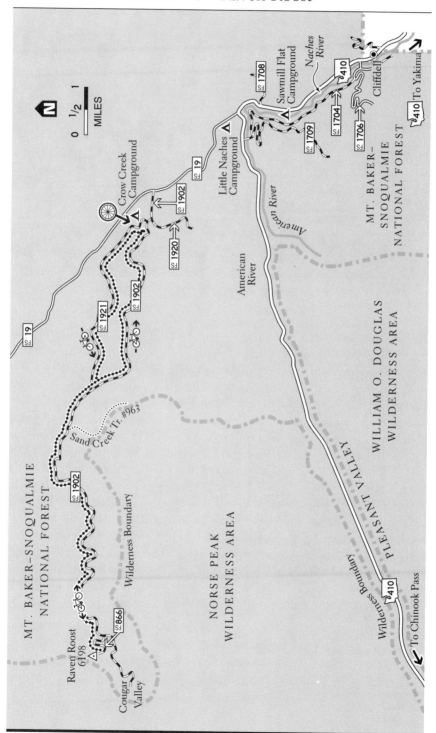

Mt. Rainier from Forest Service Road 866.

Finding the trail: From Yakima, drive north on US 12 for about 16 miles to the intersection of US 12 and WA 410. Continue straight on WA 410 where US 12 goes left toward White Pass. Follow WA 410 north for 24 miles to FS 19 (on the right, 1.2 miles north of the Sawmill Flat Campground entrance). From Enumclaw, take WA 410 east toward Chinook Pass. From the pass, continue east on WA 410 for approximately 24 miles to FS 19 (on the left, about 3.5 miles east of American River). Turn northwest onto unsigned FS 19, following the signs for Little Naches Campground. Drive up FS 19 for 2.7 miles to unsigned FS 1902. Turn left onto FS 1902, which is marked by a sign that points left and reads "Raven Roost—14 miles." Cross a concrete bridge spanning the Little Naches River and drive another 0.4 mile to an intersection where signed FS 1920 goes left toward Fifes Ridge. Turn right to stay on unmarked FS 1902; you will cross a one-lane wooden bridge over Crow Creek. Immediately after crossing this bridge, you will arrive at another intersection. The road to the left—signed "Raven Roost—13 miles"—is FS 1902. The road to the right is signed FS 1921. Turn right onto FS 1921, then turn right again into the Crow Creek Campground. Park in a site if you intend to camp; otherwise, park on the roadside.

Source of additional information:

Naches Ranger District
10061 Highway 12
Naches, WA 98937
(509) 653-2205

Notes on the trail: Exit the campground and turn right onto FS 1921. After 5.5 miles of riding you will arrive at the intersection of FS 1921 and FS 1902. Bear right onto FS 1902 toward Raven Roost. After 1 mile of pedaling on FS 1902, you will pass Sand Creek Trail #963 at a primitive campground. Stay on FS 1902 for another 6.6 miles to FS 866. Turn right onto FS 866 toward Raven Roost. Turn around at the top and return the way you came, to the intersection of FS 1902 and FS 1921. Keep right, staying on FS 1902. In another 5.3 miles, you will come to the intersection where FS 1902 meets FS 1921 again. Turn left onto FS 1921, then immediately turn right into the Crow Creek Campground to reach your vehicle.

Adventurous cyclists may wish to check out some of the off-road vehicle trails in the area. Sand Creek Trail #963 can be incorporated into the return from Raven Roost. It is indicated on the recommended district map, but like most off-road vehicle routes, it is inadequately signed in the field. Be prepared to do some route finding if you venture off the roads.

RIDE 47 · Old River Road

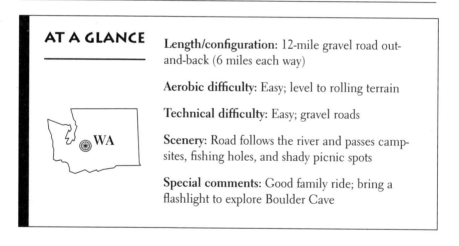

AT A GLANCE

Length/configuration: 12-mile gravel road out-and-back (6 miles each way)

Aerobic difficulty: Easy; level to rolling terrain

Technical difficulty: Easy; gravel roads

Scenery: Road follows the river and passes camp-sites, fishing holes, and shady picnic spots

Special comments: Good family ride; bring a flashlight to explore Boulder Cave

This 12-mile out-and-back trip on Old River Road offers cyclists a pleasant outing. The terrain is level to rolling, and the gravel road is in good condition. The route includes 1.5 miles of paved road cycling.

The cycling is easy along this stretch of the popular Naches River. Old River Road rolls past developed and undeveloped campsites, fishing holes, shady picnic spots, and summer homes. This route also passes the trailhead for the Boulder Cave Recreation Trail.

General location: The trailhead is approximately 40 miles northwest of Yakima, Washington.

Roving with Rover.

Elevation change: The ride begins at 2,600'. The turnaround point lies at 2,400'. Undulations in the terrain add another 200' of climbing to the ride. Total elevation gain: 400'.

Season: This circuit may be ridden year-round. Wet, cold, winter weather may be a limiting factor.

Services: Water can be found at the Boulder Cave Picnic Area, located 2.8 miles into the ride. The Whistlin' Jack Lodge in Cliffdell has food, lodging, gas, limited groceries, and a pay phone. All services are available in Yakima.

Hazards: Although traffic is generally light, you can expect some motorists traveling to homes, campsites, and the trail to the cave. Approach blind corners with caution.

Rescue index: Help can be found in Cliffdell.

Land status: Wenatchee National Forest.

Maps: The district map of the Naches Ranger District is a good guide to this ride. USGS 7.5 minute quad: Cliffdell.

RIDE 47 · Old River Road

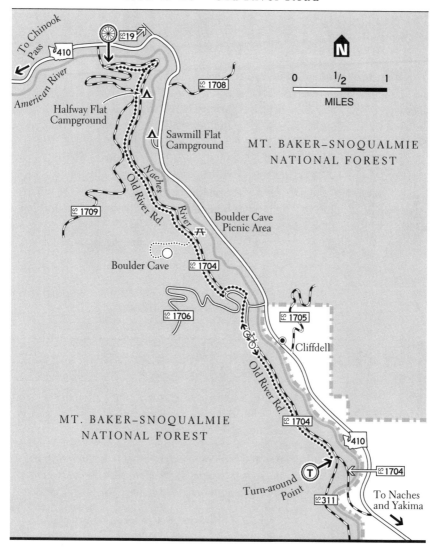

Finding the trail: From Yakima, drive north on US 12 for 16 miles to the intersection of US 12 and WA 410. Continue straight on WA 410 where US 12 goes left toward White Pass. Follow WA 410 north for 25 miles to Old River Road (on the left, 2 miles north of the Sawmill Flat Campground entrance). A sign marks this turn and directs you left toward Halfway Flat Campground and Old River Road/FS 1704. Turn left onto FS 1704 and proceed over the bridge spanning the river. Bear left after crossing the bridge, and park on the left side of FS 1704.

Source of additional information:

Naches Ranger District
10061 Highway 12
Naches, WA 98937
(509) 653-2205

Notes on the trail: Follow the river downstream on Old River Road/FS 1704. In 2.2 miles you will arrive at a sign that reads "Road Closed due to Flood Damage." Walk your bike over the earthen berm and then over a small creek bridged by a couple of planks. Ride another 0.5 mile, crossing a second berm. Soon you will arrive at the Boulder Cave Picnic Area. If you wish to explore the cave, stay to the right, toward the hiking trailhead. To remain on the route, pass through the picnic area on Old River Road. Continue straight where Swamp Creek Road/FS 1706 goes right. Go straight at the next intersection, where a spur road goes left to the highway. It is another 2 miles to the turnaround point at FS 311. Return the way you came.

Bring a flashlight and a bike lock if you plan on exploring Boulder Cave.

RIDE 48 · Little Bald Mountain

AT A GLANCE

Length/configuration: 29.8-mile combination route includes a 26.6-mile loop using gravel roads and 10.8 miles of single-track, plus a 1.6-mile gravel-road out-and-back (each way) to the summit of Little Bald Mountain

Aerobic difficulty: Advanced, due to the length of the mostly gradual 17.4-mile road climb to the top, and sharp climbing on the trail

Technical difficulty: Rough scree, rooty sections, some cliffsides and steep side-cuts

Scenery: Awe-inspiring, 360-degree views from the lookout at the top; the scenery from the trail isn't too shabby either

Special comments: Climbs and descents on both road and trail; superb views make this a great outing for the advanced rider

A 29.8-mile ride with more than 4,000 feet of climbing, the Little Bald Mountain Loop is worth every ounce of the considerable energy expended. The mostly smooth road section travels among Douglas fir, ponderosa pine, and western larch, which livens up the autumn landscape with its delicate gold hue. Views of Bald Mountain and Manastash Ridge can be seen to the east as you climb.

Your reward for topping out the road climb, actually 1.6 miles past the trailhead, is a mind-blowing view dominated by Old Scab Mountain before you and Mt. Rainier beyond it to the west; Goat Peak and American Ridge, Fifes Peak and Fifes Ridge as you turn north; Glacier Peak and the north Cascades, nearby Quartz Mountain, and distant Mt. Stuart due north; Manastash Ridge and Bethel Ridge as you turn east and south; and Mt. Aix, completing the circle. Awesome cliffs and rock formations lie below you as well.

The road section is an advanced-level (mostly for its length) 17.4-mile climb, with some steep, some level, and mostly gradual ascending sections. Descents within the climb give your legs and confidence a boost. The road is generally in good condition, with the most rocky, uneven terrain toward the top.

On the single-track the incredible views continue as you climb steeply and descend quickly, skirting the William O. Douglas Wilderness on the upper portion of trail. Sharp, rocky sections await you, including a steeply side-cut, challenging scree at the start. The trail, too, is in generally good shape, with some roots also making for some rough descending through woods and late-spring meadows.

Though we didn't do it on our research day, I was told that you can jump off the bridge on FS 1709 into the American River for a postride cool-down.

General location: You'll reach the lower trailhead about 43 miles northwest of Yakima and 100 miles southeast of Tacoma.

Elevation change: The route starts at about 2,500' elevation from the lower trailhead area. Pass the upper trailhead at 5,360' and reach the heights at 6,108'. Climbing on the trail brings total elevation gain to 4,050'.

Season: June through October, depending on conditions. Check with the Naches Ranger District office before you go out at either end of the season. You can ride the trail as an out-and-back from the lower trailhead in the spring and fall as the snows allow.

Services: Water is not available on the loop; you can fill up at Sawmill Flat and Little Naches Campgrounds, both off of WA 410 east of FS 1709. Camping is available at Halfway Flat, Sawmill Flat, Little Naches, and other area campgrounds. Food and gas can be found in Cliffdell. All services are provided in Yakima.

Hazards: Rocky, uneven trail as you descend from the upper trailhead; steep side-cuts can make falls in some sections perilous. The trail is an off-road vehicle trail, so you may meet some motos along the way.

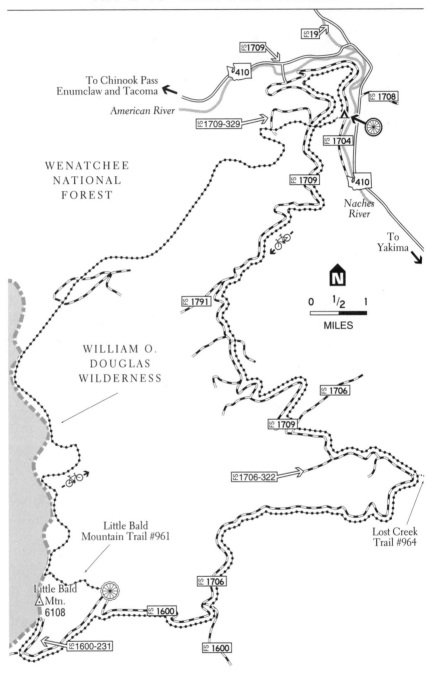

FS 19

FS 1709

410

To Chinook Pass
Enumclaw and Tacoma

American River

FS 1709-329

FS 1708

FS 1704

FS 1709

WENATCHEE
NATIONAL
FOREST

410

*Naches
River*

To
Yakima

N

0   1/2   1
MILES

FS 1791

WILLIAM O.
DOUGLAS
WILDERNESS

FS 1706

FS 1709

FS 1706-322

Little Bald
Mountain Trail #961

Lost Creek
Trail #964

FS 1706

Little Bald
△Mtn.
6108

FS 1600

FS 1600-231

FS 1600

Rescue index: Folks at the Halfway Flat Campground or at the cabins along the American River can summon help. The nearest phone is in Cliffdell.

Land status: Wenatchee National Forest, Naches Ranger District.

Maps: Both Green Trails #272 Old Scab Mtn. and the Naches Ranger District map will ably guide you. The ranger district map (revised in 1993) shows the surrounding roads in better detail but doesn't detail the small stretch of trail above the lower crossing between the top and bottom of spur road 329—an omission that common sense will render insignificant.

Finding the trail: From Yakima, take US 12 westbound for about 17 miles to the junction of WA 410. Continue straight onto WA 410, following the Naches River, and travel 24.8 miles (4.7 miles past the town of Cliffdell) to FS 1709 on your left. Turn onto FS 1709, and in 0.2 mile cross the bridge over the American River. Immediately after, make a hard left onto the lower road, FS 1704 (the ride climbs on FS 1709, the soft left here). Parallel the river on FS 1704 for 1.1 miles to the Halfway Flat Campground on your left. Veer right on the double-track next to the signboard, from where you can see the trail at the 2 o'clock position on your right, and park.

From Enumclaw, drive east on WA 410; proceed about 25 miles east of Chinook Pass to FS 1704. Turn right onto FS 1704, cross the bridge, and turn left as above. (If you make a roundhouse curve to the right past FS 19 and the Little Naches River on your left, you've gone too far. If you enter Cliffdell, you've gone almost 5 miles too far.)

Sources of additional information:

Naches Ranger District
10061 Highway 12
Naches, WA 98937
(509) 653-2205

Sagebrush Cycles
1406 Fruitvale Boulevard
Yakima, WA 98902-1927
(509) 248-5393

Greatful Tread Mountain Bike Club
118 E. Orchard Street#1
Selah, WA 98942
(509) 697-9695
http://www.ewa.net/users/jdmtnbiker/index.html

Notes on the trail: From the parking area, retrace your four-wheeled path with your two wheels for 1.1 miles to the junction of FS 1709, and switchback up and to the left before the bridge. FS 1709 is an obvious main road in good condition and is pretty easy to follow. Stay on FS 1709 through a moderately tough section to a road that veers off at the 2 o'clock position. The trail crosses spur road 329 at this point, so it's possible to start a loop here and knock 3.1 miles off of the road section and only 0.9 mile off of the trail. Stay on FS 1709 and, at 4.5 miles,

Jem Rockholt (left) and Jeremy Freisz at the top of Little Bald.

as the climb levels out, look up at the 11 o'clock position in the distance. See that little bald mountain? That's Little Bald Mountain, where you'll be in just a little while. At 5.8 miles, come to a **Y** junction. To the right is FS 1791; take the left fork, continuing on FS 1709. Pedal past more junctions, including a junction with a road on your right at 7.6 miles that looks like it could be a main road. Stay to the left on FS 1709, and in another 1.5 miles (9.1-miles total), FS 1709 ends into FS 1706, which goes both straight and downhill to the left. Stay straight, and in 0.6 mile, come to a delta junction where spur road 322 goes right. Stay to the left, continuing on FS 1706, and in another 1 mile, pass Lost Creek Trail #964 on your left. Stay on FS 1706, passing junctions, and at 14.1 miles, meet FS 1600, which goes both straight and to the left. Ride straight through the junction, and follow the road up and to the left. In another 0.6 mile, switchback up a rough section of road, passing an early-blooming meadow. In another 1.0 mile, after a left-hand switchback, come to the trailhead, with parking, on the right.

Don't start in on the trail just yet! Continue up to a junction in 1.1 miles. Directly ahead the road leads toward Clover Springs; veer right, onto FS 1600-231, and come to the top in 0.5 mile. At the top, with an antenna to the left and a well-placed railing at the end of the road, enjoy the view all around. When you've finished savoring the beauty, rage back down to the trailhead, turn left onto Little Bald Mountain Trail #961, and descend. That first left-hand switchback, loose, rocky, and exposed on a steep hillside, leads to a short, steeply sidecut scree. Soon you'll be back in the trees and climbing for about 0.8 mile. After that, roller-coaster along the boundary of the William O. Douglas Wilderness. At 2.1 miles on the trail (21.1 overall mileage), a descent brings you to a road crossing. The trail picks up about 20 feet to the left, following in the direction of the trail. Make a rough descent to another road crossing in another 100 yards and ride straight across, then shortly cross again and make a 200' climb in 0.2 mile, through some old growth on the wilderness boundary. Look for some good views to the left (southwest) on the ensuing beargrass-lined descent, with an even better look at Old Scab Mountain than before. (With the rocky cliffside trail, make sure the viewing and descending are not done simultaneously!) Make the winding descent through meadow, sparsely wooded and more densely wooded sections, and then make an 80' climb in 0.1 mile (at the 27.4-mile point). In another 1.1 miles, riding through a clear-cut, come to spur road 329 and ride about 100' to the right to the end of the road, and pick up the trail to the left that was marked, at the time of research, by two, one-foot-high, 3" diameter stumps. In another 0.4 mile, come upon spur road 329 again, near its junction with FS 1709. The trail skirts road 329 to the right, then climbs about 50 yards before it crosses FS 1709. (If you dump out onto the road here, just descend the short distance to FS 1709 and pick up the trail.) A 0.9-mile descent brings you to the ride's end.

NORTHWEST WASHINGTON
AREA RIDES

Near the southwestern Canadian border are the city of Bellingham and an excellent bike path known as the Interurban Trail. This popular rail-trail follows along the shoreline of island-studded Chuckanut Bay. It is a fun path for folks of all skill and fitness levels. At the south end of the trail, a closed gravel road heads steeply uphill to beautiful Fragrance Lake in Larrabee State Park.

Bellingham's Lake Padden Park also features riding for all skill levels. You can choose between a wide, easy, gravel path around the lake or some superb, hilly single-track. The park is just a few pedal strokes away from Lookout Mountain and the technical, user-built trails of what's known locally as Galbraith.

Southwest of Bellingham is Anacortes, on Fidalgo Island, the jumping-off point for the San Juan Islands. Classic single-tracks at Moran State Park on Orcas Island have recently been closed to mountain biking, but the San Juans are world-renowned as a destination for outstanding bicycle touring—the road riding is great. If this prospect interests you, pick up a guidebook (there are several good ones on the market) and hop a ferry to some unforgettable back-road riding.

From Anacortes, though, you don't need to hop on a boat to find great riding. Anacortes holds some first-class single-track within pedaling distance of downtown, both at Cranberry Lake and in the Heart Lake–Whistle Lake area.

East of Anacortes is Sedro Wooley, and east of Sedro Wooley is Mt. Josephine. It's a demanding ride to a summit that features close-ups of the Twin Sisters, Mt. Baker, and Mt. Shuksan. Cinch down your helmet and hold on tight—the coast back to the bottom is fast and furious!

RIDE 49 · Interurban Trail and Fragrance Lake

AT A GLANCE

WA

Length/configuration: 16-mile out-and-back on a dirt and gravel path and gravel roads (8 miles each way)

Aerobic difficulty: Easy to advanced; the Interurban Trail is mostly easy, but it includes a couple of short, steep hills; the 4-mile climb to Fragrance Lake is difficult

Technical difficulty: Easy to moderately difficult; good gravel road to Fragrance Lake; the dirt and gravel Interurban Trail is in good condition; watch for loose gravel

Scenery: The Interurban Trail passes through woods and residential areas; the road to the lake is shaded by dense second-growth forest

Special comments: Beginners and families can forego the climb to Fragrance Lake and enjoy an easy pedal on the Interurban Trail

The Interurban was an electric railway that linked the communities of Bellingham and Mt. Vernon, Washington. It ran from 1912 to 1930. In 1987, the 5.8-mile Interurban Trail was opened to pedestrians, equestrians, and cyclists.

Linking up the Interurban Trail with Fragrance Lake Road creates a good out-and-back ride (16-miles round-trip). The pedaling on the compacted dirt and gravel trail is mostly easy. The path narrows and begins to zigzag as it drops into Arroyo Park. The climb out of the park is steep, short, and fun. There is one other short, steep hill before you arrive at the south end of the trail.

The gravel road to Fragrance Lake starts out as a gentle grade, but it soon becomes a very steep climb. Fragrance Lake Road is in good condition and is closed to public motor traffic. Your primary concern will be looking out for descending cyclists as you weave and waver your way to the top. After 2.3 miles you'll reach the end of the road and a trailhead. A short hiking trail leads to and around picturesque Fragrance Lake. The return road descent is exhilarating. Back at the Interurban Trail, you can lock your bike to a tree and walk down to a beach on Samish Bay. This hike is a 1-mile round-trip.

General location: This ride starts from Old Fairhaven Parkway in South Bellingham, Washington.

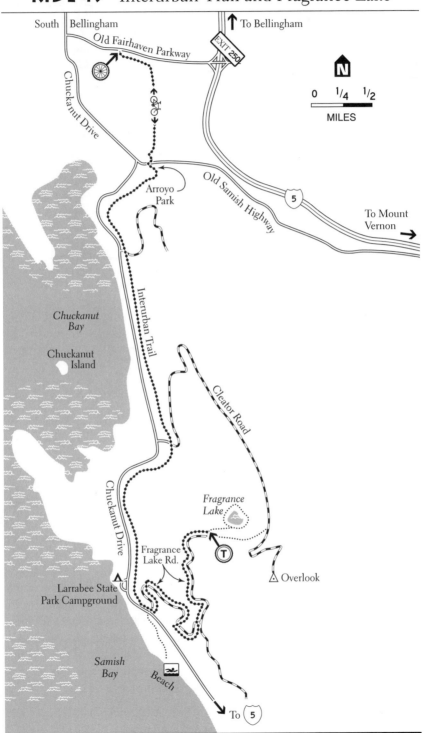

Sandy beach on Samish Bay.

Elevation change: The Interurban Trail begins at 100' and climbs to 250'. Fragrance Lake lies at 1,170'. Ups and downs over the course of the trip add about 200' of climbing to the ride. Total elevation gain: 1,270'.

Season: This ride can be enjoyed at any time of the year. July and August are nice — the route is well shaded, and ocean breezes help moderate the summer heat.

Services: There is no water available on this ride. All services are available in Bellingham.

Hazards: Trail use is heaviest on summer holiday weekends. There are some blind corners in Arroyo Park — expect other trail users to be approaching. You may be sharing the trail with equestrians. Places where the trail crosses roads are poorly marked from both the cyclist's and the motorist's perspective. Be alert for intersections and approach them cautiously. Control your speed, and watch for loose gravel while descending from the lake. Although Fragrance Lake Road is closed to most traffic, you may encounter a Larrabee State Park patrol or maintenance vehicle.

Rescue index: Help is available in Bellingham. In an emergency, assistance may be available at the campground in Larrabee State Park (off of Chuckanut Drive). The campground has a pay phone and is staffed by a host.

Land status: State park lands and public right-of-way through private property.

Maps: A map by Rex N. Brainard called "Chuckanut Mountain Roads and Trails" is a good guide to this route and can be purchased at local bike shops and sporting goods stores. USGS 7.5 minute quad: Bellingham South.

Fragrance Lake.

Finding the trail: From Interstate 5 near Bellingham, take Exit 250 and follow the signs toward Chuckanut Drive and the Old Fairhaven Historic District. This will put you on Old Fairhaven Parkway, heading west. The trailhead for the Interurban Trail is on the left side of Old Fairhaven Parkway, 0.5 mile from I-5. Park on the side of Old Fairhaven Parkway.

Source of additional information:

Whatcom County Parks and Recreation Department
3373 Mount Baker Highway
Bellingham, WA 98226
(360) 733-2900

Notes on the trail: Follow the trail to its southern terminus at Chuckanut Drive. Stay on the east side of Chuckanut Drive and walk your bike south—parallel the road, but stay off of the pavement. In 0.1 mile, bear left into a large parking area. Go to the left of the white gate and turn onto Fragrance Lake Road. Ride to the end of the road, hike to the lake, and return the way you came.

RIDE 50 · Lake Padden Loop

AT A GLANCE

Length/configuration: 2.6-mile loop on a wide gravel path

Aerobic difficulty: If you can ride a bike, you can ride it!

Technical difficulty: The only technical challenge is avoiding other users

Scenery: Lake Padden, people watching

Special comments: Good ride for families, true beginners, and those recovering from major surgery

This little jaunt is an urban, rather genteel, mountain bike ride, suitable for families and true beginners. It's only 2.6 flat, nontechnical miles around the lake, but the ride can be part of a day of riding, swimming, picnicking, fishing, paddling, ballplaying, and other activities that a lake-improved city park affords.

The gravel trail around the lake is wide and smooth, perfect for riding two-, three-, or four-abreast and chatting while riding. The ride travels along the lakeshore almost throughout, and contains numerous short accesses to the lake.

The ride can be part of a longer outing, using the technical single-track south of the lake, but the single-track is not recommended for the true beginner.

General location: Lake Padden Park is located at the south end of Bellingham and north of I-5.

Elevation change: Lake Padden is at 445' elevation. Entire elevation gain is no more than 40'.

Season: Year-round.

Services: Water is available at the park. All services are available in Bellingham.

Hazards: Locals use this trail for biking, hiking, jogging, and dog walking. Beware of the traffic, and give a greeting that reflects well on mountain bikers.

Rescue index: Assistance will most likely be found at the park. Help is available in Bellingham.

Land status: Bellingham Parks and Recreation Department.

Maps: The trail is mapped at a signboard at the end of the parking lot. If ever you ride without a map, this is the route for it. The Bellingham Parks and Recreation Department also produces a booklet of local trail maps.

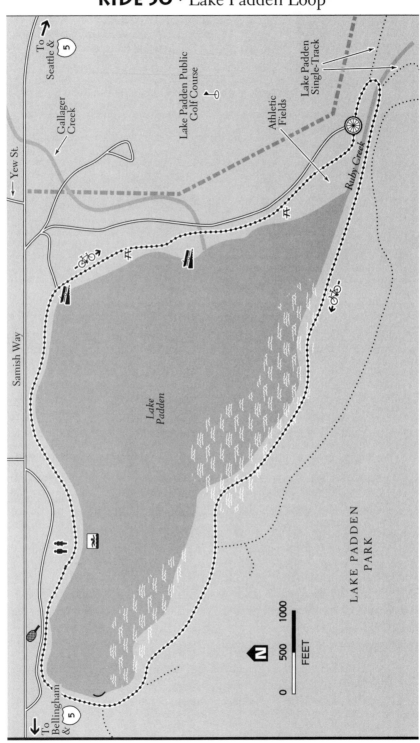

To Seattle & 5

Gallager Creek

Yew St.

Lake Padden Public Golf Course

Lake Padden Single-Track

Athletic Fields

Ruby Creek

Samish Way

Lake Padden

LAKE PADDEN PARK

N

1000

500

FEET

0

To Bellingham & 5

Lake Padden.

Finding the trail: From Seattle, take I-5 north to Exit 246/Samish Way, about 9 miles south of Bellingham's city center. Turn left (north) onto Samish Way and travel 2.5 miles to Lake Padden Park. Turn left into the park and stay right at the split, toward the picnic area (to the left is the golf course).

From the north, drive south on I-5 to Exit 252/Samish Way. Go left over I-5, and right at the signal, continuing on Samish Way. In 2.5 miles, turn right into Lake Padden Park's east entrance.

Source of additional information:

Bellingham Parks & Recreation Department
210 Lottie Street
Bellingham, WA 98225
(360) 676-6985

Notes on the trail: You can start the ride from numerous areas within the park, including the swimming area. From the far parking area, though, ride left on a wide path. In about 100', turn right onto a 20' corridor connecting the Lake Padden Loop with the single-track. At the end of the corridor, turn right. Stay near the lake on the wide path as you pass junctions along the way. Pass swimming areas, showers, rest rooms, picnic areas, and finally, the baseball diamonds, as you complete the loop.

RIDE 51 · Lake Padden Single-Track

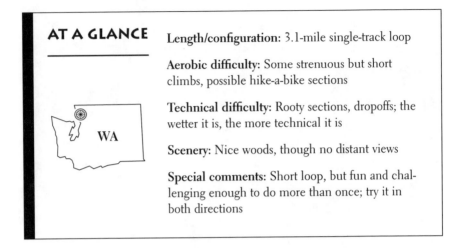

AT A GLANCE

WA

Length/configuration: 3.1-mile single-track loop

Aerobic difficulty: Some strenuous but short climbs, possible hike-a-bike sections

Technical difficulty: Rooty sections, dropoffs; the wetter it is, the more technical it is

Scenery: Nice woods, though no distant views

Special comments: Short loop, but fun and challenging enough to do more than once; try it in both directions

The 3.1-mile Lake Padden single-track loop is a sharp contrast to the wide, flat loop around the lake. It is short in length but not recommended for true beginners. Ambitious novices will find it challenging enough to appreciate the demands of true single-tracking, and short enough that it's never too far to turn back. Some walking will be required for fledgling fat-tire fanciers on some short-but-steep climbs, and on the tight switchbacks from the top of the system.

The ride is appropriate for more advanced riders, but will be a bit brief. In that case, do as they did here during the National Off-Road Bicycling Association (NORBA)-sanctioned Washington state championship races in the mid-1990s: do multiple laps.

The route starts on a gentle climb before the hard stuff comes, after passing the power lines for the first time. It meanders on good-quality trails through Douglas fir– and western red cedar–dominated landscape, along with hemlock, alder, and vine maple. The golf course and power lines under which you pass remind you, though, that you're not in the backcountry. The park sits just north of I-5 and south of Samish Way; the sounds you hear in the background are cars, but if you let your mind wander, you can pretend it's the sound of a river in the distance. Don't let your mind wander too far, though, because the rooty, technical terrain demands your attention.

This ride is a good choice for the leisure-time-impaired, because you can have a little fun and get a little exercise, while only going a little way from the center of town to get there.

General location: Lake Padden Park is located at the south end of Bellingham and north of I-5.

Elevation change: The route starts at about 450' elevation, and reaches a high point of 930'. Other climbing brings total elevation gain to about 640'.

RIDE 51 · Lake Padden Single-Track

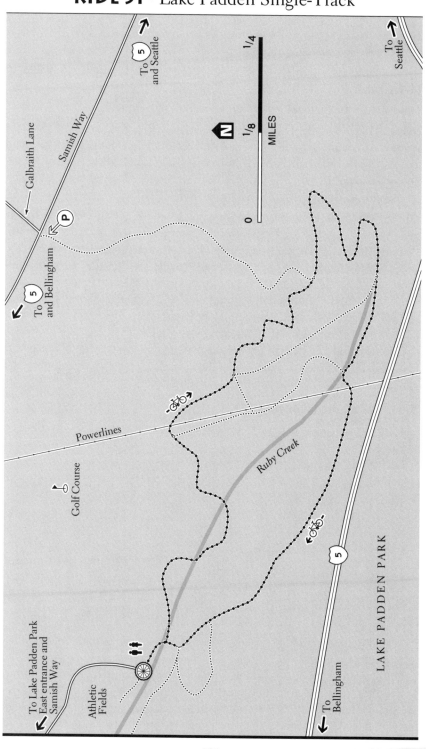

To 5 and Seattle

To Seattle

Galbraith Lane

Samish Way

N

1/4

1/8

0

MILES

P

To 5 and Bellingham

Powerlines

Golf Course

Ruby Creek

5

To Lake Padden Park East entrance and Samish Way

Athletic Fields

To Bellingham

LAKE PADDEN PARK

Season: Year-round.

Services: Water is available at the park. All services are available in Bellingham.

Hazards: Rooty sections; the wetter it is, the more technical it is. A couple of switchbacks may demand dismounts.

Rescue index: Help may be summoned at the park, and is available in Bellingham.

Land status: Bellingham Parks and Recreation Department.

Maps: The best (although not perfect) map is the *Rex Brainard: Western Lookout Mountains* map, available at local bike shops, including Baker Bike and Board. The Rex Brainard series is fun, quirky, and unorthodox; a sample notation is, "Pickup (sic) Litter—Every Litter Bit Counts." They also contain such information as calorie-expenditure and heart-rate graphs.

Finding the trail: From Seattle, drive along I-5 north to Exit 246/Samish Way (about 9 miles south of Bellingham's city center). Turn left (north) onto Samish Way and travel 2.5 miles to Lake Padden Park's east entrance. Turn left into the park and stay right at the split, toward the picnic area (to the left is the golf course). In 0.5 mile, park in the lot at the end of the road, next to the rest rooms.

From the north, drive along I-5 south to Exit 252/Samish Way. Go left over I-5, and right at the signal, continuing on Samish Way. In 2.5 miles, turn right into Lake Padden Park's east entrance.

The trails can also be accessed from a parking pullout just west of and across from Galbraith Lane, 1.2 miles east of the Lake Padden Park east entrance (the same spot from which to access the Galbraith network).

Sources of additional information:

WHIMPS (Whatcom Independent Mountain Pedalers)
P.O. Box 2961
Bellingham, WA 98227
(360) 671-4107

Baker Bike & Board
209 E. Holly Street
Bellingham, WA 98225
(360) 738-3728

Bellingham Parks & Recreation Department
210 Lottie Street
Bellingham, WA 98225
(360) 676-6985

Notes on the trail: Ride to the map board at the end of the parking lot and go left, starting on a wide dirt path. In about 100' you'll see a 20' corridor to the right connecting the Lake Padden loop and the trail on which you'll return. Ignore it for now and continue straight. The trail abruptly narrows into single-track and climbs gently. At 0.4 mile the grade gets a bit steeper but is still moderate. At 0.6 mile cross under the power line. To your right is the power line trail

A brief moment out of the trees at Lake Padden Park.

and to the left is the golf course; stay on the main trail, which immediately puts you back under the trees. Keep your eyes peeled to the left as you continue; in another 0.2 mile you'll leave the main trail and take the trail that shoots off to the left at the 8 o'clock position. Here's where some real climbing starts—gear down and grind up. In 0.4 mile, you will reach a **Y** intersection. The left fork ends at the parking area on Samish Way at Galbraith Lane in 0.5 mile; to continue the loop, go right, staying level for about 100' and then climbing the last 0.2 mile to the crest. From here, switchback down the steep, uneven, rutty, challenging, and—most of all—fun 0.3-mile section. From the bottom of the switchbacks, look for the trail to the left at 7 o'clock in 0.1 mile and take it (if you miss this turn, you'll be back to that first steep climb in another 0.1 mile). It's a fun descent here, but be careful; on a left-hand switchback I lost concentration and rammed into the tree on the far side of the turn at 15 mph—ouch! At a **T** intersection 0.2 mile from that fateful series of switchbacks, go left, cross the power lines, and continue. In another 0.1 mile, it's time to gear down again as you come to a climb that alternates between gentle and steep. The trail then drops and climbs as you twist around to a **Y** intersection, where horses are directed up and to the left, and bikes are routed to the right. In 0.1 mile meet the corridor to the right that leads you back to the parking lot. You've only gone 3.0 miles to this point, and you've probably still got a lot of energy left, so do another lap (in the opposite direction for a change of pace), take a leisurely cruise around Lake Padden, or stop and indulge yourself with a postride dip in the lake.

RIDE 52 · Galbraith

AT A GLANCE

WA

Length/configuration: Described ride is a 7.3-mile combination (2 loops tied together in a barbell configuration, with about 4 miles of single-track, plus gravel road and 0.6 mile of pavement); the gravel roads and single-track in the area can provide rides of all lengths and configurations

Aerobic difficulty: Moderate climbing on both roads and trails

Technical difficulty: Roots, rocks, drop-offs, log crossings, the works!

Scenery: Privately owned logging area includes clear-cuts and regenerated forest; views include Lummi Island, Portage Island, Orcas Island, and Bellingham

Special comments: If you can master these trails, you are a technical wizard!

The WHIMPS are anything but wimps—the Whatcom Independent Mountain Pedalers build and maintain the trails on Lookout Mountain (known among local mountain bikers as Galbraith). The trails they build are technically challenging affairs, wandering among big boulders and smaller rocks, root webs and angled roots, drop-offs and log crossings. They ride them throughout the year; the wetter the conditions, the more challenging the trails.

The network includes many short trail sections, 0.5 mile or less, that can be connected and routed in many different ways; there will undoubtedly be more by the time you read this, and if you stay generally on the west and south side of the mountain you'll find your way back down to Galbraith Lane.

This 7.3-mile route was led by WHIMPS founder and local cycling advocate Jim Sullivan. "Sully" has since moved on, but the WHIMPS remain, riding

Typical technical challenge at Galbraith. Rider: Tamara Blum.

their trails during the week and most weekends. If you can't get out to ride with the WHIMPS, then go out with a sense of adventure, and also a compass, so you'll know your general locations.

Most of the trails are named but none are marked; they're pretty easy to find, though. The names of some of the trails show the lighthearted spirit with which the club rides. The "Arsenio" Trail is so named because a tree patch along this otherwise clear-cut trail resembles the haircut of the former talk show host. Another trail, according to Sullivan, is known to the men as "Pubic Hair," but the women know it as the "Premature Trail," because, he says, just when it starts to get fun, it ends!

The network may not be there indefinitely; the landowners talk every so often about developing the land for housing and that *may* eventually become a reality.

General location: The ride's start is just south of Bellingham and north of I-5.

Elevation change: The parking area is at 730' elevation. The high point on the described ride is 1,365', though it is possible to climb to 1,790' at the high point in the trail network. Total elevation gain on the described route is about 850'.

Season: All year.

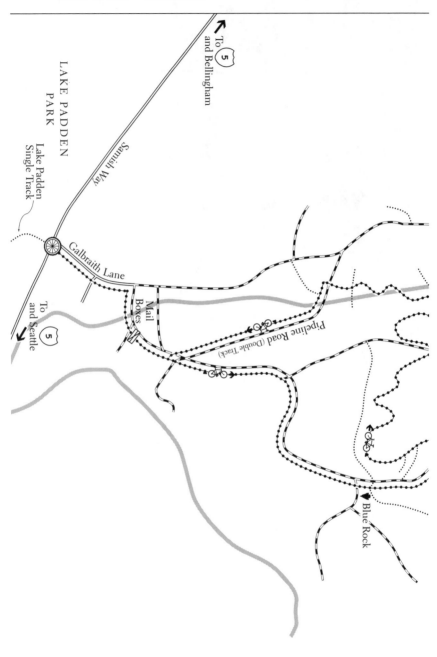

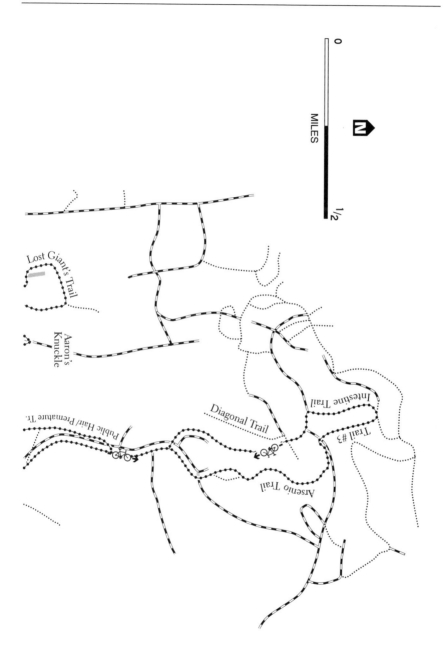

Lost Giant's Trail

Aaron's Knuckle

Public Hair/Premature Tr.

Diagonal Trail

Intestine Trail

Trail #3

Arsenio Trail

MILES

0   1/2

N

Services: Water is available at Lake Padden Park. All services are available in Bellingham.

Hazards: Galbraith is a great place to hone your technical riding skills, but be prepared to occasionally be separated from your bike.

Rescue index: Residents at the bottom of the hill may be of assistance. Help is available in Bellingham.

Land status: Land in this area has a patchwork private ownership, including the Trillium Corporation. WHIMPS member Craig Stevens said the company has a "don't ask, don't tell" policy on mountain biking, so, as is always the case, be respectful of the land on which you are riding.

Maps: No map accurately describes this area, which is constantly changing due to logging and trail-building. As a general guideline, use the *Rex Brainard: Western Lookout Mountains* map, available at Bike Shops in Bellingham.

Finding the trail: From Seattle, drive along I-5 north to Exit 246/Samish Way (about 9 miles south of Bellingham's city center). Turn left (north) onto Samish Way and travel 1.3 miles to a pullout on the left, just after Galbraith Lane to the right.

From the north, drive along I-5 south to Exit 252/Samish Way. Go left over I-5, and right at the signal, continuing on Samish Way. In 3.7 miles, park at the pulloff on the right, just before Galbraith Lane takes off to the left.

This parking area also serves as an access to the single-track at Lake Padden Park.

Sources of additional information:

WHIMPS (Whatcom Independent Mountain Pedalers)
P.O. Box 2961
Bellingham, WA 98227
(360) 671-4107

Baker Bike & Board
209 E. Holly Street
Bellingham, WA 98225
(360) 738-3728

Notes on the trail: From the parking area, ride up Galbraith Lane for 0.3 mile, and turn right at the bank of mailboxes on an unmarked private road. The road turns to gravel; in 0.1 mile, veer left at the **Y** intersection (where a private drive is to the right), go around the gate and start climbing, ignoring the spur roads and trails along the way. (You'll return on the road that comes in from the left, shortly past the gate.) As you gain elevation on the climb, look back to the west for views of Bellingham, the Chuckanut Mountains, Samish Flats, and Lummi, Portage, and Orcas Islands. At 1.4 miles, come to a **Y** junction, cleverly named "Blue Rock" for the spray-painted rock at the road split. You can go right and climb up to Lookout Mountain and the higher elevation trails, but for this ride, turn around and enjoy the view, then veer left at Blue Rock. Continue on the main road past more road and trail junctions for 0.9 mile, when the road going straight becomes overgrown and the main road turns to the left. In the next 50' the "Arsenio Trail" takes off to the right. In 0.1 mile come to a **Y** intersection; the two trails will rejoin shortly. The Arsenio Trail ends at a **T** intersection in 0.5 mile; go left, and continue on as the trail winds to the left. You'll quickly dump out onto an alder-lined skid road, from where you'll see "Arsenio" off to your left.

Follow the road past Trail #1 and Trail #2, then go right on Trail #3 (all three trails are within 100 yards). Trail #1 and Trail #2 hook back up with Trail #3 at a **T** intersection in 0.3 mile. Go left at the **T** and descend 50 yards to another **T** intersection. Turn left here, onto the Intestine Trail. In 0.5 mile, the Intestine Trail ends at a **T** intersection. Climb to the left, where, in about 100 feet, the main trail goes straight and another trail curves off to the right and climbs. Climb to the right, and in 0.1 mile, go straight at the 4-way intersection for a short taste of the Diagonal Trail. In a mere 20' a trail jumps off to the left of the Diagonal Trail. Take it as it climbs, initially paralleling the Diagonal Trail, and then to an open area in 0.2 mile. From here, look west for views of Bellingham Bay and the San Juan Islands, and northwest to Bellingham. The trail widens out into a road in another 0.1 mile, and climbs for 0.2 mile back to the road on which you made the initial climb. If you climb to the left at this junction, you're only 0.1 mile from the top of the main road and the Arsenio Trail. But go right and descend for 0.3 mile.

Just past the next gravel road to your right, find the Pubic Hair/Premature Trail to the right and hop on. The trail comes to a **Y** intersection in 0.2 mile. The left fork returns to the road; go right, continuing on the trail past some tight turns and tight squeezes through the trees as you parallel the road. In 0.1 mile after the **Y**, you'll pass two trails; stay to the right both times and wind around to the west and north on this rocky, loggy, obstacle course of a trail. After 0.7 mile of the Pubic Hair/Premature Trail, come out onto the gravel road known to the club as Aaron's Knuckle. Descend to the left a couple hundred yards, keeping an eye out to the right for the Lost Giants Trail. Turn right onto the Lost Giants Trail, and go left at the junction in 0.3 mile. After some tough log crossings, the trail ends at a **T** intersection within another 0.2 mile. Go left here, onto what starts out as a smooth trail (rare in this network). In 0.3 mile, after a log crossing, come to a 4-way junction, where the left and right junctions are not directly across from each other. Go straight until the trail ends at a **T** intersection at the double-track Pipeline Road. Take a left on Pipeline Road, through the creek and to the intersection at the bottom of the main road. Turn right, retracing the final 0.3 mile past the gate and to the ride's end.

RIDE 53 · Cranberry Lake

AT A GLANCE

WA

Length/configuration: 6.6-mile combination (out-and-back leading to a loop), mostly single-track with a few narrow dirt roads and a short stretch of gravel road; since the time of original research, a new trail has been added, making a full loop around the lake possible

Aerobic difficulty: Some short, sharp climbs, but it's not the aerobic challenge that makes for great riding . . .

Technical difficulty: . . . It's the technical challenge that does; roots and rocks abound

Scenery: The scenery, too: old-growth Douglas fir, Cranberry Lake and wetland views; you might catch glimpses of eagles, otters, and beavers as well

Special comments: Along with the Heart Lake/Whistle Lake area, the best in-town riding in the state. Great for a hike in wetter conditions, but please ride only when the trails are dry!

The Cranberry Lake trails provide some lush, classically northwest, in-town single-track suitable for the *adventurous* beginner—wimps need not apply. They're similar to the nearby Heart Lake/Whistle Lake trails—rooty, rocky, twisting, forested roller coasters—without as much steep climbing, but also without the corresponding distant views. Numerous spots along the route feature two distinct lines, or even trail splits, with a more beginner-friendly line and a more advanced, challenging, technical line.

The trails will be enjoyable for the more advanced rider, too, but true hammerheads will be more challenged by the Heart Lake/Whistle Lake network.

According to a representative from the local parks department, the Anacortes Community Forest Lands (ACFL) management plan calls for *local* use and education. They're a bit provincial about their trails here, and along those lines, I was also told that if the trails are overused, they will be restricted. The representative noted that even if an influx of riders stays on the trails and nobody skids around corners, the trails will still get worn, so please wait until the trails, not just the weather, are dry.

At the time of original research, a full loop around this area was not accessible to mountain bikes. Since then, a new trail around the northwest portion of

Cranberry Lake makes a full loop possible. Therefore, I submit both routes for your riding pleasure.

The trail network allows good explorability; numerous routes are available. Be creative, but be sensitive to the trails on which bikes are not allowed (e.g., trails immediately around the lake).

You'll know where they are by buying the ACFL map, but the trails are well signed. Interestingly, the trail signs are placed higher up than those you see on most trails (more to prevent vandalism than as a courtesy to equestrians, according to the parks rep). They are currently lowering the signs but be on the lookout; you have to adjust your mindset to watch for trail signs at a higher level than usual. Either way, take heed of the restrictions—bike access could be limited more by riding unauthorized trails than by overuse.

The Cranberry Lake trails, along with the Heart Lake/Whistle Lake trails, are part of an envisioned "Cross-Island Trail," linking Deception Pass State Park to the south, to Shannon Point, due west of the Lake. Some of the trail would go through private land, though, so it's not a sure thing. But how much local information you get depends on which local you speak to. (I spoke with some locals who were less than enthralled to find out I was from out of town. On the other hand, I was told by a couple of friendly in-towners that the bike shops in town are not good about giving info to out-of-towners, but when I visited Anacortes Cyclery, I was pointed right to the ACFL map.)

General location: Cranberry Lake is located in Anacortes, about 80 miles northwest of Seattle and 40 miles southwest of Bellingham.

Elevation change: Elevation at Cranberry Lake is 279'. The highest elevation, on Trail #116, is 600'. Total elevation gain on both routes is around 400'.

Season: Trails are rideable year-round, but wait until the good weather comes. Mountain bikers are taking the blame for trail erosion, even though most of the trail work volunteers are mountain bikers. Disregarding the park rep's caveat could result in negative long-term repercussions for mountain biking on ACFL lands.

Services: No water is available at Cranberry Lake. All services are available in Anacortes.

Hazards: Angled roots can cause problems. The trails close to the wetlands are especially vulnerable to wear. The trails are getting a lot of use, some by people who use the area for their daily walks. You've heard it before but it's worth repeating: be courteous to and be respectful of other trail users.

Rescue index: Lucky you—if you get hurt you're right in town!

Land status: Anacortes Community Forest Lands, under the jurisdiction of Anacortes Parks and Recreation.

Maps: The only map to use here is the Anacortes Community Forest Lands Trail Guide, available at the Parks Department in City Hall, the Anacortes Chamber of Commerce, Friendly Books, Watermark Books, and at Anacortes Cyclery.

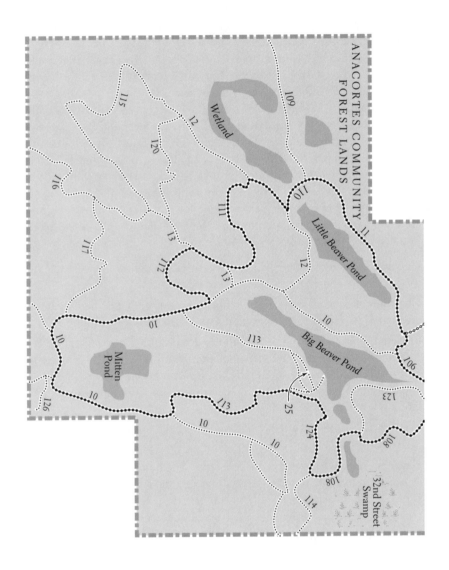

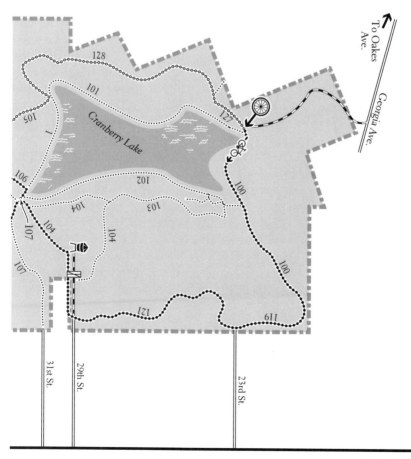

0
FEET
500
1000

Cranberry Lake

To Oakes Ave.

Georgia Ave.

128
101
105
1
106
107
107
104
104
102
103
100
100
121
119
127
100

31st St.
29th St.
23rd St.

Finding the trail: From Seattle, take I-5 north for 62 miles to WA 536 in Mt. Vernon and follow the signs toward Anacortes. WA 536 meets WA 20 in 5.3 miles; go west on WA 20, continuing west on WA 20 Spur when WA 20 turns south for 9.6 miles total, then turn right at the **T** intersection into Anacortes, staying on WA 20 Spur (Commercial Avenue). In 1.4 miles, turn left onto 12th Street. As the road curves left in 1.1 miles, 12th Street turns into Oakes Avenue. In 0.5 mile, turn left from the left turn lane onto Hartford, one street past Georgia Avenue. Turn left on West 3rd Street in 0.1 mile, then right onto Georgia Avenue in another 0.1 mile. (The more direct, though potentially more expensive option, is a left turn on Georgia Avenue, which is illegal.) In another 0.1 mile, turn right onto the gravel road toward Cranberry Lake (locked between 10 P.M. and 6 A.M.) and climb to the parking area in 0.3 mile.

From Bellingham, drive south on I-5 22 miles to WA 20 in Burlington. Drive west on WA 20 to Anacortes, and proceed as above.

Sources of additional information:

Anacortes Parks and Recreation
6th and Q Streets
P.O. Box 547
Anacortes, WA 98221
(360) 293-1918

Anacortes Cyclery
2012 Commercial Avenue
Anacortes, WA 98221-2528
(360) 293-6205

Notes on the trail: Ride around the north side of Cranberry Lake on Trail 100, greeting the anglers on shore as you pass by. Trail 100 veers northeast and then turns into Trail 119 going south. At 0.5 mile, come to a short trail split—straight ahead you can get up momentum and ride over a big boulder, or go left on a smooth path to where the trails rejoin. A junction to the left at 0.7 mile drops you onto 23rd Street; go straight (south) as Trail 119 turns into Trail 121. At 1.0 mile, on a gradual descent, veer right at the junction to continue on Trail 121. About 0.2 mile after this junction, a very short but sharp incline brings you to 29th Street, directly across from a Jehovah's Witness Kingdom Hall. Turn right here, where the pavement ends, and ride 0.1 mile up a gravel road toward a water tank and past a gate. About 10' before the water tank, Trail 104 starts to the left (the trail to the right just before the gates is a section of Trail 104 on which bikes are not allowed). Descend on Trail 104 for about 0.2 mile to a 3-way junction where the loop portion of the described combination ride begins. A hard right here is another section of Trail 104 off-limits to bikes; a soft right is where you return.

For now, go left on Trail 107, pass Trail 123 to the right, and then turn right at the **Y** intersection onto Trail 108. Follow Trail 108 to Trail 124 and turn right onto Trail 124. A slight climb on Trail 124 leads to a 4-way junction in 0.2 mile. Using your momentum from Trail 124, go left into a 50' long, sharp climb on Trail 113. Trail 113 twists, turns, and passes another junction as you ride south, continuing on Trail 113. In 0.2 mile come to the junction of Road 10, a wide gravel path that has a woodsy, single-track feel to it. Turn right on Road 10, descending by Mitten Pond to the right. (Mitten Pond is barely visible from the

Riding a bridge on Trail
108 at Cranberry Lake.

trail, but accesses along the way lead to it.) Road 10 winds to the west, and then
the north, passing some challenging terrain on intersecting trails (try them out!).
Stay on Road 10 past the junction of Trail 113; 0.1 mile past Trail 113, turn left
off of Road 10 and onto a tough little climb on Trail 112. Trail 112 rolls to a **T**
intersection at Road 13; go right at the **T** onto rocky Road 13 for just a few pedal
strokes, and then turn left onto a rocky incline on Trail 111. Trail 111 drops onto
Road 12, going north (right). Descend on Road 12 for 0.1 mile, then turn left
onto Trail 110. Be sensitive to the trail (dismount if conditions demand it) as you
ride the marshy area between the wetland and Little Beaver Pond. After the
marshy area, an angled log divides Trail 109 to the left and Road 11 (which, at
this point, is a single-track) to the right. Turn right onto Road 11, riding northeast around Little Beaver Pond. In 0.5 mile, come to the junction of Trail 105 to
the left. Here's where you can branch off for the full-lake loop: Go left on Trail
105, and in about 0.3 mile, not far after a wooden bridge, look to the right for
Trail 128, marked by a big cedar—if you miss it you'll come to a new road in
another 0.2 mile. Twist and climb around to Trail 127 in 0.6 mile and return to
the Cranberry Lake Parking area in another 0.2 mile.

To continue the combination route, continue on Road 11, past Trail 105, to the junction of Trail 106 to the left and Road 10 to the right. Go left into a short descent on Trail 106. In 0.2 mile, cross a bridge, then immediately look back and up to the right. See the trail? That's Trail 107; take it and make the steep climb back to the 3-way junction to complete the loop, and start the "back" portion of the out-and-back. At the 3-way junction, make a soft left to retrace Trail 104 back to the water tank. Ride down the road to the pavement and the Kingdom Hall, go left onto Trail 121 and wind back on Trails 119 and 100.

RIDE 54 · Heart Lake/Whistle Lake

AT A GLANCE

WA

Length/configuration: Up to 12 miles of overwhelmingly single-track, exploring all mountain bike–legal trails and other dirt in the network, plus a 1.7-mile paved road climb to the top of Mt. Erie

Aerobic difficulty: Short, steep climbs; some hike-a-bikes; the paved road climb rises 870' to the top of Fidalgo Island

Technical difficulty: Lots of rocks and roots, some on steep grades; switchbacks

Scenery: Beautiful lake overlooks, deep woods, San Juan Islands views from the high points on the trails, distant views west, south, and east from the top of Mt. Erie (road only)

Special comments: Your conduct on the trails will determine the future of mountain biking in this beautiful, challenging area.

Challenging climbs, fast and technical descents, lake views and accesses, vistas to the Olympic Peninsula, the San Juan Islands, and the high Cascades, scattered old growth in lush forestland, literally a few minutes from the heart of town—life is good in Anacortes!

Rooty, rocky, hard-packed trails and roads invite mountain bikers to wander among old growth and alder, ferns, mosses, and wildflowers.

You'll find some level stuff here, but not too much, and that's part of the fun. Middle-ring climbs, low-ring climbs, and even some hike-a-bikes are rewarded with sometimes speedy, sometimes jarring descents. Search around for views at the crests of the climbs; you'll love what you see.

I rode here twice, and both times got lost, but I enjoyed the area so much that I just kept a general idea of my location, and knew which way to go when I wanted to end. I started at the Whistle Lake side, rode across H Avenue (Heart Lake Road), wandered some more, and found my way back without worry.

I found a few descents riding down to Heart Lake Road excessively rutted, to the point where I was walking my bike downhill, but the vast majority of the trails were quite rideable, quite beautiful, and quite fun.

In addition to the trails, the 1.7-mile paved road climb up to Mt. Erie is worth your knobby-treaded effort. It's a steep, stair-step climb that leads to the highest point on Fidalgo Island. Concrete platforms, accessed by very short walkways and stairs (one near the left-hand curve that brings you to the top; another from the walkway to the left of the tower; and the third from the end of the paved road) allow you to set down your bike and check out some glorious views. Signs at the viewing areas identify the scenery below and beyond. On a clear day you can see as far east as Glacier Peak. Cool!

Like the Cranberry Lake trails, the trails here are signed about 8 feet up into the trees. As a rule, the ACFL trails are numbered in the 20s and 200s, while the Heart Lake State Park trails have a 300-series designation. The signage is much more complete in the ACFL portion of the network; on my rides, I got lost once I entered the Heart Lake trails. You can't get too lost here because the trails are self-contained, mostly bordered by paved roads and residences. Bring a compass and spring for the map booklet, and you'll know the general direction in which to return.

General location: The trailheads are located just south of the Anacortes city limits, approximately 80 miles northwest of Seattle and 40 miles southwest of Bellingham.

Elevation change: Whistle Lake is situated at 432' elevation; Heart Lake is at 332'. Mt. Erie (by road only, for bikes) tops out at 1,273', for an approximately 870' paved road climb in 1.7 miles. A tour of the all the trails will easily give you more than 1,000' of elevation gain.

Season: As with the Cranberry Lake trails, ride around here in dry conditions only, due to both political and trail concerns. Thank you.

Services: There is no potable water available along the trails; fill up in town. For a preride muffin and espresso, postride sandwich, wine, and cheese, and all manner of good eats and drinks, try The Store, a neat little shop on Commercial Avenue and 37th Street, one block south (left) of the **T** intersection at WA 20 and Commercial Avenue.

Hazards: Ride perpendicular to those angled roots so your rear wheel doesn't slip. Many blind corners can conceal hikers and equestrians, so assume there are others beyond every curve. Show the locals you're a responsible cyclist; ride in control.

A 1987 ordinance allows trail restrictions if a particular user group is causing user conflicts or trail damage. Though motorcycles are allowed on many trails,

HEART LAKE
STATE PARK

To 41st St.

To
Fidalgo Ave.

ANACORTES
COMMUNITY
FOREST LANDS

H Ave.

O Ave.

208

221

223

236

240

308

209

209

224

23

211

310

313

302

309

302

311

308

310

307

306

305

300

Heart
Lake

210
Ø

210
Ø

21

332

300

View

231

213
25
Ø

215
Ø

305

305

302

300

216

225

226

220
Ø

214

21

229
Ø

226

230

207

Sugarloaf

215
Ø

Mt. Erie Rd.

26

21

22

205

Heart Lake Rd.

ANACORTES

Mt. Erie

Tr. 216
Ø

1273

Lake
Erie

To Rosario Rd.

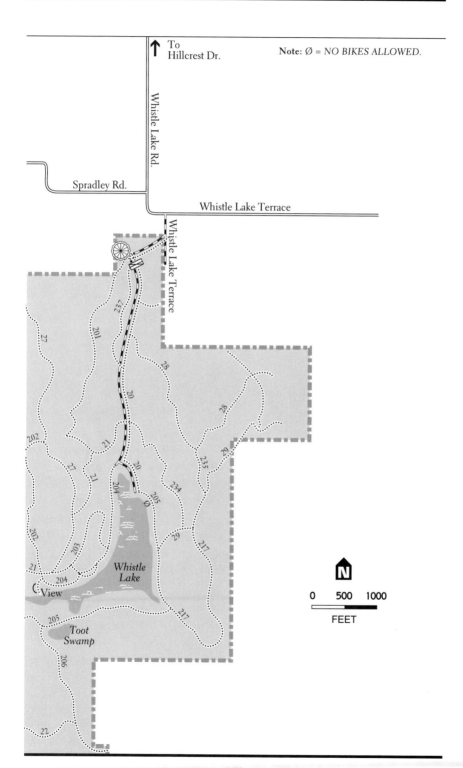

To
Hillcrest Dr.

Note: Ø = *NO BIKES ALLOWED.*

Whistle Lake Rd.

Spradley Rd.

Whistle Lake Terrace

Whistle Lake Terrace

237

201

27

28

20

28

202

21

29

27

235

21

20

234

204

205

29

217

202

203

21

204

Whistle
Lake

View

205

217

Toot
Swamp

206

22

N

0   500   1000

FEET

All this beauty and fun are just minutes away from the heart of town.

bikes potentially present more of a problem for hikers and equestrians because of their quiet nature (which is usually a plus).

Rescue index: There are residences on the way to both trailheads, and help is available in town.

Land status: Whistle Lake and Mt. Erie lie within the Anacortes Community Forest Lands, under the jurisdiction of Anacortes Parks and Recreation. In 1987 the City of Anacortes passed an ordinance annexing all city forestland into the city. The northwest area of the network is within Heart Lake State Park.

Maps: The Anacortes Community Forest Lands (ACFL) Trail Guide, available at the parks department office in City Hall, Anacortes Cyclery, and other locations around town, is a must. The booklet contains maps of both this area and the Cranberry Lake trails, and provides background on the trails, the flora and fauna, and the ACFL.

Finding the trail: From Seattle, travel north on I-5 for 62 miles to WA 536 in Mt. Vernon, then follow the signs toward Anacortes. WA 536 meets WA 20 in 5.3 miles; go west on WA 20, then WA 20 Spur (when WA 20 turns south) for 9.6 miles, then turn left at the **T** intersection onto Commercial Avenue. In 0.3 mile come to the intersection of Fidalgo Avenue. Now that you're here it's decision time.

To get to the Whistle Lake Trailhead, turn left on Fidalgo and take it as it jogs left onto Hillcrest Drive in 0.2 mile, then right again. Hillcrest Drive turns into Whistle Lake Road as it turns right in another 0.2 mile. Pass Spradley Road and a "Dead End" sign in 0.8 mile, then turn left onto Whistle Lake Terrace (where a private residence is straight ahead). Veer right on gravel Whistle Lake Terrace past the residences on the left; then, just after a wide parking pullout on your left, turn right at the junction. You'll come to the parking area, at Road 20 and Trails 201 and 237, in 0.2 mile.

To get to the Heart Lake Trailhead, turn right on Fidalgo and follow it as it quickly turns left into O Avenue. Take the first right, onto 41st Street, and travel 0.5 mile to the stop sign at H Avenue (which turns into Heart Lake Road as you head south). Turn left; in 0.5 mile you'll see a sign on your right reading "Anacortes Community Forest Land, Heart Lake Trails." Continue past it and park 0.4 mile farther at Heart Lake State Park on the right; or 0.1 mile past it at a pullout on the left, at the base of Road 21; or 0.6 mile beyond the state park, making a left turn before Mt. Erie Road and parking on the side of that access road.

From Bellingham, drive south on I-5 22 miles to WA 20 in Burlington. Drive west on WA 20 to Anacortes, and proceed as above.

Sources of additional information:

Anacortes Parks and Recreation
6th and Q Streets
P.O. Box 547
Anacortes, WA 98221
(360) 293-1918

Anacortes Cyclery
2012 Commercial Avenue
Anacortes, WA 98221-2528
(360) 293-6205

Notes on the trail: In the Whistle Lake area, bikes are allowed on all trails except Trail 205 from Roads 20 to 29; Trails 212, 213, 214, 215 (south and west of the Sugarloaf summit), 216, 220, 228, 238, 239, and Roads 24 and 25. In the Heart Lake area bikes are prohibited on Trail 210 around the lakeshore. If this sounds like a lot of trails, worry not, fellow rider; there are many, many trails on which bikes can blissfully roam.

Road (trail) 21 is a good thoroughfare to use. It's a fun trail in and of itself, but also connects to all of the areas within the forest. It widens out in places and narrows in others, and though it is designated as a road, you'll call it a trail. It starts on the Whistle Lake side via Road 20 (which *does* feel like a road) and ends with a fast descent to Heart Lake Road, 0.1 mile south of the Heart Lake State Park entrance, at a small pullout. The trail is marked by a small white gate. To access paved Mt. Erie Road, travel south of the Heart Lake State Park entrance for 0.6 mile to the left turn that accesses Mt. Erie Road. Other trails can be accessed north of Heart Lake on that side of the road.

If you're a beginner, you're best off parking on the Whistle Lake side and starting past the gate on Road 20. Ride about 0.8 mile to the north tip of the lake and veer right onto Trail 204. From there, it's a challenging 0.4 mile on Trail 204 to some great views from above Whistle Lake. This was one of my favorite trails in the network.

If you plan to wander, you'll eventually find your way back, but it may get dark by then if you start later in the day. If you find yourself on the opposite side of the network than where you started, take the pavement back. It's about 2.9 miles from the Whistle Lake Trailhead parking area to the Heart Lake State Park parking area using the "Finding the trail" directions.

RIDE 55 · Mt. Josephine

AT A GLANCE

WA

Length/configuration: 18-mile out-and-back on gravel roads (9 miles each way)

Aerobic difficulty: Moderate to advanced; a long, steady climb with short, steep pitches

Technical difficulty: Moderate; some rough, rocky sections

Scenery: A ride through privately owned forest-lands (large clear-cuts and stands of second-growth); good distant views from road

Special comments: Area is popular with off-road vehicle enthusiasts

This out-and-back ride is an 18-mile round-trip over gravel roads in fair to poor condition. The ascent is long and tiring, with a lot of moderate climbing and some short, steep pitches. The last couple of miles below the summit are the toughest. Rocky stretches of road make the return technical in places.

Although clear-cuts feature heavily in the picture, the panoramic view from the summit of Mt. Josephine is good. Twin Sisters, Mt. Baker, and Mt. Shuksan dominate the northern horizon. On a clear day you can spy Puget Sound and the Olympics to the west.

General location: This ride starts about 15 miles east of Sedro Woolley, Washington.

Elevation change: The ride begins at 570' and tops out on Mt. Josephine at 3,957'. Total elevation gain: 3,387'.

Season: Snow may linger near the top of the mountain until the middle of the summer.

Services: There is no water available on the ride. Water, food, lodging, gas, and groceries can be obtained in Sedro Woolley.

Hazards: Watch your speed on the descent, and anticipate changing road conditions. The area is popular with off-road vehicle riders.

RIDE 55 · Mt. Josephine

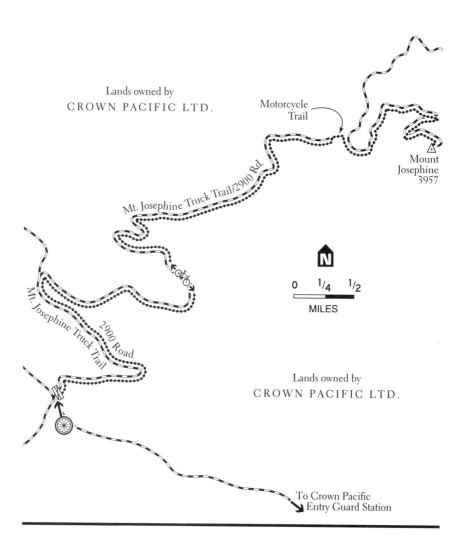

Rescue index: Access to the ride is gained through a controlled entry point at a guard station. Help can be summoned at the Crown Pacific guard station or in nearby Hamilton. To reach Hamilton, drive east on WA 20 from Cabin Creek Road and turn right after 0.6 mile.

Land status: Lands owned by Crown Pacific.

Maps: USGS 7.5 minute quads: Lyman and Hamilton.

Finding the trail: Take I-5 to Exit 230 and follow WA 20 east through Burlington and Sedro Woolley. It is 17 miles from I-5 to Cabin Creek Road. (You

Looking north to Twin Sister from Mt. Josephine.

have gone too far if you pass Crown Pacific's Hamilton office on your right.) Turn left (north) onto Cabin Creek Road and follow it for 0.2 mile to a stop sign. Turn right and proceed for 0.3 mile to an unsigned intersection. Turn left and travel 0.2 mile to a Crown Pacific entry guard station to obtain an entrance permit. Continue along the main road for another 2.5 miles to the gated Mt. Josephine Truck Trail on the right. An obscure wooden sign reads "Truck Trail/SW–HO–2900." Park on the side of the spur road that goes left here.

Source of additional information:

Crown Pacific
P.O. Box 28
Hamilton, WA 98255
(360) 826-3951

Notes on the trail: Crown Pacific encourages recreational use of its forestlands in places where such use will not conflict with logging operations. Please obtain an access permit at the guard station or at the company's Hamilton office.

Ride up the 2900 road. At intersections, follow the main road or signs that keep you on the 2900 road. Much of the cycling is through logged or burned areas that offer open views. The road enters shady woods after 5.5 miles and ends at a couple of streams in another 1.9 miles. Look to the right for a rough motor-cycle trail. Take this path through the wet area and around a trench. This path will bring you to a gravel road; turn right. Stay left at the next three intersections. The road ends just below the summit. Turn right onto an old double-track trail that switchbacks up to the top. Return the way you came.

MOUNTAIN LOOP HIGHWAY

The ambitiously named Mountain Loop Highway heads east out of Everett. This modest two-lane road takes travelers into the Darrington Ranger District of the Mt. Baker–Snoqualmie National Forest. Mountain bikers find the area laced with quiet gravel roads.

The paved portion of Mountain Loop Highway ends near Barlow Pass (one of several Barlow Passes in the Pacific Northwest). A double-track heads south from the highway and follows the Sauk River to the old mining town of Monte Cristo. The gravel road is quiet today except for the sounds of hikers and bikers. At the turn of the century, the towering granite peaks surrounding Monte Cristo were crawling with grizzled miners searching for gold. Today several footpaths lead from the town site into the Henry M. Jackson Wilderness Area.

In close proximity to Monte Cristo is the Schweitzer Creek Loop. This ride takes in a mountain lake and passes over a short stretch of trail through old-growth cedar.

Swinging north, Mountain Loop Highway becomes a gravel road and heads toward Darrington. Most of the residents of this mill town hail from the hills and hollows of North Carolina. These fun-loving people have kept their rich southern Appalachian culture alive through quilting, bluegrass music, and gospel.

A good time can be had riding to the top of nearby North Mountain. A lookout tower on the summit gets you up over the treetops, revealing a countryside that is stunning in its beauty.

RIDE 56 · Schweitzer Creek Loop

AT A GLANCE

WA

Length/configuration: 10.8-mile combination on gravel roads and a touch of trail; 6-mile loop and a 4.8-mile out-and-back (2.4 miles each way)

Aerobic difficulty: Mostly moderately difficult with a mix of steep and easy sections

Technical difficulty: The gravel roads present few difficulties; 0.3 mile of single-track (contains some obstacles)

Scenery: Logged forest; pretty streams and lakes; a bit of old-growth cedar

Special comments: Ends with fun descents (watch out for oncoming traffic)

The majority of this 10.8-mile loop (which also includes an out-and-back leg) is on gravel roads in fair to good condition. There is no warming up on this ride; you begin with steep climbing. Steep grades quickly give way to moderate ones and then to easy uphill pedaling. The outing ends with fast, twisty downhills. There is some washboarding on the steep hills.

This loop is nice, though unremarkable. You climb past some pleasant, cascading creeks near the start of the ride. Logging operations have created some openings in the forest canopy; these gaps allow glimpses of snowcapped peaks in the Boulder River Wilderness. Rounding out the highlights are a stroll to a small lake and a short trail through a stand of old-growth cedar.

General location: The trip begins near Schweitzer Creek, approximately 33 miles east of Everett, Washington.

Elevation change: The circuit starts at 1,380' and climbs to a high point of 2,800'. Undulations on the route add an estimated 200' of climbing to the outing. Total elevation gain: 1,620'

Season: The early fall is a nice time for a visit to this portion of the forest. Forest Service Road 4020 is busy with vehicles traveling to hiking trailheads, especially in the summer.

Services: There is no water available on the ride. Water is available at the Verlot Public Service Center and seasonally at Turlo Campground (across from the service center). Gas, food, lodging, and pay phones are available in Granite Falls.

RIDE 56 · Schweitzer Creek Loop

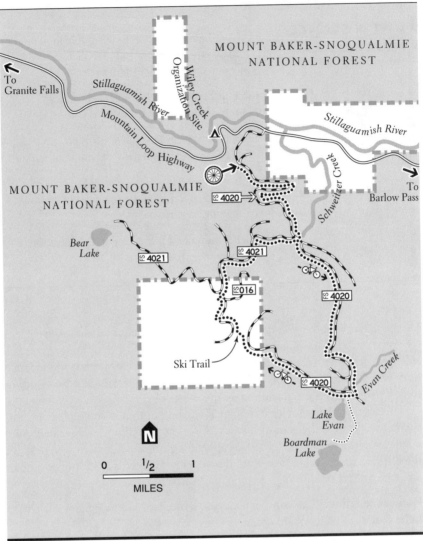

Hazards: Traffic can be heavy. Stay alert and control your speed on the descent. The route contains some blind corners.

Rescue index: Help can be found at the Verlot Public Service Center during office hours and in Granite Falls. There is a pay phone at the service center.

Land status: Mt. Baker–Snoqualmie National Forest.

Maps: The district map of the Darrington Ranger District is a good guide to the forest roads followed on this ride. The ski trail connecting FS 4020 to FS 4021 is not shown. USGS 7.5 minute quad: Mallardy Ridge.

Checking the map at Lake Evan.

Finding the trail: From Everett and Interstate 5, take Exit 194 to US 2 east. Travel east on US 2 for about 4 miles to WA 9. Turn left (north) onto WA 9 and follow it for approximately 3.5 miles to WA 92. Turn right (east) onto WA 92 toward Granite Falls. Stay on WA 92 for about 8.5 miles to the intersection of WA 92 and Mountain Loop Highway in Granite Falls. Turn left (north) onto Mountain Loop Highway. Drive approximately 11 miles on Mountain Loop Highway to the Verlot Public Service Center (on the left). Continue past the service center on Mountain Loop Highway for 4.7 miles and turn right on FS 4020. A sign here reads "Ashland Lakes Trails–5, Bear/Pinnacle Lakes Trails–6." Follow the dirt road uphill for 0.3 mile and park in the pullout on the right. There is a double-track jeep road to the left, opposite the pullout.

Sources of additional information:

Darrington Ranger District
1405 Emmens Street
Darrington, WA 98241
(360) 436-1155

Verlot Public Service Center
Granite Falls, WA 98252
(360) 691-7791

Notes on the trail: From the pullout, follow FS 4020 uphill. Continue on the main road past signed FS 4021 on the right. (You will be returning on this road.) The trailhead for Boardman Lake and Lake Evan is on the left, 4.7 miles into the ride. FS 4020 rolls up and down from this point. When the road swings north and descends, approximately 1.3 miles from the Lake Evan Trailhead, look to the left for blue diamond-shaped symbols nailed on trees. These blue diamonds mark the start of a single-track ski trail. Turn left onto the trail and follow it into the woods. You will reach an abandoned road in about 0.3 mile. The road is built out of dark, crushed rock. Turn right onto the road and go over a two-plank bridge that spans the first of several ditches. After the ditches, you will reach a dirt road with a sign for Ashland Lakes Trailhead; turn left here. Shortly you will come to unsigned FS 4021. There is a sign here for Ashland Lakes Trail and Bear/Pinnacle Lakes. Turn right onto FS 4021. At the intersection with FS 4020, turn left. Follow FS 4020 back down to your vehicle.

RIDE 57 · Monte Cristo

AT A GLANCE

WA

Length/configuration: 9-mile dirt and gravel road out-and-back (4.5 miles each way)

Aerobic difficulty: Mostly easy; a couple of moderately difficult hills

Technical difficulty: Easy to moderately difficult; a few, brief rocky stretches

Scenery: 7,000' peaks surround the historic mining town of Monte Cristo

Special comments: An excellent ride for strong families

Monte Cristo is an old mining town near the headwaters of the South Fork of the Sauk River. This easy out-and-back ride is nine miles long. It covers gentle terrain with a couple of short, moderately difficult hills. The trip follows a compacted dirt-and-gravel road in good condition. Repairs to flood-damaged sections of the road have been made with coarse rock; there are a few of these brief, extremely bumpy sections of road.

This area was the site of the Cascades' greatest gold rush. Millions of dollars worth of gold and silver ore were produced here in the late nineteenth and early twentieth centuries. A free map and walking tour brochure is available as you enter the town site. The pamphlet describes some of the town's history and provides insights into the lives of the miners. There are walking paths to old structures and relics of the "boom." The town sits below 7,000-foot peaks. Hiking trails lead into the surrounding Henry M. Jackson Wilderness.

General location: The trailhead is at Barlow Pass, about 50 miles east of Everett, Washington.

RIDE 57 · Monte Cristo

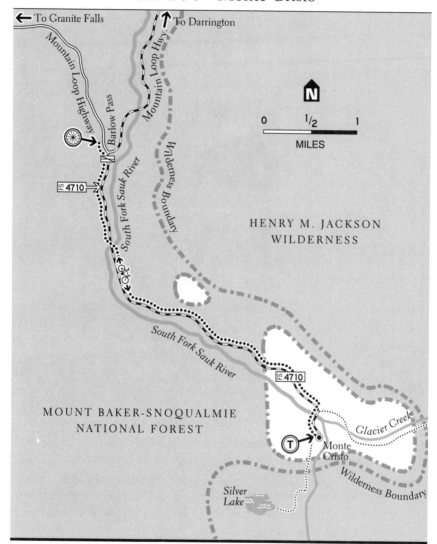

To Granite Falls

To Darrington

Mountain Loop Highway

Barlow Pass

Mountain Loop Hwy.

Wilderness Boundary

N

0   1/2   1
MILES

FS 4710

South Fork Sauk River

HENRY M. JACKSON
WILDERNESS

South Fork Sauk River

FS 4710

MOUNT BAKER-SNOQUALMIE
NATIONAL FOREST

Glacier Creek

T

Monte
Cristo

Wilderness Boundary

Silver
Lake

Elevation change: The ride starts at 2,360' and reaches a low point of 2,300' in the first mile. The road ascends to a high point of 2,760' in Monte Cristo. Additional ups and downs over the course of the ride add approximately 50' of climbing to the route. Total elevation gain: 570'.

Season: The road to Monte Cristo is generally free of snow from late May through October. The area sees its greatest influx of visitors in the summer.

Services: There is no water available on this trip. Water is available at the Ver-lot Public Service Center and seasonally at Turlo Campground (across from the

Peaks in the Henry M.
Jackson Wilderness.

service center). Verlot is on Mountain Loop Highway on the way to the trail-head. Food, lodging, groceries, and gas are available in Granite Falls.

Hazards: Short, rocky sections of road can cause handling problems, particularly on the return descent. Use extra caution while riding over these rough areas or walk your bike through them. Extend courtesy to others on the road—this is a popular day hike. Although traffic is usually very light, you may encounter motorists traveling to homes in the area.

Rescue index: Help can be found at the Verlot Public Service Center during regular business hours. The nearest pay phone is at the service center.

Land status: Forestlands and private property within the boundaries of the Mt. Baker–Snoqualmie National Forest.

Maps: The district map of the Darrington Ranger District is a good guide to this ride. USGS 7.5 minute quads: Bedal and Monte Cristo.

Finding the trail: From Everett and I-5, take Exit 194 to US 2 east. Travel east on US 2 for about 4 miles to WA 9. Turn left (north) onto WA 9 and follow it for approximately 3.5 miles to WA 92. Turn right (east) onto WA 92 toward Granite

Falls. Stay on WA 92 for about 8.5 miles to the intersection of WA 92 and Mountain Loop Highway in Granite Falls. Turn left (north) onto Mountain Loop Highway. Drive approximately 31 miles on Mountain Loop Highway to Barlow Pass. There are parking areas on both sides of the highway.

Sources of additional information:

Darrington Ranger District
1405 Emmens Street
Darrington, WA 98241
(360) 436-1155

Verlot Public Service Center
Granite Falls, WA 98252
(360) 691-7791

Notes on the trail: Pedal east from the parking area toward the beginning of FS 4710/Monte Cristo Road. Turn right onto FS 4710. Walk your bike around the gate and follow the road to Monte Cristo. Explore Monte Cristo on foot; no bikes on the trails, please. Return the way you came.

RIDE 58 · North Mountain

AT A GLANCE

Length/configuration: 13.6-mile gravel road out-and-back (6.8 miles each way)

Aerobic difficulty: Mostly easy; the road gets steeper near the top

Technical difficulty: Easy; good gravel road (gets rougher near the summit)

Scenery: On clear days, views of the Olympics, Puget Sound, and Mt. Baker

Special comments: One of the finest vantage points in the Pacific Northwest

This out-and-back ride is 13.6 miles long. The ascent to the summit of North Mountain involves mostly easy pedaling. The climb is on a nicely graded gravel road in good condition. Near the top, the road gets steeper and a little rougher.

A lookout tower at the summit of North Mountain gives you one of the finest vantage points in the Pacific Northwest. Prominent features to the southwest are Whitehorse Ridge and Three Fingers. To the east lie the Sauk Prairie and the Sauk and Suiattle Rivers. On a clear day, you can see Mount Baker, the Olympics, and Puget Sound.

RIDE 58 · North Mountain

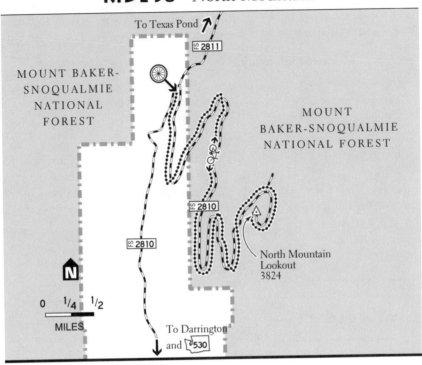

To Texas Pond

FS 2811

MOUNT BAKER-
SNOQUALMIE
NATIONAL
FOREST

MOUNT
BAKER-SNOQUALMIE
NATIONAL FOREST

FS 2810

FS 2810

North Mountain
Lookout
3824

N

0   1/4   1/2
MILES

To Darrington
and 530

General location: This ride begins near Darrington, Washington. Darrington is 32 miles east of I-5, approximately halfway between Seattle and Bellingham.

Elevation change: The ride starts at 1,960' and reaches 3,824' at the lookout. Total elevation gain: 1,864'.

Season: The road is usually clear of snow from May through October.

Services: There is no water available on the ride. Water, food, lodging, groceries, and gas can be obtained in Darrington.

Hazards: Expect some traffic on this trip, especially around sunset. Assume that sight-seeing motorists will be preoccupied. Control your speed on the descent, and watch for loose gravel.

Rescue index: Help can be found in Darrington.

Land status: Mt. Baker–Snoqualmie National Forest and state forestlands. There is also a stretch of public right-of-way through a small parcel of private property.

Maps: The district map of the Darrington Ranger District is a good guide to this ride. USGS 7.5 minute quads: Darrington and Fortson.

Finding the trail: From Bellingham, drive south on I-5 for about 45 miles to Exit 208. From Seattle, travel north on I-5 for approximately 45 miles to Exit 208. Follow WA 530 east for 32 miles to Darrington. Proceed east through

View south from the
lookout tower on North
Mountain.

Darrington to the intersection of WA 530 and Mountain Loop Highway. Turn
left (north) to continue on WA 530. You will pass the Darrington Ranger Station
on the left, then you will cross two sets of railroad tracks. FS 28 intersects with
WA 530 immediately north of the second set of tracks (1.1 miles north of the
intersection of WA 530 and Mountain Loop Highway). Turn left and follow FS 28
for 3 miles to FS 2810. Turn right onto FS 2810. You will arrive at FS 2811 (on
the left, at a switchback in FS 2810) after 3.8 miles on FS 2810. Park your vehicle
on FS 2810, on the outside of the switchback and just uphill from FS 2811.

Source of additional information:

Darrington Ranger District
1405 Emmens Street
Darrington, WA 98241
(360) 436-1155

Notes on the trail: Ride uphill on FS 2810. Shortly you will pass milepost
marker 4. Just beyond milepost marker 10, you will arrive at an intersection of
roads. Stay to the right and continue to climb on the main road. (A rough spur
road goes left and descends here.) Follow the main road to the lookout tower.
Return the way you came.

SKYKOMISH TO LAKE
WENATCHEE

The Lake Wenatchee area holds a wealth of single-track, in both the Lake Wenatchee and Entiat Ranger Districts of the Wenatchee National Forest. It is truly mountain bike nirvana, but activities are hardly limited to mountain biking. It's about a two-hour drive east of Seattle on US 2, and the popularity of the area is such that the 380,000-acre Lake Wenatchee Ranger District alone has 29 campgrounds, both private and public, from which to choose.

Though Lake Wenatchee is a hub of outdoor activity in the region, most of the choice mountain biking is northeast of the lake, east of the Chiwawa River Valley and into the Entiat Mountains. The trails are so scenic, thrilling, challenging, and plentiful here that some groups of well-prepared, iron-legged cyclists start from here and ride all the way to Lake Chelan. Shuttle vehicles await them after rides of up to 60 miles and more, all on single-track!

The Johnson Ridge Trail, in the adjoining Skykomish District of the Mt. Baker–Snoqualmie National Forest, is another story. It can be accessed off of US 2 out of Skykomish, on the way to Lake Wenatchee from the Puget Sound area. Skykomish is about 16 miles west of Stevens Pass and 40 miles west of Lake Wenatchee. As of 1998, it's the only single-track in the Skykomish Ranger District of the Mt. Baker–Snoqualmie National Forest open to mountain bikes. It physically, technically, and scenically amazes even the most experienced of riders.

Though it's the only single-track open in the area, it's well worth a stop on the way over Stevens Pass. It is most logically presented in this section, as it can be accessed off of US 2 north of Skykomish, on the way to Lake Wenatchee from the Puget Sound area. Skykomish is about 16 miles west of Stevens Pass and about 40 miles west of Lake Wenatchee.

Trailhead parking passes are required at most trailheads within both the Mt. Baker–Snoqualmie and Wenatchee National Forests. Pick yours up in town or from any ranger district office or forest service headquarters.

RIDE 59 · Johnson Ridge Trail

AT A GLANCE

Length/configuration: 8.2 mile (total mileage) out-and-back including 6.8 miles of single-track; trail ends at Henry M. Jackson Wilderness boundary; can be extended by bike from the start, and on foot at the wilderness boundary

Aerobic difficulty: A lung-busting, anaerobic fitness test

Technical difficulty: As demanding technically as it is aerobically

Scenery: Incredible Cascade views (Mt. Rainier, Mt. Stuart, and Glacier Peak are but a fraction of the list); wildflower-strewn meadows

Special comments: As of 1998, the only trail in the Skykomish Ranger District open to mountain bikes—don't ruin it by pedaling into the wilderness area

There's a saying among some hard-core mountain bikers: "If you ain't walkin', you ain't ridin'." They're talking about doing trails a little beyond your capability to test your limits. The Johnson Ridge Trail #1067 is such a test for even the most advanced mountain biker. From the first pedal stroke this 4.1-mile (each way) outing is a physical and technical challenge, first climbing on a loose, steep, rocky roadbed, and then on a hard-packed vertical trail with root and rock hurdles on steep grades. The views are worth the effort, though; the Cascades views at the start and on Sunrise Mountain are mere teasers for the panoramas from Scorpion Mountain at the far end of the route.

You can extend this trip on either side of the trail: park at the junction of Forest Service Road 65 and FS 6520 for a scenic and difficult 6.9-mile warm-up, or at the junction of FS 6520 and FS 6526 for 1.3 miles of warm-up (both have ample parking, and will make for exhilarating final descents); or stash your bike at the far end of the mountain bike legal portion of the trail and make the 0.5-mile hike down to Joan Lake, in the Henry M. Jackson Wilderness. Here's an argument for the hike: you'll be doing some walking anyway, as it was one of the most difficult trails I've ever tackled.

General location: The trail is located approximately 14 miles northeast of Skykomish, and about 30 miles northwest of Stevens Pass.

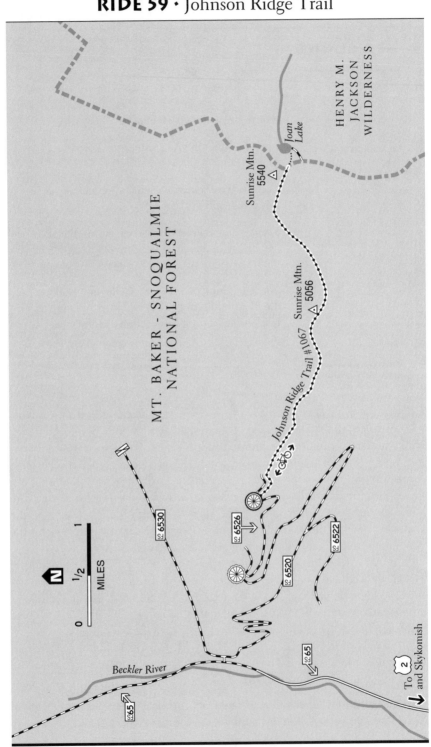

HENRY M.
JACKSON
WILDERNESS

Joan
Lake

Sunrise Mtn.
5540 △

Sunrise Mtn.
5056 △

Johnson Ridge Trail #1067

MT. BAKER - SNOQUALMIE
NATIONAL FOREST

FS 6530

FS 6526

FS 6520

FS 6522

FS 65

Beckler River

FS 65

To 2
and Skykomish

N

MILES

0   ½   1

View from the southern flank of Scorpion Mountain.

Elevation change: The lower trailhead lies at 3,600' and reaches a high elevation of 5,400' at Scorpion Mountain. Climbs in both directions add an extra 580' for a total gain of 2,380'.

Season: You'll find trail conditions best in summer and early fall. Check with the ranger district office to make sure the trail is passable.

Services: There is no water available along the ride. You'll find camping and drinking water at the Beckler River Campground on FS 65, with other campgrounds in the area. Services are available in Skykomish.

Hazards: Root and rock challenges, many on steep grades, occur throughout the ride. Some steep descents can send you flying if you're not back far enough on the saddle; better to walk them than skid down. The narrow trail at the east end of the route obscures obstacles and uneven surface.

Rescue index: Due to the relatively light use of the trail, you may not be able to flag down help until FS 65, 6.9 miles down the road, or in Skykomish, about 14 miles southwest of the trailhead.

Land status: Mt. Baker–Snoqualmie National Forest, Skykomish Ranger District.

Maps: The Mt. Baker–Snoqualmie National Forest map is an adequate guide to this ride, though it doesn't show the topography. Green Trails #143 Monte Cristo, #144 Benchmark Mtn., and the Skykomish Ranger District map do.

Finding the trail: Traveling east on US 2, proceed 0.8 mile past Skykomish to FS 65 (Beckler River Road) and turn left. Travel 6.9 miles on FS 65 to the end of the pavement, just before the one-lane bridge, and make a hard right onto FS 6520. Stay left on FS 6520 as it passes FS 6522 on the right in 2.7 miles. In 2.9 more miles turn right, as FS 6520 ends into FS 6526 (parking is available here for a warm-up road climb). From here it is 1.3 more miles to the end of FS 6526 and the trailhead. Very limited parking, for just a few vehicles, is available at the trailhead.

Skykomish is approximately 16 miles west of Stevens Pass on US 2.

Source of additional information:

Skykomish Ranger District
P.O. Box 305
Skykomish, WA 98288
(360) 677-2414
(The Ranger District office is located on US 2, about 0.3 mile east of FS 65.)

Notes on the trail: First, gear down. Then start your initial ascent to the right of the end of FS 6526 on the roadbed that starts the route. In 0.6 mile you'll see an incredibly steep, downright evil climb at the 10 o'clock position. Pass it by—the climb you're on now is tough enough! In another 0.1 mile the road curves to the left and starts to descend; the trail proper, unmarked, starts in the trees to the right (if you descend on the road you've gone too far). The beginning of the trail provides a respite from the difficult climbing thus far and yet to come. At 2.1 miles, after a steep climb, come briefly out of the trees and to a huckleberry-adorned clearing. You can look north from the trail and dismount and walk a few steps on a footpath to the right for a southern view. Back on the bike, descend sharply, about 200' in 0.2 mile. The trail then rolls steeply to a meadow at 3.2 miles. In another 0.2 mile you can sneak a view north through the trees at the crest of Sunrise Mountain. The trail becomes razor-thin and the views become clearer as you climb along the meadow on the south side of the ridge. At 4.1 miles come to a **T** junction, with Joan Lake down below. To the right is the Henry M. Jackson Wilderness, where bikes are not allowed; it's a 0.5-mile hike down to the lake. To the left is a 0.1-mile trek to the summit of Scorpion Mountain, where a near 360-degree panorama provides awe-inspiring views too numerous to list. Some dismounts will be necessary even on the return trip, so proceed with caution.

RIDE 60 · Pole Ridge

AT A GLANCE

Length/configuration: 12-mile loop on dirt and gravel roads

Aerobic difficulty: Moderately difficult; 1 mile of steep climbing

Technical difficulty: Easy to moderate; some washboarding and loose gravel on steeper sections

WA

Scenery: Forested ride with good views into the Glacier Peaks Wilderness from Pole Ridge

Special comments: Loop ends with a fun descent

This is a 12-mile loop on dirt and gravel roads. The roads are in fair condition, with some washboarding and loose gravel on the steeper hills. A good warm-up leads into a moderately difficult 5-mile climb (with about one 1 mile of steep grades). The ride ends with a 4-mile descent from Pole Ridge.

Much of the timber in this section of the forest has been logged out. There is a bright side to the clear-cuts: they open up nice vistas. The view from Pole Ridge is excellent. To the north are snowfields and mountain ranges in the Glacier Peak Wilderness.

General location: This ride begins approximately 25 miles north of Leavenworth, Washington.

Elevation change: The ride starts at 2,400' and climbs to a high point of 3,880'. Ups and downs add an estimated 200' of climbing to the loop. Total elevation gain: 1,680'.

Season: You can ride here from spring through fall. Avoid hunting season and summer holiday weekends.

Services: There is no water available on this ride. Water can be obtained seasonally at the campgrounds on Lake Wenatchee. You will pass several convenience stores on the way to the trailhead. All services are available in Leavenworth.

Hazards: Finding your way will require some route finding—many of the roads are unsigned. Control your speed on the steep descents. Stay alert for logging trucks and other vehicles. Black bears are not uncommon in this part of the forest.

Rescue index: In the summer, help is available during regular business hours at the Lake Wenatchee Ranger Station on the north shore. You may be able to summon aid at Lake Wenatchee State Park (at the eastern end of the lake). The

RIDE 60 · Pole Ridge

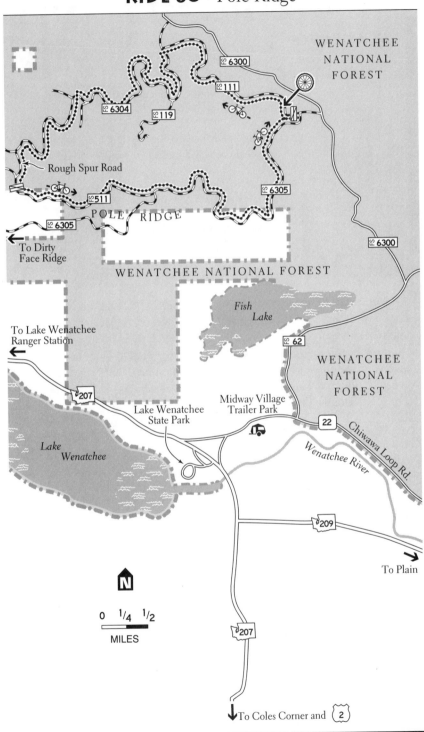

WENATCHEE
NATIONAL
FOREST

FS 6300

FS 111

FS 6304

FS 119

Rough Spur Road

FS 511

FS 6305

POLE   RIDGE

FS 6305

To Dirty
Face Ridge

WENATCHEE NATIONAL FOREST

FS 6300

Fish
Lake

WENATCHEE
NATIONAL
FOREST

FS 62

To Lake Wenatchee
Ranger Station

207

Lake Wenatchee
State Park

Midway Village
Trailer Park

22

Chiwawa Loop Rd.

Lake
Wenatchee

Wenatchee River

209

To Plain

N

0   1/4   1/2

MILES

207

To Coles Corner and 2

View into the Glacier Peaks Wilderness from Pole Ridge.

nearest pay phone is at the Midway Village Trailer Park, 5.5 miles south of the trailhead.

Land status: Wenatchee National Forest.

Maps: The district map of the Lake Wenatchee Ranger District is an adequate guide to this route. USGS 7.5 minute quads: Plain, Lake Wenatchee, Chikamin Creek, and Schaefer Lake.

Finding the trail: From locations to the west, take US 2 east to Stevens Pass. Continue east from the pass for 19 miles to WA 207 (on the left, at Coles Corner). From Leavenworth, follow US 2 north for 16 miles to Coles Corner and WA 207 (on the right). Turn north onto WA 207—follow the signs for Lake Wenatchee State Park. WA 209 goes right, toward Plain/Wenatchee, after 3.5 miles. Continue straight, staying on WA 207. Shortly you will cross the bridge over the Wenatchee River and arrive at a **Y** intersection; here, WA 207 goes left toward the ranger station and state park. Turn right and follow the road as it swings to the right and feeds into another road. Drive past Midway Village Trailer Park. At the next major intersection, 0.5 mile beyond the trailer park, turn left onto FS 62. Follow FS 62 for 2.3 miles to FS 6300. Turn left onto FS 6300 and drive 2.1 miles to FS 6305. Turn left onto gravel FS 6305 and proceed 0.3 mile to FS 111. Turn right onto FS 111 (pass through the gate) and follow the road for 0.2 mile to a borrow pit and a pullout on the left. Park in the pullout.

If FS 111 is blocked by the gate, park at the intersection of FS 6305 and FS 6300.

Source of additional information:

Lake Wenatchee Ranger District
22976 Highway 207
Leavenworth, WA 98826
(509) 763-3103

Notes on the trail: Turn left out of the parking area, following FS 111. FS 111 ends at a **T** intersection in 2 miles. Turn left here onto unsigned FS 6304. Stay on the main road as spur roads branch off. The surface of FS 6304 changes from gravel to dirt after 3.5 miles. There is also a sign here that reads "National Forest Firewood Cutting Area." Continue on FS 6304 for 0.8 mile to a high point in the road. This high point occurs after the road switchbacks hard to the right and climbs steeply (there is a clear-cut to your right). Roll over the crest and immediately turn left onto an unsigned spur road. (This turn is easy to miss—do not follow the main road downhill.) Proceed on the rough spur road past "Wildlife Habitat" signs to a gravel road (unsigned FS 511). Turn left onto FS 511 and pedal past a gate. Stay on the main road as a couple of spur roads branch off. You will arrive at a **T** intersection after a short but fast descent. Turn left onto FS 6305, which also heads to the right toward Dirtyface Ridge. Descend on FS 6305 for 3.5 miles to FS 111. Turn left onto FS 111 and ride back to your vehicle. FS 111 is easy to miss; you will quickly come to paved FS 6300 if you go too far.

RIDE 61 · Lower Chiwawa Trail

AT A GLANCE

WA

Length/configuration: 16.2-mile (total mileage) out-and-back, all single-track; 15.2-mile loop option uses 8.2 miles of single-track, with gravel road and paved road return; numerous combinations of out-and-back plus road return are possible

Aerobic difficulty: Roller-coaster all the way; some steep climbs, none longer than 0.4 mile

Technical difficulty: Some motorcycle braking bumps and whoop-de-doos

Scenery: Second-growth woods with some old-growth pine; lush creekside sections

Special comments: Intermediate ride, but an open-book test for the thrill-seeking beginner

Lower Chiwawa Trail #1548 is a sometimes steep, sometimes dusty, always fun 8.1-mile (each way) roller-coaster single-track. The off-road vehicle trail will challenge the intermediate rider and provide an adventure—with safety nets—for the hardy beginner who is willing to do a little walking. The trail parallels paved Forest Service Road 62, and then gravel FS 6210, and contains numerous bail-out points along the way if the trail provides *too* much of a challenge. (The same quality would make this a superb night ride.) If this is the case, merely hop onto the road and ride back. The trip is routed as a trail/road loop, but you can ride it as all trail, or do any number of combinations of out-and-back and road return utilizing FS 62.

The lower trailhead is south of the described route, at Deep Creek Campground, to where you can add an extra three miles each way. But by parking at the suggested area it's easier to access, all on paved roads and not far from WA 207.

General location: The ride begins approximately 25 miles north of Leavenworth and 5 miles northeast of Lake Wenatchee.

Elevation change: The route starts at 2,220' and hits the turnaround at 2,640' at the Chikamin Creek Trailhead, but constant dips and climbs on the trail bring total elevation gain to over 1,000'.

Season: The trails are rideable spring through fall. Seasonal closures that affect upper elevation trails in the area don't apply to the Lower Chiwawa Trail. Early season rains pack down the dust that kicks up during the summer.

Services: There is no water available along the route. Numerous campgrounds in the vicinity provide overnight options. Limited supplies can be obtained at the Midway Village General Store or stores along WA 207. All services are available in Leavenworth.

Hazards: This is a popular area with motorcyclists and equestrians as well as mountain bikers, so watch (and listen) for fellow trail users.

Rescue index: Someone along the trail or in any of the numerous camping areas near the route may be able to summon help. The nearest phone is at the Midway Village General Store, 3.8 miles from the ride start. The Lake Wenatchee Ranger Station is located along the north shore of Lake Wentachee on WA 207.

Land status: Wenatchee National Forest, Lake Wenatchee Ranger District.

Maps: Green Trails #146 Plain, shows this trail and some of the wealth of other trails in the area to enjoy. The Lake Wenatchee Ranger District map is also an adequate guide.

Finding the trail: From US 2 at Coles Corner (19 miles east of Stevens Pass and 16 miles west of Leavenworth), turn north on WA 207. Cross the Wenatchee River in 4.3 miles, then immediately veer right on Chiwawa Loop Road. Wind around to the right and pass the Midway Village General Store in 0.8 mile. In another 0.5 mile, turn left at Meadow Creek Road, the start of FS 62 (Chiwawa

RIDE 61 · Lower Chiwawa Trail

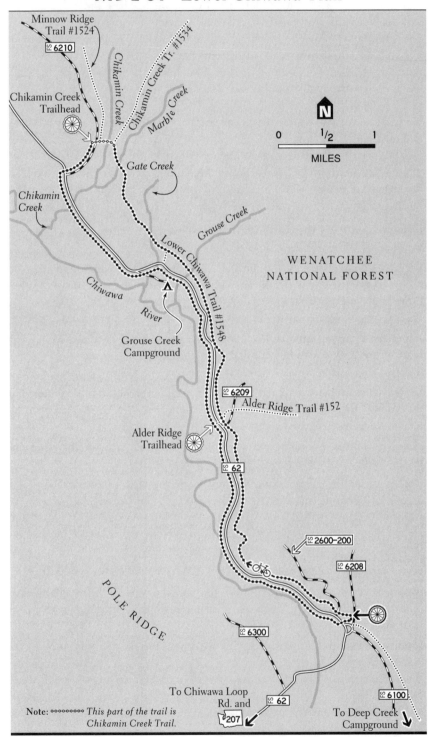

Minnow Ridge
Trail #1524

FS 6210

Chikamin Creek Tr. #1534

Chikamin Creek

Chikamin Creek
Trailhead

Marble Creek

Gate Creek

Chikamin
Creek

Grouse Creek

N

0   1/2   1
MILES

WENATCHEE
NATIONAL FOREST

Lower Chiwawa Trail #1548

Chiwawa

River

Grouse Creek
Campground

FS 6209

Alder Ridge Trail #152

Alder Ridge
Trailhead

FS 62

FS 2600-200

FS 6208

POLE RIDGE

FS 6300

To Chiwawa Loop
Rd. and

FS 62

FS 6100

207

To Deep Creek
Campground

Note: ∞∞∞∞∞∞∞ *This part of the trail is*
Chikamin Creek Trail.

Lower Chiwawa Trail.

River Road). Take FS 62 3.2 miles to FS 6208, the Goose Creek Campground turnoff, and turn right. In about 100', come to a 4-way intersection with FS 6100 to the right, FS 6208 straight ahead, and an access back to FS 6200 to the left. Turn left, and park at the pullout immediately to the left.

Source of additional information:

Lake Wenatchee Ranger District
22976 Highway 207
Leavenworth, WA 98826
(509) 763-3103

Notes on the trail: Continue up FS 6208 for 0.1 mile and turn left onto the trail. At 0.3 mile cross FS 6200-200. At 3.2 miles, after a 0.3-mile descent, come to the junction of FS 62 and FS 6209, which climbs to the right. Cross FS 6209 and continue straight. In another 0.1 mile, cross Twin Creek and the Alder Ridge (#1523) Trailhead and gear down for a steep climb. At 5.0 miles, the trail veers right on an old roadbed but with a nicely defined line guiding you through. In another mile the trail again widens out as it descends. Shortly after the road switchbacks left, look to the right, where a cinder-block reinforced switchback continues the trail. (If you miss the turn you'll make a short, rough descent to FS 62.) Descend to another creek crossing, and enjoy lush scenery and middle-ring rollers. At 7.6 miles, cross Marble Creek and exit into a granny-gear, one-switch-back climb, then come to a junction to the left in 0.1 mile. Straight ahead is Chikamin Creek Trail #1534. To get to the Chikamin Creek Trailhead, the far end of the loop, or the turnaround point for out-and-backers, turn left. Make the sweet descent to Chikamin Creek, cross the bridge, and make the tough climb out from it. Note the remnants of a misguided attempt to pave the trail on the way up. On the short, final descent to the trailhead, pass Minnow Ridge Trail #1524, which takes off to the right at a delta junction.

Out-and-backers, start your "back" portion from the trailhead. To make the full trail/road loop, exit the trailhead parking area and descend to the left on FS 6210. This is a nice, fast 0.5 mile, but watch for vehicles on the road. At the junction of FS 62 turn left, and return to FS 6208 in 6.5 miles. Turn back to the car on either of the two roads after the Alder Creek Horse Camp. Out-and-backers, near the end of the trip, look for the second of two road crossings in short order, 3.2 miles after crossing FS 6209 at its junction with FS 62. Go right on the second road, FS 6208, and ride 0.1 mile back to your vehicle.

RIDE 62 · Chikamin Creek Loop

AT A GLANCE

WA

Length/configuration: 16.4-mile loop with 8.7 miles of single-track; can route it as all single-track using Minnow Ridge Trail #1524

Aerobic difficulty: Moderate to difficult 1,960', 7.7-mile gravel-road climb; short, steep single-track climbs

Technical difficulty: Numerous creek crossings, steep side-cut sections; one fast descent with steep drops on both sides

Scenery: Distant views on the road climb and latter stretches of trail; overviews of Chikamin Creek and its lush surroundings

Special comments: Road and trail, or all single-track?—the choice is yours

This advanced-level, 16.4-mile loop can be done as all single-track, with 6.1 miles of rolling climbing on the Minnow Ridge Trail, and I would recommend it—but if you do, be sure to climb the extra 880' on the Chikamin Tie Trail to Forest Service Road 6210, so you can enjoy the same sweet 2.0-mile descent as you get by climbing the road.

The 7.7-mile gravel-road climb alternates between middle-ring and low-ring efforts. Upon reaching the trail, you're immediately rewarded with a fast, fun 2.0-mile descent on the Chikamin Tie Trail.

You can see by the references in this chapter how this route accesses many other trails and becomes the hub of many, many excellent adventures. By way of this loop you can access the Lower Chiwawa Trail and Minnow Ridge trails, the Minnow Creek Trail (tying into the Rock Creek network), and the upper Chikamin Tie Trail, which leads to the Upper Mad River Trail and the Pond Camp Tie Trail, which lead to the Mad River Trail . . . and on and on and on, for miles and miles and miles. This may just be single-track heaven; your only limits are your legs and your lungs, your desire and your imagination.

General location: The trailhead is approximately 32 miles north of Leavenworth and 12 miles northeast of Lake Wenatchee

Elevation change: The trailhead is at 2,600' elevation; you'll be at 4,350' when you turn onto the Chikamin Tie Trail, and 3,600' when you turn onto the Chikamin Creek Trail. Climbing on the trail totals, oh, about 300', for a *total* elevation gain of, oh, about 2,050'.

Season: The trails can be ridden from spring through fall, as the snows allow on the upper elevations.

Services: Water is available at the campgrounds at Lake Wenatchee, and at the stores on WA 207 and in Midway Village. All services are available in Leavenworth.

Hazards: On the Chikamin Tie Trail, switchbacks come at you while at speed, so keep your vision well ahead of your wheels. Some steep side-cuts on the Chikamin Creek Trail can be treacherous if you fall to the right. A steep descent at 13.7 miles, after the view stop, has steep drops on both sides.

Rescue index: The nearest phone is at the Midway Village General Store.

Land status: Wenatchee National Forest, Lake Wenatchee Ranger District.

Maps: Green Trails #146 Plain, or the Lake Wenatchee Ranger District map.

Finding the trail: From US 2 at Coles Corner (19 miles east of Stevens Pass and 16 miles west of Leavenworth), turn north on WA 207. Cross the Wenatchee River in 4.3 miles, then immediately veer right on Chiwawa Loop Road. Wind around to the right and pass the Midway Village General Store in 0.8 mile. Continuing 0.5 mile further, turn left at signed Meadow Creek Road, the start of FS 62 (Chiwawa Valley Road). Travel 9.2 miles up FS 62, pass a bridge over Chikamin Creek, and in another 0.3 mile, turn right onto gravel FS 6210. Climb 0.5 mile to the Chikamin Creek Trailhead parking area on your right. Turn right, and do what you do when you come to a parking area.

Source of additional information:

Lake Wenatchee Ranger District
22976 Highway 207
Leavenworth, WA 98826
(509) 763-3103

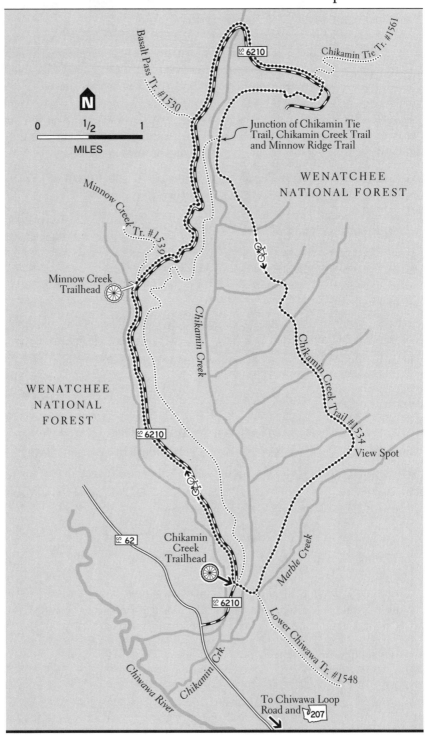

Chikamin Tie Tr. #1561

Basalt Pass Tr. #1530

FS 6210

Junction of Chikamin Tie
Trail, Chikamin Creek Trail
and Minnow Ridge Trail

WENATCHEE
NATIONAL FOREST

Minnow Creek Tr. #1539

Minnow Creek
Trailhead

Chikamin Creek

Chikamin Creek Trail #1534

View Spot

WENATCHEE
NATIONAL
FOREST

FS 6210

FS 62

Chikamin
Creek
Trailhead

Marble Creek

FS 6210

Lower Chiwawa Tr. #1548

Chiwawa River

Chikamin Crk.

To Chiwawa Loop
Road and 207

0   1/2   1
MILES

N

Notes on the trail: To ride the full single-track loop, pedal up the wide trail entrance and turn left onto the Minnow Ridge Trail in 0.1 mile. You'll meet up with the Chikamin Creek Trail in about 6.1 rolling, hilly miles. For the road/trail loop, ride back out the parking area and start your climb to the right up FS 6210, passing spur roads and trails along the way. In 2.8 miles pass the access to the Minnow Ridge Trail to the right; pass the Minnow Creek Trailhead on your left another 0.2 mile up. At 5.3 miles, pass Basalt Pass Trail #1530 on your left. Continue on FS 6210, and as the road winds south and east about a mile past the Basalt Pass Trail, enjoy some nearby views of the Entiat Mountains and some distant views to the south as you approach the trailhead. FS 6210 intersects the Chikamin Tie Trail at 7.7 miles, or 1.4 miles past the Basalt Pass Trail; it first comes down from the left and then descends to the right about 10' farther. Check your brakes, turn right, and start a fast, switchbacking, cinder-block-reinforced descent through a clear-cut. You'll be into the trees in a little over a mile, and at the junction of the Chikamin Creek Trail and the Minnow Ridge Trail in 2.0 miles. Turn left at the junction, and start the Chikamin Creek Trail with a climb. In 1.0 mile cross four Chikamin Creek feeders, and catch some distant views through a thinned area before descending to the fifth creek crossing. Keep rolling, rolling, rolling along on some fun descents and short, steep climbs. At 4.0 miles on the Chikamin Creek Trail, climb to a little landing to the left of the trail, before a descent as the trail turns right, and stop to take in the view to the east. Check your brakes again, because after the stop, you'll enjoy the fast, steep descent, with drops to both sides and extended cinder-block reinforcement on the trail. You can sneak some views to the south if you're riding in control. In the 2.2 miles of descending, only a few cranks of the pedals are necessary until you come to the junction of the Lower Chiwawa Trail straight ahead, and back to the trailhead to the right. Turn right—if you go too far, you'll switchback down to Marble Creek in 0.2 mile—and continue the descent to Chikamin Creek. From the creek, climb back to the trailhead in 0.5 mile.

RIDE 63 · Minnow Ridge Loop

AT A GLANCE

Length/configuration: 6.7-mile loop, including gravel-road climb and 3.9 miles of single-track

Aerobic difficulty: Moderate 2.8-mile, 840' road climb; some steep rollers on the trail

Technical difficulty: Small drop-offs, motorcycle braking bumps, whoop-de-doos, and some elementary-level wide switchbacks

Scenery: Second-growth woods with scattered old-growth ponderosa pines; quick glimpses of the Chiwawa River Valley and Stuart Range

Special comments: A good sampler platter for the beginner who's ready to do some serious mountain biking

WA

This 6.7-mile loop is a condensed version of the Chikamin Creek loop. If you have the time, endurance, and daylight, do the Chikamin Creek loop. If not, or if you're up for a shorter-distance night ride, this is a great choice.

Experienced beginners who are ready to tackle some serious mountain biking get a little taste of just about everything: a 2.8-mile, moderate gravel-road climb; single-track rollers that teach the use of momentum from fast descents on the ensuing climbs (gear down *before* the climb gets steep!); and some wide, rideable switchbacks, drop-offs, whoop-de-doos, and motorcycle braking bumps to hone those technical skills.

The trail surface is generally a firm hard-pack that gets dusty with weather and use. The cupped areas and braking bumps add some technical flavor to the ride.

General location: The trailhead is approximately 32 miles north of Leavenworth and 12 miles northeast of Lake Wenatchee.

Elevation change: The trailhead is at 2,600', and by the time you touch single-track you'll be at 3,440'. Climbing on the trail brings total elevation gain to about 1,020'.

Season: You can ride this route from spring through fall. The trail can get a little dusty in the summer, though the riding is good throughout the season.

Services: There is no water available along the route. Numerous campgrounds in the vicinity provide overnight options. Limited supplies can be obtained at

RIDE 63 · Minnow Ridge Loop

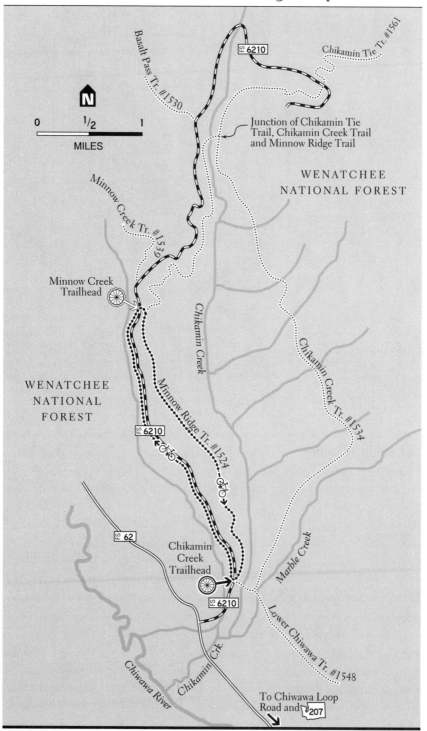

Basalt Pass Tr. #1530

FS 6210

Chikamin Tie Tr. #1561

N

0   1/2   1

MILES

Junction of Chikamin Tie
Trail, Chikamin Creek Trail
and Minnow Ridge Trail

WENATCHEE
NATIONAL FOREST

Minnow Creek Tr. #1539

Minnow Creek
Trailhead

Chikamin Creek

WENATCHEE
NATIONAL
FOREST

FS 6210

Minnow Ridge Tr. #1524

Chikamin Creek Tr. #1534

FS 62

Chikamin
Creek
Trailhead

Marble Creek

FS 6210

Lower Chiwawa Tr. #1548

Chiwawa River

Chikamin Crk.

To Chiwawa Loop
Road and 207

287

Michael Jewel cleaning a
wide switchback on
Minnow Ridge Trail.

the Midway Village General Store or stores along WA 207. All services are available in Leavenworth.

Hazards: Watch for small drop-offs and motorcycle braking bumps. It's no mystery how the bumps got here; this is a popular area with motorcyclists and equestrians, too, so be aware.

Rescue index: You'll find a phone at the Midway Village General Store, 10.5 miles from the ride's start. The Lake Wenatchee Ranger Station is located along the north shore of Lake Wentachee on WA 207. Personnel may be on duty at Lake Wenatchee State Park.

Land status: Wenatchee National Forest, Lake Wenatchee Ranger District.

Maps: Green Trails #146 Plain, and the Lake Wenatchee Ranger District map are both sufficient guides for this trip.

Finding the trail: From US 2 at Coles Corner (19 miles east of Stevens Pass and 16 miles west of Leavenworth), turn north on WA 207. Cross the Wenatchee River in 4.3 miles, then immediately veer right onto Chiwawa Loop Road. Wind around to the right and pass the Midway Village General Store in 0.8 mile. In

Minnow Ridge Trail.

another 0.5 mile, turn left at what's signed as Meadow Creek Road, and is actually the start of FS 62 (Chiwawa Valley Road). Travel 9.2 miles on FS 62, and pass a bridge over Chikamin Creek. Just 0.3 mile past the bridge, turn right onto dirt FS 6210, and drive 0.5 mile to the Chikamin Creek Trailhead parking area, which is to the right.

Source of additional information:

Lake Wenatchee Ranger District
22976 Highway 207
Leavenworth, WA 98826
(509) 763-3103

Notes on the trail: Exit the trailhead parking area and climb to the right on FS 6210. In 2.8 miles, as you're riding straight before a left-hand curve ahead of you, look to the right. You'll see the unsigned Minnow Ridge Trail #1524 as it skirts by the road at this spot; hop on here, for this is where you start the return of the loop. You can't miss it . . . but if you do, you'll come to Minnow Creek Trail #1539 to your left, and an old, overgrown access to the Minnow Ridge Trail in

0.2 mile. After a short descent to start, the trail throws its first steep climb at you, and you're on your way! At 1.7 miles on the trail, after cresting a small climb as the trail curves left, you'll come to an exposed area that allows nice views down to the Chiwawa River Valley and up to the Stuart Range; it's a lovely place to take a breather and savor the ride. Then twist and wind, descend and climb, to the switchback section; most of them have beginner-friendly, wide lines to help you around. As you come to the bottom of that section, use your momentum to propel you up a short climb to the final descent. The trail ends at a delta junction where, to the left, you access the Chikamin Creek Trail and the Lower Chiwawa Trail. Turn right here and return on the wide path to the trailhead and loop's end in 0.1 mile.

RIDE 64 · Mad Lake from the North

AT A GLANCE

Length/configuration: 16-mile (total mileage) single-track out-and-back; numerous other possibilities

Aerobic difficulty: Difficult climbing, from 4,350' to 6,200' elevation

Technical difficulty: Scree, tight switchbacks, rocky creek crossings

Scenery: Entiat Mountains landscape of imposing scree, gorgeous meadows, rock formations, and Mad Lake

Special comments: An advanced ride with advanced scenery; beginners should aspire to ride trails like this!

The highlight of this 16-mile (total mileage) out-and-back is the imposing scenery along the scree sections of the Chikamin Tie Trail. Or is it conquering the initial 1,850', 4.2-mile climb? Maybe it's reaping the reward of that climb with the super-sweet descent that ends the outing? Or perhaps it's the beautiful wildflowers of Pond Meadow, Marble Meadow, and Mad Meadow? Is it the destination of Mad Lake? You get the idea: this is an all-around excellent adventure that epitomizes great mountain biking.

A tough, no warm-up, single-track climb through the trees starts the journey. The grade generally eases up as you get warmed up, though technical riding

RIDE 64 · Mad Lake from the North

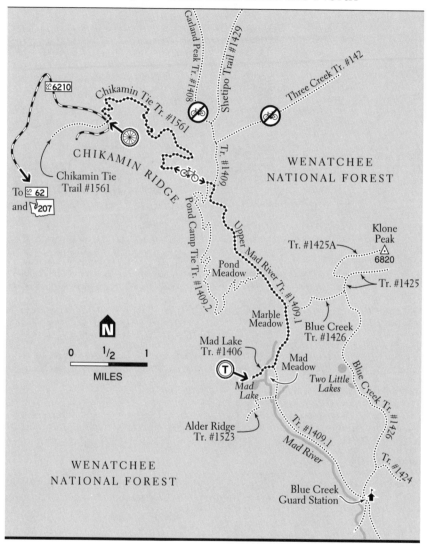

skills also come into play over roots and creeks in addition to the scree as you make your way through woods, rock formations, and views. Ease your way to Mad Lake through waves of gorgeous meadow.

The trails are in good condition, though they get dusty with sun-exposure and use. Cinder-blocked sections firm up the trail and some water crossings. Ride over them for good traction and to keep the trails from eroding.

General location: The ride starts about 40 miles north of Leavenworth and 20 miles northeast of Lake Wenatchee.

Scree along Chikamin
Tie Trail.

Elevation change: The trail starts at 4,350' elevation and crests at about 6,200' in the first 4.2 miles. Additional climbing on the trail brings total elevation gain to about 2,050'.

Season: Seasonal closures affect the upper elevation trails in this area, usually until early or mid-July. Check with the Lake Wenatchee Ranger Station or Entiat Ranger Station for the exact date. The mosquitoes'll get you if you come early in the season, so be prepared. Generally, prime time will be late August until Mother Nature says no more in October.

Services: There is no potable water available on the ride. Stock up in Leavenworth, at Coles Corner, on WA 207, or at Midway Village General Store on Chiwawa Loop Road. Camping is available at Lake Wenatchee or off of FS 62. All services are available in Leavenworth.

Hazards: Things ranging from mildly bad to really bad can happen if you fall at any point along the scree. Walk any sections on which you feel unsure.

Rescue index: The nearest phone is at the Midway Village General Store. Help can also be summoned from Lake Wenatchee State Park, or at the Lake Wenatchee Ranger Station.

Land status: Wenatchee National Forest, Lake Wenatchee and Entiat Ranger Districts.

Maps: Green Trails #146 Plain, most recently revised in 1997, shows this route most accurately.

Finding the trail: From US 2 at Coles Corner (19 miles east of Stevens Pass and 16 miles west of Leavenworth), turn north on WA 207. Cross the Wenatchee River in 4.3 miles, then immediately veer right on Chiwawa Loop Road. Wind around to the right and pass the Midway Village General Store in 0.8 mile. Continuing 0.5 mile further, turn left at Meadow Creek Road, the start of FS 62 (Chiwawa Valley Road). Travel 9.2 miles up FS 62 and pass a bridge over Chikamin Creek. In another 0.3 mile, turn right onto dirt FS 6210. Continue past spur roads and past the Chikamin Creek Trailhead on your right at 0.5 mile, Minnow Ridge Trailhead on your left at 3.5 miles, and the Basalt Pass Trailhead on your left at 5.2 miles. Cross the Chikamin Tie Trail on your left at 8.1 miles and park just beyond it to the left.

Sources of additional information:

Entiat Ranger District
2108 Entiat Way
P.O. Box 476
Entiat, WA 98822
(509) 784-1511

Lake Wenatchee Ranger District
22976 Highway 207
Leavenworth, WA 98826
(509) 763-3103

Notes on the trail: Start climbing on the Chikamin Tie Trail, a low-ring grind with a few middle-ring respites, that lifts you to the 6,200' high point of the route. At 0.7 mile, make the first of many small creek crossings; after the first three, get a taste of scree riding at 1.6 miles. Glimpses of other scree and sheer hillsides lie to the north. Shortly you'll re-enter the woods and keep climbing. You'll get a glimpse of another scree section ahead of you at 2.7 miles, but as you make a traversing climb to the west, you won't hit it until you swing back to the east in another 0.6 mile. Make the uneven climb along the scree as you catch the incredible views of a ridgeline canyon and valley on your climb up Chikamin Ridge. At 4.1 miles, pass the junction of Pond Camp Tie Trail #1409.2 on your right. (You can take the Pond Camp Tie Trail in either or both directions. This adds a steep 2.4 miles each way.) In another 0.1 mile, turn right onto Upper Mad River Trail #1409.1, heading south; after a switchbacking descent, meet up with the lower end of the Pond Camp Tie Trail in 1.7 miles. Pedal another 0.9 mile to Marble Meadow and pass the junction of Blue Creek Trail #1426 on your left, 0.9 mile beyond the Pond Camp Tie Trail junction. In 0.9 mile more you'll meet the junction of the Mad Lake Trail #1406, where you'll turn right and ride 0.4 mile to Mad Lake. Stop, reapply the mosquito repellent, eat, and enjoy. You'll need the energy to get you back to Chikamin Ridge and the exhilarating 4-mile return descent. To extend the outing you can climb to Klone Peak, a 2.9-mile (each way) side trip by way of the Blue Creek Trail, or continue south on the Upper Mad River Trail.

RIDE 65 · Rock Creek Area Trails

AT A GLANCE

WA

Length/configuration: Full-area ride can include a 10.6-mile loop, plus out-and-back-spurs of 1.9 miles, 1.7 miles, 1.4 miles, and 0.7 mile (each way), all on primo single-track

Aerobic difficulty: Extreme gain of 3,470' in 5.2 miles on the loop; out-and-back sections can provide from 200' to 1,500' of climbing—this ride is for climbers!

Technical difficulty: Creek crossings, switchbacks, and some rocks and roots on otherwise smooth trail

Scenery: Deep woods; gorgeous overlook from spur trail off Basalt Ridge Trail; views of the world from 6,000' Basalt Peak

Special comments: Trail system was not fully researched; however, what was researched was incredible—see for yourself!

First off, let me say that my schedule did not allow logging all the miles in this trail network. (When I say "logging" here I don't mean cutting down the trees.) But next, let me say that the trails I did ride—Rock Creek Trail #1509, part of Basalt Ridge Trail #1515, a spur trail to a viewpoint, Minnow Creek Trail #1539, and Finner Tie Trail—were nothing less than fantastic.

The trails in this area, unlike the Chikamin Creek and Upper Mad River areas, are off-limits to motorcycles. While those trails make for great riding, and are more extensive networks, the Rock Creek area trails are noticeably smoother. As far as I rode, there were no severe technical sections to navigate, so pure climbers will love these trails; and, of course, the steep climbs mean steep (read: fun!) descents. This is classic single-track.

Aerobically, the trails are advanced, with steep, demanding efforts; you can climb clockwise from the Rock Creek Trailhead, at 2,530 feet in elevation, to Basalt Peak, at 6,000 feet, in 5.2 miles. This clockwise route is the suggestion here, since you'd be climbing the same 3,470 feet in a mere 3.4 miles going counterclockwise.

The deep tree canopy on the Rock Creek Trail makes it a good choice for a hot day. The distant views, though, are few. Undoubtedly, as you climb higher in the network, the views get better. By the next edition of this book I will have made the ascent to Basalt Peak and will be eager to report my findings. On the

RIDE 65 · Rock Creek Area Trails

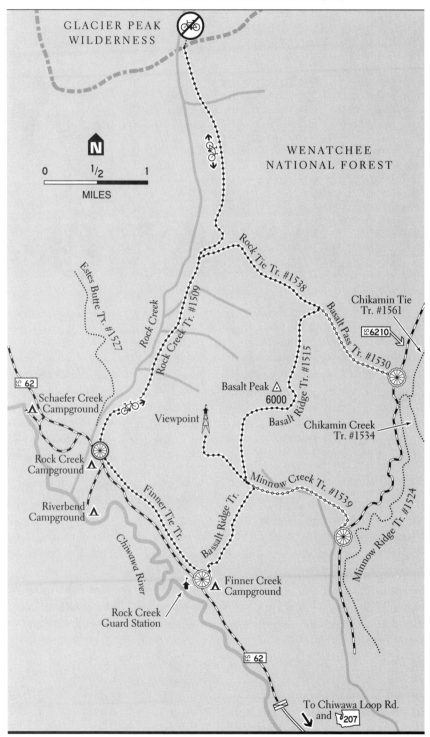

GLACIER PEAK
WILDERNESS

WENATCHEE
NATIONAL FOREST

N

0   1/2   1
MILES

Estes Butte Tr. #1527

Rock Creek

Rock Creek Tr. #1509

Rock Tie Tr. #1538

Basalt Pass Tr. #1530

Chikamin Tie
Tr. #1561

6210

FS 62

Schaefer Creek
Campground

Basalt Peak
6000

Basalt Ridge Tr. #1515

Chikamin Creek
Tr. #1534

Viewpoint

Rock Creek
Campground

Riverbend
Campground

Finner Tie Tr.

Basalt Ridge Tr.

Minnow Creek Tr. #1539

Minnow Ridge Tr. #1524

Chiwawa River

Rock Creek
Guard Station

Finner Creek
Campground

FS 62

To Chiwawa Loop Rd.
and WA 207

Rock Creek Trail.

research ride, though, an overlook at the end of a spur trail off the Basalt Ridge Trail provided a breathtaking view. The viewpoint is atop a sheer rock outcropping high above the Chiwawa River Valley, and renders incredible views to the west, north, south, and far, far, below you. If time is short, you can get to the viewpoint via a 2.6-mile out-and-back (each way) from the Minnow Creek Trail, starting on FS 6210. (See Chikamin Creek Loop for directions to the trailhead.)

General location: The Basalt Ridge Trailhead is located about 35 miles north of Leavenworth and 15 miles north of Lake Wenatchee. The Rock Creek Trailhead is 1.7 miles farther up the road.

Elevation change: The Rock Creek Trailhead sits at 2,530' elevation. The viewpoint is at 4,800', and the high point of the network, Basalt Peak, is at 6,000'. So how are your legs today?

Season: Trails this great shouldn't be ridden when wet. Wait until summer, remembering that the higher up you go, the longer it will be until the trails are snow-free and dry. Late summer and early fall are good choices for a climb to Basalt Peak.

Services: Water is available from a hand pump at the Rock Creek Guard Station. You can camp at the Rock Creek Campground, Riverbend Campground (0.3 miles from the Rock Creek Trailhead), Finner Creek Campground (at the Basalt Ridge Trailhead), and others along FS 62. Limited services are available in the Lake Wenatchee area. All services are available in Leavenworth.

Hazards: Steep side-cut sections of trail can send you tumbling a long, painful way if you fall. A few water crossings along the Rock Creek Trail and Minnow Creek Trail have steep entrances and exits; good technical skills are required to remain on the bike. You should be adept at riding steep switchbacks to ride these trails; on an unresearched portion of the Basalt Ridge Trail below the Minnow Creek Trail junction, maps indicate sections containing extremely steep switchbacks. Expect them at the upper reaches of the network as well.

Rescue index: Someone at any of the area campgrounds may be of assistance, but the nearest phone is at the Midway Village General Store.

Land status: Wenatchee National Forest, Lake Wenatchee Ranger District.

Maps: Green Trails #145 Wenatchee Lake and #146 Plain show the majority of this trail system. The upper end of the bike-legal Rock Creek Trail, to the Glacier Peak Wilderness boundary, is shown on Green Trails #113 Holden— you really don't need it for this ride. If you want to use just one map, go with the Lake Wenatchee Ranger District map. None of the maps show the spur trail to the viewpoint, as of their most recent revisions.

Finding the trail: From US 2 at Coles Corner (19 miles east of Stevens Pass and 16 miles west of Leavenworth), turn north on WA 207. Cross the Wenatchee River in 4.3 miles, then immediately veer right on Chiwawa Loop Road. Wind around to the right and pass the Midway Village General Store in 0.8 mile. Continuing 0.5 mile further, turn left at Meadow Creek Road, the start of FS 62 (Chiwawa Valley Road). Cross a bridge over Chikamin Creek in 9.2 miles and pass FS 6210 in another 0.3 mile, after which the road narrows. In 1.5 miles the pavement ends at a gate; 1.9 miles beyond the gate, pass the Basalt Ridge Trailhead on your right (across from the Rock Creek Guard Station). You'll find the Rock Creek Trailhead on your right, across from the Rock Creek Campground, in another 1.7 miles. Parking is available on either side of the road.

Source of additional information:

Lake Wenatchee Ranger District
22976 Highway 207
Leavenworth, WA 98826
(509) 763-3103

Notes on the trail: At the Rock Creek Trailhead, the Rock Creek Trail starts steeply to the left as the Finner Tie Trail comes in from the right. The climb levels out temporarily; a steep but steady grade brings you to a quick drop to the first creek crossing at 1.0 mile. A steady low-ring effort with some middle-ring respites and creek dips brings you to the junction of the Basalt Pass Trail (signed on the trail as the Rock Tie Trail #1538) at 2.5 miles. Climb to the right to continue the loop, or continue on the Rock Creek Trail for another 0.7 mile, where a difficult, two-switchback climb brings you to an elevation of 3,650'. You can ride 1.5 miles beyond the switchbacks before the trail enters the Glacier Peak Wilderness, which is off-limits to mountain bikes. A good turnaround point is an exposed creek crossing to which you descend 1.2 miles from the top of the switchbacks.

From the Rock Creek and Rock Creek Tie/Basalt Pass Trail junction, you can descend on Rock Creek Trail back to FS 6210, or climb for about 1.6 miles to the junction of the Basalt Ridge Trail, and turn right (south) for the final 1.1-mile push to Basalt Peak. From Basalt Peak, descend about 1.1 miles to the spur trail to the right that goes to the viewpoint, as the main trail switchbacks left. The 0.7-mile spur trail climbs about 300' and ends by the rocks to your left. Scamper up the rocks and be dazzled. Descend back to the main trail; from here it is 0.3 mile to the junction where the Basalt Ridge Trail is to the right and the Minnow Creek Trail is straight ahead. Turn right and descend what's mapped to be a very steep 1.6 miles, to the junction of the Finner Tie Trail. Turn right and pedal the undulating 2 miles back to the Rock Creek Trailhead or continue down the Basalt Ridge Trail and ride FS 62 back.

The Finner Tie Trail, which connects the Basalt Ridge and the Rock Creek Trails, paralleling FS 62, is just a few years old, and was the roughest of the trails I rode. It was a fun rolling trail to ride, and with time and use, it will settle in much more than it had at the time of research.

RIDE 66 · Mad Lake from the South

AT A GLANCE

Length/configuration: 18-mile (total mileage) out-and-back; 0.3-mile gravel-road start and finish — the rest is single-track

Aerobic difficulty: Strenuous climbing, mostly toward the beginning; about 1,800' of total climbing

Technical difficulty: Rocks, roots, creek crossings

Scenery: Incredible meadows, Entiat Mountains, Mad River, Mad Lake

Special comments: A great ride in itself, it can be the jump-off point to many other trails

Why are the river and lake called "Mad"? Nobody in our research party knew, but to venture a guess, we rode it in mid-August and the mosquitoes were driving us mad! If you do this trail early in the season (which here is late July), don't forget the mosquito repellent. But if possible, wait until September, when they won't be as bad. The skeeters were a small price to pay for an upper-elevation trail with incredible wildflower-covered meadows, rock

RIDE 66 · Mad Lake from the South

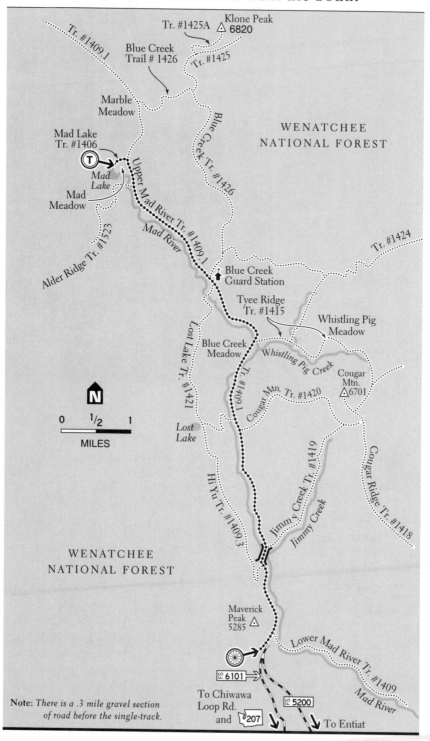

Tr. #1409.1

Klone Peak
△ 6820

Tr. #1425A

Blue Creek
Trail # 1426

Tr. #1425

Marble
Meadow

Blue Creek Tr. #1426

WENATCHEE
NATIONAL FOREST

Mad Lake
Tr. #1406

T

Mad
Lake

Upper Mad River Tr. #1409.1

Mad
Meadow

Mad River

Tr. #1424

Alder Ridge Tr. #1523

Blue Creek
Guard Station

Tyee Ridge
Tr. #1415

Whistling Pig
Meadow

N

Blue Creek
Meadow

Whistling Pig Creek

Cougar
Mtn.
△ 6701

0   1/2   1

MILES

Lost Lake Tr. #1421

Tr. #1409.1

Cougar Mtn. Tr. #1420

Lost
Lake

Jimmy Creek Tr. #1419

Cougar Ridge Tr. #1418

Hi Yu Tr. #1409.3

Jimmy Creek

WENATCHEE
NATIONAL FOREST

Maverick
Peak
5285 △

Lower Mad River Tr. #1409

FS 6101

Mad River

Note: *There is a .3 mile gravel section
of road before the single-track.*

To Chiwawa
Loop Rd.
and 🛈207

FS 5200

To Entiat

Brad Sauber, Brent McCord, and Michael Jewel relaxing at Mad Lake.

formations, Entiat Mountains views, challenging climbs, and thrilling descents; it made us anything *but* mad.

The trail—hard-packed, dusty, and with numerous cinder-blocked sections— passes many others along the way and can lead to many other explorations, but this primer on the area's upper-elevation trails is an excellent ride and is quite satisfying by itself.

It's an easy route to follow, but a difficult trail to ride. Stay on Upper Mad River Trail #1409.1 the entire way until the 0.4-mile (each way) side trip to Mad Lake; that's the easy part. The hard parts—the steep climbs and technical challenges—make it suitable for advanced riders.

General location: The trail is located approximately 32 miles north of Leavenworth, and 12 miles west of Lake Wenatchee.

Elevation change: The trail starts at 4200' elevation and climbs to 5,820'; total elevation gain is approximately 1,800'.

Season: Seasonal closures affect the trails in this area, usually until early or midJuly. Check with the Lake Wenatchee Ranger Station or Entiat Ranger Station for the exact date. The mosquitoes can be a real pain early in the season; if you have a chance, make it up in September or early October after the human and insect crowds are gone.

Services: There is no potable water available along the trail. Limited services are available at the Midway Village General Store and other stores on the way from Coles Corner. All services are available in Leavenworth.

Hazards: On our summer, weekend-day excursion, we encountered motorcyclists, equestrians, and hikers. Expect the same unless you come midweek or late in the season. Beware of the rocky sections along the trail.

Rescue index: Help can be summoned from a phone at Midway Village General Store, at Lake Wenatchee State Park, or at the Lake Wenatchee Ranger Station.

Land status: Wenatchee National Forest, Entiat Ranger District (just east of the Lake Wenatchee Ranger District boundary).

Maps: Green Trails #146 Plain, seems to be a more user-friendly guide to this trail than either the Lake Wenatchee or Entiat Ranger District maps, but any one will guide you there and back.

Finding the trail: From US 2 at Coles Corner (19 miles east of Stevens Pass and 16 miles west of Leavenworth), turn north on WA 207. Cross the Wenatchee River in 4.3 miles, then immediately veer right on Chiwawa Loop Road. Wind around to the right and pass the Midway Village General Store in 0.8 mile. Continue on Chiwawa Loop Road, past the Thousand Trails Campground and about 0.5 mile past the Chiwawa River to gravel FS 6100 back to the left (north) as Chiwawa Loop Road turns south. Turn left onto FS 6100 and travel approximately 1.5 miles to the junction of FS 6101 at Deep Creek Campground. Turn right onto FS 6101 and follow it around for about 3.7 miles, past FS 6102 to the left, FS 6105 to the right, and past FS 6104 to the left, to the junction of FS 6100-300, past Deer Camp Campground. Turn left at the junction, continuing on FS 6101, and climb about 3 miles to Maverick Saddle, at the junction of FS 6101 and FS 5200. You get views of Lake Wenatchee and Nason Ridge to the west as you climb. Parking is available off the road, at the saddle.

Sources of additional information:

Entiat Ranger District
2108 Entiat Way
P.O. Box 476
Entiat, WA 98822
(509) 784-1511

Lake Wenatchee Ranger District
22976 Highway 207
Leavenworth, WA 98826
(509) 763-3103

Notes on the trail: Start with a 0.3-mile, rough, gravel-road descent to the north of the road junction, leading you straight to Upper Mad River Trail #1409.1 and a difficult climb. (Lower Mad River Trail #1409 starts off to the right.) In 0.5 mile you get a short breather of a descent, with the Mad River down the hill to the right. At 1.5 miles, pass the junction of Hi Yu Trail #1403 on your left, and continue straight. In another 0.1 mile, after a bridge over the river, pass Jimmy

Creek Trail #1419, which veers off to the right at the 4 o'clock position. In front of you lies a large scree, and to the right are some beautiful rock formations. The trail is steep and rocky in spots, but rideable. Keep climbing and paralleling the river. At 3.5 miles, as you round a curve to the right on a log-bordered section of trail, a spur trail to a primitive campsite shoots off to the left. Just after that, pass the junction of Lost Lake Trail #1421 on your left. Less than a mile from this junction, past a creek crossing, ride along Blue Creek Meadow. Past the crossing the climb becomes more gradual (or maybe you're just warmed up now!). In 0.6 more miles, make another splash, and then pass the junction of Tyee Ridge Trail #1415. Past yet another creek crossing in 1.3 more miles, at the top of the meadow, pass the upper junction of the Lost Lake Trail on your left. In short order, come to a **Y** junction, with Blue Creek Trail #1426 to the right. (The Blue Creek Guard Station is also to the right.) Veer left, staying on the Upper Mad River Trail. In 2.1 miles, pass the junction of Alder Ridge Trail #1523 to your left as you ride through the madly beautiful Mad Meadow. In 0.3 mile from this junction, come to the junction of Mad Lake Trail #1406. Turn left and make the 0.4-mile trek to the lake. Back on the Upper Mad River Trail, explore or loop back on any of the other trails you passed on the way up, or continue north on the Upper Mad River Trail.

LEAVENWORTH RANGER DISTRICT

As you drive east on US 2, past the Lake Wenatchee turnoff (WA 207) and toward Leavenworth, the Wenatchee River meets US 2 near the Tumwater Campground, about ten miles north of Leavenworth. A drive through rugged, beautiful Tumwater Canyon, alongside the river, brings you to the Bavarian-themed town of Leavenworth. Leavenworth was a dying lumber town that literally rebuilt itself from the ground up and created a year-round tourist destination with its shopping, dining, and outdoor activities set under a gorgeous, mountainous backdrop. If you didn't know better, you'd swear you were in the Alps.

The Leavenworth Ranger District encompasses 342,000 acres within the Wenatchee National Forest, from the Cascade crest to the eastern foothills; US 2 is its main thoroughfare. The area is accessible by way of WA 970 in Cle Elum and US 97 from Ellensburg, which climbs over Blewitt Pass to meet US 2 about four miles south of Leavenworth.

As you drive further east on US 2, passing US 97, the landscape becomes more sparse. You travel through pine-dotted, boulder-strewn hillsides as the Wenatchee River descends toward its confluence with the Columbia in Wenatchee. The Devil's Gulch Trail, south of the orchards that surround the colonial-themed town of Cashmere, is a single-track on which many use a shuttle vehicle to avoid the dirt road climb but get in on a classic descent. Devil's Gulch also provides a challenging, scenic climb, and it meets the Mission Ridge Trail to form a classic single-track loop.

RIDE 67 · Wenatchee River Road

AT A GLANCE
_____

WA

Length/configuration: 8.5-mile out-and-back on a dirt and gravel road (4.25 miles each way)

Aerobic difficulty: Easy to moderately difficult (a couple of steep hills)

Technical difficulty: Easy; some sand, ruts, and rocks

Scenery: Riverside meadows and wooded forest roads

Special comments: Wildflowers in the spring and good fall color

This is an easy 8.5-mile out-and-back ride. There are a couple of steep climbs and descents, which make it a tough ride for a novice. The Wenatchee River Road is a dirt and gravel road in good condition, with some areas of rough tread and patches of loose sand. The road follows the river past many good picnic and camping spots. Wildflowers grow along the roadside; lupine, Indian paintbrush, Chinese houses, and phlox are in bloom in the late spring. Maples and other deciduous trees line the route and add some color to the fall landscape.

General location: The trailhead is located approximately 11 miles north of Leavenworth, Washington.

Elevation change: The ride begins at 1,800' and quickly descends to 1,760'. This descent is followed by a climb to the trip's high point at 2,000'. Then the road drops to the river, at 1,760'. Rolling terrain adds about 200' of climbing to the outing. Total elevation gain: 720'.

Season: The relatively low elevation of the road makes it a good early and late season trip.

Services: There is no water available on the ride. Water can be found seasonally at Tumwater Campground, 0.6 mile south of the trailhead on US 2. All services are available in Leavenworth.

Hazards: Control your speed on the descents. You may encounter limited traffic on Wenatchee River Road—residents hold keys to the locked gate.

Rescue index: Help is available in Leavenworth.

Land status: Wenatchee National Forest.

Maps: The district map of the Lake Wenatchee Ranger District is a good guide to this ride.

RIDE 67 · Wenatchee River Road

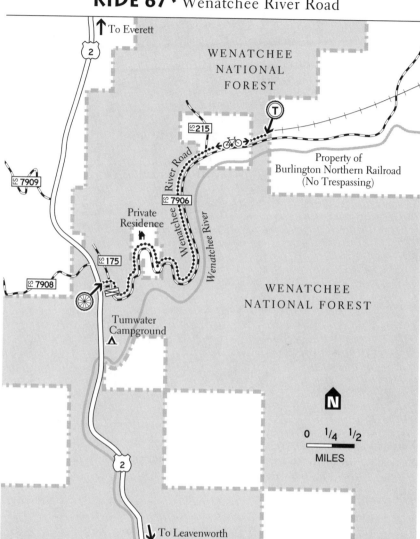

Finding the trail: From Leavenworth, follow US 2 north for 10.8 miles and turn right onto Forest Service Road 7906 (0.6 miles north of Tumwater Campground). Immediately turn left onto FS 175 and park on the side of the road.

Source of additional information:

Leavenworth Ranger District
600 Sherbourne Street (on US 2 at the east end of town)
Leavenworth, WA 98826
(509) 782-1413

Wenatchee River Road.

Notes on the trail: Follow FS 7906 to the gate. Go around the locked gate and proceed on the main road. Turn around when, after pedaling 4 miles, you arrive at a Burlington Northern Railroad "No Trespassing" sign. Return the way you came.

RIDE 68 · Boundary Butte

AT A GLANCE

WA

Length/configuration: 13-mile combination on dirt roads, gravel roads, and double-track; 6-mile loop with two out-and-back spurs, a 4.8-mile out-and-back (2.4 miles each way) and a 2.2-mile out-and-back (1.1 miles each way)

Aerobic difficulty: Moderately difficult climbing with several short steep pitches; the last pitch is a real doozy

Technical difficulty: Moderate; some rough gravel and eroded sections of double-track

Scenery: Stunning views of Icicle Ridge, the Stuart Range, and Icicle Valley

Special comments: Great wildflowers in the springtime

This 13-mile ride is a loop combined with two out-and-back legs. The first part of the trip is a climb to Boundary Butte. The grade of the climb changes from moment to moment—it is mostly easy and moderately difficult pedaling. There are about a dozen short, steep pitches (totaling less than one mile). Double-track Canyon Crest Trail makes up 2.4 miles of the route. The trail is eroded in places and quite challenging. Mounds of earth have been built across the road in an effort to divert runoff. The rest of the excursion is on dirt and gravel roads in good condition. One exception is the final 0.3 mile below the summit. This stretch is rough and extremely steep.

Views of Leavenworth, the Stuart Range, Icicle Ridge, and Icicle Valley are this ride's main attraction. Canyon Crest Trail is part of the Mountain Home Lodge trail system. This full-service lodge has a nice deck, with views of the Stuart Range to the west.

General location: This ride begins on Mountain Home Road, approximately 2 miles south of Leavenworth, Washington.

Elevation change: The ride begins at 1,600' and climbs to 3,168' at Boundary Butte. Undulations on the ride add an estimated 200' of climbing to the trip. Total elevation gain: 1,768'.

Season: Portions of the route are lined with wildflowers in the spring. You can ride here from the early spring into the late fall.

Services: All services are available in Leavenworth.

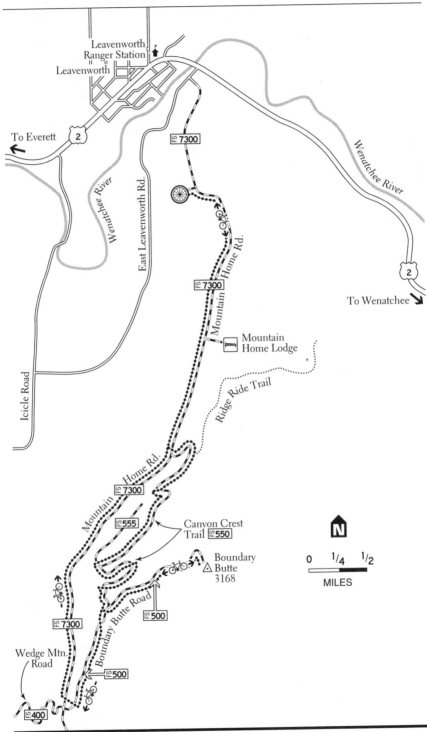

Leavenworth
Ranger Station
Leavenworth

To Everett

(2)

Wenatchee River

Wenatchee River

FS 7300

East Leavenworth Rd.

Mountain Home Rd.

FS 7300

(2)

To Wenatchee

Mountain
Home Lodge

Ridge Ride Trail

Icicle Road

Mountain Home Rd.

FS 7300

FS 555

Canyon Crest
Trail FS 550

Boundary
△ Butte
3168

N

0   1/4   1/2

MILES

Boundary Butte Road

FS 500

FS 7300

Wedge Mtn.
Road

FS 500

FS 400

The Stuart Range from
Boundary Butte.

Hazards: Watch for motorists, equestrians, hikers, and fellow mountain bikers. Watch for loose gravel on the descents.

Rescue index: Help can be obtained in Leavenworth.

Land status: Lands within the Wenatchee National Forest and public right-of-way through private property.

Maps: The district map of the Leavenworth Ranger District is a good guide to this ride. USGS 7.5 minute quad: Leavenworth.

Finding the trail: From the ranger station in Leavenworth, turn left onto US 2. Cross the bridge over the Wenatchee River and immediately turn right onto East Leavenworth Road. Take the next left onto Mountain Home Road. Soon this road changes to a gravel road and climbs very steeply. Mountain Home Road narrows as it passes a couple of large boulders. Proceed beyond the second boulder for 0.2 mile to a closed spur road on the right. Park on the side of the spur road.

Sources of additional information:

Leavenworth Ranger District
600 Sherbourne Street (on US 2 at the east end of town)
Leavenworth, WA 98826
(509) 782-1413

Mountain Home Lodge
P.O. Box 687
Leavenworth, WA 98826
(509) 548-7077

Notes on the trail: From your car, follow Mountain Home Road/FS 7300 uphill past homes and the Mountain Home Lodge. One mile past the lodge, turn left onto Canyon Crest Trail (a dirt spur road). This turn comes shortly after you pass a sign indicating that you have been traveling on FS 7300. Ride up Canyon Crest Trail to FS 555, at a **T** intersection, and turn left. At the next **T** intersection, turn left onto unsigned FS 500 and pedal to the summit. Turn around at the top and descend on FS 500. You will arrive at a major intersection of roads in 2 miles. Turn right onto unsigned FS 7300 and ride back to your vehicle.

RIDE 69 · Devil's Gulch/Mission Ridge Trail

AT A GLANCE

WA

Length/configuration: 17.8-mile single-track loop; entire length of Devil's Gulch Trail can be ridden (or shuttled) as a 23-mile gravel road and single-track loop with about 12 miles of single-track

Aerobic difficulty: Advanced-level climbing (walking?) on the upper stretch of the Devil's Gulch Trail and the start of the Mission Ridge Trail

Technical difficulty: Switchbacks, creek crossings

Scenery: Rugged rock formations, views down into central Washington, the Wenatchee Mountains, and the Entiat Mountains

Special comments: Advanced-level riding with all single-track or road/trail route options

This 17.8-mile single-track loop climbs to within 2 miles of the upper trail-head of Devil's Gulch Trail #1220, which is a screamin'-fast, popular downhill run. The gentle climb at the start of Devil's Gulch and the steep descent at the end of Mission Ridge Trail #1201 make a counterclockwise direction the preferred routing for a full single-track loop, but you can descend the entire length of the Devil's Gulch Trail by way of an 11-mile, 3,300-foot road climb, which many do as a shuttle ride. The gravel road and single-track option

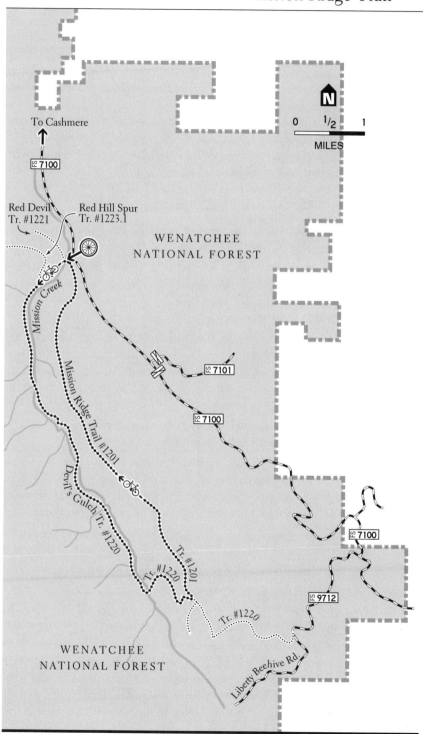

To Cashmere

FS 7100

Red Devil
Tr. #1221

Red Hill Spur
Tr. #1223.1

WENATCHEE
NATIONAL FOREST

Mission Creek

Mission Ridge Trail #1201

FS 7101

FS 7100

Devil's Gulch Tr. #1220

Tr. #1201

Tr. #1220

FS 7100

FS 9712

Tr. #1220

WENATCHEE
NATIONAL FOREST

Liberty Beehive Rd.

0   1/2   1

MILES

discussed here were not researched, but I've been told that the road route to the top of the Devil's Gulch Trail is pretty straightforward.

The trails are mostly firm and smooth; as the season progresses, dusty conditions arise on sun-exposed trail. Tree-lined creek crossings toward the start provide respites from the heat. You generate the real heat, though, as you power up the switchbacks and grind up the dry hillside to the top of the Mission Ridge Trail. The rewards for your efforts are beautiful views in all directions and a descent that gets steeper as you get lower.

The Douglas fir and ponderosa pine provide some sun protection but come prepared with plenty of water and sunscreen. Come prepared, too, with a trail park pass, as they are required at all trailheads within the Leavenworth Ranger District.

The Devil's Gulch area boasts around 60 miles of trail open to mountain bikes, including Tronsen Ridge Trail #1204, Red Hill Trail #1223, Red Hill Spur Trail #1223.1, Red Devil Trail #1221, and others.

General location: The trailhead is located about 22 miles south of Leavenworth, and 18 miles west of Wenatchee by way of Cashmere.

Elevation change: You're at 1,700' as you unload your bike. Elevation crests at 4,480' on the Mission Ridge Trail. Additional climbing pushes the total elevation gain to right around the 3,000' mark. On the road/trail loop, you'll start a rim-heating descent at 5,000' elevation.

Season: A Forest Service employee at the trailhead told me you can make the trek here in late spring when the snow melts. I'm sure he was sincere, but check with the ranger district office or the nearby Forest Service Headquarters for conditions anyway. You can come back and come back again, to reride, reroute, or explore other area trails, until midautumn.

Services: Water and most services are available in Cashmere. All services, including bike shops, are available in Wenatchee and Leavenworth.

Hazards: The Devil's Gulch Trail is a popular trail on which mountain bikers and motorcyclists may be descending at speed, so be aware of fellow riders. Beware, also, of some soft, sandy patches and water diversion ditches as you're groovin' on the descent on the Mission Ridge Trail. Don't forget sunscreen and plenty of water.

Rescue index: Help can be found in Cashmere.

Land status: Wenatchee National Forest, Leavenworth Ranger District.

Maps: The big, bulky Leavenworth Ranger District map is your best guide; photocopy this section for your outing. The 1996 revision did not show the Red Devil Trail at the bottom of the loop, but that won't stop you!

Finding the trail: From Leavenworth, drive east on US 2, passing the junction of US 97 (to Ellensburg and Cle Elum) in 4 miles and coming to the west end of Cashmere in about 12 miles. Turn right on Division Street on the west end of town, crossing over the Wenatchee River. From Wenatchee, travel west on US 2 for about 8 miles. Turn left over the river on the east side of town, and fol-

Devil's Gulch Trail.

low the road (Cottage Avenue) until it meets up with Division Street at a **T** intersection. Drive south on Division for 0.3 mile, and after a right-hand curve onto Pioneer Street, turn left onto Mission Creek Road (CR 11). At a **T** intersection in 0.5 mile, turn right, cross Mission Creek, and quickly veer left, continuing on Mission Creek Road. Driving 6.2 miles beyond the **T** intersection, Mission Creek Road turns to gravel FS 7100 as it passes FS 7104 to the right. In 1.0 mile, cross a one-lane bridge over Mission Creek and continue straight, passing a road to the right. The trailhead parking area is 1.5 miles beyond the bridge.

Sources of additional information:

Leavenworth Ranger District
600 Sherbourne Street (on US 2 at the east end of town)
Leavenworth, WA 98826
(509) 548-6977

Wenatchee National Forest Headquarters
215 Melody Lane
Wenatchee, WA 98801
(509) 662-4335

Notes on the trail: From the trailhead, pedal across the bridge over Mission Creek and onto the Devil's Gulch Trail. At 0.1 mile, pass the junction of the recently cut Red Devil Trail #1221 on the right, which Connects to Red Hill Trail #1223. In another 0.1 mile the Mission Ridge Trail, on which you'll return, joins from the left. Pass the junction of Red Hill Spur Trail #1223.1 on your right as you continue. Cross the creek at 2.8 miles, climb gradually, and cross another creek 1.7 miles farther. Keep climbing, and after a creek crossing in another 2.8 miles, start switchbacking up to the ridge. (The steep stuff begins!) On a couple of right-hand switchbacks, you can dismount, climb on the rocks, and catch some beautiful views of Tronsen Ridge's rugged landscape to the west. After 1.9 miles of climbing from the creek, make your final push on Devil's Gulch Trail and come to a 3-way junction. Devil's Gulch continues straight, but angle back to the left on the Mission Ridge Trail #1201 and continue riding/hiking the steep climb to the top. In 0.6 mile, you've done the lion's share of the climbing, and are rewarded with views of Tronson Ridge to the west, the Entiat Mountains to the north, the Columbia River and central Washington to the east, and Mission Peak to the south, as you ride on both sides of the ridge and stop to climb the rocks. The descent is broken up with some fairly steep roller coasters, but as you near the bottom, it's all downhill. Sadly, all good loops must come to an end, so rejoin the Devil's Gulch Trail and turn right to meet the trailhead in 0.2 mile.

To ride (or shuttle) the road/trail loop, continue up FS 7100 8.6 miles from the trailhead parking area and turn sharp right at the junction, staying on FS 7100. Turn right onto Liberty Beehive Road (FS 9712), 0.7 mile beyond the junction, and turn right onto the Devil's Gulch Trail after 1.8 miles on Liberty Beehive Road. Keep descending on Devil's Gulch Trail as the Mission Ridge Trail veers up to the right.

METHOW VALLEY RIDES

The Methow Valley sits in the center of northern Washington, just east of North Cascades National Park. The valley has the "east of the Cascades" advantage: dry weather. In summer, temperatures in the daytime are moderate, while nights are cool. Sunny days are the standard fare.

The drive to the valley on the North Cascades Highway/WA 20 is great. The highway takes off from Interstate 5 near Burlington, south of Bellingham. As it proceeds east, the highway passes between the north and south sections of North Cascades National Park through some of the highest and wildest mountains in the state; it is incredibly picturesque. This stretch of highway is also a favorite with experienced touring bicyclists.

Dropping 3,600 feet from Washington Pass, the highway enters the open spaces of the Methow Valley. The valley is world-famous for its network of cross-country ski trails. It is becoming equally well-known for its mountain biking. Surrounding the valley is the Okanogan National Forest, which contains hundreds of miles of outstanding single-tracks and scenic forest roads.

The valley has long been courted for its downhill ski resort potential. Developers fancy the area's plentiful snowpack, rolling hills, and high peaks. Valley residents have resisted this type of growth for over 25 years. Many would like to see the continued development of trail-based resorts. (One such resort is the elegant and already thriving Sun Mountain Lodge.) Some envision gondolas to a mountaintop for access not to alpine skiing but to a massive trail system.

This "trail-friendly" attitude gives the area a wonderful ambience. The Methow Valley Sport Trails Association has been a catalyst for community pride and trail development. The association was originally formed to maintain the area's cross-country ski trails. Now its members maintain many of the bike routes in the region as well. The association produces an excellent quarterly newsletter, "Trails," and brings the popular Methow Valley Mountain Bike Festival to the valley each October.

Winthrop is the center of tourism in the Methow Valley. The town operates on a western theme—with wooden sidewalks, storefronts, hitching posts, and so forth. It is quaint and quirky, with many fine accommodations, restaurants, and interesting shops.

Less than three miles out of Winthrop is Pearrygin Lake. Nestled in sagebrush hills, this state park provides visitors with camping and hot showers. Camping is also plentiful in the surrounding forests. Stop in at the national forest ranger station in Twisp for information.

RIDE 70 · Pearrygin Lake Loop

AT A GLANCE

Length/configuration: 11.5-mile paved road and gravel road loop; optional 2-mile (each way) gravel road side trip to Sullivan Pond

Aerobic difficulty: Moderate 700' climb

Technical difficulty: Fat tires are needed, technical skills are not

Scenery: Jagged Cascades peaks, Methow Wildlife Area

Special comments: A moderate spin that starts and ends in the heart of town

The 11.4-mile Pearrygin Lake Loop is a good introductory tour to the Winthrop area on which you can take your non-single-track riding partners. The moderate-level effort is also a good choice when your nonriding companions tour the quaint town of Winthrop and want you to leave the car in town. It's not single-track, and it's not backcountry—you can play a midride round of golf if you bring your clubs—but it's a good workout, it'll show you some pretty views, and maybe you'll catch sight of some mule deer, pheasant, and grouse in the Methow Wildlife area.

If you crave more climbing and more views than the loop affords, take the 2-mile side trip to Sullivans Pond. The pond is hardly a scenic feast but it's a wildlife watering hole, so you might score some valuable animal sighting points (valuable only for the memories and postride chat). Just past the Pearrygin State Park entrance, it starts with a 0.8-mile descent and then climbs to a scenic stop in another mile. I heard, though I didn't confirm, that some single-track takes off from the Sullivans Pond area. Ah, so little time, so many areas to explore. . . .

General location: The ride begins smack in the middle of Winthrop, where eastbound WA 20 turns south (or northbound WA 20 turns west; take your pick), 34 miles east of Washington Pass and 9 miles north of Twisp.

Elevation change: Winthrop lies at 1,800' elevation. The roads on this loop rise to a high point of 2,500', for an elevation gain of 700'.

RIDE 70 • Pearrygin Lake Loop

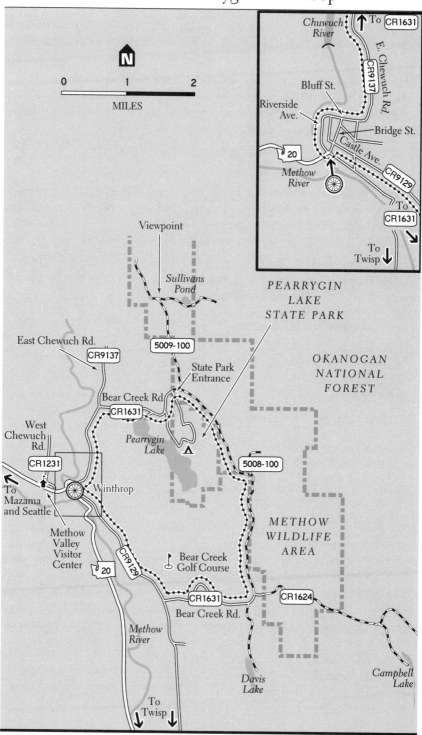

To CR1631

Chuwuch River

E. Chewuch Rd.

CR9137

Bluff St.

Riverside Ave.

Bridge St.

Castle Ave.

CR9129

20

Methow River

To CR1631

To Twisp

N

0   1   2

MILES

Viewpoint

Sullivans Pond

PEARRYGIN LAKE STATE PARK

East Chewuch Rd.

CR9137

5009-100

State Park Entrance

OKANOGAN NATIONAL FOREST

Bear Creek Rd

CR1631

West Chewuch Rd.

CR1231

Pearrygin Lake

5008-100

To Mazama and Seattle

Winthrop

Methow Valley Visitor Center

20

CR9129

Bear Creek Golf Course

METHOW WILDLIFE AREA

CR1631

Bear Creek Rd.

CR1624

Methow River

Davis Lake

Campbell Lake

To Twisp

Season: Late winter or early spring, when the snow level is low enough, to late fall or early winter, when the snow level is not yet too high.

Services: If you drain your water bottle by the 3.3-mile mark, you can fill up at Pearrygin Lake State Park, where camping is also available. All services are available in Winthrop.

Hazards: Winthrop is a popular year-round location, and the state park is a popular summer getaway, so watch for vehicles of all shapes and sizes. This is not a tree-shaded route, so in the heat of summer, go early or later in the day, or slather on the sunscreen and work on your tan.

Rescue index: Help is available along the route and in Winthrop.

Land status: Methow Wildlife Area, Okanagan County roads.

Maps: The Okanagan National Forest map is a suitable guide to the area. Green Trails #84 Twisp shows everything on the loop except the very northern tip. If you make the side trip up road 5009-100, you can use Green Trails #52 Doe Mountain. If you stay on the route and throw caution to the wind, you can get by without a map. If necessary, you can ask for directions along the way!

Finding the trail: If you go to the touristy town center of Winthrop on WA 20, you are there. Parking is available nearby.

Sources of additional information:

Winthrop Visitors Center
Building 49, US 20 (just west of the Winthrop town center)
Winthrop, WA 98862
(509) 996-4000

Methow Valley Sport Trails Association
P.O. Box 147
Winthrop, WA 98862
(509) 996-3287

Washington State Department of Wildlife
1550 Alder Street N.W.
Ephrata, WA 98823
(509) 754-4624

Notes on the trail: Start in Winthrop at the junction of WA 20 to the west and south, Riverside Avenue to the north, and steep Bridge Street to the east. Pedal north on Riverside Avenue through the north part of town. In 0.1 mile, the road winds east (right) and turns into Bluff Street, which will turn into CR 9137, East Chewuch Road. Stay on this main paved road past dirt and paved junctions on both sides. At about 1.6 miles, after a short descent and before the road curves left and is signed as Chewuch Road, turn right. You'll be climbing on paved Bear Creek Road (CR 1631) toward Pearrygin Lake State Park. Climb past private resorts and get your first view of the lake at about 2.1 miles. Pass the entrance to the state park at 3.3 miles, at which point you enter the Methow Wildlife Area and the road turns to gravel. In 0.2 mile come to a junction with

Pearrygin Lake and Cascades view from Bear Creek Road.

Wildlife Area Road 5009-100 on your left. Turn and look to the west for some beautiful views of jagged Cascades peaks. To get even better views, take the left and make the 2-mile side trip to Sullivans Pond on road 5009-100. (Start with a 0.8-mile descent, then climb about 600' in another 1.2 miles to a right-hand curve in the road. Again look to the west, and compare the view to the one down the hill. Sullivans Pond is just a short distance beyond the view, and some single-track reportedly lies just beyond Sullivans Pond.)

To continue the loop, pass road 5009-100 and continue the stair-step climb on Bear Creek Road that takes you to the top elevation on the loop in 1.5 miles, and then makes a rolling descent. Come to a **T** intersection 0.4 mile into the descent and turn right, toward Davis Lake. Shortly after the turn stop and check out the informational sign on the left about the Methow Wildlife Area. In another 0.4 mile, Davis Lake comes into view through a saddle to the south. When the road turns back to pavement, continue straight on Bear Creek Road as you pass the junction of CR 1624 (with its other side-trip possibilities, toward Campbell Lake, Beaver Creek, and Pipestone Canyon), on your left. In 1.1 miles, pass the entrance to the golf course on your right, as the descent levels out momentarily. Come to a **T** intersection in another 0.7 mile, and turn right on CR 9129, back toward town. Stay on this road for 2.2 miles, just 0.2 mile after you pass—or stop at—the Shafer Museum on your left. (The museum displays historical items and artifacts from the area.) At the four-way intersection of Bridge Street, descend 0.1 mile to the left, to the ride's end, and reward yourself with an espresso or ice cream cone from one of the nearby shops.

RIDE 71 · Methow Trail/Sun Mountain Trails

AT A GLANCE

WA

Length/configuration: Riding the Methow Trail makes for a 12.6-mile out-and-back (6.3 miles each way); the Methow Trail is comprised of double-track, gravel roads, single-track, and pavement; the Sun Mountain Trails are also varied

Aerobic difficulty: The Methow Trail is mostly easy to moderately difficult (it includes 0.3 mile of steep climbing); there are easy trails and demanding trails at Sun Mountain

Technical difficulty: The Methow Trail is comprised of mostly good riding surfaces, but it includes loose conditions, rocks, and other obstacles; Sun Mountain Trails are well maintained and sport all manner of conditions and difficulties

Scenery: Methow Trail climbs through meadows and hillsides to reach the Sun Mountain Trails; Sun Mountain Trails pass by lakes, cruise through dense timber, and roll across flowered meadows

Special comments: The Methow Valley is a special place, especially if you love to travel on trails

The 6.3-mile Methow Trail is a combination of single-tracks, double-tracks, gravel roads, and a touch of pavement. All of these parts form a link between the town of Winthrop and a concentrated network of loops known as the Sun Mountain Trails. The Sun Mountain Trails comprise 30 miles of single-tracks, double-tracks, and gravel roads used by equestrians, hikers, runners, cyclists, and cross-country skiers. You would be hard-pressed to find an area with a greater variety of routes and settings.

From the valley floor, the Methow Trail climbs west toward Patterson Lake and into the mountains. The difficulty of the climb and the technical difficulty of the trail vary constantly. There are 2.7 miles of easy, 1.2 miles of moderate, and 0.3 mile of steep ascending. In addition, there are over 2 miles of level and downhill terrain. The hardest stretch of uphill comes after about 3 miles of pedaling, where a double-track stair-steps up a drainage. Most of the ride is on good surfaces, but there are many sections of loose and/or embedded rocks and a couple of short sandy stretches.

Sun Mountain Trails offer circuits suitable to all ability levels. The easiest loops are via Chickadee, Beaver Pond, and Little Wolf Trails. Pathways that

RIDE 71 · Methow Trail / Sun Mountain Trails

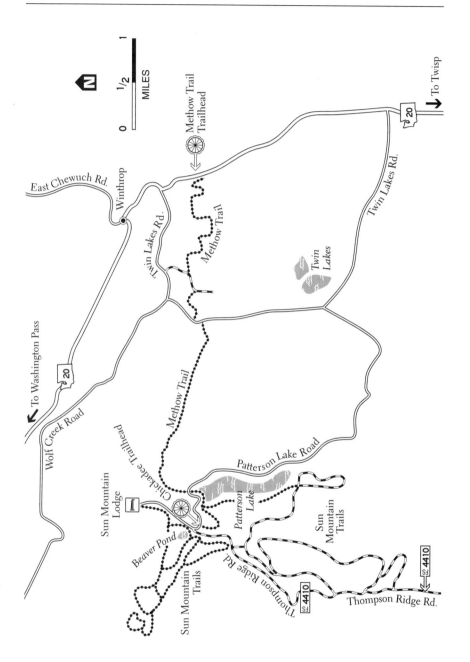

Little Wolf Trail on Sun
Mountain.

branch off from these easier routes offer cyclists some intermediate challenges. Tougher routes include the Overland, Criss-Cross, Inside Passage, Meadow Lark, and Patterson Lake Trails.

General location: The Methow Trail begins in Winthrop, Washington.

Elevation change: The trailhead for the Methow Trail lies at 1,760'. The Chickadee parking lot trailhead for the Sun Mountain Trails lies at 2,600'. Ups and downs along the way add about 200' of climbing to the ride. Total elevation gain: 1,040'. Rides on the Sun Mountain Trails can involve negligible amounts of elevation gain (Beaver Pond Loop) or sizeable doses of climbing (Thompson Ridge Road tops out at about 3,640').

Season: It is often dry enough to ride here in the late spring. Snow may begin falling in October.

Services: There is no water available on the ride. Water and all services can be found in Winthrop. The Sun Mountain Lodge offers dining and accommodations.

Hazards: Note the location of the barbed-wire gate you pass through while climbing on the Methow Trail—you will approach it from around a corner on the return. Watch for traffic on the roads. Yield to horses and pedestrians.

Rescue index: Help can be found in Winthrop.

Land status: The Methow Trail crosses private property on its way to public lands; the general public is encouraged to use the trail responsibly. The Sun Mountain Trails are in the Okanogan National Forest.

Maps: These trails are not delineated on National Forest maps or the USGS quads. We recommend the Methow Valley Sport Trails Association's "Sun Mountain Ski Trails" map and the "Summer Hiking and Mountain Biking Trail Map and Guide" produced by the Sun Mountain Lodge.

Finding the trail: The trailhead for the Methow Trail is next to WA 20 in Winthrop. To find it, drive south through town on WA 20. Follow the highway as it swings hard to the right, crossing a steel bridge over the Methow River. After you cross the bridge, bear left, staying on WA 20. From the bridge, it is about 0.5 mile to the trailhead (on the right side of the highway, across from the Cascade Inn. There is no room to park on the west side of the highway near the trailhead. Turn around and head north on the highway. Turn right and pull well off the highway to park near the "Rodeo" sign (just south of the Evergreen Grocery and Hardware).

To drive to the Chickadee Trailhead and day-use parking for the Sun Mountain Trails, drive south through Winthrop on WA 20. After crossing the steel bridge over the river, bear right and follow the signs for Sun Mountain Lodge. The parking area is on the left about 0.5 mile beyond the Patterson Lake Cabins (about 9 miles from town).

Sources of additional information:

Methow Valley Ranger Distric
P.O. Box 188
Twisp, WA 98856
(509) 997-2131

Methow Valley Sport Trails Association
P.O. Box 147
Winthrop, WA 98862
(509) 996-3287

Sun Mountain Lodge
P.O. Box 1000
Winthrop, WA 98862
(509) 996-2211

Notes on the trails: Some of the Sun Mountain Trails are closed to bikes. Kraule and Ridge are off-limits to cyclists at all times. Sunnyside and Beaver Pond are closed after 5 P.M.

At the time of our research, the Methow Trail was well marked and easy to follow. Although the Sun Mountain Trails were marked, a map and a compass were helpful directional aids.

RIDE 72 · Buck Lake Loop

AT A GLANCE

Length/configuration: 13-mile loop on paved roads, gravel roads, and dirt double-tracks

Aerobic difficulty: Moderately difficult; some brief, steep pedaling, and a short hike-a-bike section

Technical difficulty: Easy to moderately difficult; some degraded double-track; watch for loose conditions

Scenery: Woods, a small lake, and grassy hillsides awash with wildflowers in the spring and early summer

Special comments: Well-named Buck Lake is home to large numbers of deer

This 13-mile loop is moderately difficult and involves about 4.5 miles of climbing. These uphills are evenly divided between easy and moderately difficult grades; one-quarter mile is strenuous. Nearly 70 percent of the ride follows level terrain or descends. About half of the route is paved; the other half is on compacted dirt roads and gravel roads in good condition. There is a short uphill stretch of degraded double-track where you must push your bike.

Buck Lake is a nice place to camp, fish, or enjoy a picnic lunch. Deer and other wildlife are often observed near the shore. The sun-drenched hillsides south of the lake are awash with wildflowers in the spring and summer. There are some nice views of the Cub Creek and Chewuch River drainages from Forest Service Road 140.

General location: This ride starts approximately 8 miles north of Winthrop, Washington.

Elevation change: The ride begins at 2,080' and climbs to a high point of 3,260'. Ups and downs encountered along the route add about 200' of climbing to the ride. Total elevation gain: 1,380'.

Season: The roads around Buck Lake are usually free of snow by June. Locals enjoy mountain biking from the late spring through the fall. The Methow Valley is busy with tourists during the summer.

Services: There is no water available on this ride. Water and all services are available in Winthrop.

RIDE 72 · Buck Lake Loop

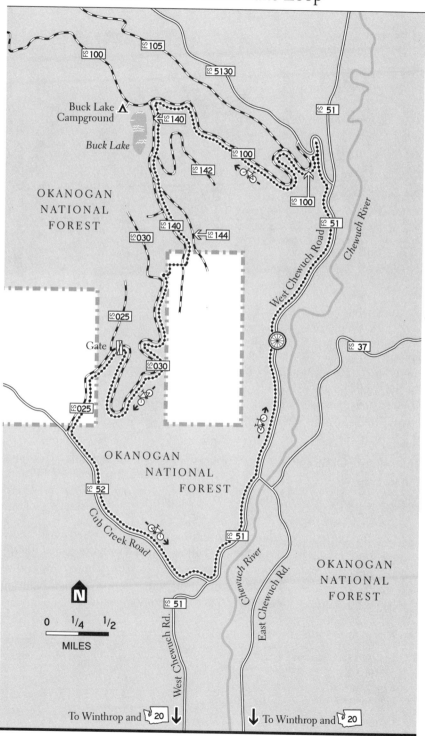

FS 105

FS 100

FS 5130

Buck Lake
Campground

FS 140

FS 51

Buck Lake

FS 100

FS 142

OKANOGAN
NATIONAL
FOREST

FS 100

FS 140

FS 51

FS 030

FS 144

West Chewuch Road

Chewuch River

FS 025

FS 37

Gate

FS 030

FS 025

OKANOGAN
NATIONAL
FOREST

FS 52

Cub Creek Road

FS 51

Chewuch River

East Chewuch Rd.

OKANOGAN
NATIONAL
FOREST

N

0   1/4   1/2
MILES

FS 51

West Chewuch Rd.

To Winthrop and 20

To Winthrop and 20

Buck Lake Loop.

Hazards: Be extra careful on the paved roads. They are quite narrow, and traffic moves along at a good clip. Wear shoes that provide good traction for the push up the double-track that connects FS 140 to FS 030; it is steep, rutted, and sandy. There are two cattle guards: one across FS 140 at Buck Lake, and one across FS 025 near its intersection with Cub Creek Road.

Rescue index: Help is available in Winthrop.

Land status: Okanogan National Forest lands and public right-of-way through private property.

Maps: The district map of the western half of the Winthrop Ranger District is a good guide to this ride. USGS 7.5 minute quad: Lewis Butte.

Finding the trail: In Winthrop, turn north onto West Chewuch Road/FS 51 (across from the Red Barn auditorium). Follow it for 7.8 miles to signed FS 015 (on the right, 0.9 mile north of the intersection of West Chewuch and East Chewuch roads). FS 015 leads downhill into the defunct Memorial Campground. Turn right onto FS 015 and park on the roadside.

Sources of additional information:

Methow Valley Ranger District
P.O. Box 188
Twisp, WA 98856
(509) 997-2131

Methow Valley Sport Trails Association
P.O. Box 147
Winthrop, WA 98862
(509) 996-3287

Notes on the trail: Follow West Chewuch Road north. Turn left onto paved FS 5130 (marked by a sign that points left toward Buck Lake), then turn left onto gravel FS 100. Climb to FS 140 and turn left to follow the sign for the boat ramp (right goes to the campground). Follow the road along the lakeshore. You will cross a cattle guard and then arrive at an unmarked intersection at the south end of the lake. Turn right. Soon the road starts to descend; follow the main road downhill. About 1 mile beyond the lake, the double-track emerges from the woods onto grassy hillsides. Ride through this more open environment for a short distance to an intersection in a group of pine trees. Look to the right for a large rock and a double-track that goes right and climbs very steeply up the hillside. Turn right and push your bike up this double-track. It tops out in 0.1 mile, swings to the left (south), and promptly comes to an intersection with another double-track that goes right (west). Continue straight and in a southerly direction; you are now on unsigned FS 030. From here, portions of the route are marked with bike route symbols. Descend on FS 030 to a locked gate. Pass around the side of the gate and immediately come to the unsigned intersection of FS 030 and FS 025. Stay left and downhill, on FS 025. You will cross a cattle guard before arriving at unsigned, paved Cub Creek Road. Turn left and follow Cub Creek Road down to West Chewuch Road. Turn left onto West Chewuch Road and pedal back to your vehicle.

RIDE 73 · Goat Wall Loop

AT A GLANCE

Length/configuration: 28-mile loop on gravel and paved roads

Aerobic difficulty: Difficult; 7-mile switchbacking climb

Technical difficulty: Moderately difficult; much of the descent is rocky and rutted

Scenery: Forest roads lead to an excellent viewpoint

Special comments: Fun climb and fun descent for strong riders

RIDE 73 · Goat Wall Loop

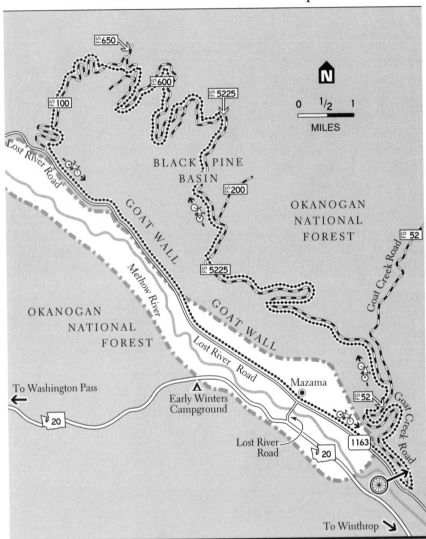

Goat Wall is a huge granite outcropping that looms high above the western end of the Methow Valley. The views from the top of this escarpment are outstanding. Below you are pasturelands and residences bordering the Methow River; above are the jagged peaks that surround Washington Pass. Fit cyclists with a taste for vistas will appreciate this demanding 28-mile road ride.

The first seven miles switchback up 2,560 feet. The ascent is evenly divided between easy and moderately difficult climbing, with about one-half mile of steep hills. This climb is followed by a 1.5-mile descent into Black Pine Basin.

The Methow Valley from Goat Wall.

Then the road rolls up and down through the basin for close to three miles and climbs again for two miles. You descend from this point to meet Lost River Road. The last eight miles are an easy paved road ride back to your vehicle.

Most of the roads are gravel and in good condition. The four miles that descend from the mountain are on a weathered dirt road that drops off like a high dive.

General location: This ride begins approximately 11.5 miles northwest of Winthrop, Washington.

Elevation change: The ride begins at 2,240' and climbs to 4,800' atop Goat Wall. A high point of 5,000' occurs after the climb out of Black Pine Basin. Undulations on the ride add an estimated 500' of climbing to the trip. Total elevation gain: 3,260'.

Season: The ride is best from the late spring through the fall.

Services: There is no water available on this ride. Water is available seasonally at the Early Winters Campground on WA 20. Phone, gas, limited groceries, and espresso are available at the Mazama Country Store. All services can be found in Winthrop.

Hazards: Stay in control while descending on FS 100; it is a steep and degraded dirt road. Ride defensively and watch for traffic at all times.

Rescue index: Help can be found in Winthrop. You may also be able to obtain assistance in Mazama.

Land status: Okanogan National Forest.

Maps: The district map of the western half of the Winthrop Ranger District is a good guide to this route. USGS 7.5 minute quads: Rendezvous Mountain, Mazama, and McLeod Mountain.

Finding the trail: From locations to the west, drive east on WA 20 from Early Winters Campground. In 1.9 miles, turn left onto Lost River Road toward Mazama. Cross the river and bear to the right onto CR 1163 in Mazama. Turn left onto gravel Goat Creek Road/FS 52 in another 1.9 miles. From locations to the east, travel west from Winthrop on WA 20. After 7 miles on WA 20, turn right onto CR 1163 (just before the bridge over the Winthrop River), where a sign directs you toward Hart's Pass and Goat Creek Road. Drive 4.5 miles on CR 1163 and turn right onto Goat Creek Road/FS 52. Proceed down FS 52 for 0.3 mile and turn right onto a spur road. Park in the clearing.

Sources of additional information:

Methow Valley Ranger District
P.O. Box 188
Twisp, WA 98856
(509) 997-2131

Methow Valley Sport Trails Association
P.O. Box 147
Winthrop, WA 98862
(509) 996-3287

Notes on the trail: Continue on FS 52 for 2.3 miles to an intersection where FS 5225 breaks off hard left and FS 52 goes straight. Turn left onto FS 5225 toward Goat Peak Lookout. Stay on the main road as spur roads break off to the left and right. Notice the mileposts that mark this road—the Goat Wall viewpoint is 0.3 mile beyond milepost 4. After checking out the view, continue on FS 5225 for nearly 5 miles to a **Y** intersection at signed FS 600. Turn right onto FS 600 and climb to the high point of the ride, which occurs at a cattle guard and a green gate. FS 600 descends briskly from this spot. Slow down after FS 600 switchbacks hard to the right, 1 mile past the cattle guard. Descend for another 0.5 mile to unmarked FS 650, which is marked by an orange, diamond-shaped symbol on a tree; the road crosses a wet, open area. Turn right onto FS 650; bear left at a fire ring and left again where an overgrown road goes right at a **T** intersection. You are now on unsigned FS 100. Rag-doll down the hill for several miles; you will emerge into a meadow near two vault toilets. Continue straight, then turn left onto unsigned, paved Lost River Road. Follow the pavement back to FS 52 and your vehicle.

RIDE 74 · Lightning Creek Trail

AT A GLANCE

WA

Length/configuration: 16-mile loop on gravel roads and single-track trail

Aerobic difficulty: Moderately difficult to advanced; demanding climb

Technical difficulty: Moderate to advanced; a fairly technical trail

Scenery: Open, sunny forest

Special comments: Good climb on forest roads and a fun single-track descent

Half of this 16-mile loop is a climb on gravel roads. The other half is a fun, fairly technical descent on single-track Lightning Creek Trail #425. The trip is short on views, but the cycling is pleasant as you pass through an open, sunny forest.

Overall, the climb on the forest roads is long and demanding. The ascent includes 4.5 miles of easy pedaling, 2.4 miles that are moderately difficult, and 1.3 miles that can be described as strenuous. There are also some short stretches of downhill and level riding. The road and trail surfaces are in good condition. Lightning Creek Trail passes through some rocky sections and some sandy areas. There are a couple of creek crossings where you are likely to get your feet wet.

General location: The trailhead is 15 miles southeast of Winthrop, Washington, and 10 miles northeast of Twisp, Washington.

Elevation change: The ride starts at 2,800' and reaches a high point of 5,200' near the Lightning Creek Trailhead. Undulations add about 300' of climbing to the loop. Total elevation gain: 2,700'.

Season: The trail is usually free of snow from mid-June through October. Avoid cycling here during hunting season.

Services: There is no water available on this ride. All services can be found in Twisp and Winthrop.

Hazards: Watch for logging trucks on the roads. Primary trail obstacles are rocks and sand. Watch for the small diversion ditches that have been carved across the trail in an effort to control erosion.

Rescue index: The nearest help is in Twisp.

Land status: Okanogan National Forest.

RIDE 74 · Lightning Creek Trail

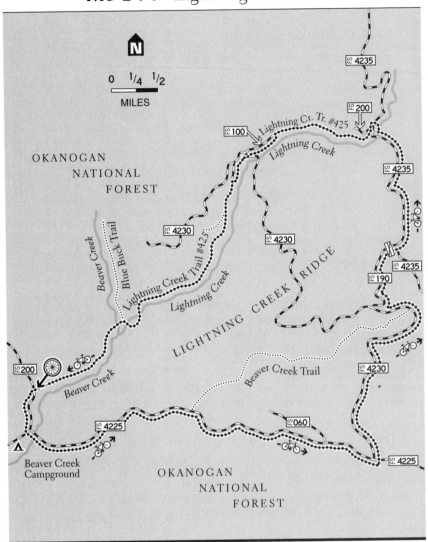

Maps: The district map of the Twisp Ranger District is a good guide to this ride. USGS 7.5 minute quads: Blue Buck Mountain and Loup Loup Summit.

Finding the trail: From Winthrop, drive south through town on WA 20. Turn left onto Eastside Winthrop–Twisp Road where WA 20 swings right to cross a steel bridge over the Methow River. (Stay on the east side of the river and follow the signs for the airport.) Proceed on Eastside Winthrop–Twisp Road for 6.5 miles to Balky Hill Road on the left. Turn left onto Balky Hill Road and travel 4.5 miles to Upper Beaver Creek Road. Go left on Upper Beaver Creek Road

Lightning Creek Trail.

and drive 3.4 miles to the intersection of FS 4225 and FS 200. Bear left up FS 200 and drive 0.4 mile to a group of campsites on the right. Turn right and park.

From Twisp, drive east on WA 20. Turn left to stay on WA 20 where WA 153 goes right toward Wenatchee. In another 2.9 miles, turn left onto Beaver Creek Road (a sign points left toward Beaver Creek). Travel 5.9 miles to the intersection of FS 4225 and FS 200. Bear left up FS 200 and drive 0.4 mile to a group of campsites on the right. Turn right and park.

Source of additional information:

Methow Valley Ranger District
P.O. Box 188
Twisp, WA 98856
(509) 997-2131

Notes on the trail: Coast down FS 200 and turn left onto FS 4225. Follow FS 4225 for 4 miles and turn left onto FS 4230. Pedal another 2.8 miles and make a right onto FS 190. After 1.2 miles on FS 190, you will pass through a gate and reach unsigned FS 4235. Turn left onto FS 4235, and stay on this road as spur roads branch off. FS 4235 crosses Lightning Creek after 1.4 miles, then intersects with FS 200 in another 0.2 mile. Go left onto FS 200 and immediately bear left to pick up the Lightning Creek Trail (do not follow FS 200). After 1.4 miles, the single-track trail enters a clear-cut and becomes more road-like. (The trail follows closed FS 100 here.) Next, the trail crosses a couple of trenches and deposits you at unsigned FS 4230. Turn right on this main road and descend a short distance (0.1 mile) to a spur road on the left (closed FS 125). Turn left onto the old road and pass through a couple more trenches. (You are now back on unsigned Lightning Creek Trail.) In another 0.8 mile you will arrive at a **Y** intersection. Stay to the left and follow the trail to your vehicle.

RIDE 75 · Twisp River Trail

AT A GLANCE

WA

Length/configuration: 13-mile loop; half single-track and half paved and gravel forest roads

Aerobic difficulty: Moderately difficult; lots of ups and downs on the single-track

Technical difficulty: Advanced; roots, rocks, drop-offs, soft sections of trail, and creek crossings

Scenery: Forested and grassy hillsides; broken views into the Lake Chelan–Sawtooth Wilderness

Special comments: Abundant wildflowers in the late spring and summer

The first half of this moderately difficult 13-mile loop is on a good single-track trail. The remainder is on well-maintained paved and gravel roads. Although the river is often audible from the trail, views of the water are rare. Clearings offer excellent vistas to Reynolds Peak in the Lake Chelan–Sawtooth Wilderness. Open, sunny areas are jammed with wildflowers in the spring and summer.

The Twisp River Trail #440 maintains a rather consistent elevation along its course. The pedaling is still demanding, however. The trail parallels the river on a forested hillside. There are no mountains to climb, but there are still plenty of ups and downs. Exposed roots, rocks, scree slopes, narrow sections, steep drop-offs, and creek crossings are encountered along the way.

General location: The trailhead is 23 miles west of Twisp, Washington.

Elevation change: The trail starts at 3,400' and quickly reaches a high point of 3,500'. Overall, the trail loses elevation as it heads east through many lesser hills

Stiletto Peak and Twisp
River Road.

and valleys. The road riding begins at 2,860' and returns to 3,400'. Undulations add approximately 500' of climbing to the ride. Total elevation gain: 1,140'.

Season: Wildflower displays in the spring and summer are often spectacular. Call ahead to check on the condition of the trail—specifically, whether or not it is dry.

Services: Water can be obtained seasonally at the Poplar Flat Campground. All services are available in Twisp.

Hazards: You will encounter obstacles and conditions typical of single-track trails. Walk your bike across scree slopes.

Rescue index: The nearest help is in Twisp.

Land status: Okanogan National Forest.

Maps: The trail was built in 1991 and was not delineated on Forest Service maps or USGS quads at the time of our research. Check with the Methow Valley Ranger District for updated maps.

Finding the trail: From WA 20 in Twisp, turn west onto Twisp River Road/FS 44. Stay on the north side of the river and drive 23 miles; park in the pullout on

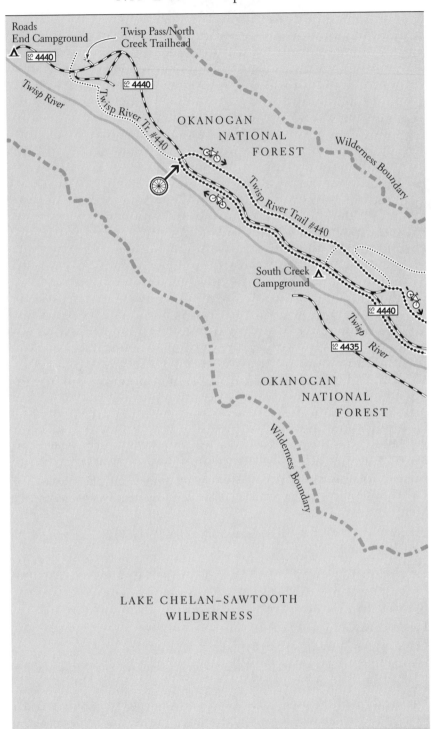

Roads
End Campground

Twisp Pass/North
Creek Trailhead

FS 4440

Twisp River

Twisp River Tr. #440

FS 4440

OKANOGAN
NATIONAL
FOREST

Wilderness Boundary

Twisp River Trail #440

South Creek
Campground

Twisp River

FS 4440

FS 4435

OKANOGAN
NATIONAL
FOREST

Wilderness Boundary

LAKE CHELAN–SAWTOOTH
WILDERNESS

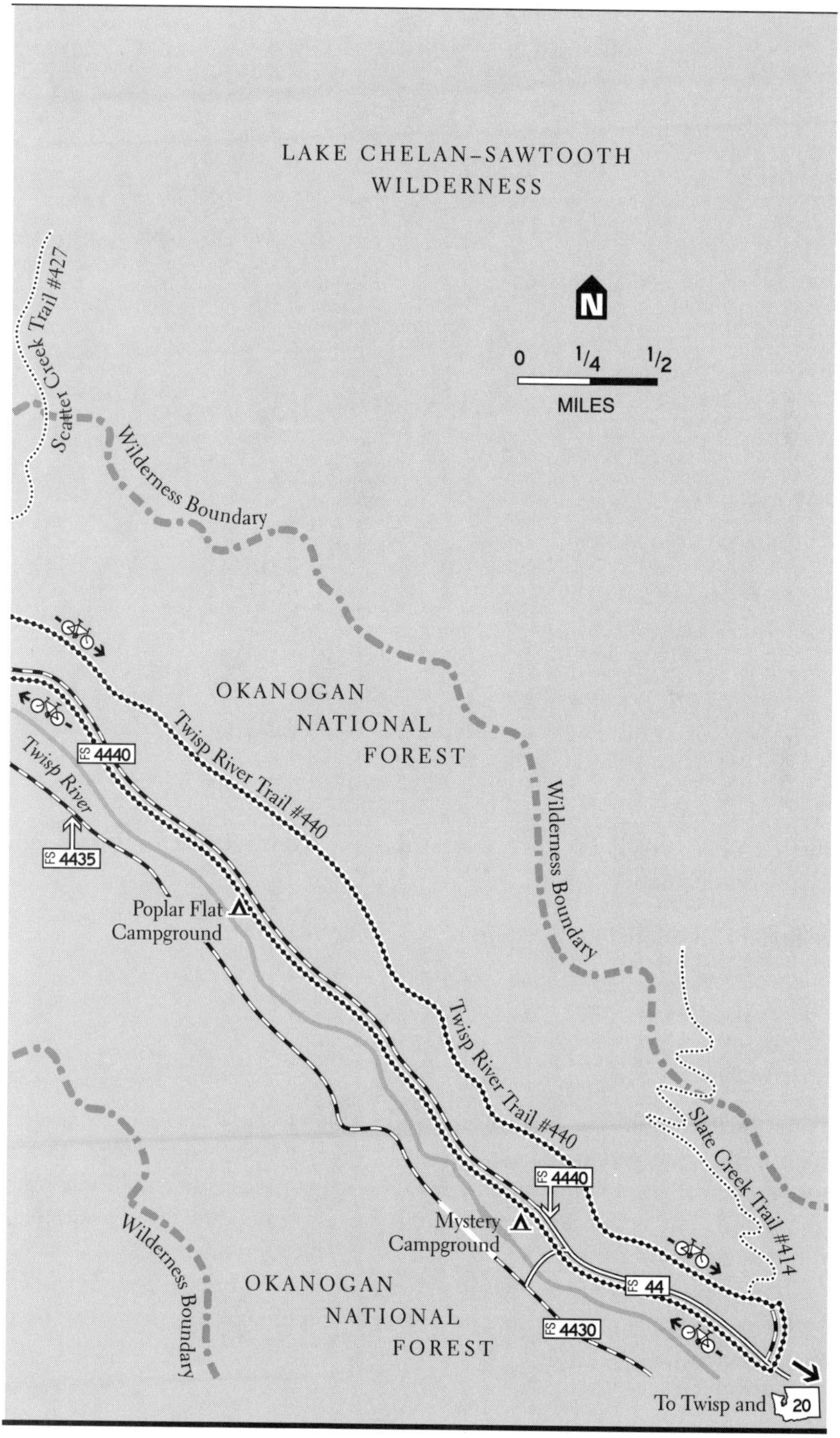

LAKE CHELAN–SAWTOOTH
WILDERNESS

N

0   1/4   1/2
MILES

Scatter Creek Trail #427

Wilderness Boundary

OKANOGAN
NATIONAL
FOREST

Twisp River Trail #440

FS 4440

Twisp River

FS 4435

Poplar Flat
Campground

Wilderness Boundary

Twisp River Trail #440

Slate Creek Trail #414

FS 4440

Mystery
Campground

FS 44

FS 4430

Wilderness Boundary

OKANOGAN
NATIONAL
FOREST

To Twisp and 20

Twisp River Trail.

the left where the Twisp River Trail crosses the road, 1.4 miles west of South Creek Campground.

Source of additional information:

Methow Valley Ranger District
P.O. Box 188
Twisp, WA 98856
(509) 997-2131

Notes on the trail: The official trailhead for the Twisp River Trail is another mile west of the parking area/trailhead that we have suggested. Heavy spring runoff had damaged portions of the trail and made passage difficult at the time of our visit. The Forest Service was in the process of building bridges and relocating segments of the trail.

The ride starts on the north side of the road, across from the recommended parking pullout. You should have little trouble finding your way along the Twisp River Trail—it is well marked. When you get to FS 44, turn right and pedal back to your vehicle.

RIDE 76 · Cooney Lake

AT A GLANCE

Length/configuration: 18.1-mile (total mileage) single-track out-and-back

Aerobic difficulty: Mostly gradual climb with some steep sections; a hearty challenge for strong intermediate riders

Technical difficulty: Rocky climbs; sections where line selection will keep you on or take you off the bike

Scenery: Eye-popping views near and at Cooney Lake, glimpses east to the Colville Indian Reservation

Special comments: Three words: beautiful, challenging, single-track (OK, so maybe it's four words)

This 18.1-mile (total mileage) out-and-back treats riders to some magnificent scenery near and at Cooney Lake. It tests intermediate-level riders and provides a great workout for advanced riders as it makes its way up the sometimes dusty, sometimes rocky trail. The climb, through stands of Douglas fir, lodgepole pine, and larch, culminates in a soothing meadow and tranquil Cooney Lake.

Bask in the beauty of the lake and the jumping cutthroat trout, the wildflower-laden meadow, and 8,000-foot-high Angel Staircase above the lake to the west before the return descent (which includes about a mile of climbing). Look east through the trees on the way back, where you'll get some views as far below and beyond as the Colville Indian Reservation.

The trail, especially in the corners, gets dusty in exposed areas as it's baked by the summer sun and ridden on by mountain bikers, motorcyclists, and equestrians. The motorcyclists, at least, give back to the trail; a sign at the trailhead notes that the trail system has been adopted and maintained by the Coulee Riders Motorcycle Association.

This ride can be a jump-off point for loop and shuttle rides using other area trails, including Eagle Lake Trail #431 and spurs #431A and #431B, Foggy Dew Ridge Trail #438, and Foggy Dew Creek Trail #417.

For the most up-to-date trail conditions, stop by the Methow Valley Ranger District office in Twisp. Then drive over to Michaelisa Espresso, a block away on WA 20. Owner Michael Marchiney, a nice guy and avid mountain biker, will serve up your favorite coffee drink and some hot tips on the local trails, if he's not out riding them himself!

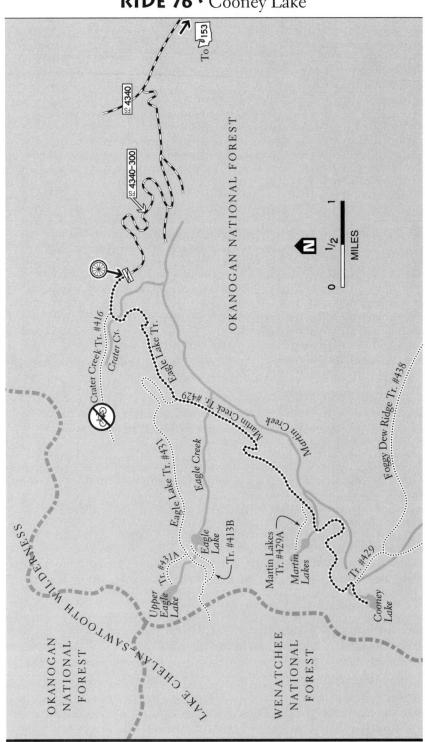

To 153

FS 4340

FS 4340-300

OKANOGAN NATIONAL FOREST

N

1/2   1
MILES
0

Crater Creek Tr. #416

Crater Cr.

Eagle Lake Tr.

Martin Creek Tr. #429

Martin Creek

Foggy Dew Ridge Tr. #438

Eagle Lake Tr. #431

Eagle Creek

Eagle Creek

Tr. #413B

Martin Lakes
Tr. #429A

Martin
Lakes

Tr. #429

Upper
Eagle
Lake

Tr. #431A

Eagle
Lake

Cooney
Lake

OKANOGAN CHELAN-SAWTOOTH WILDERNESS

LAKE CHELAN-SAWTOOTH WILDERNESS

OKANOGAN
NATIONAL
FOREST

WENATCHEE
NATIONAL
FOREST

General location: Trailhead parking is approximately 27 miles south of Twisp, 36 miles south of Winthrop, 50 miles north of Chelan, and 86 miles north of Wenatchee.

Elevation change: Starting at 4,800' elevation, the route takes you up to Cooney Lake, at a cool 7,241'. Additional climbing both ways brings total elevation gain to about 3,140'.

Season: The upper reaches of the route usually won't be snow-free and rideable until sometime in July. You'll have better chances at solitude on the trails during the week and post–Labor Day, until the end of the season in October. Check with the ranger district office for trail conditions.

Services: If you forgot water or snacks, a little store in Carlton is your last chance. Services are available in Pateros to the south, and Twisp and Winthrop to the north. Camping is available nearby.

Hazards: Rocky climbs and creek crossings, some of which demand dismounts. Your footsteps are hazardous to the grasses around Cooney Lake, so stay on the well-worn paths.

Rescue index: Maybe you'll be lucky and a motorcylist or fellow mountain biker will cross your path when you need help. If not, help can be summoned back down in the Methow Valley, at Carlton, Twisp, and Methow.

Land status: Okanagan National Forest, Methow Valley Ranger District.

Maps: Green Trails #115 Prince Creek will do the trick, while the Twisp Ranger District map shows these trails and a wealth of others in the region. (With the recent consolidation of the Winthrop and Twisp Ranger Districts into the Methow Valley Ranger District, a new district map will eventually be produced.) If you're too cheap to buy a map, the Wenatchee and Okanogan National Forests jointly produce a Sawtooth Backcountry Recreation Trails flyer showing this route and a few others in the area. (But, then, dear reader, you bought this book, so I would never hurl such epithets your way.)

Finding the trail: From Twisp, 9 miles south of Winthrop, travel south on WA 20, continuing south on WA 153 when WA 20 turns east in 2.9 miles. Pass the town of Carlton 11.1 miles south of Twisp. From Carlton, continue south on WA 153 for 3.5 miles and turn right (west) on Gold Creek Loop Road (CR 1029). In 1.5 miles turn right at the junction, onto CR 1034, Gold Creek Road. (From the south, turn left onto Gold Creek Loop Road 5.8 miles north of Methow and 17 miles north of Pateros off WA 153. Meet CR 1034 in approximately 1 mile and turn left.) In 1.1 miles continue straight and climb as the road turns into FS 4340, and follow the signs to the Crater Creek Trailhead and Eagle Lake Trail. Continue straight past the junctions to a one-lane bridge in another 4.0 miles; veer right, staying on FS 4340 as the pavement ends. Come to a **Y** junction 1.5 miles past the bridge; veer left and down on FS 4340-300. In 2.9 miles, pass a horse packing area to the left; continue straight, climbing steeply and steadily. Come to the trailhead parking area 1.6 miles past the horse packing area, and 4.4 miles total on FS 4340-300. Trailhead parking is available.

Michael Marchiney
climbing on Martin
Creek Trail.

Sources of additional information:

Methow Valley Sport Trails Association
P.O. Box 147
Winthrop, WA 98862
(509) 996-3287

Methow Valley Ranger District (formerly Twisp Ranger District)
502 Glover Street (just off of US 20)
P.O. Box 188
Twisp, WA 98856
(509) 997-2131

Winthrop Visitors Center
Building 49, US 20 (just west of the Winthrop town center)
Winthrop, WA 98862
(509) 996-4000

Notes on the trail: Click into or strap onto the pedals, and start on Eagle Lake Trail #431, steadily traversing an exposed area. Get into the trees by 0.7 mile, and cross the bridge over Crater Creek where a horse crossing goes left. After the bridge, pass the Crater Creek Trail, which climbs to your right. In another 0.3 mile an unmarked trail descends to your left; stay right and climb steadily. At 2.3 miles (1.3 miles after the unmarked trail) you've done 800' of climbing when you come to the junction of the Martin Creek Trail on the left. If you stay on the Eagle Lake Trail you'll come to Horsehead Pass in 5 miles, but turn left onto the Martin Creek Trail, and descend to Eagle Creek in 1 mile. Resume climbing past the creek. At 4.0 miles (0.7 mile after the creek) the climb levels out and traverses, and then climbs gradually, with a few steep grinders. On your right at 6.6 miles, pass Martin Lakes Trail #429A, which climbs steeply and technically to Martin Lakes in 0.6 mile. It'll be a hike-a-bike but you can make it up for some nice views if you're not spent on the return trip.

Continue on the Martin Creek Trail with a respite from the climb. Dismount for a rocky creek crossing, and then gear down for more climbing. Steep sections, including steep switchbacks, are interspersed with more gradual sections as you make your way up. The climb gets steeper, and the views more majestic, as you near the lake; at 8.1 miles you'll come to a meadow, with a rugged scree and sawtooth peaks soon filling in the picture. A few steep switchbacks signal the last of the hard climbing at 8.9 miles, just 0.1 mile from Cooney Lake. Very quickly, a creek crossing gives way to a small climb to the right. At the crest of this little climb, look down at the 1 o'clock position on the right. That is the trail on which you'll make the short final ascent to the lake. Descend less than 100' and come to the junction, where the trail takes off at a creek crossing at the 4 o'clock position. If you go straight you'll continue the Martin Creek Trail to the Foggy Dew Ridge Trail in 0.7 mile. But cut right, cross the creek, and in a few hundred feet you'll near the shore of shallow, peaceful Cooney Lake. (As mentioned, take special care not to tromp along the grassy area near the lake; in this area, the grasses take a long time to regenerate from any damage.) The descent is brisk but controlled; you want to keep those digits on the brake levers in anticipation of the rocky terrain and many turns along the way. At the Crater Lake Trail junction close to the finish, a hard left leads to the Crater Lake Trail, a soft left leads to the bridge, and straight ahead is the horse crossing. Take door number two, to the bridge, and you'll be back to the trailhead in another 0.7 mile.

COLVILLE NATIONAL FOREST

The relatively remote Colville National Forest is fast developing a reputation as a good destination for mountain biking. Tucked into the northeast corner of Washington, the forest shares borders with British Columbia to the north and Idaho to the east. Spokane lies to the south and supplies the forest with most of its visitors.

The old gold-mining town of Republic is the center of activity in the western part of the forest. South of town is the Lakes Area of the Republic Ranger District. Some of the roads and double-tracks in this part of the forest have been closed to motor traffic. These routes are slowly being absorbed back into the woods. Some are beginning to feel more like trails than roads.

The district hosts a fat-tire festival each year to promote all-terrain biking. Group rides of varying lengths and difficulties highlight the weekend. The event is held at Swan Lake Campground, an excellent base for exploring in the Lakes Area.

East of Republic on WA 20 is Sherman Pass. At 5,575 feet, it is the highest highway pass in Washington. Extending north and south from the gap is the 30-mile long Kettle Crest Trail. Many loops and shuttle rides can be created by combining Kettle Crest Trail with spur trails that drop off the ridge.

Continuing east on WA 20, you'll cross the Columbia River near Kettle Falls; pass through Colville, the region's largest community; and then enter the Little Pend Oreille Chain of Lakes Recreation Area. The region is packed with multi-use trails, good camping facilities, and resort services.

The extreme northeast corner of the forest is administered by the Sullivan Lake Ranger District. The riding on Hall Mountain above Sullivan Lake is an outstanding mix of gravel roads and single-tracks. Wildlife viewing is an added bonus in your travels through this part of the country.

Driving south from Sullivan Lake toward Spokane brings you past the Newport Ranger District. The rangers in this part of the forest are actively involved in promoting mountain biking. Cross-country ski trails and forest roads near Newport are seeing increased two-wheeled traffic from locals and visitors alike. There is an especially pleasant loop at Bead Lake; this outing features a single-track that drops out of the mountains to skirt the eastern shore of the lake.

RIDE 77 · Swan Lake Trail/Lakes Area Mountain Bike Routes

AT A GLANCE

Length/configuration: 7.6-mile loop on gravel roads, pavement, double-tracks, and single-track trails

Aerobic difficulty: Easy to moderately difficult

Technical difficulty: Easy to moderately difficult; the single-track around Swan Lake is the most technically challenging part of this ride

Scenery: Dense second-growth forest, open woodlands, small lakes

Special comments: Good camping and swimming at Swan Lake

The Lakes Area (south of Republic, Washington) offers many miles of pleasant cycling on gravel roads. Some of the roads are closed to motor vehicles, and several loops have been signed as mountain bike routes. Many of the outings are easy; others make good training rides. This chapter describes a relatively easy 7.6-mile loop. Beginners will find the circuit challenging. The route includes an excellent 1.6-mile single-track trip around Swan Lake.

The road conditions vary considerably. Much of the ride is on double-tracks that are slowly becoming trail-like. There is also riding on good gravel roads, rough spurs, and a short stretch of pavement. The trail around Swan Lake is in good shape. The single-track has some challenging sections, but pushing your bike through them is only moderately difficult.

General location: Swan Lake is approximately 15 miles southwest of Republic, Washington.

Elevation change: The ride begins at 3,700' and descends to a low point of 3,320' at Forest Service Road 350 and FS 100. From here, the route climbs to meet Swan Lake Trail at 3,640'. Ups and downs on the roads add approximately 300' of climbing to the trip. Swan Lake Trail adds about 200'. Total elevation gain: 880'.

Season: The period from spring through fall is the best time to ride in this area. Swan Lake is a popular destination on summer weekends. Avoid hunting season.

Services: There is no water available on this ride. Water, food, lodging, groceries, and gas are available in Republic.

Hazards: Expect some traffic on the main forest roads. There are areas of sand and some large ruts on FS 640. You will encounter embedded rocks, roots, and log bridges on Swan Lake Trail.

RIDE 77 · Swan Lake Trail/
Lakes Area Mountain Bike Routes

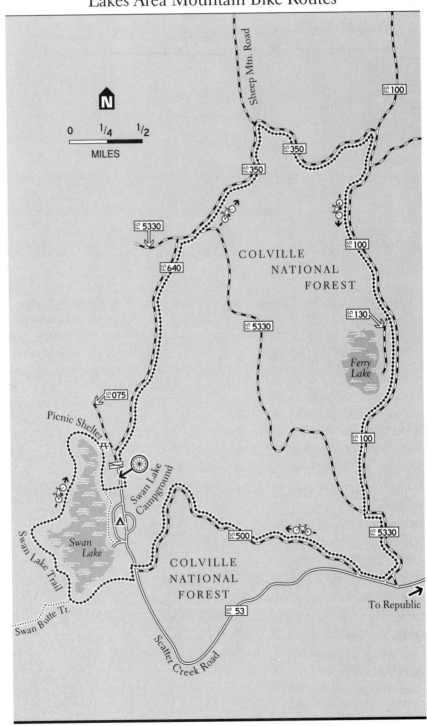

Near the south end of
Swan Lake.

Rescue index: Help can be found in Republic.

Land status: Colville National Forest.

Maps: A handout and map on the area's mountain bike opportunities can be obtained from the Republic Ranger District. USGS 7.5 minute quad: Swan Lake.

Finding the trail: From the intersection of WA 20 and WA 21 in Republic, follow WA 21 south. Turn right after 6.7 miles onto Scatter Creek Road/FS 53 toward Swan Lake. You will arrive at Swan Lake Campground in 7.3 miles. Continue straight on FS 53 for another 0.25 mile to a parking area on the left near a gate and the beginning of FS 075. Park on the left near the information board.

Source of additional information:

Republic Ranger District
P.O. Box 468
Republic, WA 99166
(509) 775-3305

Swan Lake.

Notes on the trail: From the parking area, go through the open gate on FS 075, then immediately turn right onto unsigned FS 640. This old road is blocked by a couple of large rocks and is marked with a bike symbol (as is much of the route). You will reach unsigned FS 5330 after 1 mile of pedaling. Turn right, then immediately turn left onto FS 350 at a bike symbol. Stay on the main double-track for 0.8 mile to an intersection where Sheep Mountain Road goes left. Turn right to remain on FS 350. You will reach FS 100 at a **T** intersection in another 0.5 mile. Turn right onto FS 100. Continue straight at the next juncture of roads, where FS 130 goes right toward Ferry Lake. Turn left onto FS 5330, toward Scatter Creek, at the next **T** intersection. After crossing a cattle guard, turn right at a **Y** intersection, then turn right again onto paved, unsigned FS 53/Scatter Creek Road. In 0.2 mile, turn right onto double-track FS 500, toward Swan Lake Road. Follow this road for 1.4 miles to paved FS 53/Scatter Creek Road. Turn left and immediately turn right onto Swan Lake Trail. Remain on Swan Lake Trail where Swan Butte Trail goes left, after 0.4 mile of single-track. Stay on the main trail to the picnic shelter at the north end of the lake. Continue past the shelter along the lakeshore. Just after passing the first beach, bear left onto a side trail, and stay to the left as you climb away from the water. Pass through a tent campsite; you will emerge onto FS 53 and your vehicle to the left.

RIDE 78 · Kettle Crest/Sherman Trail

AT A GLANCE

WA

Length/configuration: 17.2-mile loop on single-tracks, gravel forest roads, and paved highway

Aerobic difficulty: Difficult; some steep sections of trail; ride ends with a 5-mile climb on WA 20

Technical difficulty: Moderately difficult to advanced; Kettle Crest and Sherman Trails include tight switchbacks and degraded areas of trail

Scenery: Trails traverse grassy hillsides and travel through stands of timber; the highway passes the remains of a 20,000 acre forest fire

Special comments: Great technical single-track

This loop—a strenuous 17.2-mile ride—follows trails for 6.6 miles, gravel roads for 6.2 miles, and pavement for 4.6 miles. The most challenging part is the initial climb on Kettle Crest Trail. From Sherman Pass on WA 20, Kettle Crest Trail switchbacks up Columbia Mountain for a mile; it is steep and hoof-worn in places. Short "breaks" between the most technical spots keep it rideable. This climb is followed by a gentle traverse around Columbia Mountain and some moderately difficult (but short) climbs near Jungle Hill. Much of the descent from Kettle Crest involves tight, rocky switchbacks. Sherman Trail ties into gravel roads that lead out to WA 20. The climb back up to the pass is on a two-lane highway—a grind only a touring cyclist could love. It is actually an easy grade, but you will be taxed after 5 miles of it.

The highlights of this ride are its challenging start and miles of pleasant single-track cruising. Climbing up the highway, you look out over 20,000 acres of wasteland—the result of the 1988 White Mountain fire. On the highway there is an interpretive display about the fire. The display gives you a good excuse for taking a break from the climb, but it is hard to make devastation interesting.

General location: The trailhead is at Sherman Pass, approximately 17 miles east of Republic, Washington.

Elevation change: The ride begins at 5,600' and tops out at 6,500' on Kettle Crest Trail. The low point of the route is 4,260'. Ups and downs on the loop add approximately 300' of climbing to the trip. Total elevation gain: 2,540'.

Season: The best riding here is in the summer, after the snow has melted and the trail has had a chance to dry.

RIDE 78 · Kettle Crest / Sherman Trail

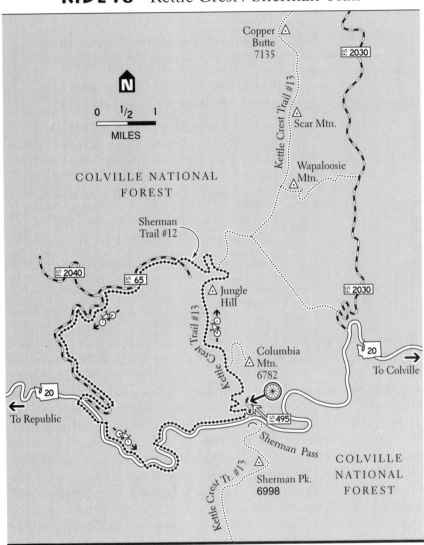

Services: There is no water available on this ride. Water, food, lodging, groceries, and gas are available in Republic. There are rest rooms and picnic tables at a roadside interpretive display on WA 20.

Hazards: Obstacles on the trails include rocks, roots, and tight switchbacks. The gravel roads contain ruts and cattle guards. The riding on WA 20 is probably the most dangerous part of the trip. Traffic is usually light, but it moves along at a good clip.

Rescue index: Help can be found in Republic.

Kettle Crest Trail.

Land status: Colville National Forest.

Maps: The forest map for the Colville National Forest is a suitable guide to this route. The USGS topographic maps are more detailed and are a better source of information. USGS 7.5 minute quads: Sherman Peak, Edds Mountain, Copper Butte, and Cooke Mountain.

Finding the trail: From locations to the west, follow WA 20 east from Republic for 17 miles to Sherman Pass. From locations to the east, take WA 20 west from Colville for 36 miles to Sherman Pass. Turn onto FS 495 at the "Trailhead" sign. Follow FS 495 north to a cul-de-sac and park your vehicle.

Source of additional information:

Republic Ranger District
P.O. Box 468
Republic, WA 99166
(509) 775-3305

Notes on the trail: From the parking area, ride back up FS 495 and turn right onto Kettle Crest Trail #13 north. After a little more than 2 miles, continue straight where Kettle Crest Trail meets Columbia Mountain Trail. Remain on Kettle Crest Trail for another 3.2 miles, through a switchbacking descent, to Sherman Trail #12. Continue straight onto Sherman Trail where Kettle Crest Trail goes right. Sherman Trail becomes overgrown and grassy after 0.6 mile. Continue straight; the trail soon switchbacks to the left and becomes obvious again. Turn right and descend when you reach FS 65. Both the descent and FS 65 end at unsigned FS 2040. Turn left onto FS 2040. Stay on the main road; you will reach WA 20 in 3.8 miles. Turn left onto the highway and climb back up to the pass.

RIDE 79 · Frater Lake

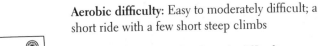

AT A GLANCE

Length/configuration: 4.3-mile loop on single-track trails and double-track roads

Aerobic difficulty: Easy to moderately difficult; a short ride with a few short steep climbs

Technical difficulty: Moderately difficult; some rough and rocky sections of road and trail

Scenery: Dense forest, rock outcroppings, meadows, and logged areas

Special comments: The Little Pend Oreille off-road vehicle trails are nearby

Frater Lake is one of the eight glacial lakes that make up the Little Pend Oreille chain in northeastern Washington. Frater Lake Trail #150 is part of a 15-mile network of cross-country ski trails. This 4.3-mile loop serves as an introduction to the mountain biking opportunities in the area. The region is also home to the Little Pend Oreille Trails, a 75-mile system of multiuse trails designated for off-road motorcycling, hiking, horseback riding, and mountain biking.

About half of the route is on single-tracks in mostly good condition. The other half is on rough double-track roads. The loop has a fairly low elevation gain, but it does contain some steep ascents and rocky stretches. Overall, the terrain is rolling, with a significant number of ups and downs. The trail winds through dense forest and boggy areas and past rocky outcrops, meadows, and clear-cuts.

General location: Frater Lake is approximately 30 miles northeast of Colville, Washington.

RIDE 79 · Frater Lake

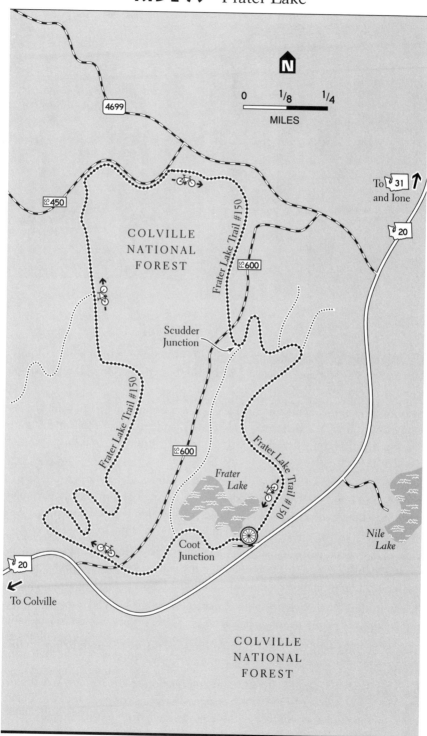

N

0   1/8   1/4
MILES

4699

To 31
and Ione

20

450

COLVILLE
NATIONAL
FOREST

Frater Lake Trail #150

FS 600

Scudder
Junction

Frater Lake Trail #150

FS 600

Frater Lake Trail #150

Frater
Lake

Nile
Lake

20

Coot
Junction

To Colville

COLVILLE
NATIONAL
FOREST

Frater Lake.

Elevation change: The ride begins at 3,220' and reaches a high point of 3,430'. Ups and downs add an estimated 200' of climbing to the loop. Total elevation gain: 410'.

Season: The Little Pend Oreille Lakes region is known for its wild berries. Gorge yourself on huckleberries, gooseberries, and currants in July and August. The trails can be boggy in the spring and early summer. Avoid busy summer weekends.

Services: There is no water available on the ride. Lodging, water, and a pay phone can be found at Beaver Lodge Resort, located approximately 4.5 miles southeast of the trailhead on WA 20. Water, food, lodging, groceries, and gas can be obtained in Ione, approximately 10 miles northeast of the trailhead on WA 31.

Hazards: Portions of the trail are open to motorcycles; remain alert for approaching traffic. Ski trails are easier to follow in the winter; keep your eyes peeled for the blue diamond-shaped symbols affixed to the trees.

Rescue index: Help is available in Colville.

Land status: Colville National Forest.

Maps: The district map of the Colville Ranger District is a useful guide to this outing. USGS 7.5 minute quad: Ione.

Finding the trail: From Colville, at the intersection of US 395 and WA 20, follow WA 20 east toward Ione and Newport. Drive just over 29 miles to Frater Lake (on the left). You will pass a cross-country skier symbol just before the lake.

Turn left off the highway to park in the pullout beside Frater Lake. From Ione, follow WA 31 south for 3.6 miles and turn right onto WA 20. Travel 6.3 miles to Frater Lake (on the right). A cross-country skier symbol is posted just before you reach the lake. Turn right to park in the pullout beside the lake.

Source of additional information:

Colville Ranger District
765 S. Main Street
Colville, WA 99114
(509) 684-7010

Notes on the trail: From the parking area, pedal past the map and boat ramp, following a trail marked with blue diamond-shaped symbols. This trail will put you on a spur road that leads into a parking area. The trail continues at the end of the parking area—it is marked with blue diamonds. Turn left for Coyote Rock Loop when you reach Coot Junction. Cross a gravel road and continue the climb to Coyote Rock. Continue past the rock for 0.6 mile to a rutted multiuse trail on the left. Continue straight on the ski trail. The route gets boggy and then arrives at FS 450. Bear right and descend on the double-track for 0.3 mile to an indistinct trail on the right. (This trail is easy to miss. While descending on FS 450, look to the right for the faint trail marked by a blue diamond. You have overshot the trail by 0.1 mile if you arrive at a **T** intersection at a gravel road.) Follow the trail into the woods and chase the blue diamonds for 0.75 mile to Scudder Junction. Turn left for Tiger Loop. Shortly you will approach a fence bounding Teepee Seed Orchard. Do not pedal up the fence line; look farther to the right to find a blue diamond on a tree. Move toward it. The trail becomes more obvious and heads into the woods. Follow the blue diamonds. You will soon reach a **Y** intersection where both trails are signed with blue diamonds. Turn right. Choose the route marked with blue diamonds at the next two intersections. This will bring you to a barbed-wire gate. Pass through the gate and turn right onto a faint trail marked with a blue diamond (which is easy to miss). Parallel the highway back to your vehicle.

RIDE 80 · Hall Mountain Loop

AT A GLANCE

Length/configuration: 24-mile loop on pavement, dirt roads, gravel roads, and single-track

Aerobic difficulty: Difficult; long ride with a long climb

Technical difficulty: Difficult; technical single-track

Scenery: Great mountain riding with excellent views into Idaho and British Columbia

Special comments: The grassy, alpine slopes near the summit of Hall Mountain are particularly beautiful

Spectacular scenery and great single-track riding highlight this loop. You can see into Idaho and British Columbia from the top of Hall Mountain. There is also a good possibility of spotting Rocky Mountain bighorn sheep; a herd that ranges on the mountain is frequently seen from the trail. The ride is 24-miles long and suited to strong, experienced cyclists.

The first 8 miles follow pavement and hard-packed dirt roads—a nice warm-up for the 7.3-mile grind that follows. This long gravel road ascent is moderately difficult, with a few short, steep pitches. Dig deep at road's end for the 2.3-mile ascent on Hall Mountain Trail. It is moderately difficult, with some steep sections and some level riding. Descending on Hall Mountain Trail is fun, but dessert is served on Noisy Creek Trail. The first 1.5 miles feel like an E-ticket ride at Disney World! Then, back to reality and 2 miles of creek crossings, rocky stretches, boggy areas, and technical climbs and descents. Noisy Creek Trail improves for a terrific 1.5-mile ending.

General location: The trailhead is located approximately 12 miles southeast of Metaline Falls, Washington.

Elevation change: The loop begins at 2,600' and reaches 2,880' at the intersection of FS 22 and FS 500. It climbs steadily on FS 500 to Hall Mountain Trail at 5,280'. Hall Mountain Trail tops out at 6,323'. Ups and downs over the course of the ride add an estimated 300' of climbing to the ride. Total elevation gain: 4,023'.

Season: This ride is good from late June through September. Windfall may be a problem in the spring; find out if the trail has been cleared.

RIDE 80 · Hall Mountain Loop

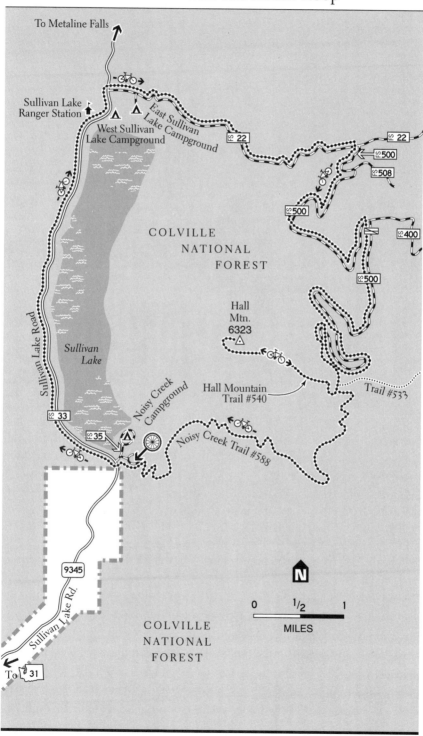

To Metaline Falls

Sullivan Lake
Ranger Station

West Sullivan
Lake Campground

East Sullivan
Lake Campground

FS 22

FS 22

FS 500

FS 508

FS 500

FS 400

FS 500

COLVILLE
NATIONAL
FOREST

Hall
Mtn.
6323

Sullivan
Lake

Sullivan Lake Road

FS 33

FS 35

Noisy Creek
Campground

Hall Mountain
Trail #540

Trail #533

Noisy Creek Trail #588

9345

Sullivan Lake Rd.

To 31

COLVILLE
NATIONAL
FOREST

N

0   1/2   1

MILES

COLVILLE
NATIONAL
FOREST

Hall Mountain Trail.

Services: Water is available seasonally at Noisy Creek Campground near the trailhead. There is a pay phone at the Sullivan Lake Ranger Station. Food, lodging, groceries, and gas can be obtained in Ione and Metaline Falls.

Hazards: Sullivan Lake Road is narrow and can get busy in the summer. In places Hall Mountain Trail narrows and drops off steeply to the side. Portions of Hall Mountain Trail contain logs that are hidden from view by tall grass. Sections of Noisy Creek Trail are narrow, scree-covered, steep, and extremely technical. Anticipate others approaching from around the next bend. Black bears and grizzly bears reside in the area.

Rescue index: Help can be found at the ranger station at Sullivan Lake during office hours. Emergency services are available in Ione and Metaline Falls.

Land status: Colville National Forest.

Maps: The district map of the Sullivan Lake Ranger District is a good guide to this ride. USGS 7.5 minute quads: Pass Creek and Metaline Falls.

Finding the trail: From the intersection of WA 20 and WA 31, follow WA 31 north. In 3.2 miles (0.4 mile south of Ione), turn right onto CR 9345/Sullivan Lake Road. This road is signed for Sullivan Lake and Sullivan Lake Ranger

Station. Follow it for about 9 miles and turn right onto FS 35 into Noisy Creek Campground. Turn right in 0.1 mile onto a gravel road (marked by a hiker symbol). Follow this road past a vault toilet and park near the Noisy Creek Trailhead.

Source of additional information:

Sullivan Lake Ranger District
12641 Sullivan Lake Road
Metaline Falls, WA 99153
(509) 446-2681

Notes on the trail: Ride back to Sullivan Lake Road and turn right. Follow the road around the lake. Pass West Sullivan Lake Campground; in 0.3 mile, turn right onto FS 22. Stay on the main road for 3.3 miles and turn right onto FS 500. FS 500 ends at the trailhead for Hall Mountain Trail #540. Follow Hall Mountain Trail (an old double-track at first). Ride past Trail #533 (on the left); you will soon arrive at Noisy Creek Trail #588 (on the left). Continue straight toward Hall Mountain (you will follow Noisy Creek Trail later). The last 0.25 mile of the trail are unrideable. Park your bike and hike to the remains of the old lookout. Return down Hall Mountain Trail to the intersection with Noisy Creek Trail and turn right. Follow Noisy Creek Trail for 5 miles to your vehicle.

RIDE 81 · Bead Lake Loop

AT A GLANCE

Length/configuration: 17.7-mile loop on gravel road and single-track trail

Aerobic difficulty: Moderately difficult to difficult; demanding climb on gravel road; trail not all downhill

Technical difficulty: Moderately difficult to difficult; some rough terrain and technical challenges

Scenery: Distant views where road passes through clear-cuts; trail travels through an old forest and beside Bead Lake

Special comments: Bead Lake Trail is fun!

Bead Lake Loop is a scenic 17.7-mile ride recommended for intermediate and advanced cyclists. It's less than an hour from Spokane to the trailhead, and well worth the drive. The gravel road climb to the trail contains numerous

RIDE 81 · Bead Lake Loop

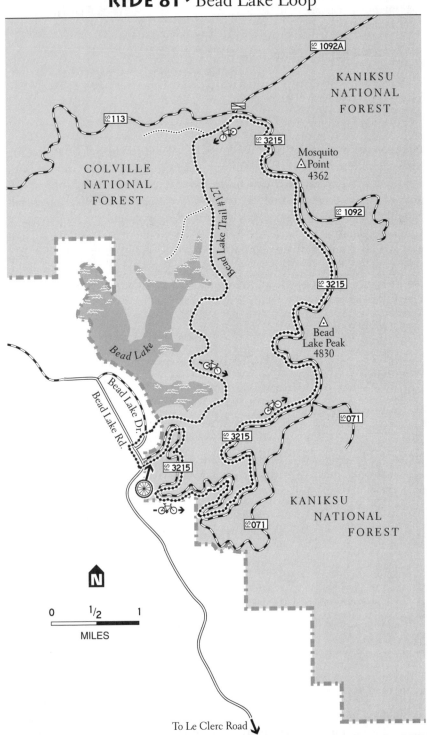

Bead Lake Loop.

fast descents, and is a fun ride in itself, but the start of the Bead Lake Trail is one of the most fun stretches of single-track I've ever been on—the initial trail descent was so magical, I half-expected gnomes to emerge from behind the lush, old-growth cedar grove while descending steeply toward the lake. You'll want to climb back up to descend it again.

Gravel roads comprise 11.7 miles of the circuit; the first 2 miles are rough and steep. The rest of the climb is easy to moderately difficult. The road surface improves, too. The last 2 miles to the trail is a fast descent, so watch for the turnoff to the left as you descend.

Six-mile long Bead Lake Trail varies in its condition. Most of it is a good, hard-packed dirt path. There are some precipitous scree slopes and five steep switchbacks by the cedar grove on the way to the lake. There is one monster climb in the last two miles of single-track.

The beginning of the ride features some nice vistas to the south of the Pend Oreille River and the Selkirks. Logging on Bead Divide has opened up some views. Below and to the west you can see Bead Lake. To the east are Idaho forests and mountains. The route passes some huge white pines.

General location: The trail begins 10 miles northeast of Newport, Washington, which is 40 miles north of Spokane.

Elevation change: The ride starts at 2,865' and reaches a high point of 4,400'. Ups and downs on the roads add approximately 300' of climbing to the trip. Undulations on the trail add about 500'. Total elevation gain: 2,335'.

Season: Portions of the trail become boggy during wet periods; plan on visiting in the summer or fall.

Services: There is no water available on the ride. Water, food, lodging, groceries, and gas are available in Newport.

Hazards: The descent on Bead Lake Trail includes steep switchbacks and scree slopes. Some sections of the trail contain an abundance of forest litter. There is also some technical single-track along the lakeshore. Some segments of the path drop off steeply to the water, and some stretches are rocky. Stay alert for traffic on the forest roads. Black bears reside in the area.

Rescue index: Help can be found in Newport.

Land status: Colville National Forest.

Maps: The Colville National Forest map is a suitable guide to this route. USGS 7.5 minute quad: Bead Lake.

Finding the trail: From Newport, follow WA 2 east through Old Town, Idaho, and cross the Pend Oreille River. At the end of the bridge, turn left onto signed Le Clerc Road. Continue for 2.7 miles and turn right onto Bead Lake Road. Follow this road for 6 miles and turn right onto FS 3215. You will reach the trailhead on the left in 0.5 mile. Park on the right or left side of the road.

Source of additional information:

Newport Ranger District
315 N. Warren Avenue
Newport, WA 99156
(509) 447-7300

Notes on the trail: Head up FS 3215. Stay on the main road for about 11 miles (spur roads go left and right). Just past the milepost 11 sign (on your right as you descend), at a clearing, look to the left for Bead Lake Trail #127. This is also the boundary between the Colville National Forest and the Idaho Panhandle National Forest; here the road designation changes from FS 3215 to FS 113. Turn left onto the single-track. In 0.3 mile, turn left at a **Y** intersection where Divide Trail goes right. Continue straight at the next intersection (in 1.4 miles), where signed Bead Lake Spur Trail goes right. A new "tie" trail connects the bottom of Bead Lake Trail with the trailhead on FS 3215. Go back up the gravel road to the intersection with Bead Lake Road. Turn left and immediately turn left again onto Bead Lake Divide/FS 3215 to return to your vehicle.

SPOKANE AREA RIDES

Spokane, the largest city between Seattle and Minneapolis, is the commercial hub of a vast mining, lumber, and agricultural region. Spokane has also emerged in the upper echelon of the nation's bike-racing centers. City officials have lured top-flight racing programs, like the 1984 and 1988 Olympic trials and the 1992 U.S. Nationals, to Spokane. Big-league mountain bike racing arrived in the form of a World Cup mountain bike event in 1994.

The mountain bike community in Spokane has, to date, not been formally organized. At the time of research, the city of 177,000 had no mountain biking club, à la other metropolitan areas in Washington, and though local riding areas are well-known, most of the trails have no commonly recognized names.

From its headwaters in northern Idaho, the Spokane River enters eastern Washington, then splits Spokane into two halves. Turning north, the river defines the western edge of the city. Here the riverside becomes a greenbelt of parks, arboretums, golf courses, and other open spaces for public enjoyment.

Riverside State Park is a wonderful recreation area on the Spokane River. Its 5,514 acres are tightly laced with single-tracks and closed roads. A footbridge near the park's campground crosses the turbulent river and offers access to the trails.

Another hotbed of mountain biking is Mt. Spokane State Park. Mt. Spokane sits in the middle of the park, and on summer weekends it crawls with mountain bikers plying their favorite trails.

Spokane also holds some good in-town riding, if you know where to look. South Hill is webbed with miles of trails, and Minnehaha Park/Beacon Hill, in northeast Spokane, treats riders to a challenging network of gravel roads and trails. Both areas come with the thrills but without the drive from town.

RIDE 82 · South Hill

AT A GLANCE

WA

Length/configuration: Up to 8.6 miles on a maze of single-track, with some wide trails and dirt roads

Aerobic difficulty: Start with a 500' descent, which you make up in the end—from the initial descent, there are steep and gradual short climbs along the way

Technical difficulty: Angled trail and a couple of tight switchbacks at the top; roots and whoop-de-doos too

Scenery: Views to the south at the ride's start, which overlooks Qualchan Golf Course and US 195; ponderosa pines, sparse vegetation down the hill

Special comments: Great riding for intermediate to advanced riders—make your own route!

South Hill, nestled in south Spokane, is a spaghetti system of interconnecting trails that can provide a different, fun ride each time out. The trails are sandy in places and, especially toward the near-barren top of the hill, are prone to erosion, but trail surface is mostly a good hardpack. The trail leading you down into the network is uneven, and there is little to catch you if you fall. You'll put out some hearty efforts as you end the ride, after the initial 500-foot descent to the base, and as much climbing as you want to do in between.

You'll notice in the ride description that many trails break off and rejoin, so take these directions as loose guidelines. Adding to the fun is the security that you really can't get too lost, as you're bordered by Hangman Creek (or Latah Creek, depending on whom, or which map, you consult) to the south and west, High Drive to the north, and a new housing development off of Hatch Road to the east. The described route is a tour of the whole system that leaves plenty of room for you to improvise according to your ability and schedule.

Among the sights are carcasses of cars that met their makers, so to speak, hurtling down from the bluff. I counted four of 'em at the time of research but they certainly didn't detract from the quality of the ride, as it is in-town, rather than backcountry, riding.

Trails are neither named nor signed but it really doesn't cause problems. In fact the "notes on the trail" make this route sound more complicated than it actually is. My advice? Just ride!

RIDE 82 · South Hill

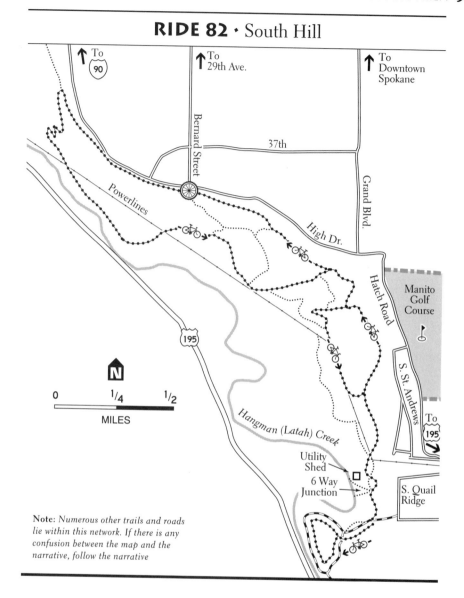

To
(90)

To
29th Ave.

To
Downtown
Spokane

Bernard Street

37th

Grand Blvd.

Powerlines

High Dr.

Hatch Road

Manito
Golf
Course

S. St. Andrews

195

To
195

N

0   1/4   1/2

MILES

Hangman (Latah) Creek

Utility
Shed

6 Way
Junction

S. Quail
Ridge

Note: *Numerous other trails and roads
lie within this network. If there is any
confusion between the map and the
narrative, follow the narrative*

General location: South Hill is located, appropriately enough, in south Spokane, south of Interstate 90 and east of US 195.

Elevation change: The initial descent is about 520', which, of course, you make up in the end. Climbing before the final ascent makes for a total elevation gain of up to 780'.

Season: Early spring through late fall, as the conditions allow.

Services: No water is available along the ride. All services are available in Spokane.

Hazards: South Hill's easy accessibility makes it a popular trail system for mountain bikers, runners, and even motorcyclists, so watch for others. With some areas prone to erosion, don't skid around corners, and be sensitive to the trail. Keep your balance at the top, too; you may tumble a long way if you fall on the angled trail.

Rescue index: You're in town, so help is available nearby.

Land status: Spokane City Parks and Recreation.

Maps: No truly accurate map of the area exists. I got a reasonable guide to the area from Spoke 'N Sport bike shop in downtown Spokane. Without being too boastful, you're holding the best map of the area in your hands right now! USGS 7.5 minute quad: Spokane Southwest.

Finding the trail: The main entrance to the trail system is at the intersection of the west 300 block of High Drive at the south end of Bernard Street in south Spokane. From I-90 eastbound, take Exit 280, the Maple Bridge exit. Get in the far right-hand lane at the exit and go south on Maple Street. Maple curves into High Drive and comes to Bernard about 4.5 miles south of I-90.

From I-90 westbound, take Exit 280A. Parallel the freeway to the second stop sign, turn left onto Maple, and proceed as above.

You can also take Grand Boulevard to its southern end and turn right; you'll come to Bernard in about six blocks. Streetside parking is available.

Sources of additional information:

Spokane Parks and Recreation Department
City Hall, 7th Floor
Park Department
808 W. Spokane Falls Boulevard
Spokane, WA 99201
(509) 625-6453

Spoke 'N Sport
212 N. Division Street
Spokane, WA 99207-1030
(509) 838-8842

Two Wheel Transit
1405 W. First Avenue
Spokane, WA 99204-0615
(509) 747-2231
(special thanks to Two Wheel Transit's Tom McFadden, my guide on the research ride)

Notes on the trail: Looking at the guard rail on High Drive at the end of Bernard Street at High Drive, take the trail to the right of the guardrail behind the ponderosa pine (the easier access is to the left). In 0.1 mile a trail switches back to the left. Pass it and continue to the next switchback—a tight, exposed turn—and continue on a steep drop. At 1.7 miles, the single-track dumps out

Tom McFadden riding South Hill.

into a double-track road. Take the double-track in the same direction the trail is taking you. The double-track ends into a trail; go straight, past another junction, and in another 30' meet a single-track that came down from the top. Go right here, and as the trail climbs sharply to the left, take any of the forks and they'll join together shortly. (The outside line is best, but erosion is likely to eliminate it in the future.) At the top of that climb go right, which starts as a double-track. It narrows a bit as a trail shoots off to the right; continue straight on the wider path. Come to a delta junction; as the trail to the left narrows, descend to the right on a wide path. As you descend and ride eastward, the trail from above crosses and another road descends, but follow the power lines at this point.

In 0.2 mile, winding to the left along a wide trail, a narrow trail shoots off to the right; they'll rejoin soon, but for now, climb on the main trail. In another 0.1 mile, come to another delta junction, and climb to the left, toward the bluff. In another 50' come to a **T** junction, where taking the left turn will bring you back up to the bluff; go right. As the trail starts descending and curving to the right, a trail goes up steeply to the left. It's just a steep dead end, but a good fitness test; try to climb it and see if you can get farther next time out. In another 0.1 mile, come to a delta junction, where the contour of the trail takes you right and down. Take it, and it will quickly bring you to a berm area—a wide path on which motorcycles have bermed out the embankments. As you wind around to the left here you can see the power lines as they go up to the east, providing the toughest climb in this network. Wind around under the power lines, and climb up the bermed section. At the top of the bermed section, as the trail winds to the right, you'll parallel another trail about 20' above it. The trails join at a 4-way intersection; descend to the right.

As the trail continues east, ride near a utility shed and stay on this trail, past the junctions, to another junction where 6—yes 6—paths converge (although in reality it's like a 4-way intersection on steroids). The main trail, the one you've been riding on, continues in a southerly direction. Take it past the 6-way junction. In 0.1 mile hit a **T** intersection at a dirt road. To the left is a new housing development, so go right on the dirt road, heading toward a short loop. In 0.1 mile, past a trail that climbs to the right, veer onto the road to the left, which makes a short loop on the "Roly Poly," or "Whoop" Trail, near the creek and the highway, back to this spot. Retrace your route back to the 6-way junction, and go right or soft left (both rejoin quickly). Continue retracing for another 0.2 mile and veer right on a short, steep climb as the main trail stays level; you'll quickly be paralleling it from above. After climbing approximately 80', now above the power lines, descend and climb again to another trail split. The trail to the left at the 11 o'clock position descends; stay straight, climbing slightly. This section of trail rolls up and down as you near the homes up on High Drive. The next junction will again bring you back to a section of trail you can retrace to the *next* junction, where you will now go right instead of retracing to the left. (If this is too confusing, just remember to keep climbing, and you'll come back up to High Drive.) The climb levels out after a left-hand switchback about 30' below the top of the bluff. Get up some momentum for the final ascent back to High Drive. Come out onto High Drive on the other side of the guard rail on which you started.

Here's another option: Descend, ride around, climb back up. Have fun!

RIDE 83 · Minnehaha Park/Beacon Hill

AT A GLANCE

WA

Length/configuration: 6.5-mile loop, including about 2.8 miles of single-track, dirt roads, and a 1.5-mile paved road return; you can make an 8-mile (total mileage) out-and-back by eliminating the pavement

Aerobic difficulty: Moderate with some short, steep climbs on both sides of Beacon Hill

Technical difficulty: Some deep **V** sections, roots, rocky sections, and boulders

Scenery: Views into Spokane and surrounding mountains from the top

Special comments: It's not backcountry riding, but way fun stuff without the drive to the backcountry

This 6.5-mile intermediate-level loop is highlighted by views from Beacon Hill into Spokane and to the surrounding mountains, as well as an ever-so-slight taste of slickrock riding at Boulder Beach. (Boulder Beach is a little rocky area where you can make short, vertical climbs and drops, and pretend you're in Moab.) Another highlight is the good visibility on the northeast side of Beacon Hill, where you can just bomb down with political correctness on your side if no other trail users are in the distance—yahoo! In this area you'll find a few deep **V** sections of steep drops followed immediately by steep rises—yet another highlight—so use your momentum to help power yourself back up.

The ride starts with a short gravel road climb out of Minnehaha Park and winds up Beacon Hill on a loose, sometimes sandy single-track through stands of ponderosa pines. From the towers and power lines at the top of Beacon Hill, the route makes rocky descents and climbs—sometimes steeply and quickly—on both trails and road, to Boulder Beach, just before the end of the dirt. From the end of the dirt portion of the route, you can loop back via Upriver Drive or the Centennial Trail, alongside the Spokane River, or return the way you came, with much more climbing on an all-dirt route. The road return is a flat, paved option.

General location: Minnehaha Park is located in northeast Spokane.

Elevation change: Minnehaha Park is at approximately 2,000' elevation. The initial climb to the top of Beacon Hill is 600', with about 300' of additional climbing before you reach the pavement.

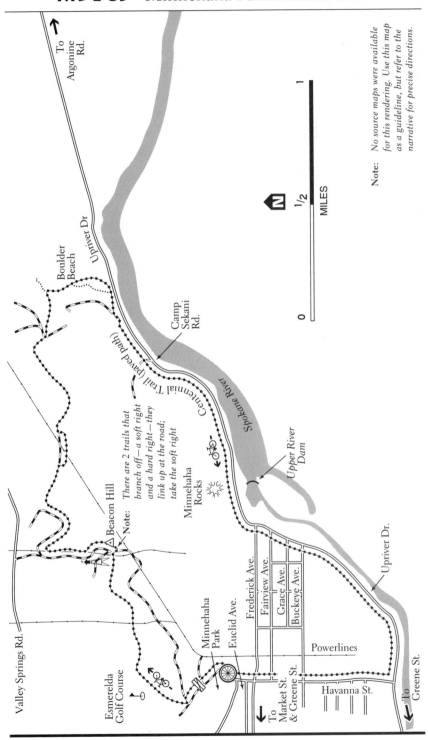

To Argonine Rd.

Uptiver Dr

Boulder Beach

Camp Sekani Rd.

Centennial Trail (paved path)

Spokane River

Upper River Dam

Minnehaha Rocks

Beacon Hill

Note: There are 2 trails that branch off — a soft right and a hard right — they link up at the road; take the soft right

Valley Springs Rd.

Esmerelda Golf Course

Minnehaha Park

Euclid Ave.

Frederick Ave.

Fairview Ave.

Grace Ave.

Buckeye Ave.

Powerlines

Upriver Dr.

To Market St. & Greene St.

Havanna St.

To Greene St.

N

0   ½   1

MILES

Note: No source maps were available for this map rendering. Use this map as a guideline, but refer to the narrative for precise directions.

John Gasioroski at
Boulder Beach.

Season: This route can be ridden any time, as the snows allow. For the described loop, you'll find suitable conditions from early spring through late fall.

Services: There is no water available along the ride. All services are available in Spokane.

Hazards: You'll find one very tight squeeze through a couple of small trees on the initial single-track section. On the steep descents and rises, be ready to dismount if you don't have the juice to get yourself all the way back up. Being so close to civilization, expect other trail users, especially on weekends.

Rescue index: Help is available in Spokane.

Land status: Spokane City Parks, Spokane County.

Maps: No accurate map of these trails exists. USGS 7.5 minute quad: Spokane Northeast.

Finding the trail: Minnehaha Park is located at the corner of Euclid Avenue and Havana Street in northeast Spokane. Traveling eastbound on I-90, take Exit 283B/Freya Street. Go north on Freya, which turns into Greene Street. (As you cross a bridge over the train tracks you can see Beacon Hill, with its power lines and transmission towers, at the 1 o'clock position.) Immediately after crossing the Spokane River, 1.6 miles from I-90, turn right on Carlisle and then veer right, to Upriver Drive. Turn left on Upriver Drive and travel 0.8 mile to Havana Street. Turn left on Havana Street, traveling north for 0.7 mile; Havana Street ends one block past Frederick Avenue, into the Minnehaha Park entrance, as Euclid Avenue turns left. Parking is available in the lower park area, near the corrugated metal building.

Sources of additional information:

> Spokane Parks and Recreation Department
> City Hall, 7th Floor
> Park Department
> 808 W. Spokane Falls Boulevard
> Spokane, WA 99201
> (509) 625-6453

> Spokane County Parks
> 1229 W. Mallon Street
> Spokane, WA 99201
> (509) 456-4730

> REI
> North 1125 Monroe Street
> Spokane, WA 99201
> (509) 328-9900

Notes on the trail: Begin by climbing the dirt road up the hill, which immediately switches back to the left, and then to the right in 0.1 mile. Go straight, past the right-hand switchback, around the green gate. Continue straight, and as the Esmerelda Golf Course comes into view below, another road switches back to the right. Just past this road, a single-track takes off at the 1 o'clock position. Take the winding single-track for 1.2 miles to the top. (At the third road crossing the trail picks up about 10' to the left.) The trail brings you up to the west side of Beacon Hill. Ride around the top for views into Spokane and the surrounding mountains, as the trees allow. Continuing the loop on the northwest side of Beacon Hill, ride under the power lines and between two chain link fences—to the left is the red and white tower—and descend 100 yards on the road. As it winds around to the left, you have the choice of a hard right and a soft right on wide trails, or staying on the road. (If you stay on the road and curve to the left, you went too far.) The hard right and the soft right link up at the bottom of the hill; take the soft right, at the 2 o'clock position. Descend here, paralleling the power lines.

This section ends onto a road that goes north, still paralleling the power lines. In about 0.3 mile come to a **Y** intersection, where the left fork climbs and the right fork stays a little lower. Go right, and stay on this road past another road that branches back toward the power lines. In the 0.2 mile on this road you have a fun little descent, and then a swing up to the left, ending at a **T** intersection.

Turn right at the **T** intersection, where you'll ride through some rocky, technical sections and some deep **V** sections. This is short-lived, though, and comes to a steep access road climb that winds around to the left and narrows out a bit.

At this point, as the hill is starting to crest, you'll see a trail straight ahead and another that curves off to the right. Take the trail to the right, where some little whoop-de-doos and some more steep, short drops and climbs await. Coming up a steep climb, you'll see a road that winds to the left and another that winds to the right, bisected by a single-track. As any true mountain biker should, take the single-track. As you crest one of the rises on this section of trail, you'll see a residential area ahead of and below you, so take the next right and make the short, steep descent to Boulder Beach. As you're riding toward Boulder Beach, you'll see paved Upriver Drive in the near distance. After playing around on the boulders, you can continue on the trail and hit the road, turning right to complete the loop, but just before Upriver Drive, you'll see a 20', sandy climb to the right. Ride (or carry) your bike up the climb, and parallel the road. In about 100 yards, a junction to the right will lead you back to Boulder Beach, but, for the loop, stay left, paralleling the road. To the left of the trail are some more boulders that beckon you to stop for a nice view of the Spokane River and Felts Field Municipal Airport beyond it. Continuing on the trail, come to a logged area, and veer left. (We had to trailblaze a few feet from here to get to the dirt road that connected to Upriver Drive, but it was easy to find.) Go left onto the dirt road, which ends shortly at Upriver Drive. Turn right on Upriver Drive, or cross the road and ride for a spell on the Centennial Trail, where some benches provide a relaxing view of the river. Wind south and west on Upriver Drive for about 1.3 miles, then turn right on Havana to return to the park.

RIDE 84 · Riverside State Park

AT A GLANCE

Length/configuration: 7.2-mile loop on single-track, dirt roads, and pavement

Aerobic difficulty: Moderately difficult

Technical difficulty: Moderately difficult; some rocks and sand

Scenery: Riverside trails; roads through open, second-growth pine forest

Special comments: There are many trails and roads to explore in Riverside State Park; the park's equestrian area and the Little Spokane River Natural Area are closed to bikes

Riverside State Park contains 8,000 acres of prime recreation land in the middle of Spokane. The area is crisscrossed with miles of trails, most of which are open to mountain bikes. The paths offer fun cycling to riders of all ability levels.

One of the most scenic trails follows the churning Spokane River past water-sculpted boulders and craggy cliffs. This 7.2-mile loop is moderately difficult. The route travels on 4.3 miles of single-track, 2.7 miles of dirt roads, and 0.2 mile of pavement. The trails and roads are in good condition, with some technical stretches of rock and sand.

General location: The park entrance is located approximately 6 miles northwest of downtown Spokane, Washington.

Elevation change: The ride begins at 1,580' and follows the river downstream to 1,480'. You reach a high point of 1,640' before dropping back to the trailhead. Ups and downs add about 300' of climbing to the loop. Total elevation gain: 460'.

Season: The riding in the park is good from the spring through the fall. Summer weekends can be very busy with fellow bikers, equestrians, runners, and walkers. Anticipate other trail users at all times.

Services: Water, a pay phone, and toilets are located in the day-use area near the beginning of the ride. All services are available in Spokane.

Hazards: Watch for rocks, soft surfaces, and other trail users. Control your speed. The trails in the park are unsigned.

Rescue index: Help can be found at the park headquarters (near the campground). Emergency services are available in Spokane.

RIDE 84 · Riverside State Park

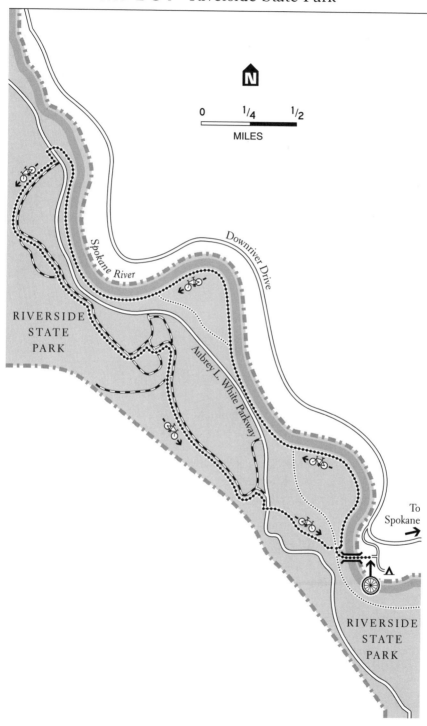

Spokane River.

Land status: Riverside State Park.

Maps: No accurate map of this area was available at the time of research.

Finding the trail: From I-90 in Spokane, take the Monroe Street exit. Drive north on Monroe Street for 1 mile to Boone Street (REI is located at this intersection). Turn left onto Boone and drive 0.4 mile, then turn right onto Maple Street. In three blocks, turn left onto Maxwell Street. Follow Maxwell Street as it swings right and becomes Downriver Drive. The road descends toward the Spokane River—stay to the left, traveling under the overpass at Meenach Drive. Continue along the east side of the river on Downriver Drive. Proceed past a municipal golf course (on the right) to the signed Riverside State Park entrance. Turn left to enter the park; follow the main road. Go past the first two day-use areas. Turn right at the third intersection—the road to the left goes to a pay phone, the campground, and park headquarters. Park in this day-use parking area.

Sources of additional information:

Riverside State Park
4427 Aubrey L. White Parkway
Spokane, WA 99205
(509) 456-3964

REI
North 1125 Monroe Street
Spokane, WA 99201
(509) 328-9900

Jerry O'Neal, Ed
Rockwell, and Kris Van
Breda Kulff in Riverside
State Park.

Notes on the trail: You may wish to forgo these directions and simply rely on the recommended map and a compass. There are miles of trails and roads to explore.

From the day-use parking area, find the paved path that leads toward the river; the path is across from the toilets. Ride down to the bridge and walk your bike across the bridge. Push your bike up the hill on the west side of the river. Stay to the right; you will pass a shelter. Bear to the right when you reach the top of the hill and ride through the basalt outcrops. Shortly you will arrive at an intersection of paths at a wooden post in the trail. Turn right toward the river; soon the trail swings left, paralleling the water. As side trails branch off, choose the trail that keeps you beside the river.

After about 3 miles of single-track, the trail climbs a hill and you'll be able to see some private residences on your right. Stay on the main trail as a faint trail goes right here. The trail climbs a little more, parallels a paved road, then turns left just beyond a white gate. You will find a trailhead sign on the right here. Turn left onto the pavement (Aubrey L. White Parkway) and ride 0.1 mile to the first gravel road on the right. Turn right onto this unsigned road. Stay on this road (heading south) as side roads branch off. The gravel road comes close to the paved road near a gate. Stay on the main gravel road and re-enter the woods. Pass a metal shed and turn left at the next intersection (the road becomes a double-track). Bear right at the next intersection and then left to stay on the main road. Begin a steep climb and stay to the right where a road comes in from the left. You will reach another intersection near the top of the hill—bear left. Descend sharply, following the main road. When you arrive at the paved road, cross it; you will regain the trail at three short, concrete posts. Stay on the trail as it hugs the hillside, climbs a little, and then descends the eroded hillside. Turn right when you come to the wooden post in the trail. Return the way you came.

RIDE 85 · Riverside State Park: "Rattlesnake"

AT A GLANCE

Length/configuration: 7.9-mile loop, including gravel road, paved road, and 2.5 miles of single-track; other, more single-track-intensive options abound

Aerobic difficulty: Single-track climbing accounts for about 1.5 miles of moderate to steep ascent; the loop finishes with a 1.8-mile moderate paved road climb

Technical difficulty: Some rocky sections near the top, with a short hike-a-bike likely

Scenery: Rock formations, ponderosa pine, Spokane River views

Special comments: A spaghetti system of trails where, because of the boundaries, you can get lost without getting *lost*

WA

A wise mountain biker once told me, "There are two kinds of people: 'loopers' and 'out-and-backers.' Loopers come full-circle, so strive to be a looper." I tend to agree with this, but I also prefer riding dirt to pavement. The described ride is a 7.9-mile single-track and paved road loop with a 0.3-mile gravel road start. It provides some rocky, hard-packed, good quality single-track, and a taste of the 37-mile long (paved) Centennial Trail, along the Spokane River. If you're like me, though, and you like to ride dirt more than pavement, do this ride as a 6.2-mile (total mileage) out-and-back, with additional trail options to increase your mileage.

The initial gravel road is a 0.3-mile, 140-foot climb to the single-track. The trail wanders another 180 feet up to the north side of Pine Bluff and down to the river through ponderosa pines, rock formations, some grassland, and low-lying shrubs.

The boundaries on this network are Pine Bluff Road to the south and west, Carlson Road to the north, the Centennial Trail to the north and west, and Seven Mile Road to the east. (As a rule of thumb, once you get to the north side of Pine Bluff, ride in a northerly direction and you will eventually drop onto the Centennial Trail.) Stay within these confines, and you're in for a great ride!

The trails in this area are not formally named. My pilot on the ride, Tom McFadden, noted that this area of Riverside Park is referred to by locals as Rattlesnake, though he had never seen any while riding in the area. He also noted that one of the trails here is referred to as "Sharp Stick in the Eye." Someone, somewhere, probably has a graphic story about that one; regardless, it sure reinforces the idea of wearing protective eyewear when you ride!

Note: Starting in 1998, Riverside State Park is conducting a park-wide trail assessment, which may lead to closures of some trails. Check with the Riverside State Park office to confirm the status of trails for mountain bikes—and get involved.

General location: This section of the Riverside State Park trail system is located approximately 12.5 miles northwest of downtown Spokane.

Elevation change: Start at 1,840' elevation at the parking area and climb to the north side of Pine Bluff at 2,160' elevation. The climb from the river, at 1,620', plus additional climbing, brings the total elevation gain to about 640'.

Season: Spring through fall, as the snows allow. This is a lesser-used section of the park, but it can still get crowded in summer.

Services: No water is available along this route. All services are available in Spokane.

Hazards: Just the names, "Rattlesnake" and "Sharp Stick in the Eye," give you something to think about. More likely, though, it will be a few rocky areas close to the top that may give you trouble.

Rescue index: There are residences near Seven Mile Road, off of the Centennial Trail. Help can be found at the park headquarters (see Ride 84, Riverside State Park, for directions), and in town.

Land status: Riverside State Park.

Maps: No accurate map of this area was available at the time of research.

Finding the trail: From Francis Avenue (WA 291) at Division Street in north Spokane, head west on Francis Avenue for 3.1 miles until it curves to the right into Nine Mile Road. Continue on Nine Mile Road for 2.0 miles and then turn left onto Seven Mile Road. In 0.8 mile cross the Spokane River. Cross another bridge 1.7 miles beyond the Spokane River, and 0.2 mile beyond the bridge, turn right onto gravel Pine Bluff Road. Park in the gravel pullout immediately to the right at the corner of Seven Mile Road and Pine Bluff Road.

Sources of additional information:

Riverside State Park
4427 Aubrey L. White Parkway
Spokane, WA 99205
(509) 456-3964

Friends of the Centennial Trail
P.O. Box 351
Spokane, WA 99910-0351
(509) 624-7188

Tom McFadden
Two Wheel Transit
1405 W. First Avenue
Spokane, WA 99204-0615
(509) 747-2231

Notes on the trail: From the parking area, start on Pine Bluff Road. At 0.1 mile cross a bridge over a creek bed and start climbing on the other side. After a 0.2-mile climb, look up and to the right; you'll soon be on the other side of that rocky bluff. Keep your eyes peeled to the right, and you'll see the start of a sweet single-track near here at the 4 o'clock position. The trail starts with a gentle climb with some easily navigable rocky sections. At 0.9 mile a clearing provides a view to the east and down to the Spokane River. At 1.1 miles, as you come to the north side of Pine Bluff, the trail becomes steeper and more uneven—a nice challenge for the technically superior rider, and a hike-a-bike for mere mortals such as your researcher. In another 0.1 mile this trail ends at a **T** intersection. Go left and climb until the trail ends in 0.2 mile at a dirt road at another **T**. The rocks to the left provide some off-the-bike adventure, while some benches to the right provide some off-the-bike relaxation. Continuing the loop, go right on the road.

The road descends and narrows into a single-track within 0.3 mile. Stay left, descending on the trail as another trail shoots off to the right. The trail descends for another 0.1 mile and then climbs about 140' in 0.4 mile. As the trail levels out, come to a **Y** junction, where the right fork descends north and the left fork traverses and rolls to the northwest. Go left, and within 0.1 mile a trail takes off at the one o'clock position. On my outing I took it, turning downhill toward the Centennial Trail; on your outing, I encourage you to explore the other option further. Continue descending as the trail passes through the middle of an old roadbed, with the trail worn distinctly through it. Finally, 3.1 miles into the journey, meet the pavement at the Carlson Trailhead of the Centennial Trail. Whether you meet the Centennial Trail here or find Carlson Road, go right, along the Centennial Trail, to continue the loop. From the Carlson Trailhead ride 3.0 miles along the Centennial Trail back to Seven Mile Road. You'll have more single-tracking opportunities along the way, though, as numerous trails take off to the right of the Centennial Trail.

In 0.8 mile from the Carlson Trailhead cross the Deep Creek Bridge. State

RIDE 85 · Riverside State Park: "Rattlesnake"

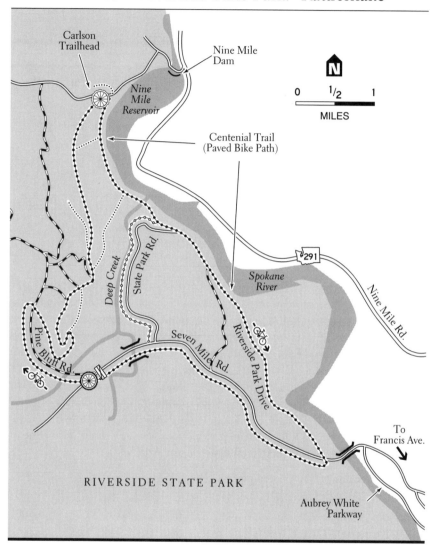

Carlson
Trailhead

Nine Mile
Dam

Nine
Mile
Reservoir

Centenial Trail
(Paved Bike Path)

Deep Creek

State Park Rd.

Spokane
River

291

Nine Mile Rd.

Pine Bluff Rd.

Seven Mile Rd.

Riverside Park Drive

To
Francis Ave.

RIVERSIDE STATE PARK

Aubrey White
Parkway

N

0   ½   1

MILES

Park Road cuts back to the right at the 4 o'clock position, 0.4 mile beyond Deep
Creek Bridge, and meets up with Seven Mile Road by way of Deep Creek
Canyon, providing yet another return option. A mile beyond this junction you
may encounter auto traffic, as cars are allowed from Seven Mile Road to a trail-
head at this point. At Seven Mile Road, turn right, and in 1.8 miles meet Pine
Bluff Road and the end of the loop.

RIDE 86 · Mt. Spokane State Park

AT A GLANCE

Length/configuration: 3.6-mile loop on double-tracks and gravel roads

Aerobic difficulty: Moderate; lots of ups and downs

Technical difficulty: Easy; roads in mostly good condition

Scenery: Dense second-growth forest

Special comments: The mountain's single-track is a big draw (see Ride 87); at the time of our last visit the trails were unmapped and unsigned

One of Mt. Spokane's chief attractions is winter recreation. Mountain biking and a spectacular summit view are the main draws for visitors during the summer months. The park's cross-country ski trails are popular with beginning mountain bikers, while miles of unmapped single-track trails delight more advanced riders.

This chapter is an introduction to the Nordic Ski Trail System on Mt. Spokane. Riders can create everything from easy outings to demanding circuits. We describe a moderately difficult 3.6-mile loop that follows double-tracks and gravel roads in good condition. Some intersections were unsigned at the time of our visit, but it looked like new signs were being installed.

General location: The trailhead for the Mt. Spokane Nordic Ski Trail System is approximately 25 miles northeast of Spokane, Washington.

Elevation change: The double-tracks take off from Selkirk Lodge at 4,500'. The high point of the trail network is about 4,800'.

Season: While some trails on the mountain may be crowded on summer week-ends, the cross-country trails receive only light use.

Services: There is no water available on the ride. Water can be found seasonally at the campground. The campground consists of 12 sites that are available on a first-come, first-served basis. All services can be obtained in Spokane.

Hazards: Anticipate some rough stretches of road and some sandy conditions.

Rescue index: There is a pay phone at Selkirk Lodge. Budget cuts have reduced the park staff to a bare minimum—you may or may not be able to obtain help at the park office. The office is on your left, just past Kirk's Lodge, as you enter the park.

Land status: Mt. Spokane State Park.

Maps: As this book went to press, a comprehensive map of bike trails on Mt. Spokane was unavailable. A map of the cross-country trails could be obtained, but it was inaccurate and hard to find. The folks in the bicycle department at the Recreational Equipment Inc. (REI) store in Spokane helped us track one down. The map in this book is a revised version of that cross-country trail map. USGS 7.5 minute quads: Mt. Spokane and Mt. Kit Carson.

Finding the trail: From I-90 in Spokane, take Exit 281 and follow Division Street north through the city. After 6 miles, bear right onto US 2, following the signs for Mt. Spokane. In another 4.3 miles, turn right onto WA 206/Mt. Spokane Park Drive. You will pass Kirk's Lodge after about 15 miles on WA 206. Go 3.5 miles beyond Kirk's Lodge and turn right into a large gravel parking lot. Proceed uphill through the parking area for 0.3 mile, and turn right to enter the upper Sno-park lot at Selkirk Lodge.

Sources of additional information:

Mt. Spokane State Park
North 26107 Mt. Spokane Park Drive
Mead, WA 99021
(509) 238-4258

Washington State Parks and Recreation Commission
7150 Cleanwater Lane, KY-11
Olympia, WA 98504-5711

Washington State Parks Information Line
(800) 562-0990 in Washington
(206) 753-2116 outside Washington
May 1 through Labor Day: Monday–Friday, 8 a.m. to 5 p.m.

REI
North 1125 Monroe Street
Spokane, WA 99201
(509) 328-9900

Notes on the trail: The following description is one of many available routes in the Mt. Spokane Nordic Ski Trail System. Stay closer to the lodge for less demanding options.

Find Valley View Trail #200 in the southwest corner of the parking lot. Follow it to Junction 1. Stay to the right at Junction 1 and pick up Larch Trail #200. When you arrive at Junction 2, bear right to get on Silver Trail #200. After 0.8 mile on Silver Trail, you will come around the back side of Nova Hut and arrive at an intersection. Turn left and ride a short distance to Junction 3. Turn left and follow the main road back to the Sno-park lot at Selkirk Lodge.

For deeper explorations into the system of trails, turn right at Junction 3. We followed the main road to Junction 5 and went left to ride on Shadow Mountain Trail #220. We got lost several times on this trail — it is interlaced with off-road

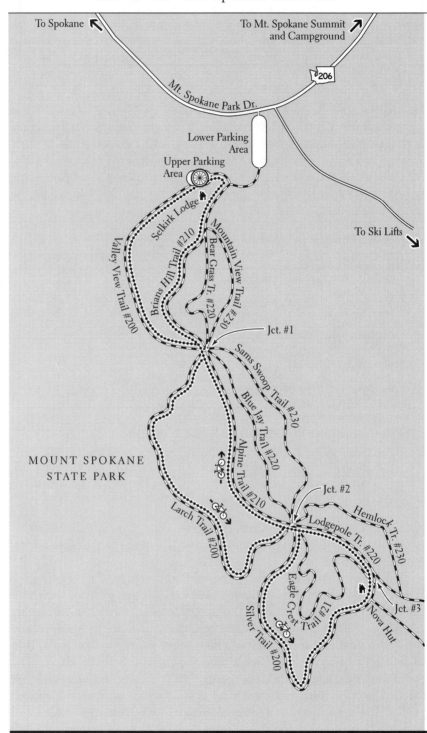

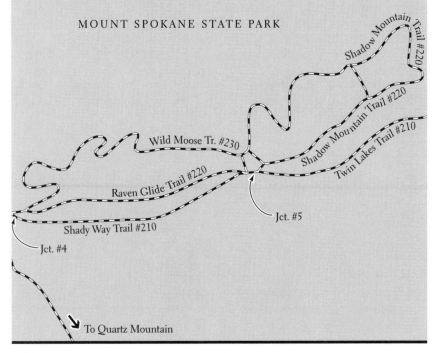

MOUNT SPOKANE STATE PARK

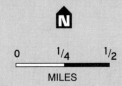

0   1/4   1/2
MILES

Shadow Mountain Trail #220

Shadow Mountain Trail #220

Twin Lakes Trail #210

Wild Moose Tr. #230

Raven Glide Trail #220

Jct. #5

Shady Way Trail #210

Jct. #4

To Quartz Mountain

Mt. Spokane State Park.

vehicle and snowmobile routes. There are some nice views to the south from this double-track.

Information about the single-track opportunities on Mt. Spokane is hard to find. The park staff is eager to promote the trail network but lacks funding for signage and maps.

RIDE 87 · Mt. Spokane State Park: Mt. Kit Carson/
Day Mountain Loop

AT A GLANCE

Length/configuration: 7.4-mile loop, including wooded dirt roads and 1.9 miles of single-track

Aerobic difficulty: The 5.5 miles of dirt roads make for a pleasant, undulating climb of about 1,300'

Technical difficulty: Some rough single-track at the top; ruts, small drop-offs

Scenery: Deep woods; a clear-cut on the climb provides a distant view

Special comments: Fun, good-quality single-track; good explorability

The gravel roads, double-track, and cross-country ski trails at Mt. Spokane provide great riding and excellent explorability; this ride highlights some bona fide single-track within the park.

Local two-wheel tour leader Joe Nollette and John Gasioroski of REI in Spokane led this 7.4-mile outing. It treats riders to a pleasant, moderate, dirt road climb through pretty woods containing a variety of firs, western hemlock, western white pine, and cottonwood. The road section is broken up with numerous flats and descents, and leads to a thrilling 1.9-mile single-track descent. A beginner should have few problems on the climb; the rough upper section of the single-track, with some ruts and small drop-offs, will prove challenging. For those with sensitive bottoms, the trail smoothes out after the first creek crossing.

It's a fun ride for the more advanced cyclist as well, and the route provides many opportunities to explore. One suggestion is using Trail 105, a wide trail 0.7 mile past Kirk's Lodge, just past the park entrance; the top of Trail 105 connects with the start of the described route to add two-plus miles of wide trail (each way) with steep grades. Another scenic suggestion is starting up the hill at Selkirk Lodge (as directed in Ride 86) and riding south to "Hole-in-the-Rock," a beautiful, mushroom-shaped rock formation on Quartz Mountain. It'll take some route-finding—or just talk to Joe Nollette, and he'll get you there.

General location: The loop starts just off the main road into Mt. Spokane State Park, about 25 miles northeast of Spokane.

RIDE 87 · Mt. Spokane State Park: Mt. Kit Carson/Day Mtn. Loop

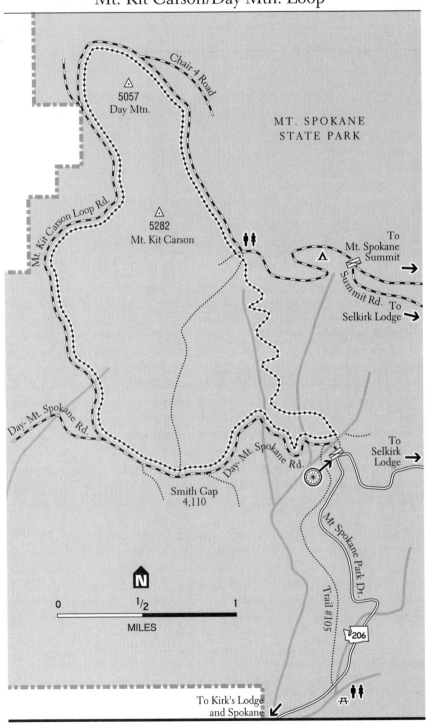

Chair 4 Road

5057
Day Mtn.

MT. SPOKANE
STATE PARK

Mt. Kit Carson Loop Rd.

5282
Mt. Kit Carson

To
Mt. Spokane
Summit

Summit Rd. To
Selkirk Lodge

Day- Mt. Spokane Rd.

Day- Mt. Spokane Rd.

To
Selkirk
Lodge

Smith Gap
4,110

Mt. Spokane Park Dr.

N

0   ¹/₂   1

MILES

Trail #105

206

To Kirk's Lodge
and Spokane

A mid-October winter wonderland on Mt. Kit Carson Loop Road.

Elevation change: From the start of the route at 3,897' elevation, you'll be rolling onto the trail at 4,920'. Descents along the way add an extra 160' of climbing, for a total gain of 1,183'.

Season: After the snow melts until the snows come again, usually April through October. On our research outing in mid-October, we encountered some snow at the top of the road but the trail was snow-free and in good shape.

Services: There is no water available along the route. A campground in the park consists of 12 sites, available on a first-come, first-serve basis. Water can be found seasonally in the campground. All services can be obtained in Spokane.

Hazards: The first part of the single-track is a bit rough and rooty, but it smoothes out as you descend.

Rescue index: There's a pay phone just down the road at Kirk's Lodge. Help may be available at the park office, just past Kirk's Lodge, at the entrance to the park.

Land status: Mt. Spokane State Park.

Maps: At the time of research, a detailed map of the trails at Mt. Spokane Park was not available. The best map I found was the Northwest Map Service Spokane County Road & Recreational Map. It's a decent general guide, though not complete, and without the topography of the area.

Finding the trail: From I-90 in Spokane, take Exit 281 and follow Division Street north through the city. After 6 miles, veer right at the **Y** intersection onto US 2, following the signs to Mt. Spokane State Park. In another 4.3 miles, turn right onto WA 206 (Mt. Spokane Park Drive). After 15.0 miles, pass Kirk's Lodge

Joe Nollette at Hole-in-the-Rock.

on the left. You can park at the pullout at the base of Trail 105, 0.7 mile past Kirk's Lodge, to extend the trip, but for the described loop, travel 2.2 miles beyond Kirk's Lodge until you see a candy-cane-striped gate on your left, as the road switchbacks right. Park near the gate.

Sources of additional information:

Mt. Spokane State Park
North 26107 Mt. Spokane Park Drive
Mead, WA 99021
(509) 238-4258

REI
North 1125 Monroe Street
Spokane, WA 99201
(509) 328-9900

Joe Nollette
Northwest Off-Road Adventures
P.O. Box 1255
Spokane, WA 99210-1255
(509) 326-5016

Northwest Map and Travel Book Center
525 W. Sprague Avenue
Spokane, WA 99204
(509) 455-6981
(they don't know much about mountain biking, but it's the best map store in town)

Notes on the trail: Ride around the candy-cane-striped gate onto Day–Mt. Spokane Road. Pass the trail on which you finish the loop on your right, and then Trail 105 on your left, in the first 0.1 mile. The smooth road climb starts with a descent and contains short descents throughout; the climbs are mostly middle-ring efforts for intermediate-level cyclists. At 1.2 miles, as you wind around to the right, you'll see trails in both directions to explore, but for the described route, stay on the main road. From here the road descends; stay to the right, on Mt. Kit Carson Loop Road, as Day–Mt. Spokane Road goes left. At 3.7 miles (2.5 miles from the trail junction), Chair 4 Road veers downhill to the left, but stay on Mt. Kit Carson Loop Road. Pedaling 1.8 miles beyond that junction, the road makes an **S** curve, first to the left and then to the right, and then to the left again. Your landmark here is a cylindrical pit toilet on the right. A hard right on the trail at the 4 o'clock position climbs to the top of Mt. Kit Carson; but take the soft right at the 1 o'clock position, to the left of the toilet, onto the unmarked trail. Once on the trail, the only intersection to negotiate is after a water crossing; as a trail comes in from the left at the 7 o'clock position, keep descending as the trail winds to the right. In 0.1 mile, meet Day–Mt. Spokane Road and turn left to the ride's end. To extend the ride, angle back on Day-Mt. Spokane Road to pick up Trail 105.

SERIES AFTERWORD

LAND-USE CONTROVERSY

A few years ago I wrote a long piece on this issue for *Sierra* magazine that entailed calling literally dozens of government land managers, game wardens, mountain bikers, and local officials to get a feeling for how riders were being welcomed on the trails. All that I've seen personally since, and heard from my authors, indicates there hasn't been much change. We're still considered the new kid on the block. We have less of a right to the trails than horses and hikers, and we're excluded from many areas, including

a) wilderness areas
b) national parks (except on roads, and those paths specifically marked "bike path")
c) national monuments (except on roads open to the public)
d) most state parks and monuments (except on roads, and those paths specifically marked "bike path")
e) an increasing number of urban and county parks, especially in California (except on roads, and those paths specifically marked "bike path")

Frankly, I have little difficulty with these exclusions and would, in fact, restrict our presence from some trails I've ridden (one time) due to the environmental damage and chance of blindsiding the many walkers and hikers I met up with along the way. But these are my personal views. The author of this volume and mountain bikers as a group may hold different opinions.

You can do your part in keeping us from being excluded from even more trails by riding responsibly. Many local and national off-road bicycle organizations have been formed with exactly this in mind, and one of the largest—the National Off-Road Bicycle Association (NORBA)—offers the following code of behavior for mountain bikers:

1. I will yield the right of way to other nonmotorized recreationists. I realize that people judge all cyclists by my actions.
2. I will slow down and use caution when approaching or overtaking another cyclist and will make my presence known well in advance.
3. I will maintain control of my speed at all times and will approach turns in anticipation of someone around the bend.
4. I will stay on designated trails to avoid trampling native vegetation and minimize potential erosion to trails by not using muddy trails or short-cutting switchbacks.
5. I will not disturb wildlife or livestock.
6. I will not litter. I will pack out what I pack in, and pack out more than my share whenever possible.
7. I will respect public and private property, including trail-use signs and no trespassing signs, and I will leave gates as I have found them.
8. I will always be self-sufficient and my destination and travel speed will be determined by my ability, my equipment, the terrain, and the present and potential weather conditions.
9. I will not travel solo when bikepacking in remote areas. I will leave word of my destination and when I plan to return.
10. I will observe the practice of minimum impact bicycling by "taking only pictures and memories and leaving only waffle prints."
11. I will always wear a helmet when I ride.

Now, I have a problem with some of these—number nine, for instance. The most enjoyable mountain biking I've ever done has been solo. And as for leaving word of destination and time of return, I've enjoyed living in such a way as to say, "I'm off to pedal Colorado. See you in the fall." Of course it's senseless to take needless risks, and I plan a ride and pack my gear with this in mind. But for me number nine smacks too much of the "never-out-of-touch" mentality. And getting away from civilization, deep into the wilds, is, for many people, what mountain biking's all about.

All in all, however, NORBA's list is good, and surely we mountain bikers would be liked more, and excluded less, if we followed the suggestions. But let me offer a "code of ethics" I much prefer, one given to cyclists by Utah's Wasatch-Cache National Forest office.

Study a Forest Map Before You Ride
Currently, bicycles are permitted on roads and developed trails within the Wasatch-Cache National Forest except in designated Wilderness. If your route crosses private land, it is your responsibility to obtain right-of-way permission from the landowner.

Keep Groups Small
Riding in large groups degrades the outdoor experience for others, can disturb wildlife, and usually leads to greater resource damage.

Avoid Riding on Wet Trails
Bicycle tires leave ruts in wet trails. These ruts concentrate runoff and accelerate erosion. Postponing a ride when the trails are wet will preserve the trails for future use.

Stay on Roads and Trails
Riding off-trail destroys vegetation and damages the soil.

Always Yield to Others
Trails are shared by hikers, horses, and bicycles. Move off the trail to allow horses to pass and stop to allow hikers adequate room to share the trail. Simply yelling "Bicycle!" is not acceptable.

Control Your Speed
Excessive speed endangers yourself and other forest users.

Avoid Wheel Lock-up and Spin-out
Steep terrain is especially vulnerable to trail wear. Locking brakes on steep descents or when stopping needlessly damages trails. If a slope is steep enough to require locking wheels and skidding, dismount and walk your bicycle. Likewise, if an ascent is so steep your rear wheel slips and spins, dismount and walk your bicycle.

Protect Waterbars and Switchbacks
Waterbars, the rock and log drains built to direct water off trails, protect trails from erosion. When you encounter a waterbar, ride directly over the top or dismount and walk your bicycle. Riding around the ends of waterbars destroys them and speeds erosion. Skidding around switchback corners shortens trail life. Slow down for switchback corners and keep your wheels rolling.

If You Abuse It, You Lose It
Mountain bikers are relative newcomers to the forest and must prove themselves responsible trail users. By following the guidelines above, and by participating in trail maintenance service projects, bicyclists can help avoid closures that would prevent them from using trails.

I've never seen a better trail-etiquette list for mountain bikers. So have fun. Be careful. And don't screw up things for the next rider.

Dennis Coello
Series Editor

GLOSSARY

This short list of terms does not contain all the words used by mountain bike enthusiasts when discussing their sport. But it should serve as an introduction to the lingo you'll hear on the trails.

ATB	all-terrain bike; this, like "fat-tire bike," is another name for a mountain bike
ATV	all-terrain vehicle; this usually refers to the loud, fume-spewing three- or four-wheeled motorized vehicles you will not enjoy meeting on the trail—except, of course, if you crash and have to hitch a ride out on one
BLM	Bureau of Land Management, an agency of the federal government
blaze	a mark on a tree made by chipping away a piece of the bark, usually done to designate a trail; such trails are sometimes described as "blazed"
blind corner	a curve in the road or trail that conceals bikers, hikers, equestrians, and other traffic
blowdown	see "windfall"
buffed	used to describe a very smooth trail
catching air	taking a jump in such a way that both wheels of the bike are off the ground at the same time
cattle guard	a grate of parallel steel bars or pipes set at ground level and suspended over a ditch; cows can't cross them (their little feet slip through the openings between the pipes), but pedestrians and vehicles can pass over cattle guards with little difficulty
clean	while this may describe what you and your bike won't be after following many trails, the term is most often used as

a verb to denote the action of pedaling a tough section of trail successfully

combination this type of route may combine two or more configurations; for example, a point-to-point route may integrate a scenic loop or an out-and-back spur midway through the ride; likewise, an out-and-back may have a loop at its farthest point (this configuration looks like a cherry with a stem attached; the stem is the out-and-back, the fruit is the terminus loop); or a loop route may have multiple out-and-back spurs and/or loops to the side; mileage for a combination route is for the total distance to complete the ride

cupped a concave trail; higher on the sides than in the middle

dab touching the ground with a foot or hand

deadfall a tangled mass of fallen trees or branches

diversion ditch a usually narrow, shallow ditch dug across or around a trail; funneling the water in this manner keeps it from destroying the trail

double-track the dual tracks made by a jeep or other vehicle, with grass or weeds or rocks between; mountain bikers can ride in either of the tracks, but you will of course find that whichever one you choose, and no matter how many times you change back and forth, the other track will appear to offer smoother travel

dugway a steep, unpaved, switchbacked descent

endo flipping end over end

feathering using a light touch on the brake lever, hitting it lightly many times rather than very hard or locking the brake

four-wheel-drive this refers to any vehicle with drive-wheel capability on all four wheels (a jeep, for instance, has four-wheel drive as compared with a two-wheel-drive passenger car), or to a rough road or trail that requires four-wheel-drive capability (or a one-wheel-drive mountain bike!) to negotiate it

game trail the usually narrow trail made by deer, elk, or other game

gated everyone knows what a gate is, and how many variations exist upon this theme; well, if a trail is described as "gated" it simply has a gate across it; don't forget that the rule is if you find a gate closed, close it behind you; if you find one open, leave it that way

Giardia	shorthand for *Giardia lamblia*, and known as the "back-packer's bane" until we mountain bikers expropriated it; this is a waterborne parasite that begins its life cycle when swallowed, and one to four weeks later has its host (you) bloated, vomiting, shivering with chills, and living in the bathroom; the disease can be avoided by "treating" (purifying) the water you acquire along the trail (see "Hitting the Trail" in the Introduction)
gnarly	a term thankfully used less and less these days, it refers to tough trails
graded	refers to a dirt road that has been smoothed out by the use of a wide blade on earth-moving equipment; "blading" gets rid of the teeth-chattering, much-cursed washboards found on so many dirt roads after heavy vehicle use
hammer	to ride very hard
hardpack	a trail in which the dirt surface is packed down hard; such trails make for good and fast riding, and very painful landings; bikers most often use "hardpack" as both a noun and adjective, and "hard-packed" as an adjective only (the grammar lesson will help you when diagramming sentences in camp)
hike-a-bike	what you do when the road or trail becomes too steep or rough to remain in the saddle
jeep road, jeep trail	a rough road or trail passable only with four-wheel-drive capability (or a horse or mountain bike)
kamikaze	while this once referred primarily to those Japanese fliers who quaffed a glass of sake, then flew off as human bombs in suicide missions against U.S. naval vessels, it has more recently been applied to the idiot mountain bikers who, far less honorably, scream down hiking trails, endangering the physical and mental safety of the walking, biking, and equestrian traffic they meet; deck guns were necessary to stop the Japanese kamikaze pilots, but a bike pump or walking staff in the spokes is sufficient for the current-day kamikazes who threaten to get us all kicked off the trails
low-ring climb	a climb using the smallest of a mountain bike's front chainring; a steep climb
low-ring climb	a climb using the middle ring of a mountain bike's front chainring; a moderate climb

loop	this route configuration is characterized by riding from the designated trailhead to a distant point, then returning to the trailhead via a different route (or simply continuing on the same in a circle route) without doubling back; you always move forward across new terrain but return to the starting point when finished; mileage is for the entire loop from the trailhead back to trailhead
multi-purpose	a BLM designation of land which is open to many uses; mountain biking is allowed
off-camber	a trail that slopes in the opposite direction than one would prefer for safety's sake; for example, on a side-cut trail the slope is away from the hill—the inside of the trail is higher, so it helps you fall downhill if your balance isn't perfect
ORV/OHV	a motorized off-road vehicle
out-and-back	a ride where you will return on the same trail you pedaled out; while this might sound far more boring than a loop route, many trails look very different when pedaled in the opposite direction
pack stock	horses, mules, llamas, etc., carrying provisions along the trails
point-to-point	a vehicle shuttle (or similar assistance) is required for this type of route, which is ridden from the designated trail-head to a distant location, or endpoint, where the route ends; total mileage is for the one-way trip from the trail-head to endpoint
portage	to carry your bike on your person
pummy	soil with high pumice content produced by volcanic activity in the Pacific Northwest and elsewhere; light in consistency and easily pedaled; trails with such soil often become thick with dust
quads	bikers use this term to refer both to the extensor muscle in the front of the thigh (which is separated into four parts) and to USGS maps; the expression "Nice quads!" refers always to the former, however, except in those instances when the speaker is an engineer
recreation opportunity guides (R.O.G.)	handouts which identify and describe resources available to the public on national forest lands (camping facilities, trails, wildlife viewing opportunities, etc.); often available for the asking

at Forest Service ranger stations throughout the Pacific Northwest

runoff	rainwater or snowmelt
salal	an evergreen shrub (*Gaultheria shallon*) belonging to the family, *ericaceae*, that is native to western North America and bears pink or white flowers followed by edible purple berries
scree	an accumulation of loose stones or rocky debris lying on a slope or at the base of a hill or cliff
side-cut trail	a trail cut on the side of a hill
signed	a "signed" trail has signs in place of blazes
single-track	a single, narrow path through grass or brush or over rocky terrain, often created by deer, elk, or backpackers; single-track riding is some of the best fun around
skid road	the path created when loggers drag trees through the forest with heavy equipment
slickrock	the rock-hard, compacted sandstone that is great to ride and even prettier to look at; you'll appreciate it even more if you think of it as a petrified sand dune or seabed (which it is), and if the rider before you hasn't left tire marks (from unnecessary skidding) or granola bar wrappers behind
snowmelt	runoff produced by the melting of snow
snowpack	unmelted snow accumulated over weeks or months of winter—or over years in high-mountain terrain
spur	a road or trail that intersects the main trail you're following
squid	one who skids
stair-step climb	a climb punctuated by a series of level or near-level sections
switchback	a zigzagging road or trail designed to assist in traversing steep terrain; mountain bikers should not skid through switchbacks
talus	the rocky debris at the base of a cliff, or a slope formed by an accumulation of this rocky debris
tank trap	a steep-sided ditch (or series of ditches) used to block access to a road or trail; often used in conjunction with high mounds of excavated material

technical	terrain that is difficult to ride due not to its grade (steepness) but to its obstacles—rocks, roots, logs, ledges, loose soil . . .
topo	short for topographical map, the kind that shows both linear distance and elevation gain and loss; "topo" is pronounced with both vowels long
trashed	a trail that has been destroyed (same term used no matter what has destroyed it . . . cattle, horses, or even mountain bikers riding when the ground was too wet)
two-track	*see double-track*
two-wheel-drive	this refers to any vehicle with drive-wheel capability on only two wheels (a passenger car, for instance, has two-wheel drive); a two-wheel-drive road is a road or trail easily traveled by an ordinary car
waterbar	an earth, rock, or wooden structure that funnels water off trails to reduce erosion
washboarded	a road that is surfaced with many ridges spaced closely together, like the ripples on a washboard; these make for very rough riding, and even worse driving in a car or jeep
whoop-de-doo	closely spaced dips or undulations in a trail; these are often encountered in areas traveled heavily by ORVs
wilderness area	land that is officially set aside by the federal government to remain natural—pure, pristine, and untrammeled by any vehicle, including mountain bikes; though mountain bikes had not been born in 1964 (when the United States Congress passed the Wilderness Act, establishing the National Wilderness Preservation system), they are considered a "form of mechanical transport" and are thereby excluded; in short, stay out
windchill	a reference to the wind's cooling effect upon exposed flesh; for example, if the temperature is 10 degrees Fahrenheit and the wind is blowing at 20 miles per hour, the windchill (that is, the actual temperature to which your skin reacts) is minus 32 degrees; if you are riding in wet conditions things are even worse, for the windchill would then be minus 74 degrees!
windfall	anything (trees, limbs, brush, fellow bikers . . .) blown down by the wind

INDEX

ALAN BENNETT graduated from the University of Missouri with a degree in journalism in 1985. He traded his thin tires for knobbies in his native southern

California in 1988. He wrote for *Southwest Cycling* magazine and became its editor in 1990. After moving to Oregon in 1993, he authored a mountain biking column in *Oregon Cycling* magazine. He is past president and treasurer of the Disciples of Dirt/ Eugene Off-Road Cyclists, as well as a dedicated Kiwanis Club member in his hometown of Creswell, Oregon. When he's not riding or writing, he manages the office of his wife, Tamara, who has a chiropractic practice in Creswell.

CHRIS and **LAURIE LEMAN** make their home in Ketchum, Idaho. Laurie was born in Vancouver, British Columbia and holds a degree from Simon Fraser

University. She is employed as a waitress and freelance writer and helps coach the Sun Valley Nordic Ski Team. Chris is from Detroit, graduated from Michigan State University, and earns a living as a carpenter. They met while working as bicycle tour leaders in the Canadian Rockies.